The Design Manual

DAVID WHITBREAD was the Head of Graphic Design at the University of Canberra and the Design Director of the Australian Government Publishing Service. With a Bachelor of Arts in Graphic Design (Swinburne), he has also run his own design consultancy, David Whitbread Design, until 2004 when he became the Director of Corporate Communications, then Web and Design for an Australian Government department. David has taught graphic design at the Canberra Institute of Technology and has run seminars and workshops on design in Canberra, Sydney, Melbourne and Brisbane.

He was art director and one of the co-authors of the Australian Government's *Style Manual for Authors, Editors and Printers* (6th edition, Wiley, 2002) and wrote a monthly 'Design' column in *Australian MacWorld* for 11 years.

His work has received recognition in the Australian Book Publishers Association Design Awards, the National Print Awards and, with *The Design Manual*, the Australian Awards for Excellence in Educational Publishing. He received an Industry Award for Excellence in 2001 and has been a member of the Australian Graphic Design Association since its foundation.

He lives in Canberra with Brigid and their daughters, Kathleen, Maggie and Elizabeth.

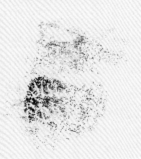

Further resources for The Design Manual are online at
www.thedesignmanual.net

The Design Manual

Revised and expanded edition

DAVID WHITBREAD

UNSW PRESS

For Brigid, Kathleen, Maggie and Elizabeth

Some of the material in this book has been previously published by Niche Media Pty Ltd in *Australian MacWorld*, *Australian MacUser* and *MacNews*. David Whitbread would like to thank the editors at Niche for their support over the years: Matthew JC Powell, Steven Noble, Richard Foxworthy, Jeremy Templer and Mike Hanlon.

A UNSW Press book

Published by
University of New South Wales Press Ltd
University of New South Wales
Sydney NSW 2052
Australia
www.unswpress.com.au

© David Whitbread 2001, 2009
First published 2001
Reprinted 2002
Reprinted 2004
Reprinted 2005
Reprinted 2007
Revised and expanded edition 2009

Design
David Whitbread

Cover illustrator
Julie Bradley

Diagrams
Louise Dews

Photographs
Andrew Sikorsky,
Art Atelier

Fonts supplied by
FontShop Australia
South Melbourne
www.fontshop.com.au

Printer
Everbest, China

National Library of Australia
Cataloguing-in-Publication entry:
Author: Whitbread, David, 1960–
Title: The design manual /David Whitbread.
Edition: 2nd ed.
ISBN: 978 174223 000 9 (pbk.)
Notes: Includes index.
Subjects: Design – Handbooks, manuals, etc.
          Desktop publishing – Handbooks, manuals, etc.
          Computer drawing – Handbooks, manuals, etc.
          Layout (Printing) – Handbooks, manuals, etc.
          Web sites – Design – Handbooks, manuals, etc.
Dewey Number: 745.4

Contents

Preface   *xi*

Acknowledgments   *xiii*

PURPOSE   *1*

What does design do?   *2*
Good design   *2*
Audiences   *4*
Styling   *7*

Real communication   *9*
Clarity   *12*
Words   *14*

How we read   *17*
Multiple entry points   *19*
Hypertext and film technique   *19*
Visual processing   *20*

Visual literacy   *21*
Using metaphors   *23*

Why print?   *25*
Why personalise?   *25*
How do you maximise the power of paper?   *25*

Any colour as long as it's green   *29*
What decisions can help reduce the
   environmental impact of print?   *29*
But it's not just print   *30*

**Designing for international audiences
and cultural difference**   *32*

Accessibility   *34*

PROCESS *37*

The design process *38*
Briefing *39*
Research *41*
Conceptualisation and idea generation *42*
Testing *44*
Prototyping *45*
Presentation *46*
Approvals *47*
Production management *47*
Launch *48*
Evaluation *49*
Design effectiveness *49*

PROJECTS *51*

Publications *52*
Books, reports and annual reports *52*
Newsletters, journals and magazines *59*
Pamphlets and brochures *65*
Catalogues *67*
Menus *70*
Programs *72*
Orders of service *73*
Comics and graphic novels *73*
Proposals *75*

Corporate identity and branding *77*
Brand evolution *78*
A design audit *79*
Identifiers *82*
Corporate typefaces *85*
Corporate colour palette *86*
Attitude *87*
Corporate identity manual *87*
Stationery *92*
Forms *98*
Signage *104*
Exhibitions, trade shows and conferences *106*

Screen-based media *109*
Multimedia *110*
Websites *124*
Email newsletters, e-books and e-zines *141*

Advertising and marketing   *143*
Posters   *146*
Postcards   *147*
Flyers, information sheets and handbills   *148*
Small-space press ads   *149*
Classified ads   *150*
Magazine and display ads   *151*
Direct-mail advertising   *152*
Packaging   *153*

PRODUCTION   *157*

Layout   *158*
Eye flow   *161*
Spatial relationships   *163*
Dominance   *164*
Simplicity   *164*
Unity   *168*
Balance   *171*
Freestyle layout   *173*
Grids   *174*
Formats   *179*
Imagery   *183*
Contrast   *196*
Scale   *197*
Tone   *197*
Repetition, pattern and texture   *198*
Direction   *199*
Borders and rules   *199*
Space and pace   *200*
Traditional and modern layouts   *203*

Four ways to save a failing design   *206*
Increase tonal contrast   *206*
Redistribute space   *206*
Alter scale relationships   *207*
Repeat something   *207*

Typography   *209*
Type categories   *212*
Typefaces, families and fonts   *223*
Type selection   *228*
Leading/linespacing   *231*
Letterspacing   *234*
Using type variation   *237*

Punctuation   *245*
Text formatting   *253*
Page furniture   *268*
Display type   *272*
Style sheets   *275*

Colour   *280*
Colour coding   *281*
Colour reproduction   *282*
Halftones, stipples, screens and reverses   *282*
Limited colour   *284*

Colour systems   *287*
Process colour (CMYK)   *287*
Pantone colour system   *290*
RGB and hexadecimal colour   *293*
The problem with colour systems   *295*

Prepress   *297*
Finished artwork preparation   *297*
Trapping   *300*
File management   *301*
Imposition   *301*
Output resolution   *303*
Proofing   *305*

Printing   *307*
Offset lithography   *309*
Screenless printing/collotype   *310*
Laser printing, photocopying and xerography   *310*
Digital printing   *312*
'On-demand' or 'just-in-time' printing   *312*
Variable data printing   *313*
Lenticular printing   *315*
Letterpress   *316*
Gravure   *317*
Engraving   *318*
Screen printing   *318*
Flexography   *319*
Selecting a printer   *319*
Identifying the cause of print problems   *319*

Paper   *321*
Paper specification   *323*
Uncoated and specialty grades   *325*

Finishing processes and embellishment   *328*
Varnishes   *328*
Coatings   *329*
Folding   *330*
Guillotining/trimming/drilling   *330*
Collating and gathering   *330*
Numbering   *331*
Binding   *331*
Office binding styles   *335*
Craft bindings   *336*
Foils   *338*
Embossing and debossing   *338*
Thermography   *339*
Die-cutting, scoring and perforation   *339*
Laser cutting   *340*
Pop-ups   *340*

PROFESSIONALISM   *343*

Using a designer   *344*
Selecting a contractor   *344*
Commissioning a contractor   *344*
A career in design   *349*
Creativity   *351*
Studio management   *353*
Ethical considerations   *354*

Index   *356*

Preface

The Design Manual explores many areas of a professional graphic designer's tasks. It focuses on the whats, whens and whys of graphic design, rather than the hows, wheres and whos.

The book looks at the underlying brief and the assumptions made when someone commissions a design project. Many other publications exist to show you how to use software, for example, or where and who to look to for inspiration. *The Design Manual* explains the many techniques available to you for creating a design with impact and a professional edge, and when you might use those techniques most effectively.

A variety of people will find the manual useful, including:
- professional graphic designers, editors and desktop publishers
- business people and public servants
- volunteers in community groups
- printers and imagesetters
- students of graphic design, marketing, communications, website and desktop publishing.

Not every section in the manual will be useful for everyone. Nor is it aimed at teaching everyone how to print, how to use particular software or to completely prepare a document to prepress level or to upload it to the Internet. What this book does discuss is how to make design decisions that best use these processes and to recognise their possibilities and limitations.

The Design Manual looks at graphic design in all media – and looks at the environmental impact of designers' decisions. As far as possible, it discusses the processes, elements, tools and techniques of graphic design in contemporary communication and marketing.

It also acknowledges other design 'voices' in margin quotes and in idiosyncratic 'Read more about it' lists that appear throughout the text. The margins also contain numerous checklists and tips for designing cheaper, faster and smarter.

As a teacher of graphic design, I have always needed a resource for my students that would go beyond fashion and beyond media choice – so I hope this book has gone some of the way to providing that.

The Design Manual was originally commissioned by the Australian Government Publishing Service as a companion volume to their *Style Manual for Authors, Editors and Printers*. As such, it was to do for designers what successive editions of the *Style Manual* have done for Australian editors and writers – and public servants – for 40 years: to provide guidance and recommendations as a practical reference for preparing publications.

So, as I had written a 'Design' column for a number of years – originally in Niche Media's *MacNews*, which then became *Australian MacUser* and ultimately *Australian MacWorld* – it was agreed that the past columns would become the basis for this publication.

Through a series of events, the book came to be published by Robin Derricourt of UNSW Press. It has been a delight to publish this book with the excellent – and patient – staff of UNSW Press, who have been so supportive and committed to its production.

I hope *The Design Manual* provides you with the sort of assistance you need – wherever you find yourself in the field of graphic design – and that you will turn back to it to be confident that you have fully considered your project and its design possibilities.

Acknowledgments

Like all books, *The Design Manual* did not write itself. There are so many people who have been influential in my design thinking, learning, doing and communicating over many years, that to list names would be fraught with the very real possibility that people would be left out.

I would like to offer my sincere thanks to the following groups of people who have supported, inspired, challenged and helped me to my present understanding – and ask them to hang in there for the future:

- my wife Brigid and daughters Kathleen, Maggie and Elizabeth
- my parents and the Whitbread, Proudman, Russell, Watson, Gumley, Baker and Taylor families
- staff and fellow students of the Graphic Design Department at Swinburne
- clients of and colleagues in the Design Studio, Editorial Section and Publishing Operations at the Australian Government Publishing Service
- teaching colleagues and students at the University of Canberra and the Canberra Institute of Technology
- the principals, my teachers, peers and friends at Melrose High School and Stirling College
- attendees at my seminars and workshops
- colleagues at Snooks & Co. and Mirrabooka Marketing and Design
- colleagues in the Australian Graphic Design Association
- editors at Niche Media
- colleagues in the Communications Branch and staff at the Australian Government Department of Education, Employment and Workplace Relations
- the editors, production and marketing staff, and management of UNSW Press
- the people who have generously read the drafts of *The Design Manual* and provided valuable contributions, particularly Philippa Hays and Liam Camilleri

- the production staff and sponsors (listed on the imprint page) and design studios who have generously supported this publication (noted throughout)
- the many printers, typesetters and prepress specialists, editors and authors, photographers and illustrators, paper reps and website developers who have provided their work, skill and patience to an inquisitive designer.

Thank you.

Purpose

What does design do?

'... there is always tension in good design; a tension between opposing forces represented by the creative and the prosaic, for design must work as few other artistic endeavours must work. It must work at many levels, at a practical level and at an imaginary level, with subtlety and obviousness, with clarity and suggestiveness, and with simplicity and complexity all intertwined in time and space.'

Steve Bright in
Hail!Storm

'Design is the process of making experiences ... Products, services and experiences already evoke meaning (even if companies do so accidentally or intuitively).'

Nathan Shedroff in *Designing Meaningful Experiences*, September 2006

'... designers are what theorist Pierre Bourdieu calls "cultural intermediaries": people who interpret and mediate the aspirations of society and produce cultural artefacts to satisfy it.'

Jonathan Baldwin in *Visual Communication: From Theory to Practice*

A graphic designer is 'a form-giver to a message'.

Dr KC Yeoh in *Designer*, 12, Singapore, 2006

Design is not an optional extra. If something has been presented in a visual form, it has been designed. Thus, everyone who presents information in a chosen form has made design decisions.

You can't say, 'Oh, we haven't got the time or money to design this – let's just get it out there!' because you will still put the material together in some visual form. Without considerations of the design decisions you're making or their effectiveness, you may as well forget the project. A project that doesn't meet its objectives, doesn't communicate to its potential audience and doesn't get seen, doesn't perform. It is a wasted opportunity, wasted time and wasted money. And you probably still have to communicate that message! So take the time now to consider design and its impact on every piece of communication you send and receive.

Good design

Whether design is used effectively (what might be called 'good' design) or ineffectively ('bad' design) is up to you. Effective design is described as the organisation of material which communicates information to a selected person (the 'audience' or 'receiver') using the visual language most appropriate to that person, the information itself, and the information source or author (the 'sender'). When you design, you are attempting to give your project its logical structure and, as a consequence of that, its logical form.

The term 'graphic design' was first used by an American designer, William Addison Dwiggins, in 1922, when he used it to describe his activities as 'bringing order and visual form to printed material'. It is still one of the best definitions, but we would probably be more broad in our media selection and embrace contemporary visual media

– television, film and particularly electronic publishing – in addition to 'printed material'.

Design is used as a communication tool to:
- attract attention and arouse interest
- separate the particular message from the many other messages people receive daily
- make your message stronger, more effective and perhaps even memorable
- save money by achieving maximum communication value from whatever resources are available.

Design is not cosmetic. Design will not hide a poorly written text, an out-of-focus photograph, an ill-conceived chart or a jerky animation. The reader must be able to understand the text, the illustrations and the concept.

But what attracts a reader? Stuff that is relevant to their life at that moment gets their attention. This explains why, when you're in the market for a fridge, suddenly you see white goods ads on television, banner ads on the web and catalogues in your mailbox. They were always there but, until you were actively interested in the product, you were filtering out the irrelevant messages in your environment; blocking them, clicking through or discarding them.

READ MORE ABOUT IT

Philip B Meggs, *Type and image: The language of graphic design*, Van Nostrand Reinhold, New York, 1989, ISBN 0 422 25846 1.

Peter Bonnici, *Visual language: The hidden medium of communication*, RotoVision SA, Crans-Pres-Celigny, Switzerland, 1999, ISBN 2 88046 388 2.

Jonathan Baldwin & Lucienne Roberts, *Visual communication: From theory to practice*, AVA Publishing SA, Lausanne, Switzerland, 2006, ISBN 2-940373-09-4.

Alice Twemlow, *What is graphic design for?*, RotoVision SA, Mies, Switzerland, 2006, ISBN 2-940361-07-X.

Sean Hall, *This means this, this means that: A user's guide to semiotics*, Laurence King, London, 2007, ISBN 978-1-85669-521-3.

Mark Oldach, *Creativity for graphic designers: A real-world guide to idea generation – from defining your message to selecting the best idea for your printed piece*, North Light Books, Cincinnati, 1995, ISBN 0 89134 583 3.

John Newcomb, *The book of graphic problem-solving: How to get visual ideas when you need them*, RR Bowker Co., New York, 1984, ISBN 0 8352 1895 3.

Steven Heller & Mirko Ilic, *The anatomy of design: Uncovering the influences and inspirations in modern graphic design*, Rockport Publishers, Gloucester, Mass., 2007, ISBN 978-1-59253-212-4.

'Good design is iterative, the result of removing the unnecessary until only the real value remains.'

David Sleight, AListApart.com, 9 May 2007

Massimo Vignelli, speaking at the international design conference *Sydney Design 99*, reminded his audience of semiotic theory when he indicated that design must be:
- semantically correct
- systematically consistent
- pragmatically understood by the user

and
- visually powerful
- intellectually elegant
- timeless.

Key semiotic concepts
- Sender (who)
- Intention (with what aim)
- Message (says what)
- Transmission (by which means)
- Noise (with what interference)
- Receiver (to whom)
- Destination (with what results)

Sean Hall in *This Means This, This Means That*

Audiences

Anything that tries to communicate should be able to be understood. The way material is written, with a logical order and appropriate language, and the way it looks will attract and hold the attention of the desired reader.

Know your reader. Awareness of your readership and all the previous experience a reader brings to the text must have a bearing on the way you design the text.

Since design is the organisation of material to communicate with a selected person, it follows that you should know all you can about that person. Consider the following when preparing a profile of your reader:
- age – and the implied cultural influences and education levels
- life experiences – and family background
- language – words, tone and usage
- visual literacy – comprehension level of symbols and metaphors.

Correct assumptions about what will attract and move the audience can ease many production decisions, not the least being finance. The job you conceive of as a full-colour brochure may be quite wrong for your audience, who may simply need a web page.

Other decisions such as the final approval of the manuscript or acceptance of a rough design should be made, not on your own aesthetic terms or your personal preferences, but rather by considering the profile of the expected readers.

There may be more audiences than you initially consider. For example, if children are the primary audience, there is usually the secondary audience of parents, teachers, peers and siblings, and perhaps even tertiary audiences of grandparents, aunts and uncles.

Use language your primary audience will understand, but ensure it is appropriate for your relationship to them. There can be an awkward moment when you realise you've used the wrong language even though the vernacular may have been chosen to make an audience feel more comfortable – the audience may feel that this is the wrong way for you to speak to them!

Choose images that will attract the primary audience and use visual language that they will understand. Then modify or allow the text and design to reflect what you know to be

'Much, if not most, graphic design is about communicating messages, and many of those messages are intended to persuade. This places its practice clearly in the realm of politics, broadly defined, even when the message is not about "political" issues.'

Michael Bierut, quoted in *Visual Communication: From Theory to Practice*

'Attention is:
□ selective
□ capable of being divided
□ limited.'

Debbie MacInnis, MarketingProfs. com, 15 January 2008

'I'd like to see more of a focus on aesthetics. Any form of dissent has to have a sense of the carnival. If this is the world we want, it has to be full of joy and laughter.'

Anita Roddick, quoted in *Worthwhile* magazine, May 2004

'Can design touch someone's heart?'

Stefan Sagmeister

the requirements of your secondary and tertiary audiences.

By tailoring information to the user or receiver of that information, the final form the information takes might be different from what you like. But if your assumptions about the audience are accurate and you have an appropriate message and format for them, the material will be well designed.

There is a broad array of information about your intended audience that is useful to consider. The traditional descriptors or audience 'metrics' that define market segments are:
- *demographics*, which include age, gender, religion, sexual preference, language, income, education and family
- *psychographics*, which include values, beliefs, habits, attitudes, activities and behaviours – particularly looking into lifestyle choices and consumption patterns
- *geographics*, which include physical location, nationality and its impact on their lifestyle
- *ethnographics*, which include how they live and work within the community they identify with.

You need to beware of grouping people into stereotypes – and assuming for all members of that particular group that their experiences and responses will be the same. 'Real' people have individual distinctive qualities and will go against their 'type' on occasion. It can help to think of a set of audience descriptive criteria as creating an 'archetype' rather than a stereotype.

There are some further distinctions that are useful for designers when considering their audiences and how they like to receive information. Anne Kiran, the anthropologist who works with Microsoft Corporation, has usefully divided people into two categories: 'digital natives' who have been born into a world with Internet access, computers and mobile devices; and 'digital immigrants' who have adopted such technologies during their lives. The two groups use technology differently and have expectations of it that are often different.

To better understand an audience – and to help your client to better describe or understand their audience – you can create an individual profile that demonstrates select features of a group. This is often called a 'persona' and, as there are usually a number of audiences, it can be worth creating a persona that represents each of your distinct audiences. In that way, you can discuss the development

First things first

Inspired by the original 'First things first' manifesto written in London in 1964 by Ken Garland and signed by 21 other visual communicators, this is an extract from the *First things first manifesto 2000* signed by 33 contemporary visual communicators which appeared in full in *Adbusters*, *Émigré*, AIGA *Journal*, *Eye*, *Blueprint*, *Items* and *Form* magazines:

'Designers who devote their efforts primarily to advertising, marketing and brand development are supporting, and implicitly endorsing, a mental environment so saturated with commercial messages that it is changing the very way citizen-consumers speak, think, feel, respond and interact. To some extent we are all helping draft a reductive and immeasurably harmful code of public discourse.

'There are pursuits more worthy of our problem-solving skills. Unprecedented environmental, social and cultural crises demand our attention. Many cultural interventions, social marketing campaigns, books, magazines, exhibitions, educational tools, television programmes, films, charitable causes and other information design projects urgently require our expertise and help.

'We propose a reversal of priorities in favour of more useful, lasting and democratic forms of communication – a mindshift away from product marketing and toward the exploration and production of a new kind of meaning. The scope of debate is shrinking; it must expand. Consumerism is running uncontested; it must be challenged by other perspectives expressed, in part, through the visual languages and resources of design.'

of your concepts and how certain personas will respond to the message. It creates a 'shorthand' reference to a set of audience metrics.

Personas will be given a name that is culturally accurate and gender-specific. As it can help to picture your audience, you can select a photograph of a person of similar age, sex and ethnicity to represent your persona. Then you create a one-page file note, 'back-story' or backgrounder that describes that person's life, describing the experiences that bring them to the point where they need your product.

Obviously this will pick up a number of the distinguishing preferences and feelings, responses and moods of your audience generally. It will describe the individual's motivations, goals, expectations, attitudes, experiences and preferences, likes and dislikes. You might profile a 'typical day' in their life, describing who they deal with and how.

The idea is to create a believable description of a person who could represent an audience segment.

Create four to six personas that represent a cross-section of your market segments. In this way, you and your client can come to 'know' them individually and discuss how they will respond to your project. It can help you to determine how to present information and is particularly influential in website development, though the process is applicable to all sorts of projects.

Developing a set of presentation boards that graphically depict the personas with their written descriptions can help your team to keep the people they are designing for in mind.

Another way of using presentation boards is to create 'mood boards'. These are graphic presentation boards that collect images from magazines, catalogues or websites that show the surroundings in which your project will ultimately find itself. The images are collaged into an inspirational presentation so a quick viewing of the boards can accurately describe the marketplace, competing products and the lifestyle choices of your audiences.

Alternatively, mood boards can conjure a feeling that helps you to capture the experience of your project – so they can be idea generators in themselves. They can help create an atmosphere for your design or the experience of it, based on a fantasy place rather than a real place. They are used extensively in product, film and interior design

'Know what you want to say and who you want to say it to. Say it clearly and engagingly in a way that your audience is able to hear it. Be consistent and brave.'

Jane Caro, 'Marketing made easy, but not foolproof', in AFR *Boss*, December 2003

'Design is constantly evolving, responding to changing consumer demands, and is subject to criticism from clients, end-users, peers and critics – none of whom uses the same criteria by which to judge it.'

Lucienne Roberts in *Visual Communication: From Theory to Practice*

'Beautiful solutions don't require the biggest budgets ... At the end of the day, it's about editing and getting down to the essence of a piece of communication, and matching the solution to the problem.'

Bill Grant in *Step Inside Design*, vol. 24, no. 2, March/April 2008 to collect appropriate textures, colours, objects, styles and atmospheric images that 'capture' a historical, cultural or fantastic realm.

When you can see the context in which your project will find itself, it can lead you to more considered decisions about how the project can succeed with its audience.

For example, a British government agency realised that, instead of using expensive television advertising buys with short generalised messages, it could reach parents more effectively through supermarket distribution of a range of pamphlets. By partnering with a national supermarket chain, and installing free pamphlet racks within each supermarket, the government agency was able to extend its information 'reach' and 'depth' without blowing its budget.

So, understanding how receptive to your message your intended audience will be in certain moments of their life, you can increase the effectiveness of both your communication and your client's budget. But you have to do the research – so you really know.

READ MORE ABOUT IT

Henry Steiner & Ken Haas, *Cross-cultural design: Communicating in the global marketplace*, Thames & Hudson, London, 1995, ISBN 0 8230 0545 3.

John Pruitt & Tamara Adlin, *The persona lifecycle: Keeping people in mind throughout product design*, Morgan Kaufmann Publishing, San Francisco, 2006, ISBN 0-12-566251-3.

Stereotypes

We need to be sceptical of labels such as baby boomers, generations X and Y that obscure the variety of life experience.

'Generational groups are never natural realities; they are manufactured. Importantly, most people resent being defined by a generational stereotype. Boomers dislike it as much as those who are lumped in the categories of Generations X or Y ... It's important for management philosophies to move beyond these stereotypes of generations and recognise that they are divisive and condescending.'

Kate Crawford, quoted in AFR *Boss*, October 2006

Styling

Design is often mistaken for styling. Styling at its worst is a surface or cosmetic treatment – creating form for the sake of form. However, for a designer, an understanding of styling is essential if it is to be used effectively.

Styles and concepts rarely exist in a void – they have value in the associations they trigger:

- their original political context
- their original social context
- their nostalgia value.

To provide the correct triggers, you need to know the audience's life experiences and attitudes.

Styles can stimulate memories, even for those with a 'learned' response to the stimuli. For example, audiences too young to 'remember' can recognise the fashion, music, and architectural and graphic styles of a historical period through exposure to museums, personal recollection by older relatives, print, film and video. But it is often more than just historical association; it can be emotional as well. Typefaces, imagery reproduction techniques and colour palettes all have associations – the response is often intuitive, not necessarily conscious.

Styling is a great tool in that it brings with it these associations which can add great dimension to a piece. If you can harness the appropriate associations, you can create powerful designs. Advertisers and film-makers use styling extensively to unlock an audience's past experiences, so there is a layer on which to build their story. It is a sort of visual shorthand where the viewer fills in detail, meeting the concept and enhancing it intellectually by connecting the combination of triggers that have been supplied.

'Styling is as crucial to good branding work as design, and maybe more so, but it's not a replacement for it.'

Adam Greenfield, AListApart.com, 7 December 2001

Sean Adams interviews Jennifer Morla of San Francisco in *Step Inside Design*, vol. 22, no. 4, July/August 2006:
Your work navigates a variety of cultural concepts, producing solutions that are clearly appropriate for the clients' specific culture. None of the work ever feels like it is a veneer. It all seems to grow organically from within the project's origin and criteria. Is that one of your priorities for significant design?
Jennifer Morla:
It is *the* priority. I always strive to find the appropriate narrative so that the solution doesn't turn into a stylistic conceit.

READ MORE ABOUT IT

Philip B Meggs & Alston W Purvis, *Meggs' history of graphic design*, 4th edn, John Wiley & Sons, Hoboken, New Jersey, 2006, ISBN 978-0-471-69902-6.

Richard Hollis, *Graphic design: A concise history*, Thames & Hudson, London, 1994, ISBN 0 500 20270 2.

Roxane Jubert, *Typography and graphic design: From antiquity to the present*, Flammarion, Paris, 2006, ISBN 10: 2080305239, ISBN 13: 9782080305237.

Laurel Harper, *Graphic radicals/Radical graphics*, Chronicle Books, San Francisco, 1999, ISBN 0 8118 1680 X.

Alan Livingston & Isabella Livingston, *The Thames and Hudson encyclopedia of graphic design and designers*, Thames & Hudson, London, 1992, ISBN 0 500 20259 1.

Steven Heller & Seymour Chwast, *Graphic style: From Victorian to post-modern*, Thames & Hudson, London, 1988, ISBN 0 500 23525 2.

Steven Heller & Louise Fili, *Stylepedia: A guide to graphic design mannerisms, quirks, and conceits*, Chronicle Books, San Francisco, 2006, ISBN-13: 978-0-8118-3346-2.

James Craig & Bruce Barton, *Thirty centuries of graphic design: An illustrated survey*, Watson-Guptill Publications, New York, 1987, ISBN 0 8230 5355 5.

Edward M Gottschall, *Typographic communications today*, MIT Press, Cambridge, Mass., 1989, ISBN 0 262 07114 2.

Ronald Labuz, *Contemporary graphic design*, Van Nostrand Reinhold, New York, 1991, ISBN 0 442 31887 1.

Donald Albrecht, Ellen Lupton & Steve Skov Holt, *Design culture now*, Laurence King, London, 2000, ISBN 1 85669 210 8.

Liz McQuiston, *Graphic agitation*, Phaidon, London, 1995, ISBN 879-0714834580.

Liz McQuiston, *Graphic agitation 2: Social and political graphics in the digital age*, Phaidon, London, 2004, ISBN 978-0714841773.

Kalle Lasn, *Design anarchy*, Adbuster Media, Vancouver, 2006, ISBN 978-0974680095.

Real communication

Communication happens on different levels: the emotive and the intellectual. Experience and moods modify it. As a designer and communicator you must try to satisfy all these levels. Will the gut reaction meet the intellectual rigour the reader brings to the message?

Different types of message get different levels of intellectual involvement. Consider the way you approach these different types of messages: political, social and cultural, educational and commercial. Also consider how welcome those messages are at various times: when relaxing, when studying, at the movies, under pressure at work.

Yet in many cases, a client or boss simply wants a design to communicate a message clearly through a visual medium. Why all the fuss?

The first priority of all graphic design is to get attention. To do that, you must break free of all the competing imagery and messages in the marketplace – the 'noise' – and direct your message to the people most likely to respond to it with images and design that appeal to them.

Texture, colour, imagery and text are used to intrigue, astound, seduce or provoke that second glance that brings the subject to a reader's attention. The second glance keeps the reader from going past your material. Some designers do it with complexity, some with simplicity, some with boldness, some with subtlety – however you do it, do it you must.

In any market there are usually multiple voices, each vying for the attention of prospective purchasers or users of the message. To stand out from the crowd, your 'voice' must be distinct. Against a children's choir, a bass voice will stand out. In a pet shop window's display of white rabbits, a black rabbit will stand out. In a stand of black-and-white brochures, a colour brochure will stand out. This is separation.

In *Visual Information for Everyday Use*, Harm Zwaga, Theo Boersema and Henriëtte Hoonhout define information as 'data organised in such a way that it can be used by people to serve their goals. The actual organization of the data evokes in the user a meaning. This organization can come into being because the user generates the interrelation between the perceived data, i.e., attaches a meaning to a set of data. The organization can also come into being because somebody else has processed and presented the data in such a way that it evokes in everybody else (ideally) the intended meaning ...'

To break free of competing imagery, you need to assess the visual form of the competition; that is, material that surrounds yours or that your reader will be aware of. Then you need to distinguish yours dramatically. If the competition is multicolour, yours should be black and white. If theirs is illustrative or photographic, yours should be flat colour. If theirs is highly patterned or textured, yours should be flat. If theirs is glossy, yours should be matt. If theirs is homey, yours should be high-tech. This involves research and an understanding of the marketplace into which your communication is going.

So you separate your material, but what else gets attention? Pictures get attention. But not every picture gets equal attention, and in a world with vast numbers of pictures, the impact of 'just a picture' is lessened. In a world where digital manipulation distorts the supposed 'truth' of a photograph, the impact of a picture is lessened even further.

But the impact of a *good* picture is not lessened. If you can find a picture that tells your story with drama, surprise and relevance, you're on a winner. Many pictures do not have these three attributes – so build them in.

Multidimensionality is attractive; layering imagery and text achieves this with implied foreground and background interaction. The juxtaposition of imagery, too, can be surprising or ironic. The incorporation of type into the imagery can mean that both the verbal and visual messages are simultaneously read – and that added dimension can be an advantage when it is competing with moving images and sound.

The design of multipicture images has gone beyond the ordinary collage that might have been used in the past. You might design a hybrid image that in itself would stop a viewer because of its clever distortion of reality. But is that enough? Not when everyone is doing it. One way to compete with the plethora of hybrid images is to 'separate'. Simplicity and understatement can be attractive in a sea of dynamic imagery; a quiet, plain, minimal statement can succeed.

Some magazines have found that one way of getting attention at the newsstand is to use 'novelty' inks and finishes – fluorescent colours, holograms in laser-etched foils, and metallic inks.

A small, well-chosen area of colour can be very powerful in a layout. Just look at some Chinese *sumi-e*, black ink paintings, where the signature block of the artist is printed in red. That little red block is very powerful as a layout element, even though it takes up a tiny area in relation to the surrounding illustration.

As layout technique, a favourite for impact is accentuated scale relationships. If all around you is big, be small. If you have an image of something big like an elephant, reduce it to be the full stop in your enormous headline. Blow up a fingerprint to full-page size to create an interesting graphic, then run tiny type through the spaces.

Another way of looking at this is the old stand-by technique used by photographers and art directors – conceal something that is easily recognised (usually a zoom in on a detail or texture) or reveal something that is not easily recognised (have you seen those stop-motion photos of a bullet going through an apple or a sugar cube dropped in a cup of coffee?).

Intrigue your audience. Hit them in the eyes with a graphic that is impossible to ignore – and leave your competition back at the starting gate.

But avoid over-design. Actually, 'over-design' is a misnomer – 'over-styled' is normally a more accurate description – but 'over-design' is convenient because we recognise the implication that there is too much design intervention between content and audience. What defines 'too much'? When the design begins to be noticed as 'the design' and the content is ignored or hidden, effectively camouflaged, the product has been over-designed. This veneer of 'being designed' is the problem – what should enhance actually detracts or disguises.

So ask yourself if your message will be sought out by your intended audience. This is where most design effort goes, and many designs stop there! Once the reader is attracted, is the designer's job done? What about the communication part? Whether the product is entertainment, information or education, designers must spend as much time formatting the text and pictures to keep the reader involved as they did in attracting the reader's attention in the first place. The mass audience is not likely to spend time trying to find the headline, the beginning of the article, the price, the coupon, the caption, the phone number, the dates ...

Many of the most effective designs are so simple you hardly notice that they have been designed. The design

Element of surprise

'The end results should contain the element of surprise – the unknown, the curious, the unexpected, spontaneous, conflicting, provocative, ambiguous, contradictory, colourful, intuitive accents that contribute to the emotional quotient of the final gestalt, be it momentary or infinite.'

Rita Siow in *Desktop*, 221, October 2006

Being provocative

☐ Be visual.
☐ Be different – break patterns and expectations.
☐ Be daring.
☐ Change things regularly.
☐ Inspire curiosity.
☐ Pose a challenge.
☐ Be controversial and committed.
☐ Be fun.
☐ Help them have hi-res experiences.
☐ Your turn.

Kathy Sierra on her *Creating passionate users* blog, 13 September 2006

DOING IT SMARTER
When not to design

Making the choice not to design is sometimes as important as knowing how to use design effectively. For example, mass-market fiction publishers use cover design to attract attention to a book and to communicate its content by doing it with genre imagery and typography that alerts the appropriate audience. However, graphics can be unwelcome intrusions between the covers.

At what other times do readers resent the imposition of design on communication? In websites, slow-loading images and pages are resented when a reference page or an online form is needed. Readers don't want to play with or admire the information, they just want to give or get it and get out. Compulsory forms or paperwork, either on-screen or in print, need to be designed for accuracy and speed.

This is not really 'not designing', but knowing when to pull back and let the communication between author and reader happen naturally. When interest is piqued, design. When interest has peaked, don't.

fits the subject so comfortably, so perfectly, that you would never believe someone laboured over it – and in many cases, you don't even notice the occasional flaw.

READ MORE ABOUT IT
Beryl McAlhone & David Stuart, *A smile in the mind: Witty thinking in graphic design*, Phaidon, London, 1996, ISBN 0 7148 3812 8.
Bob Gill, *Forget all the rules you ever learned about graphic design: Including the ones in this book*, Watson-Guptill Publications, New York, 1991, ISBN 0 8230 1863 6.
Steven Heller & Gail Anderson, *Graphic wit: The art of humor in design*, Watson-Guptill Publications, New York, 1991, ISBN 0 8230 2161 0.
Robin Landa, *Graphic design solutions*, Delmar Publishers, New York, 1996, ISBN 0 8273 6352 4.
Ellen Lupton & J Abbott Miller, *Design, writing, research: Writing on graphic design*, Kiosk, New York, 1996, ISBN 1 56898 047 7.
Karen D Fishler, *On edge: Breaking the boundaries of graphic design*, Rockport Publishers, Gloucester, Mass., 1998, ISBN 1 56496 454 X.

Clarity

To bring a message home effectively, clarity of ideas, logical sequence, relevant visual supporting images, appropriate use of language and legible and readable typography are essential. But even assuming these have been achieved, a publication can still be ignored.

Clarity of expression and presentation do not necessarily have the power to attract attention. If the message doesn't get attention, the time spent preparing it clearly has been wasted. Clear communication will give people more information in a shorter period of time once you have their attention.

Having attracted a reader's attention, the material should then be presented in such a way that it communicates clearly and maintains the reader's interest. But you must assess when clarity – the unambiguous, fast and accurate communication of ideas – takes over from attention-getting.

The techniques of information architecture are user-focused and based on questions such as: What current knowledge or interest or awareness do readers bring to the text? How are readers likely to want the information? How are readers likely to search for it? Once they have it, what will they do with it?

The interesting aspect of these questions is that our standard information organisation systems, based on chronology or alphabetical or numerical listings, rarely provide the appropriate 'way in' to the information from a user's perspective. Information analysts try to find the best way to access information for a majority of people. Rather than assuming the knowledge of the educated specialist in that sort of information, information designers use associations or recognised forms and sequences of information retrieval based on their broader audience's experiences.

They also use visual literacy extensively – diagrams, abbreviations, summaries, coding and symbol systems, quick references and cross-referencing systems. Incredibly complex material can often be presented more clearly in a diagram, flow chart or graph or, in many cases, a combination of these.

Flow charts, for example, allow you to ask questions along the way to identify in finer detail the sort of information or way through the information the reader needs. These are used to identify problems and potential solutions in the troubleshooting sections of manuals for electrical products, for example.

Knowing when and how to use diagrams and other information-organising systems can open the door to real communication. Nouns (naming words) can usually be illustrated – places can be mapped or photographed, people can be shown in portraits or caricatured, things can be photographed or illustrated, processes and abstract concepts can sometimes be charted. Quotes can indicate the possibility of a sound file (either documentary or historical recording or as the basis of a script to be recorded by voice talent). Comparisons of numbers often imply the potential for graphs.

READ MORE ABOUT IT

Richard Saul Wurman, *Information anxiety: What to do when information doesn't tell you what you need to know*, Pan Books, London, 1989, ISBN 0 330 31097 6.

Kim Baer, *Information design workbook: Graphic approaches, solutions, and inspiration + 30 case studies*, Rockport Publishers, Beverly, Mass., 2008, ISBN 978-1-59253-410-4.

Richard Saul Wurman, *Follow the yellow brick road: Learning to give, take, and use instructions*, Bantam Books, New York, 1992, ISBN 0 553 07425 3.

Richard Saul Wurman, *Information architecture*, Graphis Press Corporation, Zurich, 1996, ISBN 3 85709 458 3.

Rick Poynor, *Typography now: The next wave*, Internos Books, London, 1991, 'Introduction', ISBN 0 904 866 904.

According to Richard Saul Wurman in *Information Architecture*, there are five ways to organise information, which can be remembered by the acronym LATCH:

L   by location
A   by alphabet
T   by time (many museum shows are organised by timeline)
C   by category (the way department stores are organised)
H   by hierarchy, from the largest to the smallest of something, from the reddest to the lightest red, from the densest to the least dense, and so on.

The main way you organise something is by deciding how you want it to be found.

'Clutter is a failure of design, not an attribute of information.'

Edward Tufte, quoted by Kim Baer in *Information Design Workbook*

'It gives you what you want, when you want it, rather than everything you could ever want, even when you don't.'

Marissa Mayer, responsible for Google's look and feel, quoted by Linda Tischler in 'The beauty of simplicity', *Fast Company*, issue 100, November 2005

'Less isn't more; just enough is more.'

Milton Glaser, quoted by Joe Duffy, who went on to say, '"Just enough" contains an aesthetic component that differentiates one experience from another.'

Words

1.2 seconds. According to some sources, that's all the time you have to seduce potential customers with a piece of printed matter. At 1.3 seconds, they've turned the page, zoomed past your billboard, passed the bus, or their attention has been drawn by a competing message.

Let's say we are happy with our ability to grab people's attention with an arresting graphic image, a vibrant colour scheme or a stand-out graphic pattern. That's used a glance. How do you get them to land within the rest of our allotted 1.2 seconds and perhaps choose to stay a while?

Presumably the attraction has worked because the graphic accurately isolated the audience that is most likely to be interested in our message. We then have to generate interest – and we most often do that with words. But this is still the seduction phase – despite its brevity – and we usually need to use more words to say what readers need to know than it's possible to read in the remaining time.

But think about the mode of attention those potential readers are using. They are skimming and dipping, like a hummingbird, hovering over our message. They are skimming words, too. The words they need to find are signposts for the greater ideas contained. We use headings as signposts in text. But our readers are not into the text yet – they're still hovering. Marketers understand that words like 'you' and 'new' are good attractors. But for determining ultimate interest (and therefore landing rights), there are certain words in a headline that work harder than others. Our readers should be able to find these and find them fast.

We can use type variation to allow certain words in a headline to be found quickly. They can be:
· larger
· a different colour
· a different typeface
· positioned more prominently
· have more space around them.

Finding words that jump out means we are encouraging cross-reading; that is, reading out of sequence. Most writers care about their words being presented in the correct order and do not appreciate cross-readings, but cross-reading can communicate faster. If successful, it can encourage more readers to read further into the author's text. The graphic techniques listed above enable readers to keep reading

'The aim of an information design project, and in fact of every design project, is to develop a viable product: a product that compares well with competing products, or serves a specific unique purpose.

This means that a new product should satisfy at reasonable costs not only the needs of the user, but also those of the client/producer, and, when applicable, those of the distributor and retailer. Also the consequences of the introduction of the product for the environment may play a role in the development process. From the point of view of the user this relates to appropriate pricing, easy availability, convenience of use, aesthetic appeal, and safety in disposal.'

Harm Zwarga, Theo Boersema and Henriëtte Hoonhout in their introduction to *Visual Information for Everyday Use* continuously, as is most often desired by authors, but also allow 'attractive' words to jump out and trap them.

Since our language is cluttered with words of less importance, how do we analyse a piece of text in terms of each word's ability to attract a person? Let's look at the positioning statement for the Loud festival:

> Loud: Australia's first national media festival of youth culture and the arts

The most important word, for advertising recognition purposes, is the name of the festival, *Loud*. The three least important words are *of, and* and *the*. We almost have a tautology with the words *Australia's* and *national*. Why would we want to keep both? What do they each bring to the message? *Australia's* is definitive; *national* implies that the festival is big and encompassing, not just a localised festival that occurs somewhere in Australia. But the fact that posters and advertising are most likely to be placed pretty much exclusively in Australia seems to indicate that both words are less important in the scheme of things. Now, who cares that it's the *first* festival? It could communicate that it's an exciting development and 'new', so it's okay but not clear. Numerical labelling from second onwards usually reminds people of past success.

But really, those first three words in the placement line are not giving people information they need to decide their potential involvement in the festival.

So *media festival* ends up being important: *media* because it defines where the festival is taking place (in media events); *festival* because it defines the product. *Youth culture* is equally important because it defines the audience for participation and involvement. *Arts* is less important because it can be considered a subset of culture.

So, in briefly analysing an 11-word positioning line, we find only four words that are necessary for identification in the skimming process.

An easy way to isolate them is to use type distinction (in this case, bolding the five important words out of the 12) and also use well-chosen line breaks that place these words to dominate:

> **Loud**: Australia's first national
> **media festival** of
> **youth culture** and the arts

Why avoid the familiar?

'... the use of familiar phrases and messages undermines your company's brand. "Hey, these guys sound just like everyone else." You can't afford to sound like everyone else. You need to find a unique voice for your company ... Unique language, used to express a new message, will make all the difference in engaging a reader's attention and interest.'

> Nick Usborne in 'Copy and content: Avoiding what's familiar', MarketingProfs.com, 21 June 2006

Writing in plain language

Most readers prefer to read text that clearly and unambiguously explains new ideas or concepts. They do not want to guess or run to a dictionary to seek clarification in each paragraph. So there has been a movement towards plain language since the 1970s.

Even in fields like law, public administration and academia, where there are expectations that language will conform to tradition, there is a push for more readily accessible language.

One of the techniques recommended for writing in plain language is to imagine that you're writing a letter to 'Dear Mum'. In this way, your writing will retain respect for your reader but also explain complex ideas in more conversational language – and you're more likely to explain specialist terms, rather than assuming knowledge.

Plain language is more imperative now, as readers demand ever faster access to the information they need.

An editor should ensure that the author's message comes across 'in such a way not just that your reader understands you but such that they cannot misunderstand you'.

Quintilian, 1st century AD, quoted by Robert Nichols in *The Canberra Editor*, February 2006

There are many other more interesting graphic techniques for allowing those words to dominate. But for those people who have chosen to stop hovering and land on our message, the whole sequence should be able to be reread in context to get the full intent and nuance of the message as the author had intended.

Of course, authors too should realise their responsibility to use clear communication and as few words as are necessary to convey information to their busy, distracted readers.

READ MORE ABOUT IT

Don Watson, *Death sentence: The decay of public language*, Vintage, Sydney, 2004, ISBN 1 74051 278 2.

Don Watson, *Watson's dictionary of weasel words, contemporary clichés, cant and management jargon*, Vintage, Sydney, 2005, ISBN 1-74051-366-5.

How we read

Rarely, these days, do we sit down with a book, open it to the first page and read through to the last at one sitting. Some new fiction writers who are experimenting with non-linear narrative forms are even challenging this. With the pace of life we are embracing, we snatch moments to read and, if it is a rewarding read, we come back for more snatched moments until we've finished.

More often though, the bulk of text remains unread because our lives, our bookshelves, our magazine racks, our email in-boxes and online bookmark lists are too full to make that return visit. So even in our screen-based reading, most remains unread – indeed, with the World Wide Web, it would be impossible to read everything that is available to us – even on our very favourite blogs or our company's intranet.

We flip though publications or scroll websites, scanning for points of interest, spending a bit of time with each one. It is very much related to our embracing of film and, even more specifically, video. Scanning a book is like fast-forwarding to the interesting bit. It is said that children can watch a program in fast-forward and still give a comprehensive rundown of the content or plot that is very close to the actual. It is termed 'video literacy' – and the traditional, word-based approach to the design of text-based information finds it hard to compete.

In fiction, authors like Jackie Collins and Matthew Reilly understand this video literacy and write short scenes, editing and splicing them in much the same way as a scriptwriter or film editor does. Museum curators and exhibit designers also understand this. The concepts of strolling through different rooms and experiencing the exhibits in different lighting, media and atmosphere is very much like being in a video – you are pacing your own documentary. It is easy to see the appeal of the dynamic, blockbuster exhibit when comparing it with the passive museum experience of yesteryear.

This is not to say there is no room for a diversity of approaches, but the mass audience receives information in a manner that is significantly different from old assumptions. If you are communicating to a broad audience base, you need to recognise the motivations of that broader audience. Presentation technique has a major impact on what readers will choose to spend their time on. Where previously a reader's interest was enough and a page was passive, now page designers, on paper or on-screen, are faced with the same challenge as museum curators and film directors – how to involve the modern audience?

Consider why people read what they read. People read fiction mostly as a voluntary activity and are therefore usually motivated because they have selected the material. Their reading is often sustained reading due to the nature of plot and character-based narrative.

The text has to be clear and comfortable to read – the design should almost be 'invisible'. That is, the text design should not disturb the flow of the author's ideas from the page to the motivated reader. If a person is really interested in the subject, it doesn't matter what it looks like.

But, with reports, instruction manuals, websites, forms, contracts, journals, magazines, newspapers and advertising material, readers are often *required* to read the material or *need* to read the material in order to make a purchase or policy decision, or to determine what their next move will be. This is very often not really 'voluntary' reading – readers may be required for work purposes to read something of little personal interest or may feel obliged to read material that holds little appeal. So readers will often resort to scanning the text because sustained reading is difficult when motivation is lacking. Good design is essential to encourage readers to continue. The text must be 'made' interesting, or even entertaining, to motivate readers – because people read best when they are motivated.

With non-fiction or information-based text, few people read from beginning to end. They are more likely to check a contents list and jump to a specific section; flick through, scroll or skim for subjects of interest and graze the information; or check an index or do an advanced word-search to find very specific subject areas.

So how do readers become interested in a subject? Good design can awaken interest and sustain it.

Multiple entry points

By using a series of signposts, a reader can be encouraged to stop at each one. Traditionally, these signposts were called headings and subheadings and it was a poor writer who had to use many of them, but this, too, has changed. It is essential to use many headings – and so many levels now exist that we refer to the lot as a heading hierarchy. All they really do is provide multiple entry points to the information.

We also use pull-quotes. They draw attention to author opinions, as distinct from signpost headings, which draw attention to subject areas. A pull-quote is a quote suspended within the page, often out of context, but intriguing and provocative enough to encourage the reader to dip further into the text. It need not be a complete quote – it is there to whet the reader's appetite and trap them into reading the text.

Pictures are entry points, too. A reader gets more information more quickly from photographs than from text. Pictures are therefore the most powerful entry points. Furthermore, the size of a picture indicates its relative power, though subject matter also determines this.

This power of the picture has now redefined the power of the caption. Captions were simply labels so you could read the main text and refer to the appropriate picture when necessary.

Captions have now moved beyond simple labelling – they are longer and contain editorial opinion rather than a bald description and together with the photographs they become almost a summary of main points expressed in the text. This is so the casual reader (operating on fast-forward) catches the main points of the text.

Hypertext and film technique

The story behind the story (which in multimedia programs and websites is literally on another layer that can be brought forward when selected) also has three print equivalents: boxed text, sidebars, or, in multipage articles and documents, separate double-page spreads of related material. In all cases, a coloured background often distinguishes this from the main text. Readers get pushed through the text by the pace in the design of the article and sometimes by very obvious means: arrows, numbers and flowchart-inspired connections. These are all ways of streamlining access to information (or fast-forwarding).

There are also layout techniques that are the equivalents of both the cross-dissolve (an overlap of two images, one fading out as the other fades in) and the split screen (two images viewed concurrently). We have always had juxtaposition, where the brain seeks to connect images that are placed side by side, making sense of the placement. A more recent development, due to the emergence of photographic manipulation software, is layering, the overlapping of text and text, or text and image, or image and image. It is one of the most hotly argued graphic techniques in use.

Layering creates greater involvement with the text and its content by challenging the reader to comprehend the visual interpretation and to understand or make the links that determined the juxtaposition. This, in turn, slows readers down and makes them concentrate on the content.

On the other hand, layering can negate content because the reader will simply avoid the confrontation by turning the page, closing the publication or clicking the next hot link.

Visual processing

Aoccdrnig to rsceearh at Cmabirdge Uinvertisy, it deosn't mttaer in waht oredr the ltteers in a wrod are, the olny iprmoatnt tihng is taht the frist and lsat ltteer be at the rghit pclae. The rset can be a ttoal mses and you can sitll raed it wouthit a porbelm. The huamn mnid deos not raed ervey lteter by istlef, but preecievs the wrod as a wlohe.

Freshly peppered
Freshly prepared

When we are reading, we are actually processing a complex set of symbols made up of letters, numbers and punctuation marks which are associated with spoken language. 'Typography' is the technique and art of working with these symbols.

In order to communicate effectively using type, it is essential to understand two most important typographic concepts: legibility and readability.

Legible symbols are those that bear the correct identifying features; their form can be recognised instantly. For example, the triangular form of a capital A enables our recognition of the symbol – if you deviate from a triangular form, you are limiting its legibility and the speed with which a reader will process it.

Readability depends on how easily the arrangement of the symbols can be processed by the reader. We read by recognising the shape of words, not by identifying the individual letterforms that make up words. This explains how we can misread words: the word we misread is often similar in word shape to the word we substituted.

Of the two, readability is more important than legibility. After all, even with doctors' writing, as long as pharmacists prepare the correct dosage of the correct prescription, it doesn't matter whether they can recognise each individual letter in each word. The end justifies the means.

So readability is paramount. Legibility serves readability.

Visual literacy

A valuable adjunct to our language skills is the plethora of symbols we use daily, a realm beyond the alphabet and numbers. We use these symbols so regularly that we hardly notice how extensively they operate in our lives.

A symbol is anything that has, over time and with agreed common usage, come to represent something.

When we're driving, for example, we use a whole different language, based on simple geometric shapes and colour. The red octagon means 'stop'; the upside-down white triangle with a red stripe around the edge means 'give way' or 'yield'; the green circle means 'go'; the red circle also means 'stop'; the unbroken yellow or white lines mean 'do not pass'.

In some cases, like the stop sign, the word 'stop' is also part of the symbol – but how often do we actually read it? If the word was removed or in another language, the symbol would still be understood.

Colour can also be symbolic. Would you give a wedding invitation a thick black border? What about a blue danger or warning sign? How about a red dot on a cold tap?

For multidimensional designs, you can incorporate an army of visual devices, such as symbols, pictograms and dingbats.

In the commercial world, symbols are widely used to identify a particular product or company. They are called logotypes and logos if they involve a letterform, symbols if they are abstract shapes, or pictograms if they are representational.

Many of these symbols also use colour – Coca-Cola red; McDonald's yellow arches; Australia Post red. (By the way, these are logos, because they all represent type in some form, either by whole word or an initial.)

What about a horizontal white rectangle with a red circle in the middle? Flags like the Japanese flag use symbolism and colour distinction as well. The Canadian flag uses a pictogram of a maple leaf. Five interweaving coloured rings on a white ground provide a symbol for the Olympics.

Actually, the Olympics have given us some of the most refined pictogram-based symbol systems, starting with Masaru Katzumie's highly stylised sports and public facilities symbol set for the Tokyo Olympics in 1964. Probably the most complete set of pictogram-based symbols was Otl Aicher's Olympic set for Munich in 1972, which was later developed into extensive hospital, airport and other public signage system sets.

All these symbols are abbreviating information; they are condensing an identity. It's a type of visual shorthand that works most effectively.

Another example of visual shorthand is the star ratings of movies in newspaper film review columns. Star ratings effectively summarise the film so you decide whether you want to see it – based entirely on a number of stars.

Accommodation guides also use similar visual shorthand to rate accommodation options and to describe the facilities available – whether there is a restaurant or laundry, video hire or swimming pool, and payment options like Visa or MasterCard. Similarly, travel and restaurant guides use this system to advise readers of the relative expense of an attraction or meal by using multiple dollar signs; the quality of the food, by using multiple chef's hats; even symbols representing different cuisines.

When you walk through an airport anywhere in the world, you will be able to find baggage claim areas, the toilets, post boxes and money changing counters simply by reading the pictograms.

A pictogram is like a simplified drawing of an object. It can be a complex silhouette like Queen Elizabeth's bust on British stamps, or the kangaroo road sign, or a simple representation like the sun and clouds on television weather maps. It can be an indicator of the appropriate cuisine with which to serve particular wines or it can tell you how to wash and iron a piece of clothing. There are also symbols that have developed from pictograms, like zodiac signs for horoscopes, Egyptian hieroglyphics and Chinese characters.

This process – from representation to simplification to the development of a symbol – is how written language came to be developed. It is believed that Cretan pictograms may have influenced the early Phoenician alphabet upon which the Greeks modelled the Western alphabet we recognise today.

The term 'map reading' also implies a specialised area of visual literacy. Flow charts and instructional diagrams such as 'How to construct your model aeroplane' use similar 'reading' skills. There are conventions in comic book design that we now understand 'intuitively', such as thought balloon and speech balloon stylings.

We can use these reading styles to convert information that is new or foreign into a format that is understandable. The format of a diagram, map or chart, perhaps also incorporating other symbols like a rating system or pictograms, can speed our understanding because it relies on our visual literacy skills.

Using metaphors

A metaphor describes something new in terms of something we already know. An example of a written metaphor is 'The rain's soft fingers caressed the lovers'. Here the text has 'personified' the rain (described it as if it were a person with fingers). The metaphor tells us the rain was not beating down, but was light and even misty.

Metaphors can be tools for effective communication because we 'intuitively' recognise the familiar metaphor and can use or read the new product easily.

You can use metaphors in print design. When a catalogue takes the form of a product encyclopedia – in which products are listed alphabetically and described with diagrams, photographs and text that is akin to that found in an encyclopedia – we might intuitively use it like we would an actual encyclopedia. We might even keep it on our reference shelf!

A campaign aimed at teenagers might be written in graphic novel form, and illustrated and formatted in that style, to be more acceptable to its intended audience than a more traditional pamphlet might be.

A plant nursery and garden shop might use the metaphor of a naturalist's journal to present its catalogue to its garden club members.

In website design, the use of metaphor is more clearly defined and more widely discussed; a gallery, exhibition or trade show can provide a good metaphor for a website. A gallery includes many elements:

- the general exhibitions that are always there and which draw on the gallery's central collection
- changing special exhibitions
- a lounge where visitors can meet
- behind-the-scenes collections which can be accessed by those with special permission
- the curators' offices, where they provide direct consultation on specialist matters
- special events and performances that bring other art forms into the gallery
- a café
- a shop.

These attributes of a gallery translate into a great metaphor for a website, with these direct equivalents:

- the website's main content describing the organisation's main products and services
- regularly updated, special focus sections describing new products or features
- a registered users' chat line where regular visitors can meet other regular users
- a section that is firewalled which contains information and documents that only registered users can access
- email links that enable visitors to contact people in the organisation directly and get individual responses to requests
- hyperlinks to other sites that complement the site and broaden the scope of its offerings
- a visitors' resting place that may have light information, blogs, games or community bulletin boards
- a place to buy merchandise.

Some excellent cooking CD-ROMs and websites use the recipe card index metaphor. This has so influenced site navigation, possibly through the influence of Amazon's tabs, to the extent that the top navigation bar in most websites mimics a tabbed divider.

Usability is enhanced through recognition of the metaphor. The best metaphors sit comfortably with and do not intrude upon information. They should enable fast and intuitive access to it.

Why print?

These days, we are trying to do more with each dollar and focus our efforts on creating predictable outcomes. More than ever, we need to understand what it is that motivates people to pick up a brochure, to fan through a book or to read an advertisement. Print doesn't compete with a computer screen, it plays a different game altogether.

Why personalise?

Direct mail companies know the value of addressed mail is in its implied personal appeal. Feeling important and unique is part of the value of receiving a letter addressed specifically to us. Recent statistics from the post office have shown that more than half of addressed mail is electronically generated. This sort of personalisation is becoming more feasible as digital colour printing becomes faster and more financially viable. Databases are readily accessed through mailing houses and other list sellers.

It means that the whole experience receives greater attention, no matter how jaded we are about computer personalisation. Intellectually we may know that our name has been inserted by a database, and we may recognise the signature has been digitally scanned and not hand-signed with a ballpoint pen, but we are still intrigued that the message may hold something of interest for us, because someone recognised that the people on that mailing list presumably had some similar characteristics and were thus appropriate choices for the mailing, so the chances are good that there may actually be something here of interest.

How do you maximise the power of paper?

Computers may have sound, and whirr, hum and click, but so, too, does print – the rip of an envelope, the flick of pages, the crackle of sheets of paper, the rasp of paper

'Printed matter is available everywhere, but no bookstore has every book in print and no newsstand has every magazine. If a library has one certain book and it is checked out, access to the information in it is zero. Texts stored electronically are almost instantaneously transmittable and thus available to anyone, anywhere ... [Yet,] no instructional tool is less expensive to produce than print.'

Frank Romano in 'Print media versus new media', *ProPrint*, May 2008 against paper when the letter comes out of the envelope. The pleasurable sounds of interaction with paper allow print to engage a further and unexpected sense.

But by far the most appealing and luxurious pleasure of print belongs to the tactile experience. By skilful paper selection, the sense of touch can be a major interactive feature of print that transcends the tactile experience from a computer.

Largely, it is this tactile quality of print that determines its appeal; you can touch it and enjoy the transition of surface textures that the use of textural contrasts can give. From smooth to rough, from slippery to suede, from hard to soft, from ripples to stripes, from linen to hessian, from thick to thin, from flimsy to sturdy, from sandpaper to glass – papers can achieve all these combinations. Some papers even have different temperatures – translucent films and tracing papers are often cooler to the touch than other paper stocks.

With stationery, it is also an economical way of introducing additional colour, as stationery systems often require that two pieces be seen together. Making these pieces complement each other in both colour and texture can increase the impact of the system.

For example, the interaction of letterhead and envelope is very important. Letters have involvement too – they must be opened to reveal the contents. There is therefore a tactile response to the opening of the envelope and the aural involvement from the sound of ripping paper.

Do not underestimate the appeal of sound. Ray Black, an Australian advertising guru, pointed to research indicating that one of the things that milk drinkers like about drinking milk is the sound of milk tumbling into the glass. When you next see a milk advertisement, listen to the soundtrack – background noise is reduced to allow your ears to focus on this pleasant aural experience.

Continuing the opening of our letter, there are envelopes that have a different colour inside from that on the outside – why? And why are they used for things like wedding invitations and special announcements? Because they have that unexpectedness that can surprise and subliminally make the receiver feel more special – just what people want their sales letters to achieve.

Just contrasting the paper of the letterhead with the envelope also achieves this. Or, as many great designs are showing, you can print colour on the back of the letterhead: a pattern, texture, illustration or photograph. This heightens the pleasure of opening the letter. It becomes a sequence of colour and textural transitions that lead to the letter inside. Think of your envelope as a cocoon that gradually reveals its contents – your message. By using a sequence of paper and colours in a job, you maximise the effect.

For a publication, the cover and the text paper stocks should contrast, usually in weight with the cover heavier – in order to protect the text pages – but also in texture with the cover either smoother or more textural. You lose an opportunity to give pleasure to the reader if the cover and text papers are identical to the touch.

Endpapers have also made a comeback for this reason. Endpapers used to have a specific task – to hold the book onto the cover or case of hardbacks. They were glued to the inside cover and glued down the edge of the title page.

Fake endpapers, a pattern or texture printed on the inside front and back cover, are sometimes created in softback brochures and books to give this visual surprise or delight.

Sometimes a specialty paper insert, like an onionskin (a thin, semi-translucent white paper) or a tracing paper also create a pleasant effect – when lifted they can reveal the true colours of the next page. They can even reveal 'secret' messages: if you had printed text in the same colour as an area of flat colour on the next page, it will not be seen until you turn the page; in the same way, the text on the previous page can vanish as you lie it over a similar flat colour area on the preceding page.

Binding techniques such as comb binding or spiral binding enable multiple paper stocks to be used in this way without production complications.

You might also incorporate a surprise element like a pop-up or a cut-out which are both achieved by die-cutting. These interactive playthings can keep attention focused. They are the print equivalent of an on-screen clickable animation or hyperlink.

How can you increase the tactile qualities?

If you introduce some finishing processes like embossing, thermography or lamination (the touchy-feely ones), you further extend the tactile experience. This will maximise the ability of print to engage the audience in a manner that only print can achieve. It will often cost a bit more to use these different papers and the alternative binding and finishing techniques, but you will find they are that much more effective in communicating the message and encouraging the reader's interaction with the message. There remains just one decision: is the additional response worth the additional expenditure?

Part of the magic of really good graphic design is its ability to reveal something unexpectedly. Even more now, this element of surprise or delight should be considered for printed materials because it helps print to successfully compete with video and sound products.

The designer is the conjurer who creates surprise enough to communicate a message to the receiver. In websites, there are live graphics and links that achieve this. In print, there is the turning of pages that achieves the same thing – revelation.

A further aspect of the power of print is a sentiment so often forgotten or neglected by busy designers: it can be treasurable. Print can be an end in itself; a reader may treasure the printed object as a life-enhancing thing of beauty. This has the added bonus of an economic imperative – if the printed item is not valued or at least saved, it may not be displayed; if it is not displayed, it cannot keep its message in front of viewers for maximum cost-effectiveness. Yet it also fills one of the environmental imperatives: that objects should be able to be used and reused, recycled or, at least, reduce the environmental impact in their production. If a printed object is treasurable, it will not end up as landfill.

Any colour as long as it's green

Consider some basic practical action you can take to help conserve resources. First, simply ask whether what you're producing should be produced at all and, if so, whether it should be produced in a printed form. Screen-based publishing – particularly on the World Wide Web – is a viable alternative if your intended audience has access and will find or seek your message. There are increasing expectations that much information will be available in this way.

If we are realistic, we must acknowledge that much of our printed product very swiftly becomes landfill. How much packaging have you disposed of, or even separated for recycling, this week? How many letterbox drops, community newspapers and catalogues have been glanced at and promptly binned? How many office memos, newsletters and brochures have gone into the office waste bin?

The concept of something being so beautiful, so essential, so special, that you can't bring yourself to part with it is a challenge to all designers and clients. But if that is our new criterion for design justification, just how much printed product would we produce? Perhaps only a small percentage of what is presently gobbling up resources.

What decisions can help reduce the environmental impact of print?

There have been many developments as awareness of the long-term environmental impact of some well-established printing processes has been realised. All processes involving chemicals have been modified or radically re-thought to reduce the amount of chemical residue that can seep into our environment from printing processes.

The evolution of proofing systems to create computer-to-plate (CtP) systems has saved numerous film and chemical processes – and dropped chemical and water usage by up to 90%, as reported in *ProPrint* (November 2007).

CHECKLIST
**Environmental impact
of print**

☐ Does it need to be printed or packaged at all?
☐ How few copies are actually needed? (don't print 'extras')
☐ Have you proofread carefully? (to avoid reprinting due to error)
☐ Can it be smaller? (uses less paper)
☐ Can it be lighter? (uses less paper)
☐ Is the paper high in or even 100% post-consumer waste?
☐ Is it off-white? (saves bleaching processes)
☐ Is it free of chlorine bleaches?
☐ Is the paper manufactured locally? (avoids the environmental impact of transportation)
☐ Can it be self-covered? (not using a heavier weight for the cover saves paper)
☐ Does your printer use computer-to-plate technology? (avoids chemical platemaking processes and use of film)
☐ Is it waterless printing? (most friendly printing process)
☐ Are vegetable or soy-based inks used? (most friendly ink)
☐ Is it aqueous coated? (most friendly gloss)
☐ Is it stapled? (most friendly binding)
☐ Was it printed in one pass? (less wastage)
☐ Is your printer local? (avoids the environmental impact of transportation)

Avoid:
☐ paper made from virgin fibre unless from sustainable forest practices
☐ metallic and fluorescent inks
☐ large area of foil stamp
☐ lamination and UV varnish.

Adapted from *Creative Review*, vol. 27, no. 4, April 2007 and *Desktop*, 239, June 2008

Printing inks were originally based on petrochemicals, but now there are soy inks as a more biofriendly alternative. They perform well on press, hold colour consistency and even go further by about 10%.

Papers with recycled content have also evolved from the originally unpredictable printing surface to having predictable and consistent print results. But many paper-making processes have been revised. For example, the amount of chlorine used in bleaching processes has been minimised or completely replaced with alternative bleaching. Carbon dioxide emissions and energy consumption in the processes have also been reduced.

While numerous finishing processes (like lamination and foil stamping) limited the ability of the resources to be recycled, there are finishing processes that have minimal impact on the paper fibres, allowing it to be recycled: laser cutting, die-cutting and folding.

On-screen proofing or 'soft-proofing' enables designers and clients to clear numerous levels of proof without resorting to printouts and physical delivery. Proofs can be viewed online or sent as attachments in emails until the final stage when, sometimes, it is useful to see one final 'hard copy proof' – sometimes a 'machine proof', where it has been printed on the actual machine and paper specified so it looks exactly as the finished product will.

Other opportunities that computer-based production management systems enable include the potential to create a document in one location but print locally in each market to avoid the impact on the environment of distribution by truck or plane. This has the effect of reducing a client's 'carbon footprint' and is made more viable with low-cost, short-run printing and the developing predictable standards.

But it's not just print

It is worth bearing in mind that there is carbon emission from computing, using the Internet and CD-ROM production, for example, so print is not the only culprit. We should be seriously questioning the need to produce a message at all and minimising any environmental impact its production may involve.

In terms of minimising energy use and carbon dioxide production, Matthew Magain in 'Carbon currency' (*Desktop*,

239, June 2008) suggests you could consider purchasing energy from renewable resources like solar, wind or hydroelectric energy sources. You could also consider LCD screens instead of CRT monitors; laptops instead of desktop machines; online resources instead of printed training manuals.

Another action you could take is to turn your machines off when they are not in use and also consider how you might dispose of outdated equipment so metals and other resources can be recovered and recycled.

READ MORE ABOUT IT

Poppy Evans, *The complete guide to eco-friendly design*, North Light Books, Cincinnati, 1997, ISBN 0 89134 724 0.

Anne Chick, *The graphic designer's greenbook*, Graphis Press, Zurich, 1992, ISBN 3 85709 433 8.

Eco design: Environmentally sound packaging and graphic design, Rockport Publishers, Rockport, Mass., 1995, ISBN 1 56496 083 8.

Lee Chartier & Scott Mason, *Creating great designs on a limited budget*, North Light Books, Cincinnati, 1995, ISBN 0 89134 607 4.

Betsy Newberry & Kate York, *Fresh ideas in limited budget design*, North Light Books, Cincinnati, 1998, ISBN 0 89134 840 9.

Mary Pretzer, *Creative low-budget publication design*, North Light Books, Cincinnati, 1999, ISBN 0 89134 847 6.

Steven Heller & Anne Fink, *Low budget, high quality design*, Watson-Guptill, New York, 1992, ISBN 0 8230 2880 1.

Bryn Mulholland Mooth (ed.), *'How' idea file: 50 low budget design solutions*, North Light Books, Cincinnati, 1994, ISBN 0 89134 625 2.

Rockport Publishers, *Graphic design (on a limited budget): Cutting costs creatively for the client*, Rockport Publishers, Rockport, Mass., 1995, ISBN 1 56496 175 3.

'There is a need to consider the entire life cycle of the packaging, as well as the product it contains and wider supply chain, with the aim being to optimise material and energy flows as well as the recovery of value from waste.'

Gavin Williams, from the Packaging Council of Australia, quoted in *Desktop*, 240, July 2008

Sustainability

'Development that meets the needs of the present without compromising the ability of future generations to meet their own needs.'

World Commission on Environment and Development, 1987

CHECKLIST

Beyond just green

Social criteria:

- ☐ Socially desirable
- ☐ Culturally acceptable
- ☐ Psychologically nurturing

Financial criteria:

- ☐ Economically sustainable
- ☐ Technologically feasible
- ☐ Operationally viable

Environmental criteria:

- ☐ Environmentally robust
- ☐ Generationally sensitive
- ☐ Capable of continuous learning

From *The Dictionary of Sustainable Management*, SustainabilityDictionary.com, 24 April 2007

Designing for international audiences and cultural difference

'Western visual communication is deeply affected by our convention of writing from left to right ... The writing directions of culture vary: from right to left or from left to right, from top to bottom or in circular fashion from the centre to the outside. Consequently different values and meanings exert their influence beyond writing, and inform the meanings accorded to different compositional patterns, the amount of use made of them, and so on. In other words, we assume that the elements, such as "centre" or "margin", "top" or "bottom", will play a role in the visual semiotics of any culture, but with meanings and values that are likely to differ depending on that culture's histories of use of visual space, writing included.'

> Gunther Kress and Theo van Leeuwin in *Reading Images: The Grammar of Visual Design*

What is the influence of place on a designer and the work they produce? What are the considerations that need to be given for audiences in different parts of the world that they may understand a message in a given form?

Is there a particular way of seeing and representing the world that is distinguishable from how designers in other nations see and represent the world? What role do design traditions and history have in communicating in the contemporary world?

It is well known that colours carry meanings. Many carry opposite meanings in different cultures: death can be represented by black or white; yellow can represent fear or optimism; red can represent energy, good luck or horror.

Different cultures have different colour traditions.

European – and therefore Western – traditions include the complex symbolism and colour systems of heraldry from the Middle Ages, with rules about what colours needed to be separated and which could appear side by side. Yellow and white represented gold and silver respectively and, therefore, the metals never appeared beside each other but were separated by grounds of other colours.

Red and gold are the dominant colours in Asian – and many Eastern – traditions. They denote good luck and prosperity and are used in business, decor and greetings.

Indigenous cultures use different colour palettes again, usually based on the natural materials available locally that created pigments, technique and objects. The art and craft traditions included writing and decoration, story recording and diagram systems.

But the wholesale adoption of Indigenous styles and imagery needs to avoid appropriation and faddism – it can be insulting or diminish traditional and spiritual meanings. All cultures wish to protect the integrity of their past; many also want their traditional modes of expression to continue to evolve and tell their stories and convey what is important to them in contemporary ways.

There is always a tension between the protectors of tradition and the people at the edge who are challenging the traditional ways in order to maintain their relevance and advance them.

However, references to Indigenous style can be handled with cultural sensitivity – and the active involvement of the Indigenous community in deciding what can be shared, how and when.

Bright colour palettes are not so different when used by Australians, Jamaicans, Californians or Tibetans. But they can be applied with different attitudes and traditions. In Australia and Jamaica, application or technique is probably more casual and humorous than in either California or Tibet.

Worldwide, in art and design, there have been challenges to taboo subjects. The depiction of intimate body parts and sexual imagery is culturally charged to varying degrees in many traditions.

Defy visual conventions at your peril. In the West, left to right indicates moving forward and right to left indicates moving backwards. Growth is shown to increase from bottom to top.

In many traditions there is an equivalent tension between what we can call classicism and modernism. In Western design, it is embodied in the tension between symmetry and asymmetry, serif and sans serif typefaces. It can also be a tension between formality and informality, pattern or decoration and simplicity.

To be more inclusive of multicultural audiences, imagery selection is becoming more inclusive. A wide variety of ages, races and family types and a more even representation of the sexes – even a nod towards more inclusive treatment of diverse lifestyle choices, from sexual preferences to religious beliefs and practices – now grace the pages of our magazines and our television screens.

This move to greater inclusivity means that people from all traditions and social groups start seeing themselves represented. So designers have a significant role to play in image selection to continue this acknowledgment of the variety of humanity.

READ MORE ABOUT IT
Anistatia R Miller, Jared M Brown & Cheryl Dangel Cullen, *Global graphics: Symbols: Designing with symbols for an international market*, Rockport Publishers, Rockport, Mass., 2000, ISBN 1-56496-512-0.
LK Peterson & Cheryl Dangel Cullen, *Global graphics: Color: Designing with color for an international market*, Rockport Publishers, Rockport, Mass., 2000, ISBN 1-56496-293-8.
Gunther Kress & Theo van Leeuwin, *Reading images: The grammar of visual design*, 2nd edn, Routledge, Abingdon, UK, 2006, ISBN 9-78-415-31915-7.

Accessibility

'... "design exclusion" takes several forms: older and disabled people suffer from it; so do economically vulnerable groups and those affected by changing technologies and work practices.'

Roger Coleman, 'An introduction to inclusive design', DesignCouncil. org.uk, 26 April 2007

As people are beginning to see themselves more in representation, they are also being considered more in terms of their different abilities and desires or need to access information. Accessibility describes the ability of people with different needs and preferences being able to configure and receive information in the method that best suits them.

When people think of accessibility, they probably think immediately of website design for people with disability. They think of 'assistive technologies' like screen-readers and the need to provide alternative forms of information that describe imagery and interpret tables and graphs. However, web accessibility is greater than this. It also accommodates:

- browser choice (the different presentation settings)
- viewing preferences (images switched off or enlarged text, even colours turned off)
- the limitations of dial-up and broadband technology
- the reconfiguring of content for mobile and hand-held devices
- options for mouse or tab key navigation.

But above all, accessibility is about equity for all members of your intended audience. It can be the provision of sound files or printed brochures. It can be the awareness of multilingual audiences and the production of content in multiple languages – or the development of diagrams and storyboards with minimal dependence on written text for people with lower literacy or educational levels. It can be the provision of braille alternatives printed in hot-melt adhesive dots or embossing on the surface of a printed product.

And online, it is always about reducing file size – to ensure access for people in areas of reduced bandwidth, using older hardware or earlier software versions – by effective minimalisation of file resolution and providing alternative file formats.

It can also be clearly separating different clickable options on-screen so older users can accurately select what they want without accidentally clicking on another nearby link. Jakob Nielsen has looked into some of the issues facing seniors (people over 65 years of age) who use the web – and often they are not so steady or agile with the mouse and will be frustrated by the need to click or drag with precision.

There are ways you can test the accessibility of your information.

Simply checking whether your index will help you to get to the appropriate reference in a book will often let you know whether your audience will be served or hindered.

Turning off the images in your website and trying to navigate through text links will soon identify a few flaws in your logic.

Switching your site or your document to greyscale will immediately identify problems for people with colour blindness – maybe your coding should include a symbol as well as colour to distinguish different information and almost certainly you should increase the tonal contrast in your site. So carefully consider the way different colours interact when reduced to greyscale.

If you are carefully designing with your audience in mind, you will know your product is accessible to the members of that audience.

Accessibility?
'... if you take it as a fundamental requirement that you may have people of all educational and literacy levels, all language levels, some even unable to speak your language, all standing in a room, you need to find multiple points of entry to a single story for all these people, each of whom has different experiential requirements.'

Ralph Appelbaum on exhibition design, quoted by Lakshmi Bhaskaran

Process

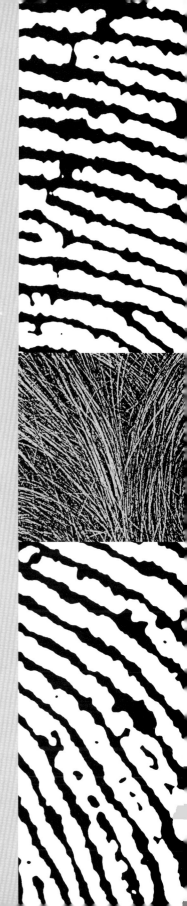

The design process

Wim Nijhuis and Theo Boersema in *Visual Information for Everyday Use*, discuss the design process in terms of a cycle of:

- problem identification and definition
- analysis and observation
- synthesis and reasoning
- simulation and testing
- evaluation and decision on viability and usefulness
- acceptance of the design or iteration of the process to improve the design.

'Our job is to give the client, on time and on cost, not what he wants, but what he never dreamed he wanted; and when he gets it, he recognises it as something he wanted all the time.'

Dewys Landon, quoted by Tom Peters in *The Circle of Innovation*

'Design is a user-focused, prototype-driven development process that simplifies complexity and achieves success through collaboration.'

Peter Lawrence, FastCompany. com, 2005

A design project will start with a full definition of the project and its context for the originators of the project. That is, it will outline where the project sits in relation to other activities of the originator or client. This is discussed at an initial briefing and is often followed by a period of research and analysis that further defines the project.

The next part of the process involves idea generation that will seek to cover all aspects of the project but is really a technique of gathering options. These are referred to as scribbles and thumbnails. They are often annotated with production notes. From these deliberations and ideas, roughs or visuals are developed.

The roughs are presented to the client for approval before finalising the design. Sometimes there will be more than one concept or rough visual for consideration at this stage – to show the client different possibilities.

In the case of publications, there might be just a cover and two pages to show how the interior pages might look. In a magazine, there might be representative spreads from each different type of section. In the case of websites, there will be a home page design and probably some representative pages from one channel of the site – showing how the levels of the site interact. This will accompany a full site map of the information architecture.

On approval of the rough, there may be another stage where the design is developed further to take into account all the nuances within the project and create comprehensive visuals, finished roughs or prototypes. After presentation, when these are approved, there may be a testing phase.

Focus groups or a short market test may be undertaken to verify the decision or to seek feedback from representatives of the actual market for the product.

There may be some iterative fine-tuning of the design following the feedback.

Then the production phase begins. Production entails the finalisation of all artwork and preparation of the job, proofing processes, and final approval before printing, embellishing, finishing and distribution (for print) or alpha and beta testing and uploading (for electronic publishing).

There should always be an evaluation of the final product and consideration of whether it met its objectives as outlined in the briefing meetings and any developments throughout the process. This may identify areas for future work.

Briefing

A brief is like a list of client wishes or requirements. It is not a solution – rather, it defines a problem. Some clients supply a written brief and back-up material about their organisation or product. Other clients give a verbal briefing when prompted by the questions at a briefing meeting.

A working title that will serve as a recognition title for both parties is needed, and a thorough description of the job. What is the reason for the project? Maybe it's a public relations exercise. It could be educational or instructional; or advice about a public safety issue. In some cases, such as annual reports, it is a statutory requirement as well as a public document.

You will need to identify any external requirements of it. These can be limitations imposed by law, by time, by other suppliers.

Discuss the audiences for the project. It helps to list the most important reader to the least important. Readers may be students, members of the media, children, the aged, businesspeople, parents, teachers, residents of a particular region, members of a community, members of parliament, industry leaders, unionists, public servants, academics, taxpayers, and so on.

Consider the ultimate distribution to gain an understanding of how the audience will receive the message. It may be available free or for purchase; on the Internet, hand-delivered or by mail; available at the newsagent or post office; by phone telesales; advertised on television or radio; subscribed to or sold over the counter; exclusive from a particular outlet or event; or any combination of these.

Imagine how it is likely to be used. Most people will scan or skim it, some will read cover-to-cover, some will only

What makes great creativity?
'The ability to delight people in solving a problem. Usually it's about taking an approach to something we never thought about before.'

Jim Stengel, quoted by Tim Burrowes in *B&T*, 27 June 2008.

'Some briefings are delivered with great clarity and the designer is aware of the [commissioner's] intentions for a specific audience; other briefings are consultations in which opinions are sought, reviewed, and contemplated. Some initial meetings are exploratory and open-ended, working on the basis that if able minds come together with an embryonic [project idea] they will bounce ideas off one another, resulting in an approach that would not have been conceived by a single person. If the brief is woolly and ill-informed, the designer may need to turn interrogator, peppering the commissioner with questions in search of the [project's] essence.'

    Andrew Haslam, who was talking about publishers and books in *Book Design*

'There are several key elements required. Firstly you need a clear and precise briefing from your client. This then needs to be transferred and communicated into a clear design brief, then implemented into strategic creative solutions that are clear and understood. The ability to reproduce and be applied accordingly is just as important.'

    John Gomez in *Desktop*, issue 224, February 2007

read summaries, and some will use it as reference.

Is there a single, most important message the audience should receive? There should also be a short description of the sort of material involved and the viewpoint that is being expressed.

Discuss the feel, look or tone of the communication. Should it be light or heavy? simple or complex? quality, earthy, lavish, playful or traditional? In addition to these considerations, what aspect/s of corporate personality – innovative, traditional, caring, progressive, high tech, friendly – need to be projected?

If it is a part of an ongoing project, samples of previous projects should be supplied for reference at the briefing. Digital files or job files on them should also be tabled or handed over to the designer, in order for the continuation of the project to be successful.

If it exists, a corporate style manual that specifies logo usage, typefaces, colours, editorial preferences and design formats should be made available for the designer.

Discuss formats that are expected to be used and whether there is room for variation. There may be existing contracts for supply, for example, that make deviations from the format difficult.

Sample text should be available, even if only in rough draft. If not, is there an indicator of the expected amount of content and how will it be supplied? If it is supplied on disk, formats and programs should be discussed. Also, note whether the text has been or will need to be edited.

Existing images might also be supplied or available, so it helps to discuss how they will be supplied and in what formats.

Preferences for colour, design style and type style should be discussed, and it is handy to have samples of designs that are liked and disliked to discuss different approaches.

Some individuals and organisations have a commitment to environmental responsibility that may mean using and documenting environmentally friendly processes and materials. This needs to be discussed upfront, so that appropriate decisions can be made with regard to supply and specifications.

There may also be special instructions that will enable the design to work into projects in the future. For example, film poster artwork is often used for DVD covers and CD covers (for the soundtrack), press advertisements and wide-screen advertisements. These are all different formats – vertical, horizontal and square and as separated elements – so there is a production complication.

What is the deadline? In discussion, is it realistic? Maybe the desired timing requires some trimming of the expectations, or a considerable overtime budget.

And what exactly are the expected deliverables? One, two or three concepts first? Followed by a full mock-up or prototype for approval?

Finally, what is the budget? Can the described job be completed successfully for that amount? Does it include print costs, programming, replication, distribution, design, illustration, photography and technical time, or are there other budgets for some aspects of the job?

You might also discuss copyright and intellectual property issues. If the commissioning client wants full rights, rather than just the reproduction rights for a particular use, you will need to negotiate the purchase of exclusive rights.

This meeting can become quite lengthy. It may be divided into stages in order to cover all the issues. It will largely depend on the nature of the task.

Research

Paul Nini describes the research component as an investigation and planning phase that identifies needs and problems, gathers and analyses information, and develops possible strategies. The research should cover the topic, the industry context and the audience needs and wants.

Research can be from *primary sources* where you seek information directly from people who know (interviews) or observe behaviour directly (structured experimentation and observation). Alternatively, it can be from *secondary sources* like existing research, documentaries or published material.

While research into the project themes or audiences may be supplied, it is always useful to conduct a little of your own research – or test the assumptions or conclusions of the supplied research.

Research can be also used for developmental purposes – to understand the context of the marketplace into which a product or project is going and what the market needs; what they already know or understand; how they prefer to receive messages ...

CHECKLIST
A brief
Documents:

Client details

☐ Contact names, direct phone numbers, fax numbers and email addresses
☐ Full legal name of the company
☐ Postal and street addresses
☐ Background information about the organisation, its industry and competitors
☐ Website URL (for further background information)

Project description

☐ Name, usage
☐ Sizes, quantity
☐ Price/budget
☐ Any preferences/limitations: colours, images, corporate standards, existing materials, environmental concerns
☐ Launch date/deadlines

Marketing objectives and strategy

☐ Intended market description: age, sex, social group, occupation, location
☐ Benefit/s to buyer/user
☐ Distribution method

Don't forget there is visual research in addition to general research. This is where you might look at how other designers have responded to similar briefs – historically and currently – even if not in the same industry sector as your project. Visual research can help you to give an authentic feel to materials that are supposed to reference a particular culture or audience. There are many resources available to you, including photo and image libraries, libraries, online collections and private collections. Your client may have an industry-specific collection that they can give you access to.

READ MORE ABOUT IT

Timothy Samara, *Design evolution: Theory into practice: A handbook of basic design principles applied in contemporary design*, Rockport, Beverly, Mass., 2008, ISBN 978-1-59253-387-9.

Paul J Nini, 'Sharpening one's axe: Making a case for a comprehensive approach to research in the graphic design process', *Visual:design:scholarship*, the research journal of the Australian Graphic Design Association, vol. 1, no. 2, 2005, AGDA.com.au, ISSN 1833-2226.

Conceptualisation and idea generation

Arguably the bit of the process that most people assume is the whole process, coming up with creative ideas, is the essence of your work as a graphic designer. Who knows where ideas come from? Certainly, relying on an act of divine intervention or happy accident on every brief is no sound basis for a career. You will need to define your own process for generating ideas.

Word association

This often involves making and exploring connections between the elements of a project. It can often be useful to use extensive word association techniques, where you seek synonyms and antonyms for each element in a message. While synonyms provide you with words that mean the same, antonyms are words that mean the opposite – and it can often be useful to think how to communicate backwards – how not to do something or how to un-do it. Which concepts lend themselves to imagery? Use a dictionary, thesaurus or encyclopedia to find alternatives.

Hackneyed or clichéd visual ideas

What images are expected? What connections are obvious? What is the stereotypical response to the project? What is the way this project would have been designed in the past?

You need to document these ideas – get them onto a piece of paper – in order to be able to move on from them.

Some of them may provide a direction to explore: Can you exaggerate the idea? What can you add to it to make it unique? Can you make it a hyper-real historical reference? Would that be appropriate? How can you update it?

Some of them are best forgotten; but some are capable of being reinterpreted or refreshed for a new audience.

Visual puns

Making visual puns usually relies on grouping images or type in a particular shape to express an idea beyond the individual elements. Visual puns do not have to be laugh-out-loud funny; they are usually more subtle.

From Bradbury Thompson's visual pun that featured on a US stamp in 1984

For example, the spine title on *A Smile in the Mind* is set in bold black capitals on white except for the final letter which is a bold capital D set in red. Running down the spine, when on a shelf, it looks like red lips smiling with white teeth and neatly conveys the concept expressed in the title. Of course, to achieve the same impact on the front cover, where the title runs horizontally, the designer has artfully turned the D on its side in the same way – just as easily read but, more importantly, conveying the concept.

Visual puns usually rely on a combination of two or more images and their considered placement to convey an additional idea. This is one of the most useful techniques for generating effective, creative ideas.

Use visual language and symbols

Combining subject-specific imagery with generic visual symbols can create a new idea. Often the incorporation of flags, road signs or other symbols can enhance the concept. You then need to develop the stylistic expression of the resulting idea.

Creating three options

Clients will often want to see more than one rough. If the brief has been sufficiently detailed, you should have enough information to be able to generate a number of alternative solutions. While you will do your own discarding, you will probably come up with a selection of ideas you think could be effective. (Usually you will have a favourite but you should only present ideas that you know will address the brief and be successful for the client on their selection.)

An approach to presenting multiple ideas could be to consider an image-dominant design and a type-dominant design. Then you might consider a traditional or conservative approach and a leading-edge or fashionable approach. You now have at least four options (you will often have numerous image possibilities).

Testing

Do people get it? Sometimes, as designers, we can become too close to an idea and lose our ability to see it as our audience will. You can try random testing on passersby to see if they 'get it'. Of course, it helps if they represent the intended audience, but sometimes it can be surprising just how broadly understood the design messages are – across audiences. This gives you some quick, anecdotal evidence as to the success of your concept.

A more formal process of testing is to enlist research companies to assemble focus groups that represent the intended audience and, with a facilitator trying not to lead them but to seek their opinions, listen to every word and watch their responses to different designs.

A useful tip if focus groups are discussing multiple options is to name each design, rather than coding them alphanumerically. The use of nicknames (usually positive rather than negative, with allusions to particular graphic elements or some memorable feature of each design) allows the meeting to use shorthand when referring to it in discussion. If you don't name them something positive, someone in the group may give it a name with a negative connotation – like the 'cockroach' logo!

One technique of testing is *A/B testing*, where designs are compared against a control version and, in each iteration of the testing, only one element of the design is changed and a preference sought. This can give clear indications of the impact of minor changes – should it be coloured? should it be large? should it be reworded? These would be tested separately in A/B testing – and compared to the 'control' version – without any of these features.

The alternative method to this is called *multivariate testing* and compares many changing elements concurrently. It can often lead to more useful qualitative information but can be more difficult to isolate the specific influence that improves the response to the design.

You should analyse the responses and consider the effectiveness of each design. A group will not necessarily select the best design, but they will make a number of useful comments that may enable designs to be improved or indicate which ones are strong front-runners.

Prototyping

The more 'real' your design looks, the more convincing it will often be.

Prototypes require all sorts of production skills, often working with alternative materials and combining new mock-ups with existing products.

Fortunately, digital printing has enabled output quality to be very high, at reasonable cost and speed.

Sometimes, it can be appropriate to present a design in context – take an author or publisher client to a bookshop where your rough has been put on a shelf and ask them to find it! (Clear this with the shop and prepare it earlier.) Similarly, with fast-moving consumer goods, shelving them and meeting at a supermarket or in someone's kitchen pantry – even listening to shoppers discuss them if they happen to reach for the product. (Obviously, this could backfire, but it's still useful feedback.)

You can demonstrate packaging as a prototype or, if it's impractical or too expensive, on-screen. With 3-D software, you can give clients the tools to turn or tilt the package, altering the lighting and viewpoint.

Websites can be provided as a series of prototype screen-shots on a CD-ROM that, when clicked in order, give a semblance of the final experience. These are often created in layers in an illustration or photo manipulation program. When assembled in a PDF, linked fields or text on each page can link to other pages in the sequence to demonstrate how a site might work.

For large-scale multimedia projects, a prototype can be a working document with active roll-overs and links that, in a few screens, demonstrates how the project will ultimately look and work.

FLAT MOUNTING

Rough

Tape*

Mount board

Tape

Flap

* tape or glue or spray adhesive

WINDOW MOUNTING

Mount board

Tape

Acetate

Rough

Tape

Backing sheet

Tape

Flap

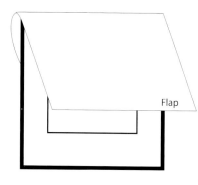

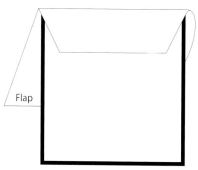

Flap

Flap

Presentation

At the presentation meeting, the designer should repeat the brief, succinctly reminding clients of their requirements, and cite some of the research considered that lead directly to design decisions taken.

Describing where concepts have come from and how that relates to both the brief and the intended audience's expected reactions – both emotive and rational responses – should set the scene for a presentation.

Staging the presentation of alternative designs is important as well. Often, you would start with the more expected response and build to the more creative, unless you wanted to create an initial surprise. You need to assess which style of presentation your client – and, at this stage, it is often a board or committee – will prefer. Sometimes starting big means your other alternatives are disappointing.

Some silence on initial viewing allows clients to weigh the brief and to view the design, going over the introductory remarks in their head. Discuss any comments and details as they arise.

Often it is valuable for clients to take a design away without making any decisions. A contact appointment should be made so there is a clear decision period. This may be determined by the production schedule.

Design justification/rationale

Rationales should be incisive and concise, but thoroughly cover the original brief. They should explain the thinking behind the design solution.

A rationale should describe effects, not specifics. When discussing colour, it should describe feelings/effects in palettes, not descriptions of the actual colours, which can plainly be seen. Regarding text, it should not mention specific typefaces (unless they are corporate faces) but it may describe the impression that the type gives. It should describe the effect of the layout, not the dynamics – words like 'traditional' and 'strong' describe symmetry, 'dynamic' and 'modern' or 'contemporary' describe asymmetry. In regard to image selection, it should explain why the image was chosen, relating it to the content or the feel of the document/item as requested in the brief. In short, it should not be full of design jargon.

The rationale is often attached to the rough on the back or, better still, on the inside flap, opposite the rough. It can be in the email accompanying the electronic proofs.

Speak the language of the boardroom or the client, not about your design but about how it answers their problem and addresses their brief to you. Use their language.

READ MORE ABOUT IT

Anistatia R Miller & Jared M Brown, *Graphic design speak: A visual dictionary for designers and clients*, Rockport, Gloucester, Mass., 1999, ISBN 1 56496 602 X.

Approvals

Approval is required at each step of a design development process. Designers need to keep checking in with the client in order to ensure that their work is accurate and meeting expectations. Both parties should also keep a record of the approval at each stage.

The record is usually a signed and dated sheet of paper with approval to commence the next stage or instructions for any changes noted. It is filed by the designer as part of the job record.

Everything should be checked: text and image content should be complete, accurate and in the correct order; type and layout should be consistent and accurate; colours and production specifications should be clear; the design should embody and complete the agreed design roughs or prototype.

Clearance, of course, becomes more important towards the production stage of the process, as it becomes considerably more costly to make alterations once a design goes into production – and such changes can delay the product's launch.

Production management

Designers monitor the production of their designs in order to guarantee the quality of the final product and ensure its timely delivery. This may involve supervising contractors, late-night press checks, or negotiating your job's priority to meet a launch deadline.

Developing a relationship with various suppliers will assist you at this stage. Ensure accurate specifications for

CHECKLIST
Design presentation techniques

☐ Mounting techniques for print or screen projects:
  – flat mount with images affixed flush on a set of usually black boards
  – window mount, like framing, with a window cut in the board and the image affixed in the 'window', sometimes with clear acetate to protect the surface of the image or give it a high gloss to match the final product
  – portfolio sleeves, where the images are presented in plastic sleeves in a presentation folio
☐ 3D mock-ups and prototypes for products, packaging, signage and exhibitions

Consider:

☐ a clear 'pocket' which snugly holds a mock-up
☐ light card flaps on each board in order to stage the 'reveal'
☐ an attached design justification, either on the back or on the inside flap.

estimates and quotes, advise your client of the supplier most likely to meet the highest quality production for the specific needs of your project (which will likely mean different suppliers for different types of jobs), and advise suppliers of the acceptance (or non-acceptance) of their quotes to assist in their forward planning.

Keep everyone in the loop. The designer will often have the integration role between all the parties in a production workflow. They will also often maintain quality control.

Proofing

Most suppliers will provide a proof against which you compare the approved files you provided to them. Both designers and clients will normally sign-off these proofs before printing or replication. If there is any suspicion that the proofs are inaccurate, you should note it and request a further proof. There are many points in the conversion of electronic files that can compromise the accuracy of the output, so be sure that you make no assumptions and, in each case, examine the proofs with care.

Launch

Usually you will also include distribution and delivery details in your specifications to your supplier. Often there will be numerous destinations for delivery and time-critical points that ensure product launches are successful. These may also involve multiple suppliers – for example, when a book is launched, a web version may need to be simultaneously uploaded; or, when a corporate identity is announced, it may involve publications and promotional products, a website and intranet, simultaneously available in multiple locations.

There may also be security issues where the job is 'under embargo' until a particular time and date – meaning that it legally doesn't exist until that point and no one can quote from it, distribute it or sell it. The reason 'embargoed' copies are given to people – usually journalists or opinion leaders in appropriate fields – is so there can be instant, informed discussion on release. Think of the worldwide printing, distribution and security around the simultaneous release of the later Harry Potter books.

Often there will also be event logistics to consider. Events managers will assist you in planning how you will reveal

Tom Peters on his blog talks about designers being 'dreamers with deadlines' – 'creative and loose ... with hardass deliverables' – and Richard Lipscombe quotes Aaron Cohen: 'The secret to good design is implementation and the secret to implementation is good design.'

TomPeters.com, 28 May 2008

the product at the right time to your invited audience. They will stage-manage the presentation to achieve maximum audience impact and newsworthiness. At the least, it will usually involve sound technicians, caterers and sales staff.

Evaluation

Once your product has been launched and distributed widely, you should review the process and the product against its initial objectives. Has it been successful, partially successful or unsuccessful? What do you need to do next to ensure your objectives will be met?

This evaluation can be a personal review process involving the main players – but it should also probably involve a more formal review process where testing or focus groups provide external feedback to you. This can inform future developments and possibly indicate the potential for future projects or refinements.

If, for example, there were unexpected additional expenses, maybe in evaluation you can identify where in the process the expense occurred and plan to avoid a similar situation in future – or budget for it if it is likely to be unavoidable.

Design effectiveness

There are a number of ways to measure the effectiveness of a design. You can base its effectiveness on an increased number of sales or an increased number of purchases or visits; or a heightened awareness of your organisation – your audience may have an improved impression; you may have increased your credibility with them.

If it is a new version of an existing product – an updated website, a new corporate identity, a revised package or a new edition of a publication – you can use statistics from previous distribution of the product to compare the results.

Alternatively, it may be a qualitative result – your audience may spend longer and go deeper into your site, recommend you to friends, read more of your text, fill out your forms more accurately or not make as many errors.

To accurately determine the amount of this improvement that is owed to the new design, you want other factors to be equivalent – advertising and promotions at the same level as they were previously.

'Recent research by the [UK] Design Council provides evidence of a link between design expenditure and economic performance. It reveals that for every £100 a design business spends on design, turnover is increased by £225, and that rapidly growing businesses are six times more likely than static ones to see design as integral, and twice as likely to have increased their investment in design.'

From the Design Council's *Design in Britain 2005–06*, cited by the Design Skills Advisory Panel in *High Level Skills for Higher Value* (online), Design Council and Creative and Cultural Skills, London, 2007

Another indicator of success might be an increased market share – that is where the design has attracted purchasers or users from competitors to your organisation or introduced enough new users to tilt the figures in your favour. Sometimes a new product will increase sales across a sector by reviving what was a stagnant market.

If you have commissioned initial research, you can often continue that research throughout the project and into the first months of introduction. This is called *tracking research* and measures the change of opinion or influence brought about by the introduction of your new product.

Projects

Publications

Steven Howard in *Corporate Image Management* describes the most important trend as 'moving from a need for content to a desire for context ... Today's problem is that there is too much raw information and data available ... The need of the immediate future is to package and deliver the content in a meaningful and timely manner.'

'Many documents fail because they are so ugly that no one will read them or so confusing that no one can understand them ... most of us have encountered documents that confuse and confound us, frustrating even highly educated readers. Poor documents are so commonplace that deciphering bad writing and bad visual design have become part of the coping skills needed to navigate in the so-called information age.'

Karen A Schriver in *Dynamics in Document Design*

'Publication' is a generic term that describes all printed information that an organisation or individual puts out. With all publication design, the aim is to make the information easy and enjoyable for the reader to digest. It should be user-friendly.

The term 'document' used to mean the same thing, but has come to mean, more specifically, an electronic text or image file.

There is often a great amount of information sadly disguised as boring, difficult-to-understand text – but this can be an authoring problem. A designer's task is to make the best of whatever text is presented and help the reader to find that information easily.

One of the main concerns of the publication designer is headings – the main point of information retrieval for the reader. Attention should also be given to making the contents list clear – no matter how complex or how simple. Equally, indexes require attention, although, as with references and bibliographies, there are fairly standard ways of organising them that have been proven to be successful.

For statistical information, a reader looks to graphs and tables. Both can be dramatically improved by clear typography. A graph shows patterns and contrasts in a quickly identifiable way. A table provides far more specific information that only some readers will use for further study and interpretation.

It helps to have a clear idea of who the intended audience for the publication is likely to be, and design text that will enable them to find what they are seeking.

Books, reports and annual reports

The book represents pure typography – the shaping and placement of words to convey the author's intent with a subtle style, clarity and appropriateness.

When designing long documents, such as books and reports, the most important decisions are those which most affect the readability of the document. Choice of typeface size and weight will often determine how wide the text column will need to be and what sort of line spacing is needed. You may need multiple columns on a wide page. You might need to create standard ways of incorporating graphics. You may choose a low-reflective paper to make the book easier to read. You might suggest to the author or editor that more headings are needed through the publication for easier access to information.

Type selection for books tends to favour classic typeface designs, because they have proven their readability and are considered anonymous enough not to drag attention to themselves. Contemporary fonts will sometimes have a graphic detail that distracts.

Books and reports often have one main column of text to a page. They may have a side column for margin notes, like this book.

There is very little you can do to establish a design 'presence' in a book's main text, because, once you have chosen the typeface, you should follow the decisions that will maximise its readability, which is paramount. Where a designer can influence the look of the book is in imagery selection and the decisions made on headings, titles, formatting and page furniture.

Report style with numbered paragraphs

You might assume you should use the numbered paragraph report styling because all the literature you receive is in that form. Be careful of this assumption – people avoid reading material that looks daunting. Even highly educated, articulate and technical audiences find it difficult to keep up with all the reading they are required to do. Anything that is a disincentive minimises effective communication.

Don't let tradition get in the way of communication. Even in scientific reports and technical manuals, the so-called report style that uses numbered paragraphs is appropriate *only* if the numbered sections, chapters, headings and paragraphs serve a function. This function is usually to do with convenience, accuracy and cost savings in cross-referencing within the document; convenience and cost-effectiveness for complex indexes; and for ease of

CHECKLIST
Attention-getting devices
(in roughly descending order from most to least)
☐ Photographs
☐ Drawings and illustrations
☐ Cartoons
☐ Collage and montage
☐ Maps, diagrams and flow charts
☐ Graphs (line, pie, bar, scatter)
☐ Pictograms and symbols
☐ Runarounds/contoured illustrations
☐ Captions
☐ Decorative type treatments
  – titles and headings
  – drop initials
☐ Colour
  – splashes
  – bars and rules
  – background tints
☐ Pull-quotes
☐ Sidebars and boxed text
☐ Bullets, arrows and other dingbats
☐ Reversed headings
☐ Texture and pattern
☐ Decorative borders
☐ Body copy (main text)
☐ Space

reference that avoids confusion in meetings ('Please turn to paragraph 4.12 to compare the definitions').

If a document meets any of these provisos, it's best to number the paragraphs and make the numbering clear for fast reference. The numbers might be bold or in a different typeface. Usually, blocked paragraphs with space between are used in this styling. For the first line of all headings and paragraphs, there is also usually a tab set that will accommodate the longest number string followed by an em space.

Try to avoid more than three subdivisions within the numbering. Even paragraph 4.12.97 (chapter 4, heading 12, paragraph 97) is getting a little extreme. When you add parts or sections to the front end of this numbering system, it begins to get too unwieldy for clear understanding and defeats its own purpose.

Using that same example, the chapter is simply numbered 4, not 4.0.0. The main heading is numbered 4.12, not 4.12.0. It is also best not to put a full stop after the paragraph number.

Consider the introduction of alphanumeric coding if it will help the reader find the references faster. Alpha coding instead of chapter numbers looks less complex – compare D12.97 with 4.12.97.

Paragraph numbering should be inserted towards the end of the writing stage or even when the final manuscript is approved. If it is done too early, various changes and paragraph insertions and deletions can create numbering hassles later.

For technical and training manuals that are revised and updated regularly – particularly for ring-binder insertion – the numbering should start with each chapter or discrete updatable part of the document, otherwise many pages may need to be reprinted simply to accommodate paragraph renumbering.

In all cases where there are no cross-references, or where cross-references and the index are by page number, avoid numbered sections, headings and paragraphs. This will make a more inviting and readable publication. Chapter numbering is traditional, even though it may serve no useful purpose.

The numbered paragraph form persists in technical documents. This is due to the assumption that many people within those areas expect to see this format. There is a pretentious view that the format identifies a certain type of reader or expert. It is time for change. Even people in those technical areas will read better and faster without the imposition of the numbering system. So break the mould now in publications where numbering is irrelevant.

Certainly, retain paragraph numbering in publications where it enhances the usability of the text, but do not confuse usability with readability.

The problem for readability is that the number interrupts text flow. To partially avoid this imposition on the text, the numbers can be within a wider margin, rather than in the body of the text. Keeping numbers and text appropriately linked is achieved with a hanging indent. The point size of the number can be reduced, as it will have sufficient space around it to stand out. For layout purposes, it is wise to increase the size of the right margin and decrease the size of the left margin, so that the main body of the text appears centred on the page area.

Series

There are three main considerations for series design:

- accommodation of different titles, subtitles and author names on covers, spines and title pages
- colour coding for ease of identification (particularly for staff at an information counter)
- stylistic consistency of illustrations, photograph selection and text treatment.

If you are designing a series of publications, discuss with the author all the likely titles and subtitles in the series so you can accommodate their different lengths. For example, in a series of pamphlets for a veterinary hospital, it's easy to design for the words 'cat' and 'dog' in the title, but 'budgerigar' can create problems. With author names, always design to accommodate both a long name and a short one, such as Eva Cox and Oodgeroo Noonuccal or even a hyphenated surname like Annette Macarthur-Onslow.

If you intend colour-coding the series – that is, associating a particular colour with a particular title – select a palette of colours for the purpose. Keep this in a file with the series style sheets. You can even have colour coding within colour coding, depending on your hierarchy – a series on animals of the world might divide into domestic animals and wild animals and then might subdivide into

DOING IT SMARTER
Complex indexes
If a complex index is to be indexed by page number, there can be considerable production downtime while the index is prepared after the page proofs have been finalised. An indexer obviously cannot complete the index until the final pagination is complete.

In the case of a manual or a report that has a critical schedule, it might be more appropriate for the index to be created using paragraph numbers rather than page numbers. The index can then be prepared concurrently with the production process and depends only on final manuscript, which is earlier in the production process than final pagination.

CHECKLIST
Order of publication
[square brackets indicate option]

The cover

- ☐ Front cover
  - – title, subtitle, author
  - – publisher's logo, series title
- ☐ Spine (reads from top to bottom)
  - – title, [subtitle], author
  - – publisher's logo, [series title]
- ☐ Back cover
  - – blurb, review quotes and author biography
  - – bar code and ISBN/ISSN
  - – recommended retail price
- ☐ Dustjacket flaps
  - – blurb or teaser copy (front flap)
  - – author biography and portrait (back flap)
  - – ISBN/ISSN
  - – recommended retail price
- ☐ Endpaper (or inside front and back covers)
  - – [*Ex Libris* block on inside front]

The preliminary pages

- ☐ Bastard or half-title
  - – title
  - – testimonials, reviews, author blurb or teaser copy
- (roman numerals start numbering here but are not printed)
- ☐ Frontispiece (verso of half-title, i.e. left of title page)
  - – a picture with caption
- ☐ Title page
  - – title, subtitle, series title and author/s
  - – publisher, place of publication, [date]

A title page should not be too much of a jolt from the cover but should also ease the reader into the text design. An easy way of achieving this is to use the title block layout from the cover and add further information in the text styling.

- ☐ Imprint page (verso of title page)
  - – © copyright owner's name, year of first publication
  - – reprint information: number of reprint, date
  - – ISBN (International Standard Book Number of ten or 13 digits)
  - – ISSN (International Standard Series Number of eight digits); annual reports may have both an ISSN, because they are a series, and an ISBN for the individual title
  - – production details such as the names of the editor, designer, production manager, printer
  - – sometimes a colophon appears here with the typographical and reproduction details, e.g. the paper stock/s used, the typeface/s used, the printing process used
  - – cataloguing-in-publication data (available from national and significant libraries)
- ☐ Dedication and/or appropriate quotation (on any page in the preliminary pages)
- ☐ Foreword (by a guest writer; note 'Foreword' not 'Forward')
- ☐ Contents at a glance (if the full contents is very detailed)
- ☐ Contents list, list of illustrations, list of tables
- (roman numerals start appearing on second contents page)

- Preface (author tells why book exists)
- Acknowledgments/Appreciation (author's and/or publisher's thanks to contributors or advisers)
- How to use this book
- Description of activities/objectives
- Organisation chart
- Mission and vision statements
- Financial highlights
- Summary (sometimes called 'Executive summary')
- Conclusions and recommendations
- Chairperson's statement
- Introduction (usually by author)
- Glossary (sometimes here if short)
- List of abbreviations used in the text
- (roman numerals finish here)

The text

- Page 1 (arabic numerals start here)
  - parts divide into chapters

Page 1 is always a right-hand page (recto). It might be a part-title page. So if chapters will always start on a recto page, page 3 would be the first chapter title and first page of actual text. If chapters can start on either a verso or recto page, page 2 would be the first chapter title and first page of the text. Part-title pages always start on a recto page and often have full-bleed colour to identify them quickly when the reader is flicking through the book.

The endmatter

- Financial statements
- Supplementary information
- Appendixes
- References (if not at the end of each chapter)
- Illustration sources (if not in the acknowledgments or within captions)
- Glossary (optional and more traditional placement)
- Bibliography (if not throughout the text, as in this book)
- Index
- Colophon (describes production details – optional placement)

particular species. Choose a colour for each division and a palette of colours that work with that colour for the subdivisions.

READ MORE ABOUT IT

Andrew Haslam, *Book design*, Laurence King Publishing, London, 2006, ISBN 978 1 85669 473 5.

Lakshmi Bhaskaran, *What is publication design?*, RotoVision SA, Mies, Switzerland, 2006, ISBN 978-2-940361-46-5.

Bruce Welch, *Guide to book production: A step-by-step guide to successful and cost effective book production* (rev. edn), Hale & Iremonger, Alexandria, NSW, 2003, ISBN 086806712-1.

Rob Carter, *Working with computer type 1: Books, magazines, newsletters*, RotoVision SA, Crans-Pres-Celigny, Switzerland, 1995, ISBN 2 88046 230 4.

Chris Foges (ed.), *Magazine design*, RotoVision SA, Crans-Pres-Celigny, Switzerland, 1999, ISBN 2 88046 450 1.

William Owen, *Modern magazine design*, Rizzoli, New York, 1991, ISBN 0 8478 1385 1.

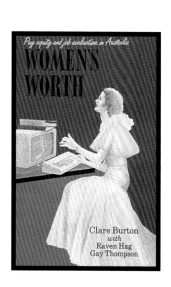

A book cover that uses allusion to a past style to convey something of the book's content.
Client: AGPS Press
Studio: AGPS Design Studio
Designer: David Whitbread
Illustrator: Mandy Orr

Covers

Cover design is like designing a miniature poster. An image needs to attract readers who are browsing in a bookshop or surfing an online bookshop or scanning a catalogue. Because of the usually severe reduction of the design used for reproduction in book catalogues, and the lower resolution when they are reduced and published on-screen in a website, titles are often larger and tracked wider for greater clarity in reduction. Consider, too, the placement in book racks – titles are usually in the top half of the cover.

Magazine covers must have general appeal and, if they are to compete in a newsagency, clarity from a distance. When considering which models to put on a cover, editors consider not only who will be attracted when a model is used, but who will be alienated. A model who has cross-over appeal, that is, who appeals to numerous audiences – young, old, males and females – will have better drawing power for a general or mass-market title. Note that it is hard for illustration to compete with photography in the newsagency!

'Teaser copy' is devised to encourage readers to pick up a copy and find a subject of interest to them if the cover picture is not sufficient. In books, the 'teaser' is often the back cover blurb but, increasingly, reviewers' 'sound-bites' are appearing on the front cover and some books even have the first paragraph on the front cover to get readers hooked straight away.

Covers can also have 'attitude' – they can make a statement about their subjects or their content or, most importantly, their readers. They attract their intended readers by appealing to their visual senses – and most markets are maturing in their visual awareness, so what in the past would have been considered avant garde or experimental is now almost mainstream.

Marketing considerations often affect design decision making in book covers as well. For example, authors may have their name above the title or larger than the title as a marketing requirement, where the author's name is deemed to be the most saleable information on the cover. This might also be a contractual arrangement, where the author's contract states a particular size and position for their name in relation to the title. Mass-market paperbacks clearly demonstrate this. Titles and illustrations in many genres take a back seat to author identification.

With genre titles, there is often a visual coding that distinguishes, say, a romance from a thriller. Within genres, there can be sub-genres. The romance genre breaks into hospital romances, time-travel romances, holiday romances, historical romances, and so on.

Consider the differences in each of the following categories: adventure, war, crime, mystery, horror, epic, romance, future, science fiction, science fantasy, historical, classics, chick lit, teen novels. Each will have distinguishing characteristics that attract particular readers or, more importantly, purchasers.

Even in annual reports there are the equivalents of 'genres': steady-as-she-goes years, innovative years, traditional-values years, what-we-do reports, focus-on-our-people reports, negative-earnings years, merger years, and so on.

You can go against the genre styling, of course. Many books that sit in the general reading sections of bookshops and newsagents could find a place in a genre section if packaged appropriately, but the publisher has chosen to aim for a general audience rather than a niche audience.

Newsletters, journals and magazines

The typography of newsletters, journals and magazines is complex – and because they need to be recreated each issue, a comprehensive style sheet is necessary. Create templates

DOING IT SMARTER
Spine titles
The title on a spine reads from top to bottom. When the book is side-bound or saddle-stapled, there is consequently no spine dimension on which to print the title. It is recommended that the spine title be printed on the back cover, about 5 mm from the spine or binding, again reading from top to bottom. This enables people to read the title without removing the book fully from the shelf.

Newsletters, journals, magazines
[square brackets indicate option]

Cover/front page

☐ Masthead/banner
The masthead (called the 'banner' in the United States) is the nameplate of
the publication. It encapsulates the character and content of the document.
It must be distinctive so that it immediately identifies the publication from
others. It often needs to work with the company logo or symbol that will be
alongside or within the title. It is often a different typeface from the rest of the
newsletter and usually the largest piece of type in the publication.
  It can run vertically in a side column in newsletters and journals, but there
is a danger in this – it is too easy to avoid reading vertical text. In magazines
and newspapers, it should be positioned in the top quarter of the front page,
to work in newsagent racks.

☐ Volume, number
In a monthly, the volume will contain 12 issues; in a quarterly, the volume will
contain four issues. The issues start from the month of the first issue (so they
do not necessarily coincide with the months of the year – issue 1 need not be
in January, as a volume need not represent a calendar year). These days, some
people prefer to number their issues sequentially, ignoring the convention of
volumes.
  Some designers prefer to make the issue number a feature, finding it makes
a stronger masthead. Ensure your design can accommodate two and three
numerals, as issues will quickly reach 10 and could exceed 99 in just over eight
years for monthlies and in just under two years for weeklies!

☐ Bar code

☐ Date (usually only month and year), price
Date and price information is usually linked to the masthead with the issue
numbering or it can be placed with the bar code. It is necessary information
but not important to your reader, so it can be small.

☐ Teaser copy
Teaser copy is a listing of a number of feature article topics and can
incorporate page numbers for easy access. Usually, there is a hierarchy of
teasers; the more popular or important topics are closer to the top, in larger
type and in a more attractive colour.

☐ Spine (reads from top to bottom)
  – name of publication, [positioning line]
  – volume, number, date
  – publisher's logo
  – [feature article topics]

The preliminary pages

☐ Contents list
Often divided into the departments of the magazine, the contents list
may not be arranged chronologically through the magazine but by level of
importance to the reader, so cover stories and feature articles are often listed
first, followed by special supplements, regular columns and listings. There
will usually be the title, a brief description of the content, the author's name
and the page number. Sometimes there will be an illustration from the story
for recognition purposes. That picture will also have a caption with the page
number, in case people are looking at the pictures and not reading the list.

☐ Editorial
Treat the editorial the same as the text. An editorial is usually an opinion or an

introduction of the content, a commentary rather than a presentation of new facts.

- □ Profiles of contributors
- □ Letters to the editor
  The text of the letter is usually in the same type as the text of the newsletter, but the salutation ('Dear Editor') and the sign-off can be treated differently. Often salutations are discarded. You will need to design another level of text for the editor to respond to any issues raised in the letter (so the response cannot be confused with the letters). Italics are often used for responses.
- □ Publisher's information
  - – name of publisher and production staff (editor, art director, contributors)
  - – mailing address
  - – telephone number/s
  - – fax number/s
  - – email addresses
  - – website URL
  - – the number of issues a year
  - – how to subscribe (including price and any discounts)
  - – how to advertise
  - – advertising contacts
  - – guide for contributors (how to submit articles)
  - – copyright information, i.e. ISSN/ISBN

  Americans call the listing of publisher information the 'masthead'; the English call it the 'colophon'; and in Australia it is sometimes referred to as the 'skite box'. It is mostly in very small type. In a newsletter or newspaper, it is often a long thin column on the second page or back page. Often it is on the verso of a contents list and opposite the editorial in a magazine. In a journal, it is mostly on the verso of the title and sometimes on the back page or inside cover.
- □ Running heads/feet (headers and footers in computer terminology)
  - – name of publication
  - – date and/or issue number
  - – folio (page number)
  - – article title on recto pages (in journal)

The text

- □ Department headings
  There will be department headings that separate distinct subject categories – editorial, letters, news, notes, reviews, hints, personnel, recipes, puzzles, and so on. They are usually quite small at the top of the page or column. They sometimes incorporate little illustrations or symbols for visual identification.
- □ News in brief
  News sections can require different heading levels and typography as they are often set on narrower column measure than feature articles. They may need a dateline: 'Canberra, Monday – The Prime Minister ...'
- □ Pull-quotes
- □ Boxed text
- □ Calendar of events
- □ Listings of suppliers, advertisers
- □ Classified advertising
- □ Feature article headings
  Feature articles will probably have three levels of heading – the main title and two levels of subheading within the article. The main heading for feature

articles can be a standard style or vary with each article. Both approaches can work, but the latter is more design-involved, so can slow production. The two headings within are usually, in order, a bold heading about the same size as the text and an italic heading the same size and width as the text.

☐ Author/writer/contributor by-lines

Sometimes the by-line will just be the author's name. It is usually smaller than the text, often set in capitals, and frequently has a particular layout relationship to the article heading. However, by-lines sometimes include more information about the author (a short 'bio') which needs to be treated as a separate level of information to the text – say, in the secondary typeface or, more usually, in italics. Some magazines and newsletters prefer to feature all their contributors' photos and bios on a page upfront, often following the editorial.

☐ Lead paragraphs

The lead paragraph is the first paragraph of a story and summarises the content of the story, introducing the subject, its coverage and sometimes the author. It is usually set in a larger size than the text, often to a different width (say, to a double-column width). This is a gentle way to ease the reader into the text.

☐ Abstract

In journals, there is often an outline of the content and description of the author's approach to the paper contained in an abstract of 100–200 words that precedes the main text. This is often set in italics in the same size as the text.

☐ Body copy (main text)

This is the most important type decision, as the reader will read more text than any other level of information. It must be easy to read. Spend time deciding on typeface, its size, its width and, most importantly, its leading. Decide whether you will indent paragraphs or space them.

☐ Dot points

☐ Table styling

☐ Diagram style and labelling style

☐ Captions

Captions are sometimes smaller than the text and sometimes in italics. They are mostly positioned underneath the photograph or occasionally in a narrow column to the right of the photograph. There is much flexibility in caption typography. Decorative fonts might be used to continue a design theme into the typography of feature articles.

☐ Continuation lines

There are two styles required here for the lines that direct the reader to the page where the article is continued and to identify, once the reader is on that continuation page, which article is being continued. They can be as simple as 'To p. 5' and 'From p. 1', or they may read 'Continued on page 5' and 'Name of article. From page 1'. Use them sparingly, because there is a considerable reader frustration factor with articles that jump through magazines and, unless they are considerably hooked, people will simply stop reading the article at the jump point.

☐ End-of-article symbol

Sometimes the end-of-article symbol is based on the masthead title design or is simply a small square block. It is useful to indicate to your reader that an article is complete.

that establish column width options and include on the master pages the running heads and folios.

In newsletter and newspaper design, consider the impact of folding. It may alter where the first article starts or photographs are placed (say, to avoid folding through the headline or faces). Also consider the impact of mailing regulations and the inclusion of a mailing label. Post offices provide guidelines for the positioning of mailing labels. Even the weight of the paper stock will have a cost impact at the distribution end – if the post office charges extra because the weight of each issue takes it up into the next charge, it can have a significant impact on finances. If the publication will have international subscribers, consider international mailing costs as well.

Custom magazines

There are a number of success stories in custom magazines or client publishing. In-flight magazines such as Qantas's *The Australian Way* are well known and readily recognised custom magazines. Some company newsletters evolve into magazines. There are now magazines published by health insurance companies, community clubs, government organisations, retail stores, shopping malls, video shops, and so on.

Corporate magazines are popular with their readers for many reasons. They are already purchasers of the product or service and can catch up with the latest offerings; their interests in purchasing or belonging will probably mean that there is a range of related information that further identifies them with that entity so their interests may be linked.

Supermarket magazines are an example of corporations capitalising on their market. Their magazine is available only in the store (thus using an existing distribution network and saving external distribution costs). The retailer links with wholesalers and other corporations to cross-promote products. Existing customer profiles provide the intended audience or readership in order to up-sell. The magazine also reinforces television advertising.

Not all custom magazines are sold. Many are free to current members or customers. The information becomes a tangible representation of membership – available only to those 'in the know', underlining that corporate 'You are special to us' message.

As another tool in the marketing kit, the custom magazine has some strengths that are hard to ignore. Understanding that it is easier and cheaper to generate a return purchase from an existing buyer than to generate a new lead, the custom magazine is able to keep the organisation's name in the purchaser's mind. Recognising that a purchase decision is usually the result of about nine prior encounters with a product, the magazine has an ability to add to the tally of those encounters. The printed magazine has a longer shelf life than newspapers, suburban newspapers, letterbox drops and pamphlets – and is likely to be dipped into more times by potentially more people (in doctors' surgeries, waiting rooms and living rooms around the nation), giving greater value for the investment.

The subject matter covered will most likely have a resonance with the reader, too, since there is already a relationship. As with any other type of magazine, develop a profile of the reader – this will already be on the marketing documentation – customers and potential customers, suppliers and staff.

Often there will be an introduction by the CEO as well as an editorial. The CEO will want to warmly embrace the reader with the image of the caring, responsible organisation. The editor will want to imply editorial freedom from the originating organisation – thereby gaining more credibility as a 'real' magazine and enhancing the image of the product as a magazine, rather than as a brochure or, worse, a catalogue. The perception of distance from the originating organisation is a fine line to walk. There must be sufficient corporate identification and image enhancement to warrant the expenditure.

Of course, the advertising policy will often be quite restrictive. Certainly, competitors do not get a look in. The type of advertising allowed must be decided on and offered to particular businesses or organisations that fit the profile of the magazine's marketplace. This, too, is a fine line to walk – a magazine is expected to have advertising, but a reader wants to be able to find the articles! Advertising also helps defray publishing costs. The magazine publisher may not need to make a profit out of their custom magazine itself, but it might want its production to be as close to cost-neutral as possible. The designers must keep this in mind and work within the publisher's policy.

The editor will probably commission a few feature articles for each issue and have a few regular columns in addition to the expected new product round-up, news pages and product reviews. You can use involving devices such as games pages and cartoon strips, and market penetration tracking devices such as competitions.

A custom magazine should fit the corporate image program. It will have, in most cases, a separate identity. It does not have to follow corporate style manuals, grid systems or even typefaces. However, somewhere upfront – either on the cover or the content page – the organisation needs to be identified using its logo and colours.

It is in the corporate identity's interest that the logo and masthead work in close proximity. This does not mean the logo must be a component of the masthead. Although this is often done, it is done more in newsletters than in custom magazines.

Sometimes this corporate awareness is achieved simply by having a luxurious amount of the company's own advertising scattered through the magazine. This helps to maintain the image of the magazine's editorial freedom.

Pamphlets and brochures

'Pamphlet' in Australia translates as the traditional form of a two-fold, six-panel pamphlet at 1/3 A4 (210 × 99 mm), generally referred to as 'A4 folded to DL' ('DL' being the size of the envelope it fits into: 110 × 220 mm). The 1/3 A4 pamphlet is now so entrenched that if a client asks for a pamphlet and gets another size, a designer has a lot of explaining to do! And reasonably so, since most pamphlet racks and counter boxes are now made for the size and DL envelopes make its mailing cost-effective.

The standard requirements for producing a pamphlet are a front cover that is visually interesting and distinctive and a panel design that continues the style established by the cover.

There are two possible methods of folding – the concertina fold or the gate fold, which give the panels a different order. The panels are considered in relation to one another to ensure they remain interesting as readers progress through the pamphlet's content.

Because of their ephemeral nature and the speed with which readers process them, pamphlets should have a

Pamphlet printing
A pamphlet can be cheaper if it can be produced by a quick printer on a pre-cut A4 sheet of paper. This can be done provided there are no bleed areas – where colour extends off the page – and there is a gripper edge of 10 mm along one edge of the sheet on both sides and about 5 mm clearance on all other edges on both sides.

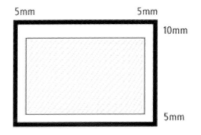

It can be cheaper still if there is no halftone work (photographs to scan and add in) and it can be printed directly from a good-quality laser print.

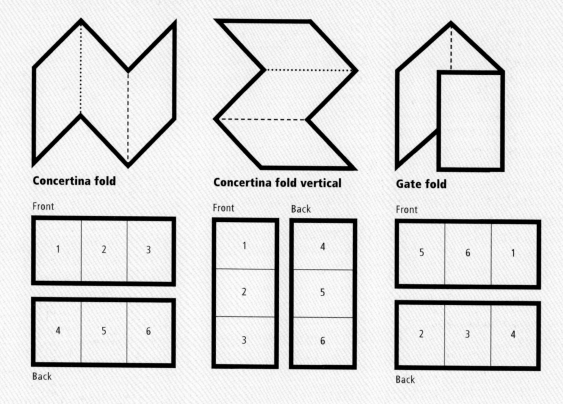

Concertina fold

Front

| 1 | 2 | 3 |

| 4 | 5 | 6 |

Back

Concertina fold vertical

Front   Back

1		4
2		5
3		6

Gate fold

Front

| 5 | 6 | 1 |

| 2 | 3 | 4 |

Back

DOING IT SMARTER
Material to consider for panel 5 in a gate-folded pamphlet

When you open a gated-folded pamphlet, panel 2 is on the left with panel 5 on the right. Opening panel 5 reveals panels 3 and 4. So panel 5 has been seen out of sequence and higher in priority than its number would suggest. As a result, it is often used for material that stands alone, such as:

□ guarantee
□ endorsements
□ order or booking form
□ quote
□ personal invitation (signed)
□ summary of features
□ special offer.

DOING IT SMARTER
Pamphlet covers

The front panel of a pamphlet is often not first seen in its entirety – it will need to be removed from the rack or box. So attract attention to it in the top third of the front cover. Photos can attract attention (but just a bit of sky and cloud, with the main subject obscured by the pamphlet in front, will not cut it these days!). Perhaps put a subject heading at the top of the pamphlet.

Some designers have made excellent use of die-cut shapes – like an arched doorway or the roof of the Sydney Opera House sailing over the top of the other pamphlets in the rack.

Remember, too, that a pamphlet in a letterbox drop or on tables for pick-up will sometimes be seen first from the back. So make the back outer panel attractive, too: let it tell some of the story, or just repeat the front information, perhaps adding the usual address, phone numbers, website URL, map and other contact information. In this way, whichever way someone receives the pamphlet, some of the message gets through – even if people never open it further or just glance at it as it lands in the bin.

series of headings that effectively summarise the content
of the pamphlet, including any special offers that might be
made. Often, readers will scan only the headings and miss
material that is within the body text.

Experimental techniques can be used on ephemeral
work like pamphlets where getting attention quickly
and cost-effectively is the main requirement. Varying
the 1/3 A4 pamphlet size or format in some way will
have a greater impact. For example, 1/4 A4 will still fit
into the pamphlet racks and DL envelopes – it may even
suit the information better to have eight panels instead
of the 1/3 A4's six panels. Perhaps turn the pamphlet
around 90° and open it like a letter. Remember that
the title will probably need to be readable in a rack
– you can repeat the title sideways, if necessary, to
accommodate this use.

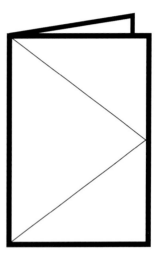

If the pamphlet does not need to be read in a rack and
is dropped into a letterbox, try a triangular format. Most
people will open a triangular format just to see how it
works. If you fold an A4 sheet in half to A5 and then
trim the top and bottom at 30° angles, you will create an
equilateral triangle. There is some paper wastage, but the
organisation can preprint bookmarks or coupons on the
bits trimmed off, so the paper will not be wasted.

Catalogues

A catalogue can be as simple as a table with columns for
each product's name, description and price, photocopied
onto an A4 sheet of paper. Or it can be a large brochure in
magazine format with editorial content and sumptuous
illustrations.

If a catalogue is a complex inventory of a company's
products, it can be contained in a binder that is designed
to accept regular update sheets. Dividers that identify a
particular product range can separate the literature. This
sort of catalogue is more often for trade use, rather than for
the general public.

The catalogue's colour palette and design can be varied
according to the image of the company, its products,
and the type of shopper who frequents its stores. It can
be understated and stylish, or brash and loud; visually
exciting and distracting, or sparse and clean; funky, hip and
streetwise, or logical, thorough and nerdy.

Of course, encouraging buyers to go online to get further product information and to order directly requires great accuracy between website content, product codes and catalogue content. But it also provides an opportunity to focus printed catalogues on new products, seasonal promotions or product ranges for niche markets. The website can contain the comprehensive product range as an online resource with the opportunity to order direct.

Catalogues are often seasonal, and seasons are usually associated with particular colour palettes. The spring and summer catalogues will use clear bright colour and lots of white space. In contrast, Christmas catalogues, even in the height of summer in the southern hemisphere, will probably use lots of rich, warm colours and soft-focus photography – filters can give everything a golden, nostalgic, northern hemisphere Christmas glow. The autumn and winter catalogues will usually use warm, dark, rustic colours.

Many catalogues include hints for the customer that involve the products for sale: care and maintenance advice; fashion tips or accessorising options; hints for enhancing business or home life; recipes or activity sheets; guides to collecting complete sets; endorsements by famous users; fictitious stories; and interviews with the makers or with company staff to give that 'personal' touch – effectively a seal of quality.

Most photography in catalogues is shot in a studio. Here, light is controllable, helping the photographer capture truer colours and finer details. Sometimes a catalogue will have a full shot of a product, a sequence of detail shots, and a swatch of available colours, each keyed with its name: sand, midnight, jade, charcoal ... Each photograph is then labelled or captioned with the product description and purchase information.

If there is more than one product in the photograph, each will be alpha-coded either per page, per double-page spread, or consecutively throughout the catalogue. Using a separate coding table for each double-page spread is preferable because any last-minute changes in product availability will force coding changes only to that one spread, rather than to the whole catalogue.

Some organisations use their inventory codes to resolve ordering issues, but they can often be long sets of numbers and letters that not only can look intrusive when superimposed over the photography, but can be incorrectly copied onto order forms. The coding therefore is often alphabetical rather than numeric, supporting 26 products across a double-page spread. Then the order form will usually ask for a page number and a product code. This means that multiple products will share the same letter code, so to avoid misquoted page numbers (and, truthfully, in how may catalogues can you find the page number that easily anyway?), you can introduce hybrid alphanumeric (A1, A2, B1) or double-letter (AA, AB, BA) codes.

Consider what the organisation is trying to achieve with the catalogue. Is it to get more people through the doors for a two-week blitz? Is it to get phone orders immediately with credit card payments? Is it to get postal orders? Is it to increase awareness of the product range and build the organisation's reputation so it is thought of whenever someone is in the market for that product?

Each of these motivations has implications for the catalogue's design, so find out what the organisation's motivation is. It's frustrating when a reader decides to buy something from a catalogue, but cannot find complete information or even a telephone inquiries number or website address – only an inconvenient shop address or postal options. The vendor loses the sale.

If the intention is to get people into the store, maybe a coupon that is redeemable only in-store will do it. These coupons can be used by the store to gain some valuable feedback on its customer base and the effectiveness or otherwise of its advertising. The store can count how many coupons are returned from a particular catalogue (a simple code can be placed in the corner of each coupon). If shoppers need to write their names and addresses or even just their postcodes on the coupon before they redeem it, the store can find the boundaries of its catchment area, or whether its offer was more attractive to men or to women. Next time, the store can focus on a particular area where it has found advertising to be effective.

Order forms need to be easy to use. People must be able to fill in the order form quickly and accurately. Codes must be able to fit comfortably in handwriting in the allotted space. Product descriptions need not be too long and should probably follow the code in the original product description in the catalogue, so the prospective buyer doesn't have to search for the description or, worse, make

CHECKLIST
Catalogues
- [ ] Picture of product (photograph or illustration)
- [ ] Product code keyed to picture
- [ ] Description and brand
- [ ] Price, colours, sizes and materials
- [ ] Special deals or original price
- [ ] Product order code
- [ ] Colour-matched swatches
- [ ] Availability
- [ ] Sizing details
- [ ] Supply and shipping options and prices
- [ ] Payment options
- [ ] Order form
- [ ] Location listings and maps
- [ ] Contact information including phone number, postal address, freepost address, fax, email and website addresses
- [ ] Legal requirements
- [ ] Editorial content [optional]
- [ ] Hints [optional]
- [ ] Guarantees
- [ ] Product endorsements
- [ ] Special offers
- [ ] Coupons
- [ ] Return policy

one up from the blurb. If it is likely that a special promotion will be sought by most buyers, preprint its product code, description and price on the order form. Leave sufficient room for addresses, credit card numbers and signatures.

Menus

If you need to prepare a menu for a dinner for an organisation or for a local restaurant or even for your own restaurant, you might want to consider some typographical decisions that have an impact on the image you are trying to project.

Maintaining a consistent identity is important. So much consideration has gone into the creation of an atmosphere through décor, lighting and entertainment, and the preparation of a selection of dishes and complementary drinks to tempt the palate, it is a shame to break the experience with a poorly conceived menu.

A set of good-quality, long-life menu covers that link with the restaurant logo, décor and table settings and will withstand the rigours of restaurant use is a good investment (and it might be useful to suggest this to the client). The internal pages can then be the only reprinted and discarded pieces with daily, weekly or seasonal menu changes, saving both money and the environment.

You need to make design decisions that make the updating of the internal pages fast and accurate. Usually that means avoiding illustration and relying on type to do the job. Creating a style sheet also speeds the process.

We've all experienced the following frustrations: the prices are too far away from the name of the dish and the dishes are too cramped on the sheet to accurately identify the corresponding price; the descriptions are too small to be comfortably read in the low light of the restaurant; we can't find the drinks list when the waiter has just asked, 'And would you like drinks with that?'; and there is not enough space between the entries, so we associate the price above the dish with it instead of the price below its description.

Consequently, there are four type decisions that need to be made when designing the style sheet for a menu:
· part headings that signal the courses or parts of the meal: appetiser, entrée, main, dessert, side orders, drinks ...
· cuisine headings that indicate the type or style of food: seafood, vegetarian, Malay, Szechuan, pasta, cocktails,

sparkling wines ...

- name of the dish
- description of the dish and its price.

The first and second are signpost headings – they need to jump out quickly to propel diners through the menu to their preferences. You can use more decorative typefaces, but keep them in a style that is compatible and reinforces the style of the logo typeface. For country kitchens, perhaps Caslon Antique; for wedding menus, script typefaces (usually kept large – 18 points or more – and lower case for ease of legibility); and for French restaurants, maybe art-nouveau-inspired type.

The name and description of the dish need to be comfortably read and are treated like body text – easy-to-read typefaces. This is where handwriting, though quaint and stylish, can be a hindrance to a good menu. Legibility is important. Classic typefaces are usually good, readable typefaces for this information.

Distinguish the name of the dish from its description by using normal text against italics, or bold text against normal text, or small capitals against lower case. You can use rules to separate the dishes to avoid some reading difficulties. In your style sheet for the dish name, create the rule above the name. It is just as effective to add a set amount of space between entries. This can be as little as 3 points and still work successfully.

Many menus are created like the contents lists in old-fashioned books, with dot leaders from the end of the description, or from the end of the name of the dish, to the price. There are occasional bizarre designs where 'Rice' is 16 cm of dots from its price! This is not a good look – or good communication. Try to avoid using dot leaders. There is a false sense that the so-called neatness of justified columns means we must accept this foolish spacing. There is no rule that says a menu must fill the full page width, so a narrower text block may resolve the need for dot leaders. In this case, look for the longest dish name and leave a 5 mm space and key in the price. The resulting line width can become the text block width for the menu. Generous margins can add to the experience.

Prices can be set an em space away from the dish name or a few spaces away. The only problem with this reader-friendly decision is that the price can get lost in the menu and this is a negative for those who are price-conscious.

If the prices are all full-dollar prices, do not include the decimal points and zeros. '$10' is better than '$10.00', although psychologically '$9.95' is preferred.

Programs

Regional and suburban theatre groups, community orchestras, amateur dramatic societies, churches and schools – as well as professional production companies and promoters – present productions that require often complex and fast publishing skills when it comes to preparing the program for the concert, show or event.

There are typographic, layout and production issues to consider. The program should be an adequate souvenir and collector's piece, as well as an official or historic record for the organisation and the local community. It should be cheap enough to print within the usually limited budgets and it should add to the whole perception of the event by the community.

Further complications are sometimes required by the performance rights and clauses in professional contracts regarding the size of an author's or actor's name in relation to the size of the title of the production.

The usual difficulty is coming up with an appropriate typographic treatment for the hierarchy of information that a program contains, creating easily understood and identified listings of production personnel, orchestra and cast, and being a bit theatrical as well!

Type selection and even photo treatments are different, for example, for old-time music hall and a piece of experimental, improv-based theatre. The florid and eclectic mix of fonts and faces that remind people of Edwardian and Victorian printing styles adds an ambience to the entire production for the music hall, where the song-sheet/program is as much a part of the action as the actors. In the same way, decorative borders for each page and possibly even different decorative frames for each photograph – even the use of an oval frame or a *vignette* (fading edges) – help maintain the whole production's illusion of the latter 19th century.

As a contrast, the modern line and detached impersonality of a sans serif typeface like Univers used in an idiosyncratic and perhaps unexpected or risky way helps define the nature of the improv performance. Awkwardly cropped or positioned images, with a bit of overlapping or dramatic interrelationships between the text and the images, also enhance the illusion of the production being a bit daring or unconventional.

Orders of service

Orders of service for weddings and weekly church services have their own design issues. With a wedding service, there is the desire to make a worthy souvenir. Including a list of the bridal party and the words of the readings and songs can make it a pleasant keepsake. Using a different paper that links with the invitations or placecards can tie in the range of wedding stationery, and incorporating photographs or illustrations can further personalise the order of service.

With a church service, there is often the need to fit a large amount of material but avoid unnecessary additional production costs. Consider the use of columns, narrow margins and different type sizes (larger and lower case for responses and smaller for announcements).

Another issue for orders of service is copyright infringement of song lyrics (and this includes hymns). Respect copyright laws – permission to reproduce must be sought as required (usually the song or hymn book will have instruction as to how to seek this permission on the back of its title page). The citation should be at the foot of the reproduced words with the copyright symbol, ©. Then list the owner of the copyright – it may not necessarily be the author, but a publisher or a company.

Comics and graphic novels

Comics tell a story or communicate information through pictures and text. The sequence of panels shows the progression of time and implies change between each panel: the change of time, completion or continuation of movement, a new location or action, or a change in a point of view. In this way, comics work with the reader and expect them to fill in the gaps. Different text techniques like voice balloons, thought balloons and brief location and time descriptors are often incorporated into the illustrations. There can also be linking passages of descriptive text between sequences in the story and introductory text to set the context.

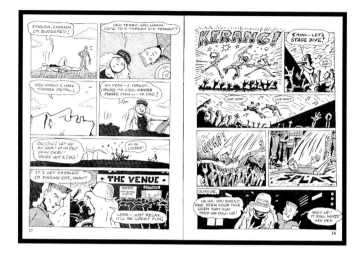

Streetwize Comics present educational
messages in a more accessible format
for their audience.
Clients: Mental Health Services Unit, NSW
Department of Health and SA Minister for
Youth Affairs
Written and designed by Streetwize Comics

Scripting conventions
Authors will use lower case for
instructions to their illustrator and
capitals for all dialogue and caption
copy.

Comics, and the further development of the genre that
refers to illustrated strip books as graphic novels, can
be used to communicate more effectively to a visually
sophisticated audience that is not necessarily reading other
forms. The comic can be a more attractive medium than
traditional text, particularly for younger audiences. Complex
information can be presented more effectively in a comic
strip, as assembly and installation instructions for many
appliances demonstrate.

The graphic novel is grander in scope than the comic.
The best graphic novels use a complex mix of text, pictorial
and film conventions. This enables them to have more
layers of detail and even more engagement of the reader.
Often the juxtaposition of different forms of narrative will
maintain the reader's interest.

The visual conventions of comics and graphic novels
relate strongly to visual literacy as learnt through
exposure to film and video. Using film conventions and
even appropriating the storyboarding technique used to
plan film, information can be presented with dialogue
– even sound effects have conventions based on type
variation.

Backgrounds and foregrounds can have different
characteristics. Backgrounds can be drawn with the same
qualities as the characters or they can comment on a
character's inner life by being drawn in different styles as
the mood and atmosphere changes. Illustratively, there is
no specific style preferred: comic, realistic, semi-abstract,

watercolour, oil painting, cut paper, collage, computer-
rendered, 3-D modelled, photographic, found objects
– anything goes.

The interpretation of style here is another visual
language, where conventions denote how a particular line
is viewed: it could be languid, neurotic, feeble or shrill,
depending on its drawn quality. The reader understands
these conventions and 'reads' this level of comment or
description intuitively.

READ MORE ABOUT IT

Scott McCloud, *Understanding comics: The invisible art*, Tundra Publishing,
    Northampton, Massachusetts, 1993, ISBN 1 56862 019 5.
Mike Chinn, *Writing and illustrating the graphic novel: Everything you wanted
    to know to create great works*, Quarto/New Burlington Books, London, 2004,
    ISBN 1-86155-471-0.
Will Eisner, *Comics and sequential art*, expanded edition, Poorhouse Press,
    Tamarac, Florida, 1990, ISBN 0 9614728 0 2.
Roger Sabin, *Comics, comix and graphic novels*, Phaidon, London, 1996,
    ISBN 0 7148 3008 9.
Mark Salisbury, *Artists on comic art*, Titan, London, 2000, ISBN 1 84023 186 6.
Stan Lee & John Buscema, *How to draw comics the Marvel way*, Simon &
    Schuster, New York, 1978, ISBN 0 671 53077 1.
Gregor Krisztian & Nesrin Schlempp-Ülker, *Visualising ideas: From scribbles to
    storyboards*, Thames & Hudson, London, 2006, ISBN 0-500-28612-4.
Rod Tokely & Dillon Naylor, *Zap! Splat! Ka-pow!: Make your own comic*,
    Omnibus Books, Norwood, South Australia, 1999, ISBN 1 86291 397 8.
Grant Morrison & Dave McKean, *Arkham Asylum*, DC Comics, New York, 1989,
    ISBN 0 930289 56 0.
Jill Bossert, *Children's book illustration: Step-by-step techniques: A unique
    guide from the masters*, RotoVision S, Crans-Pres-Celigny, 1998,
    ISBN 2 88046 335 1.

Proposals

Presentations to clients, curricula vitae, information packs,
interim reports and submissions, proposals and tender
documents have become a part of corporate life. Keep them
simple for speedy, hassle-free production. Often they need
to be produced in short order and perform on boardroom
tables in a competitive situation.

The designer can help make a competitive submission
by attending to the details and being prepared for them.
Preprinted material can be incorporated to 'dress up' the
presentation. Using a combination of overprints and
carefully templated components, a well-designed piece
can showcase the organisation's professionalism. The

Proposal production

Paper selection

- ☐ Front and back covers (maybe with a window to read a title?)
- ☐ Dividers (with generic headings?)
- ☐ Text pages

Sources:

- ☐ Stationery by the piece
- ☐ Giftwrap
- ☐ Preprints
- ☐ Handmade papers
- ☐ Tracing paper/film
- ☐ Acetate

Printing method

- ☐ Laser printing
- ☐ Photocopying

Binding

- ☐ Side-bound
- ☐ Saddle-stitched

with:

- ☐ Staples
- ☐ Wire
- ☐ Rings
- ☐ Plastic comb
- ☐ Ribbon, cotton, twine

Other techniques to consider

- ☐ Colour coding
- ☐ Cutting and folding (windows)

Standard information sheets

- ☐ Description of the organisation
- ☐ Vision and mission statements
- ☐ Organisation structure
- ☐ Bios/curricula vitae of senior team members (with photos?)
- ☐ Case studies/profiles of previous successful projects
- ☐ Letters of commendation

Check consistency

- ☐ Spelling
  - – names
  - – titles
- ☐ Figures
  - – calculations
  - – phone numbers
  - – prices

proposal must look impressive and professional and the receiver should marvel that it could be put together so effectively in such a short period of time – your reputation will be enhanced.

A proposal needs to be packaged competitively – but also needs to be able to be produced quickly. Prepared dividers and folders allow easy updating of the content.

Designers: Louise Dews, David Whitbread

Corporate identity and branding

The corporate image of any organisation is a complex mix of outsider and insider views of that organisation. The views are determined through encounters and experiences with the organisation. The encounters range through advertising on television to 'Positions Vacant', from letters to reports, from Christmas cards to staff newsletters. The experiences are usually person-to-person dealings, either by email, letter, phone or in person.

When referring to corporate identity, it is often forgotten that the print or visual identity is really only a part of an organisation's image. But it is probably the easiest part to control.

Many organisations appear to not understand how their visual identity works for them or, in many cases, against them. The identity affects not only outsiders' views of an organisation but also insiders'. It can help the organisation establish a perception of itself as worthwhile, trustworthy, professional, forward-thinking, up-to-date – alternatively, it can look fly-by-night, cheap, tasteless or muddled.

It can also be an effective, shorthand way of informing people. Once a look that is associated with the organisation has been established, people automatically remember that and the basic information doesn't have to be reiterated.

One of the assumptions many organisations make is that if they use the same symbol on everything they produce, it will fulfil the requirements of a visual identity. Money and a great deal of time is spent by management and designers working out a symbol design, and by the time a solution has been agreed, the budget is depleted. The actual 'nuts and bolts' of the identity – arguably the most important part of corporate visual identity is the application – are hurriedly thrown together for a launch and the value of the image is greatly reduced or, worse, totally lost.

To create an effective corporate visual identity, the standards must be applied consistently and creatively over

'Design makes business strategy visible, compelling, relevant and thereby measurable, increasing market share and generating brand loyalty.'

Ken Cato

'At a minimum, the identity system should create something memorable and distinctive about the organisation, something that enables the organisation to stand out from the crowd. In the best executions, a corporate identity system will provide a unique position platform for the organisation, something that allows customers and others to develop a feeling of familiarity with the organisation.'

Steven Howard in *Corporate Image Management*

'This is also where the hard work begins for the creative mind – to empower logic with imagination and then arrive at a solution that satisfies the criteria of communication relevance, distinction, understanding, engagement, memorability, charisma and an uplifting aesthetic, with the practicalities for implementation, and within a time and budget framework.'

Richard Henderson, 'The intellect vs intuition debate', in *B&T*, 7 March 2008

The 10 Cs of Branding
1   Competent
2   Credible
3   Clear
4   Compelling
5   Consistent
6   Constant
7   Confident
8   Connected
9   Committed
10 Current.

William Arruda, MarketingProfs. com, 19 September 2006

'At Gallup we refer to the sales and marketing communications as the "brand promise," and the quality of the products and services as the "brand experience." A company will be able to create a growing number of loyal customers only if its brand experience matches or exceeds its brand promise.'

Marcus Buckingham and Curt Coffman in *First, Break All the Rules*

'The research demonstrates that taste, touch, and smell are intimately involved in creating a great brand experience and continued loyalty. The role of sound to create an emotional response is well documented [think film soundtracks]. Sight may convey information well, but even at best it creates a less deeply felt emotional response.'

Martin Lindstrom in *Brand Sense*

time. It can be as simple as a corporate typeface with a standard expression of the name of the organisation and colour. Provided it is consistently applied, it should be effective. However, usually an identity has a number of components that are detailed for each manifestation of the identity in a corporate identity manual.

Brand evolution

Sometimes a visual identity needs a refresh. The point to remember here is that a visual identity will often have established a valuable recognition factor by your clients, markets, suppliers and staff. So you need to be careful not to lose the value of that recognition and the existing credibility your identity may have.

So why would you consider a refresh? Maybe your competitors have just refreshed theirs; or they may have spent considerable money establishing a new identity in your market that you think may make you appear less competitive. You might find that the existing identity is not working well in new media or that it has production limitations which need to be resolved. It may no longer represent the variety of work or product you produce.

Evolution of the identity, rather than a new identity, is called for. Research what elements of the identity are current and sending the correct messages to your markets; and identify which elements are working against you, creating limitations or miscommunicating in the marketplace.

It is worth considering Masaaki Imai's Japanese management philosophy of *kaizen*, which is based on continual, gradual or incremental improvement, for corporate identity evolution. For example, you can phase in a modified identity – maybe a spruced up logo and revised colour palette, a fresh corporate typeface and set of templates and style sheets – over a period of time. It is often cheaper and your markets gradually realise the identity has morphed into a fresher one.

READ MORE ABOUT IT

Wally Ollins, *Corporate identity: Making business strategy visible through design*, Thames & Hudson, London, 1989, ISBN 0 500 01472 8.

V+K Publishing, *The image of a company: Manual for corporate identity*, Architecture Design and Technology Press, London, 1990, ISBN 1 85454 404 7.

Per Mollerup, *Marks of excellence: The history and taxonomy of trademarks*, Phaidon, London, n.d., ISBN 0 7148 3838 1.

Marc English, *Designing identity: Graphic design as a business strategy*, Rockport Publishers, Gloucester, Mass., 1998, ISBN 1 56496 388 8.

Steven Howard, *Corporate image management: A marketing discipline for the 21st century*, Butterworth-Heinemann Asia, Singapore, 1998, ISBN 9 810 08085 9.

Peter Steidl & Garry Emery, *Corporate image and identity strategies: Designing the corporate future*, Business & Professional Publishing, Sydney, 1997, ISBN 1 875680 43 8.

Flett Henderson & Arnold, *How image can make your business more successful*, FHA, Melbourne, n.d.

Martin Lindstrom, *Brand sense: Build powerful brands through touch, taste, smell, sight and sound*, Free Press, New York, 2005, ISBN 978-0-7432-6784-7.

B Joseph Pine II & James H Gilmore, *The experience economy: Work is theatre and every business a stage*, Harvard Business School Press, Boston, Mass., 1999, ISBN 978-0-87584-819-8.

Emily Schrubbe-Potts, *Designing brands: Graphic success through graphic distinction*, Rockport Publishers, Gloucester, Mass., 2000, ISBN 1 56496 668 2.

Anistatia R Miller & Jared M Brown, *What logos do and how they do it*, Rockport Publishers, Gloucester, Mass., 1998, ISBN 1 56496 382 9.

Catherine Fishel, *Redesigning identity: Graphic design strategies for success*, Rockport Publishers, Gloucester, Mass., 2000, ISBN 1 56496 624 0.

Naomi Klein, *No logo: Taking aim at the brand bullies*, Flamingo, London, 2000, ISBN 0 00 255919 6.

Jean-Marie Floch (translated by Pierre van Osselaer & Alec McHoul), *Visual identities*, Continuum, London, 2000, ISBN 0-8264-4739-2.

A design audit

Regardless of whether the organisation is a one-person operation such as a small office/home office, a school, church or community group, a multinational business, or a government department, the image is projected by a set of pieces like a giant jigsaw puzzle. Do they fit together, or is it just a frustrating mess like that bag of old jigsaw bits out in the garage – maybe two jigsaws mixed together with a few missing pieces and a few that are broken?

Are your design efforts reinforcing the organisation's current image in the marketplace? Do they reflect the changes taking place in the organisation and its desired image? If not, what can you do to fix the situation?

The image is projected at its most important level by the staff – in their understanding and consideration of buyers, suppliers and each other. It is evidenced in their telephone manner, their welcoming smile, their demeanour, attitude and ultimately in the job they do. But design, too, at all levels of an organisation, must serve the whole. Image projection occurs through even the smallest and seemingly least important piece of the organisation's identity.

'Telling the story is about designing marketing communications to deliver on the promise all the while being clever, savvy, authentic, and true to the brand. It's about treating consumers as being interesting and interested.'

John Moore, quoted in WorthwhileMag.com, August 2004

CHECKLIST
Brand management
(in roughly chronological order of product life cycle)
- ☐ Research and product development
- ☐ Product placement
  - – market
  - – audience
  - – pricing
- ☐ Positioning statements
- ☐ Creation of mood boards
  - – associated lifestyle
  - – attitudes
  - – colours and tone
- ☐ Naming
  - – research internationally for rights
  - – appropriateness of meanings in translation
- ☐ Logo development
- ☐ Product launch
- ☐ Marketing, public relations, advertising and sales
- ☐ Research and monitoring
- ☐ Line extension
  - – seasonal extension
- ☐ Endorsements, sponsorships and strategic alliances
- ☐ Brand guardianship
- ☐ Long-term strategy

Based in part on a seminar by Carlo Pagoda of Primo Angeli Inc. in Canberra, March 2000

It needs to be consistently projected in print, on-screen, in-store and on packaging, as well as in your locations, on your vehicles and in your people.

In a worst-case scenario, maybe your design efforts are running counter to the organisation's other materials and its stated objectives. A design audit looks at the visual manifestation of the organisation's image through the array of identity materials that represent the organisation to its various markets and enables a designer to identify the successes and failures and to ultimately fine-tune the image being presented.

Markets

People sometimes assume their market is only the people who will use the product or the organisation's services. These people may be considered the primary audience, but there are many secondary and tertiary markets to be considered. Anyone who has an operational relationship with the organisation is a receiver of its image:

- users of the service or product
- purchasers (who are not necessarily the end users)
- staff, their families and friends
- suppliers
- competitors
- potential employees
- community.

Collection of evidence

A design audit is based on a collection of all the materials produced by the organisation where its identity is in view – or even where it isn't (it may have been forgotten on some pieces). There should be a central collection point so that at any moment it can be accessed and assessed.

Assessment

Collecting the material can be a difficult task – but it does not end there! You need to assess whether each of those pieces is adding to the full story about the organisation or whether it is hindering the message. Then do something about it.

'If you can wow your customers, they'll keep coming back – and do your marketing for you.'

Kym Illman

'Don't assume you can wow a customer with the big picture at the expense of details.'

Bill Capodagli and Lynn Jackson in *The Disney Way*

Customer journey mapping

Map the journey of a customer's relationship with your organisation, product or brand. In a document, flow chart or spreadsheet, detail all of a customer's possible interactions with your brand or your organisation. These interactions are called 'touchpoints' and need to be considered across multiple 'channels' – media, staff, in-store, in print, online, and so on.

Describe their physical and emotional interaction at each point – the level of their involvement with you – and what that could mean in planning to improve your business.

CHECKLIST
Manifestations of corporate identity

Stationery range

□ Letterheads
□ Continuation sheets (second-page letterhead)
□ Memorandum sheets
□ Minute papers
□ Media releases
□ Facsimile cover sheets
□ Business cards
□ With compliments slips
□ Envelopes
□ Folders
□ Pads and Post-it notes
□ Email signature blocks

Advertising and marketing materials

□ Television commercials
□ Radio commercials and recorded messages
□ Website/s
□ Podcasts and vodcasts
□ Screen-based information systems, such as CD-ROMs and DVDs
□ Newspaper advertisements
  – display ads
  – classified ads
□ Magazine advertisements
□ Listings in print or online resources like the *Yellow Pages*
□ Direct-mail packs
□ Posters and billboards
□ Taxi and bus advertising
□ Exhibitions and trade show displays
□ Promotional calendars and giftware
□ Greeting cards
□ Promotional and training videos
□ Telephone answering system
□ Product packaging
□ Point-of-sale promotional materials

Publications

□ Technical manuals and instructional materials
□ Staff manuals and corporate planning documents
□ Reports and research documents
□ Annual reports and prospectuses
□ Proposals
□ Newsletters
□ E-zines and email newsletters
□ Intranet pages
□ Brochures and pamphlets
□ Flyers, circulars, inserts and handbills
□ Catalogues and price lists
□ Product literature and updates
□ Guidebooks and programs
□ Menus and orders of service

Various internal and external forms

□ Screen-based information systems and databases
□ Application forms
□ Order forms, purchase orders and price lists
□ Invoices and statements
□ Contracts
□ Job records and time sheets
□ Cheques and receipts
□ Requisition and packaging slips
□ Questionnaires, surveys and return-mail cards

Signage

□ External building signage
□ Car park signage
□ Directional signage within buildings
□ Foyer identification
□ Room identification and name plates
□ Door labelling
□ Hours of business
□ Vehicles
□ Umbrellas and sandwich boards
□ Exhibitions, trade shows and displays
□ Lecterns
□ Banners

Uniforms and corporate wardrobe

□ Counter and sales staff
□ Office staff and senior staff
□ Ushers and serving staff
□ Delivery and receiving staff
□ Ties and scarves
□ T-shirts
□ Name tags

Other

□ Email signature blocks
□ Packaging, bags, mailing labels and wrapping paper
□ Product labelling, swing tags and tickets
□ Certificates
□ Presentation materials
  – PowerPoint slides and computer presentations
  – handouts
  – charts and diagrams
□ Interiors
  – office décor
  – retail stores
  – warehousing facilities
    – counters and booths
    – tea rooms and bathrooms
    – workshops

**Options for developing
corporate marks**

- ☐ Symbols
- ☐ Pictogram
- ☐ Silhouette
- ☐ Picture
- ☐ Logotype (full title)
- ☐ Initial/s (one letter or an acronym)
- ☐ Monogram (interlinked initials)
- ☐ Mascot or character
- ☐ Heraldic mark
- ☐ Visual pun

CHECKLIST

Brand distinction

- ☐ Icons (set)
- ☐ Colour (palette/coding)
- ☐ Shape (Coca-Cola bottle)
- ☐ Aroma (chocolates, bakeries, perfume counters, coffee shops)
- ☐ Language (name and unique words like McDonald's 'McNuggets')
- ☐ Sound (soundtrack, unique ringtones, jingles and 'Shweppervescence')
- ☐ Navigation
- ☐ Illustration style (or even Disney's 'hidden Mickeys')
- ☐ Service features
- ☐ Traditions (Christmas)
- ☐ Rituals (New Zealand All Blacks' *haka*)
- ☐ Touch (temperature and texture)
- ☐ Consistency across print, screen, in-store and packaging

From Martin Lindstrom in *Brand Sense*

Identifiers

You need to design an icon, logo or corporate symbol for the future. It must have a quality that will not date or is, at least, updatable. This usually translates into something using 'pure' shapes and 'classic' fonts because they will never date.

Design identifiers by cutting out paper shapes rather than by drawing by hand. This forces you to consider shape over line. Use the shape tools rather than the line tools. You can progressively simplify a silhouette in order to create an effective icon. Think Colonel Sanders for KFC.

Using a thick black marker, draw your symbol on a recipe card. If the symbol doesn't work because you can't fit all the detail, you know you have too much detail! You need to simplify it until it fits.

There is a test that says a good logo is able to be drawn quickly from memory by anyone using a biro. Think Nike. Think McDonald's. The wisest way to create icons is to resist the temptation to reinvent the wheel. Use readily recognised concepts in original ways.

Good logos, symbols and icons generally fall into a standard frame (square, circle, triangle, octagon and rectangle), so start by deciding on the desired frame. If you are creating a suite of icons for a program or website, you may decide that the frame will symbolise a specific type of feature. For example, the square might represent a graphic, the circle might be a sound bite, and the triangle may be an animatic.

Be careful that the triangle does not confuse the reader with a directional implication: when pointing to the right the triangle symbolises 'forward' movement, and when pointing to the left it symbolises 'backward' movement (from the familiar video and sound system interface).

Road signs use subset coding with colour coding as well. For example, round white signs are usually speed-related, rectangular green signs are usually geographical information, and diamond yellow signs show something of the road ahead.

The frame decision should be made before you create the internal detail that identifies the icon's specific role, because designing an icon to fit a square does not mean it will necessarily sit comfortably in a triangle if you later decide to alter the frame.

When you start defining the image inside that will identify specific features, again create the image with shapes rather than lines. Lines tempt you to put too much detail and nuance into the picture – you don't have the luxury of nuance in a 5 mm square graphic that is output on a computer screen! Equally, you can't achieve the detail when you're stitching the logo into a cloth badge or corporate wardrobe. By concentrating on shape, you will find it easier to create a successful icon.

You can certainly use curves, but on a website the graphic will probably be pixelated for the site to maintain its speed of draw, so consider simplifying detail. Fortunately, anti-aliasing can smooth the appearance of curves on-screen.

There are few standard icons that use type forms within them: P for parking; i for information; $ for money. In word-processing and page-layout programs, by necessity, more were created: B for bold; U for underline; *I* for italic. Letterforms imply language dependence and this is why they are normally avoided. Even the $ for money is a culturally specific icon, just as the £ (pound sign), € (euro sign) and ¥ (yen sign) represent other currencies.

But you do not need to worry so much about incorporating letterforms into icons if you know that the person reading the site, program or signage will be using the same language.

Individualising icons
To further customise icons and make them fit the feel of the site, the style of the interface, or the corporate identity you are designing, you can do some texture mapping and apply colours that link the icons stylistically to the rest of the screen display or stationery. But consider this a separate issue – the icon should work in black on white, with no texture and no colour and, preferably, be simple enough for anyone to sketch for someone else to recognise. Think Nike tick. Adding the texture and colour is a decision made on the overall appearance of the interface or range.

Beware the icons becoming lost if they are integrated too well. The user still needs to be able to find them quickly. A soft shadow, for example, is often used to 'lift' the icon off its background.

Logos = God
'A carefully considered logo will do the following:
- Identify (be distinct and therefore memorable)
- Create desirable associations (whether via content, form, or both) while avoiding negative ones
- Harmonize with the company's products, services and culture to avoid dissonance
- Reflect the company in an elastic way that allows for shifts in the logo's meaning
- Work easily and inexpensively in all media.'

Mark Holland in 'Logos = God', *Communication Arts*, vol. 41, no. 6, Design Annual, November 1999

'Your logo is not your brand. Your logo only represents your brand ... Your logo is nothing more (and certainly, nothing less) than a visual mark that represents your brand. It allows people with money to find you, remember you and differentiate you from a billion other businesses. And while your logo is not your brand, its design and consistent use will affect how your brand will be perceived.'

Jared McCarthy, 'Logos: What makes them work', MarketingProfs.com, 15 January 2008

Symbols

Symbols have an inherent problem – time is needed to establish association of the symbol with the organisation. They are, by definition, abstract. They need to be presented, explained or associated very strongly with a logo initially to enable that 'automatic' association to develop. Symbols nearly always have to be used in tandem with a logotype until recognition is instant. Once that recognition is achieved, the logotype can be dropped from many uses and the symbol can stand alone.

Logotypes/logos

A logotype, as its name implies, incorporates letterforms. Usually it is developed as a format in which the title of the organisation will consistently appear. It can be an initial, an acronym or an abbreviated version of the full title. There is usually a limited range of options developed by the designer for its use with the symbol.

Often the logo has an 'individualising' feature – this can be spacing, kerning, ligature or swash idiosyncrasy – that will be a unique feature of the identity. Westinghouse famously created an *st* ligature which cleverly controlled the spacing for signwriters and commercial artists who were reproducing their logo.

When considering the type characteristics, always look at the words in capitals and in lower case as well. Sometimes, looking at the optional letterforms that you can get in italic letterforms is also advisable. For example, in some typefaces, you can find a great *f*, *g* or *&* in italics. It is also quite acceptable to mix these letterforms in a logotype, as the mixture can provide that individualising feature.

Often the letterspacing and leading of the typography in a logo will be more extreme than in text setting. Characters might share a letterstroke; there might need to be a dotless i for a descender on the line above to sit comfortably with the line below; optical leading may mean that lines are unevenly leaded. Avoid having text lines too close to the logo or running off it – most designers recommend particular spatial relationships between logo, symbol and surrounding text and images.

Initials

Some organisations choose to use a single initial or a group of initials that may or may not make an acronym. In these

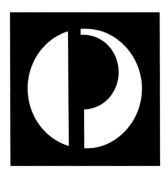

The Australia Post logo incorporates the P from Post and also the subtle pictogram of a horn, associated with town criers in medieval times and used in many European postal identities. Designed in 1975 by Pieter Huveneers

'... bricolage means calling upon a number of already established forms, some of which may be fixed forms. However ... [it] does not lead to the production of merely stereotyped discourse. Rather, in this case, the selection and exploitation of the facts of usage and the products of history lead to a kind of creativity that constitutes the originality of bricolage ...'

Jean-Marie Floch in *Visual Identities*

cases, the letterform/s need to be carefully chosen and applied. Usually initials will also be used with a logotype of the full name of the organisation.

Monograms

Another technique of creating a logotype is to create a monogram. This is a decorative interweaving or interlinking of the initial letterforms of a person or company name – look at the Volkswagen logo. This technique was very popular in the 19th century and you can see extant uses of it in the monograms for some unions, fire brigades and municipalities.

Mascots/promotional characters

Where would Australian advertising history be without Louie the Fly, Bertie the Aeroplane, Chesty Bond, the Redheads, Zig and Zag, the St George Dragon and the Gobbledok? What about sporting team mascots? For that matter, where would world advertising history be without Snap, Crackle and Pop, Leo the Paddle Pop Lion, Sam Toucan, the Michelin Man, the Jolly Green Giant, Ronald McDonald and the Hamburglar?

Constable Kenny Koala
Courtesy: Australian Federal Police Museum

Corporate characters can provide liveliness to advertising materials, and often hired actors attend promotional events in character, which can be more successful than just a logo.

Characters often become a way for an organisation to communicate to a junior audience. Junior audiences, of course, have captive secondary audiences like parents, guardians and older siblings that might get the message through the junior members of the household. Constable Kenny Koala of the Australian Federal Police has had comic strips and kids columns in local papers, a television career, personal appearances at schools, fetes and community events, appeared in colouring competitions and conveyed many safety messages.

Corporate typefaces

A 'support' typeface that is a clear face for text or forms setting – a face that is easy to read – is often selected to complement the logotype and symbol. For this role, it is usually best to stick to traditional faces, or faces that have been developed from traditional matrices, to avoid dating the identity when a face goes out of fashion.

Markets for identity

Choose a name for a nightclub such as 'Jitters Night Club'. Prepare three designs using the same wording. The market for each is different, but the product is essentially the same – a good night out on the town with great music, dance floor and bar. You need to differentiate the designs for each nightclub by using appropriate imagery, type, colour and style. The nightclubs are:

☐ upstairs at the local football club, next door to its bistro

☐ on the 30th floor of an exclusive, five-star international hotel in the CBD

☐ below street level in the most alternative, counter-cultural areas just out of the city centre.

What you produce must immediately communicate to the intended audience for each of these venues. What age is the clientele? What price do they expect to pay? What style of dress should they wear? What occasions would be appropriate to celebrate there? What time of night will things really start happening? What style of music are they likely to hear?

Design can help to identify all these characteristics by manipulating the choice of type and its layout, the style of illustration (if illustration is needed at all) and the colour palette chosen.

Ask a few people to identify which is which. You'll soon know whether you succeeded.

This is a great exercise if you're developing corporate logotypes, or if you're working on book titles, CD packaging, film titles and show posters.

This face should be used in all stationery: letterheads, business cards, with compliments slips, forms and internal memos. With cascading style sheets in web documents, it might continue into the website too. It also should be used with its various fonts in all publications: annual reports, staff newsletters, corporate plan documents, reports, product literature, brochures, pamphlets – in fact, any publication that could be considered a corporate document.

Some organisations choose more than one 'support' typeface, often due to the requirement that internal documents use system-loaded fonts only or websites use fonts readily available on readers' systems. Microsoft has developed and freely released some excellent fonts like Verdana for this reason.

Corporate colour palette

Another significant association in a visual identity is the colour or colours selected to represent an organisation. Starting with the colour used in the symbol and logotype, develop a suite or palette of colours that can be used for different purposes.

Code separate parts of the organisation with colours: stationery from Head Office can use the symbol with a dark-blue stripe; Research and Development can use the symbol with a bottle-green stripe; Marketing can use maroon; Manufacturing can use burnt orange. Annual report sections can then use the colour code to identify responsibility in organisation charts and graphs. The colours can also be used in signage for each of the sections, or on nametags to identify which part of the organisation a staff member represents.

For websites and intranets, it can be useful to also use the pale tints of that colour set, in order to maintain sufficient contrast.

There are colours that are considered trustworthy, colours that attract attention, colours that employees will wear and colours they won't ... You may need to create a variation on the print and screen colour palette when it comes to designing uniforms, because some palettes do not translate well into clothing. This is why those print and screen corporate colours are often relegated to ties, T-shirts, pockets, caps, nametags and scarves, rather than suits, shirts, skirts and jackets.

Attitude

An organisation which presents a consistent attitude to its markets is well on the way to establishing an effective corporate image. If the attitude is right, a more visually diverse identity can be presented. There is great flexibility with:

- attitude
- a colour palette
- a standard range of symbol and logotype applications.

An image can be projected in a more interesting way by having some in-built flexibility, so ground rules for the use of symbols, logotypes, typefaces and colours should be laid down, thus giving a set of principles for picture selection and layout that define the attitude the organisation wishes to project.

All this is dealing in intangibles and trying to make them tangible. How do you project excitement and dynamism consistently? How do you plan for it so it doesn't become stale and dated? How does the design maintain its integrity with traditional markets but also encourage new markets to discover it?

You can build an element of fashion awareness into the identity, which enables you to portray fashionable images and use fashionable patterns and colour combinations while maintaining the presence of the corporate palette. Even type treatments that are based on contemporary or fashionable practices can fit if the corporate typeface/s are used in contemporary ways. Leave room for the addition of stand-alone typographic statements so that corporate identification is made in body copy rather than in display text setting.

Always maintain a level of respect for the organisation's investment, but this doesn't mean you can't allow some play with the symbol and logotypes – don't compromise them, but have some fun with them. Can your symbol be cropped? The Qantas kangaroo has been known to party ...

Corporate identity manual

Creating a cohesive corporate styling across the corporate identity means maintaining control and effectively managing each manifestation of that identity. To do that, many organisations create an identity manual. It can be as simple as a four-page pamphlet or a job file that contains

Brand extension

Extension of a brand often involves extension of the visual identity as well. When companies introduce further products or 'home brands' on 'private labels', it often involves the repurposing of logos, maybe streamlining or modifying a logo to make it more or less sophisticated (depending on whether the product extension is to be more or less expensive) and extension of corporate colour palettes. Layout variation and support font selection will extend the range of acceptable variants within the tightly controlled categories.

The categories often include a generic or cheaper brand and a 'select', exclusive or premium brand. Both will have different design requirements based on the aspirations of the intended market for the product selection. Some unscrupulous operators engage in 'copycat' branding where the designs for the private label mimic the existing market leader's branding – however, this can compromise your original brand.

Why are so many businesses – particularly global retailers – moving to private labels? As they don't need to advertise their products because their generic brand advertising will get people into the store, they can realise a saving of up to 25% of normal marketing costs, which the branded competitors will spend. They also rely on their reputation for sourcing products their customers appreciate and are happy to pass on some of that saving to their customer in return for loyalty (but they still make more profit due to the greater margins).

Some ideas from 'The brand snatchers', *Business Review Weekly*, 8 November 2007 bits and pieces that enables the identity to be applied appropriately. It can be a bound volume running, in some cases, to hundreds of pages. All identity manuals cover the same material to a greater or lesser extent, depending on the complexity of the identity and the number of likely users or people who will eventually apply the identity.

In the case of multinational corporations that wish to project a cohesive identity in all their marketplaces through the world, the answer has been to define all elements of what is often termed a 'monolithic' corporate identity. The idea is to keep it a practical document: if something isn't 'useful', it's not in the manual!

Contents generally fall into three categories, though these are of varying sizes:
- identifiers
- what to do
- what not to do.

There can be varying levels of detail, from pernickety to casual, broad-brush description.

Aside from the usual title pages and introductions (preferably from the managing director, CEO, department head, headmaster, priest or president), the first section is usually on corporate identifiers. Corporate identifiers might include a symbol, a logotype, typefaces and colour palette.

The symbol might be provided in both its solid form and an outline form. It will be in black on white and white on black (its reverse), single-colour forms and as full-colour versions. It will be shown in conjunction with type and on different coloured backgrounds.

Sometimes, the reverse version of the symbol or logo may require some fiddling in order for the logo to read clearly. For example, in pictograms like KFC's Colonel Sanders face, when reversed, the parts that represent shadows on the face become the lightest areas and become harder to 'read'. So the 'reverse' version is redrawn to balance the shadow areas and flesh areas so the face still reads as a face.

The logotype might include various renditions of the company name and its divisional identification. There might be an initial format as well as the full name. The divisions might appear under or to the right of the full name in particular configurations.

Corporate typefaces include the full font of the typeface used in the logotype. All other corporate text might appear in, say, only two other fonts, so those other fonts and the principal weights would also be included. There might be a description of when to use particular weights, sizes and spacing guides.

The colour palette might be more than just the colours in the symbol and logo. There might be colour coding for corporate divisions. There might be slight variations when printing in Pantone inks, CMYK inks and in screen colours for websites and television advertising. There might also be slight colour variations for printed colours when printing on matt or gloss papers.

The section on identifiers gives all the standard specifications for reproduction, and can include details of various suppliers, all templates and digital files for accurate reproduction. It can specify file naming conventions and storage locations (including folders, drives and servers).

The application section includes specifications for individual pieces of the identity: print and digital applications for stationery, forms, publications, press advertising, packaging, giftware, signage, uniforms, websites, television graphics.

In the case of stationery, there are specifications for all type and measurements for accurate recreation of the templates. Any grids used are described and specified in detail for accurate drawing but are also usually supplied as templates.

A sort of mini style manual might be included, indicating not only typing guides for positioning text on the letterhead, but also writing guides for different types of letters, memos, minutes, email headers and signature blocks, and web page wireframes, content description and writing style. These need to define your organisation's preferences from the expression of corporate addresses to the accepted abbreviations for internal use.

In the case of forms, standards are described in detail and samples shown for signature blocks, section dividers, colour coding, questions and instructional layout.

Press advertising standards include details of the borders and symbol/logotype combinations used in classified advertising and display advertising. Company mottoes, taglines or positioning statements are specified in particular typefaces and positioned in various grids.

Publications might include annual reports, technical manuals, newsletters, product literature, or any number

Corporate identifiers

Logo for Canberra Couriers
Client: Rod Whitbread

Logo for Proudman Building
Contractors
Clients: Sean and Brenda Proudman

Symbol for the Australian Amateur
Music Theatre Awards
Client: Coralie Wood

Logo for Tuggeranong Veterinary
Hospital
Clients: Kym and Malcolm McKnown

Logo for Maison de Parfum, a perfume
retail store
Client: Nina Gayne

Pictogram for the Canberra Area
Theatre (CAT) Awards
Clients: Kate Peters, Coralie Wood

HAIRAFFAIR

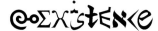

Logo for a hairdressing salon
Client: John Martone

Symbol for Priority One Consulting
Clients: Karen McKenzie, Sue Bennet

Logo for a CD and concert
Client: Colin Hoorweg, Muzair Productions

All identities on this page designed by the author

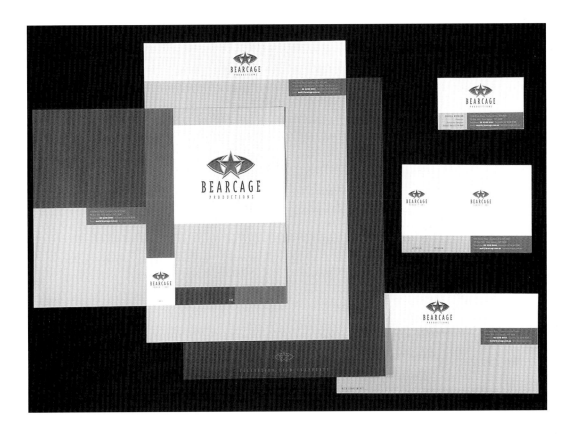

Stationery programs

Bearcage Productions stationery
(above) includes video labels and
covers
Studio: Swell Design Group

Priority One Consulting (left) uses a
full-colour sticker for the logo to be
hand-applied to envelopes, business
cards and letterhead.
Clients: Karen McKenzie, Sue Bennet
Designer: David Whitbread

of brochures. Full style sheets and grid templates can be included.

Signage can be for buildings (both internal and external), car parks, exhibitions and displays, trade shows, vehicles, equipment and machinery.

Uniforms can be for office staff, ushers, technical staff, work crews. The accessories can be diverse and can include some of the corporate giftware: cuff links, scarves, hard hats, safety clothing, spray jackets, waistcoats, T-shirts, ties and tiepins, caps, brooches, nametags, medallions.

For signage, packaging and uniforms, particular materials and fabrics might be specified. Grids for symbol/logo application and spacing in relation to building or box corners can be devised. Suppliers can be noted and combinations of colours, materials and finishes can be specified.

In addition to including what should be done, it is useful to have a section on what should not be done. Often this will feature particular colour combinations that will not work. For example, if a background colour is the same as one of the stripes in the logo, it could cause an incorrect reading of the logo. There are many mistakes that can be made. There might be incorrect proportions used where the logo swamps the symbol. Sometimes, cramming the logo or allowing it to bleed off a page is inadvisable. This section is usually a small but important section as it helps to further define the corporate standards for consistent image control.

Stationery

A4 is the standard sheet for laser printers and photocopiers. But, of course, pieces of stationery can be any size, provided they do what is needed of them. You could feed all sorts of odd-shaped papers through a typewriter (triangular, square, parallelograms, even circles), but there are fewer options with laser printers – and with filing systems at the receiver's end – all accommodating the assumed A4 sheet. Optional sizes, though, can provide interesting format options for information and, consequently, can help a message stand out from its competitors.

Many stationery items will be based on the letterhead design which is usually printed on an A4 sheet. You can avoid printing many different pieces of stationery by preparing templates that overprint the letterhead sheet.

In this way, a letterhead can quickly become an order, an invoice, a receipt.

Letterheads

A letterhead is normally A4 folded to 1/3 A4 and posted in a DL envelope. But an alternative is to fold the long side of an A4 letter in half to A5 and then fold the long side of that in half again to A6. This fits another standard envelope, the C6 envelope.

A letterhead is a preprinted sheet that contains all the contact information that the receiver might need, presented in an appropriate way to establish and maintain the corporate identity. This will often include the symbol and logo printed in corporate colours. All the information and corporate identification will appear in the margins surrounding the text area where the letter is typed.

The back of the letterhead is often considered an appropriate place for some corporate identification or imagery as well. It can distinguish the organisation if there is an impressive look to the letterhead as it comes out of an envelope.

The main text area for the overprinted letter usually starts about one-third of the way down the page with a generous left margin of about 30 mm or more (for filing purposes at the receiver's end and for the sender's records) and a narrow right margin. Often the address of the receiver, the date of the letter and the salutation have specific alignments within the top third that are determined to complement the letterhead design or to align with the window in a standard window envelope.

Positioning is often defined in a digital template that is loaded onto an organisation's intranet with a typing guide, so that anyone about to prepare a letter can meet the standards. A small rule or even a dot at one of the fold points makes folding to one-third for the DL envelope easier for staff.

Continuation sheets
When a letter spills over into an extra page, the organisation may choose to have a continuation sheet printed with the logo. Usually this has simply the corporate logo positioned appropriately, often smaller than the letterhead and in a similar position to the letterhead, and rarely with any textual information preprinted. The template

CHECKLIST
Letterhead
- [ ] A4
- [ ] Organisation/business name
- [ ] Corporate symbols/logos
- [ ] Postal address
- [ ] Location address
- [ ] Phone number/s
- [ ] Fax number
- [ ] General email address
- [ ] Website address (URL)
- [ ] Positioning statement/slogan
- [ ] Other locations
- [ ] Senior staff/board members/ partners
- [ ] Affiliates
- [ ] Sales tax registration numbers
- [ ] Business or company registration numbers
- [ ] Registered business address (which can be different to location)
- [ ] Your ref./Our ref. (this is for filing systems of senders and receivers)
- [ ] Fold mark

CHECKLIST
Invoice or 'Tax invoice'
As letterhead but, depending on your business, it may also feature the following:
- [ ] Product code and description
- [ ] Quantity
- [ ] Price (including applicable tax)
- [ ] Total
- [ ] Any legal requirements

CHECKLIST
Fax sheet
□ A4
□ Organisation/business name
□ Corporate symbols/logos in solid
   black version
□ From (person)
□ Fax number (sender)
□ To (person)
□ Fax number (receiver)
□ Re (subject)
□ Number of pages in transmission
□ Message (area)
□ Postal address
□ Location address
□ Phone number/s
□ General email address
□ Website address (URL)
□ Positioning statement/slogan
□ Other locations
□ Senior staff/board members/
   partners
□ Business or company registration
   numbers

for the continuation pages will probably advise a letter identification line to start the second page, which includes the date of the letter, maybe the initials of the sender, and the page number expressed simply as '2' or '2 of 3' as preferred.

Overprint templates
With careful design, a letterhead can become the basis of a stationery range that includes a diverse number of corporate papers. The assumption these days is that the letterhead, if printed at all, will be overprinted to address a number of other uses: receipts, invoices, orders, memos, minute papers, media releases, etc.

In order to standardise the layouts for letters and all other uses, a series of templates are created, usually in a word-processing program. The templates embed margins, fonts, style sheets and positioning guides for particular content. Non-printing text can also give instructions to your staff so they will apply standards in consistent ways.

When selecting fonts for overprinting in these templates, ensure you have chosen fonts that are loaded on the system in all your offices (called 'system fonts') so that you do not have to compromise the look of your stationery by accepting alternative fonts.

When preparing the templates, identify how many levels of information are required – including standard and occasional requirements for each document type – and prepare a customised style sheet with preset type specifications, spacing and indenting for all.

You may need to train staff in how to use each of the templates, as this sort of standardisation is often introduced where people have had their own ways of doing things and may not understand all the new formatting options and how they are applied through a style sheet.

READ MORE ABOUT IT
Roger Walton, *Design rules for letterheads: Over 75 examples from the simple to the spectacular*, Harper Design International, New York, 2004, ISBN 0-06-058906-X.
Chris Foges (ed.), *Letterheads and business cards*, RotoVision SA, Crans-Pres-Celigny, Switzerland, 1999, ISBN 2 88946 390 4.
Rob Carter, *Working with computer type 2: Logotypes, stationery systems, visual identity*, RotoVision SA, Crans-Pres-Celigny, Switzerland, 1996, ISBN 2 88046 231 2.

Fax sheets

A fax sheet, which is the first page of a facsimile transmission, tells the receiver who the fax comes from and how long it is. It can serve as an introductory sheet or the actual message may start on it. It is often available only as a template on in-house systems or sometimes is preprinted. It prints in black only – with no tonal variation – on white paper as it needs to consider the clarity of output at the receivers' machines. Receivers will not necessarily be able to receive fine detail, so the design is often more solid than the letterhead – the text and symbol/logo are larger for clarity when bitmapped by the receiver's printer. Sometimes designers will use sans serif type for the fax because it is clearer than a serif type in transmission.

Sometimes the sheet is preprinted with the assumption that some will quickly fill in the required information by hand as they add it as a cover page to the document they are sending at the fax machine. But it is more likely that the organisation would prefer a generic fax sheet blank for installation onto all computers or downloadable from the intranet for staff to fill in on-screen and print out when needed.

Memoranda sheets and minute papers

Memos and minute papers do not need full organisational contact information like letterheads because they are mostly internal documents, but they will usually have corporate identification and a standardised look to their presentation.

The memo is headed by a standard set of four references: the names of the receiver and the sender, the subject of the memo, and the date.

The minute paper has the place and date of the meeting it documents and the title of the group that met. It lists those who attended and who apologised for not attending and the people who will receive copies of the minutes. The minutes follow the agenda of the meeting, each agenda item a numbered heading followed by brief descriptive text. Sometimes the agenda items will be followed by action points that define what action was agreed, who was to take the action and by when. This is often in a contrasting typeface to the text – so it is easily found. Usually minutes conclude with a reference to the next meeting's date, time and place.

CHECKLIST
Minute paper
- ☐ A4
- ☐ Organisation/business name
- ☐ Committee name
- ☐ Corporate symbols/logos
- ☐ Minute *or* Minute paper
- ☐ Date, time and place of meeting
- ☐ Present (list of people in attendance)
- ☐ Apologies (list of people unable to attend)
- ☐ cc (list of people who will receive copies of the minutes)
- ☐ Text (area – usually numbered paragraphs following the agenda)

CHECKLIST
Memorandum
- ☐ A4
- ☐ Organisation/business name
- ☐ Committee name
- ☐ Corporate symbols/logos
- ☐ To (person)
- ☐ From (person)
- ☐ Re (subject)
- ☐ Date
- ☐ Memorandum *or* Memo
- ☐ Text (area – usually numbered paragraphs)

The cost of a preprint and colours can be avoided because they are internal documents. By providing staff with on-screen generic memo and minute blanks, they can generate the document and email them. They are often read electronically but usually printed out for discussion and verification at the following meetings.

Media releases

'Media release' is preferred to 'Press release' in order to encompass television, radio and online media, as well as the traditional 'press', which were specifically the print media; that is, newspapers and magazines.

A media release is very similar in feel to a letterhead and includes much the same corporate information, but it is often designed in a more lively or dynamic manner. A media release needs to stand out when received. It often has coloured bands at the top or in the margins that distinguish it from a letterhead. If often needs to work in a corporate folder or a specially designed media kit.

It must have a clear space for identification of the sender (usually the person to whom the media can direct further inquiries) and contact phone number/s or email address. It also defines when the news can be released: 'For immediate release' or 'For release on [date]' or 'Under embargo until [date]'.

Its text has an appropriate headline and the details written in descending order of importance. It should still have a clear blank text area for scanning of the release to be effective, but that is less important now as it is often emailed or available as an online resource on the organisation's website. The media need to be encouraged to use it, so make it easy for them.

Business cards

A business card can be one of the most effective advertising investments a person can make – it is an advertisement that people carry around in their pockets that reminds them of both the individual and the organisation. A business card can also be one of the biggest design headaches because, like small press ads, there is only a small area and usually too much information to fit into it.

The standard size for a business card is changing from 50 × 90 mm to 55 × 85 mm, because wallets are now designed for credit cards. People often keep their cards in their wallet to distribute – and the recipient often puts the card into a wallet. Make sure the ones you design fit.

This size variation has helped the design to be more flexible – there are greater possibilities, the most popular of which is simply turning the card from a horizontal to a vertical format. This often suits the information levels.

Some companies have realised the potential of the business card as a greater advertising tool. Some cards are printed on the back – restaurants might have a map showing their location; organisations might have a mission statement, corporate philosophy, guarantee or motto; some advertise new products; some service companies outline their areas of expertise; some list the date and time of your next appointment; and some offer discounts. With all this extra information, some have a folded card or are miniature booklets.

Be careful how small the type gets on the business card – people need to read it easily. Consider tracking the type a little wider when it gets down to those small sizes.

Coloured or textured paper stocks, varnish or laminate, photographs, heat-raised lettering and multicoloured logos all get more attention and the recipient is more likely to keep the card – an ad in someone's pocket is a constant reminder.

With compliments slips

Designed for a short personal message, the 'with compliments' slip contains the same amount of information as the letterhead plus a salutation line. It leaves an area for a short handwritten message to be added – this is a personal response sheet.

Envelopes

All the information required by postal regulations is a return address and a stamp area or Postage Paid artwork where a stamp would go, but usually organisations include the name of the organisation, the symbol/logotype and some form of graphic that fits the corporate stationery range. Information is provided for identification or to encourage opening, so it can include teaser copy and imagery. You can contact your local post office to be certain an envelope design meets the postal regulations and mailing standards. Sometimes print area is limited in order to not confuse automatic mail sorting machines. The post

CHECKLIST
Business cards
- [ ] 55 × 85 mm *or* 50 × 90 mm *or* 45 × 90 mm
- [ ] Organisation/business name
- [ ] Corporate symbols/logos
- [ ] Personal name
- [ ] Position
- [ ] Personal phone number
- [ ] Personal email address
- [ ] Postal address
- [ ] Location address
- [ ] Phone number/s
- [ ] Fax number
- [ ] General email address
- [ ] Website address (URL)
- [ ] Positioning statement/slogan
- [ ] Other locations
- [ ] Senior staff/board members/ partners
- [ ] Company or business registration numbers

CHECKLIST
With compliments slip
- [ ] 1/3 A4 or A6
- [ ] Organisation/business name
- [ ] Corporate symbols/logos
- [ ] With compliments *or* With compliments of ... (name and/or position) *or* With our compliments *or* Compliments
- [ ] Postal address
- [ ] Location address
- [ ] Phone number/s
- [ ] Fax number
- [ ] General email address
- [ ] Website address (URL)
- [ ] Positioning statement/slogan
- [ ] Other locations
- [ ] Senior staff/board members/ partners

1/3	1/3	1/3
Image area	Address area	Stamp area

15 mm

Envelope
☐ DL *or* C6 (though there are numerous standard sizes)
☐ Organisation/business name
☐ Corporate symbols/logos
☐ Postal address
☐ Postage paid artwork (as required) in the stamp zone
☐ Positioning statement/slogan
☐ Teaser copy

Media kits
☐ Folder
☐ Media releases
☐ Photographs for reproduction
☐ Background briefings or information sheets on:
  – organisation
  – products
  – personnel
☐ Contact information
☐ Gimmick (as a memory trigger)
☐ Pad and pen

Folder dies
Ask your printer what folder dies are available and if you can have a blank to design the surfaces for. Using a standard die will save money. Select a sturdy paper stock that folds without cracking and choose a stock colour that fits the corporate palette (if it's well chosen, this can save you printing an extra colour).

office can also supply artwork specifications for reply paid cards and registered self-mailed newsletters.

Labels, stickers and seals

Stickers can be an inexpensive method of getting corporate identification onto many pieces of stationery with little outlay. They can be used as seals on certificates and envelopes. Instead of printing the logo in colour on each piece of stationery, the one logo sticker can be printed and hand applied to business cards, letterheads and envelopes. This is appropriate for smaller businesses and organisations, but can be frustrating for an organisation that uses much stationery.

Folders and media kits

Folders with corporate identification are handy for presentations to clients, for in-house training session materials and for public distribution at trade shows. There should be appropriate corporate identification room for a business card to be inserted inside and they should comfortably accommodate a number of A4 sheets without them spilling out. So the size is usually A4+ (305 × 220 mm).

The number of internal pockets and whether they will be along the short or long side of the folder needs to be considered. One pocket may need diagonal cuts for business card insertion. You might also consider a spine if there are to be a number of inclusions.

For a media launch, there may be a suite of materials including badges, corporate gifts, stickers, and a pad and printed information sheets. Information sheets can be overprinted on media releases, minute paper or continuation sheets, run-on copies of advertisements, memoranda or letterhead to maintain corporate identification without too much additional expense.

Forms

A form might be a simple name and address registration with a few tick boxes in a pamphlet or return card, or a more detailed order form, or even a questionnaire that runs to booklet size. It can also be a response vehicle at the end of a website. On-screen forms have similar design issues to paper-based forms.

   Once a form has been drafted, and the information it contains analysed and logically grouped, the task of designing it for ease of use begins. Users don't want to spend a great amount of time with forms, so it is best to sacrifice graphic interest to utilitarian aims. Keep it simple.

   By sketching a plan for the form, you can work with modules of particular sets of information. You can create a logical flow to the form that presents the information in a sequence that suits. You can also work on the tonal arrangement of instructions, headings and fill-in boxes to create a form that is welcoming.

   There are at least two users of a form: the person who fills in the information and the person who needs to read that entered information and transfer it to some other media or generate a report or commence an action as a result of the information given. Both users need to be able to find information quickly and accurately.

   When a form is printed, it is useful to print it in a colour different from the pen colour likely to be used by the person filling it in. Blue and black are the most usual ink colours that people use to fill in forms but, for example, some forms are filled in only at an organisation's premises, so the organisation can ensure that the only writing implement available suits their forms. In election booths, it is pencils. In banks, black pens.

   If a form is filled in on-screen, the ground provided for the user to type in information should be sufficient for most users to be able to read what they've entered. Usually more information can be entered than the ground will display, but there is a frustration factor if the complete entry can't be reread – so at least provide a scroll bar.

   Sometimes you need to separate distinct parts of the form from others as some parts will be filled in by all respondents and some parts by only a few. You need to identify these clearly so respondents can move logically through the form. Use numbers, coding, arrows and directions to other sections as necessary. Directional information should be clear. Rules, bands and bars of tone and colour can help this segmentation into the logical sections of information needed. Colour coding can also be effective here if the budget allows. Sans serif headings reversed out of solid black rules can separate sections.

   A pattern of stripes can distinguish one question from another by changing background tone for each second question. This will stripe the form but also make the divisions clear. It also saves dot leaders to answer boxes.

Instructions need to be obvious and easy to digest. Set a style for this level of information – it should be easily distinguished from the body of the form. Further instructions can be given in a narrow column or sidebar. Typographic styling for them should be distinct from other stylings. This effectively codes the instructions as such.

To ascertain whether your design works, test the form with a few different people to see whether they fill it out accurately. If not, analyse why the mistakes were made and determine how you can fix them. Poorly conceived and prepared forms can collect inaccurate and ultimately unusable information.

Give specific directions for information that might be filled in by people from different countries – particularly in Internet forms. Specifying 'DD/MM/YYYY' (Australian and English preference) or 'MM/DD/YYYY' (US preference) helps dates. Use 'given name' (rather than 'Christian name' or 'first name') and 'family name' (rather than 'surname') – this is more multiculturally aware and respectful. Title options should include 'Mr/Ms/Mrs/Miss' and might include 'Prof./Dr/Rev.' and 'Other' depending on the likely respondents to the questions.

Using appropriate icons can also speed communication. The icons must be clear and unambiguous. For example, a paper clip icon can indicate that the user needs to attach something to the form.

For readability, lower-case type is recommended. We read it faster and more accurately than text set in all capitals. Do not slow down the user of the form by putting instructions and important information in capitals. Rather, distinguish that information typographically, using the type variations available to you, altering typeface, font and size.

For continuous reading, serif typefaces are recommended. But in a form there is not usually much continuous reading. So sans serif is recommended for its greater legibility (the clarity and speed with which you can recognise the letter shapes). Sans serif type is also easier to read on-screen and at small sizes because of its constant stroke thickness – and you often need to fit a form into a limited page area.

READ MORE ABOUT IT
David Sless, *Name and address please: A guide for form designers*, Proceedings of seminar conducted by Communication Research Institute of Australia, Canberra, 1987.
Harm JG Zwaga, Theo Boersema & Henriëtte CM Hoonhout (eds), *Visual information for everyday use: Design and research perspectives*, Taylor & Francis, London, 1999, ISBN 0 7484 0670 0.
Robert Barnett, *Forms for people: Designing forms that people can use*, Robert Barnett & Associates, Belconnen, ACT, 2005, ISBN 0 9586 3842 X.

Response area

It is important that the user of the form knows where to write the information. How many times have you got to the bottom of a printed form, only to realise that all your answers were written on the line above the identified piece of information instead of the line underneath? To avoid this sort of confusion, it can help to have white boxes for the user to fill in. To help them stand out, a light shade of grey or, preferably, another colour should be used in the background of the form. If printing a second colour, do not use anything heavier than 20%. If your form is printed in only one colour, do not go heavier than 10% – the dots start to distort the letterforms and inhibit legibility.

On-screen forms have variable text areas where the respondent can key in their answers which scroll across and down to accommodate the extra length.

Other response modes are tick boxes (print) and check boxes (online) which allow the user to select multiple responses to the one question. Radio buttons (which can also be white on a tinted background and are filled by hand or when clicked) usually only allow one response for each question. Sliding scales (strongly agree/strongly disagree, and so on) have numbers circled by users or radio buttons that are coloured in by hand or clicked online.

Numbers in scales should be tabbed with an even amount of space between each. An explanation of the grading system should be clearly indicated in an instruction preceding the scales – and should be easy to find for each question. Repeat it on each page or screen on which that scale is used – and be consistent throughout a particular form. If 1 is 'strongly agree' and 5 is 'strongly disagree', and it swaps in the next question, you jeopardise the accuracy of the answers as people make assumptions and don't read instructions.

You might also indicate which answers are required or optional. This is often indicated with a red asterisk.

DOING IT SMARTER
Tick box options
Respondents are most likely to tick boxes – even if asked to cross them! Tick boxes might follow the word they apply to in a one-line entry:

YES ☐   NO ☐   UNDECIDED ☐

They might be aligned at the left following the answer code number:

13 ☐   YES
14 ☐   NO
15 ☐   UNDECIDED

DOING IT SMARTER
Response boxes
The minimum width recommended for handwritten responses allows 5 mm for each written character. For these standard requests, the recommended width is:

☐ Given names	40 mm each
☐ Family name	50 mm
☐ Address	140 mm
☐ Business address	210 mm
☐ Postcode/zip code	20 mm/30 mm
☐ Phone numbers	50 mm
☐ Fax number	50 mm
☐ Email address	100 mm
☐ Web URL	80 mm
☐ Credit card number	80 mm
☐ Date	40 mm
☐ Signature	70 mm wide and 20 mm deep

For all other blocks a depth of 7 mm should be sufficient.

On-screen, you can deny progression to the next page until the required fields are filled.

On printed forms for handwritten response, it is not necessary to have little nicks or little boxes for each letter in address lines – like those that are sometimes provided for credit card numbers. A clear, white area of sufficient size for the information is appropriate and tends to ensure fewer errors.

Alignment and the appropriate clustering of information is important in forms so connections are clear to the user. Consistency in the way questions are asked is important within the same form or from the same organisation. If users are likely to be filling in more than one form, it can be frustrating to have inconsistent methods of asking for name, address and birth date. Internal consistency makes forms faster to fill in accurately and the resulting information more reliable.

Forms production

Black is the easiest colour to read for text. But other colours are acceptable, provided you use the deepest hues: chocolate brown, navy blue, maroon, royal purple and bottle green. This enables you to use a range of tints, particularly if you choose to print black and a second colour. You then have all the tints of black and the other colour and the option of printing black over the second colour, reversing the second colour through black, and reversing through black and its tints and the second colour and its tints.

Limit the use of a second colour to tinting the background and/or colouring bars to separate sections. It is better not to use it for large amounts of text – better to use it as a coding device for levels of information and as a way of making the form look more interesting.

The paper should be matt, rather than gloss – ballpoints, pencils and markers all write better on matt paper.

The users' needs should determine all your decisions. And you should be testing how successfully the form can be used at each iteration. It need not be expensive market testing; often just asking a friend to fill out a proof will identify some required changes. You might also do a limited 'live' test with a small selection of real users before printing the final run or letting the site go live. This may require them to fill out digitally printed proofs or a CD-based test or development site.

CHECKLIST
Forms design elements

Printed forms

☐ Branding and initial instructions
☐ Section dividers [may be numbered]
☐ Instructions
☐ Questions
☐ Response fields that accommodate handwriting and the length of the expected answers
☐ Line numbering if required to code answers that may be referred to later ('Subtract line 26 from line 14 to determine your tax refund')
☐ For processing staff, you may need to include answer codes
☐ Tick boxes, scale bars for answers
☐ Arrows to direct people from a section or answer to another required response
☐ Instructions for any attachments required
☐ Signature and date blocks
☐ Form submission details
☐ Office-use-only fields

Online forms

☐ Branding and initial instructions including privacy statements
☐ Section dividers [may be numbered, but more likely to be linked pages]
☐ Instructions
☐ Password if necessary
☐ Questions
☐ Text entry fields probably with a limited number of characters using a 'maxlength' specification – for example, credit card numbers would have a maxlength of 16
☐ A coloured asterisk beside text entry fields and other required answers
☐ Scroll bars on long text entry fields so respondents can review and edit their answers
☐ Auto-filled fields (linked from previous answers) as necessary
☐ Check boxes, radio buttons, pull-down menus – with scroll bars on long menus – and scale bars with radio buttons for answers
☐ Links to a section or answer that requires another response
☐ An animated thermometer that progressively indicates how much of the survey the respondent has completed
☐ Pop-up reminders that required answers have not been given
☐ 'Submit' button

Instructions for completion

Print clearly. Illegible, unclear or incomplete application forms may delay processing.

Note
All expenses incurred must

Applicant's details

Name
SURNAME
GIVEN NAMES

Designation

Section/Branch

Are you a permanent officer?
☐ YES   ☐ NO

Previous location
TOWN

New location
TOWN

Date of formal notification

Date commenced duty at

Section of a form showing instruction zone and fill-in zone
Designer: Louise Dews

Signage

Wayfinding systems are signposted using a combination of symbols and text. In areas where there will be users who speak many languages, signs need to be non-language-dependent. At airports, hospitals, stadiums and car parks – and to a lesser extent, theatres and universities – people rely on pictograms, numbering, symbol systems and colour codings with multilingual maps or computer information kiosks.

Clarity and speed of communication are paramount. Imagine how visitors or users will move in the spaces and what information they will want at any particular point. Understand their mental state – whether they will be nervous, late, relaxed, or urgently seeking assistance.

Signage should also enhance the spaces it adorns. In corporate identification, it needs to be consistent with other manifestations of the identity. The logo may need to be rejigged into a three-dimensional form. In foyers of head offices and particularly in retail outlets and trade shows, 3-D logos are a part of the fit-out.

There are different levels of production for signage, as the nature of the signage environment dictates. Permanent displays use different materials and finishes from changing displays. Low-traffic areas use different surfaces from high-traffic areas. There are public safety issues as well as public convenience to be considered.

READ MORE ABOUT IT

Edo Smitshuijzen, *Signage design manual*, Lars Müller Publishers, Baden, 2007, ISBN 978-3-03778-096-1.

Andreas Uebele, *Signage systems and information graphics: A professional sourcebook*, Thames & Hudson, London, 2007, ISBN 978-0-500-51379-8.

Cheryl Dangel Cullen, *Large graphics: Design innovation for oversized spaces*, Rockport Publishers, Gloucester, Mass., 2000, ISBN 1 56496 692 5.

James Grayson Trulove, *This way: Signage design for public spaces*, Rockport Publishers, Gloucester, Mass., 2000, ISBN 1 56496 752 2.

Sign gallery: From the editors of 'Signs of the Times' magazine, ST Publications, Cincinnati, 1997, ISBN 0 944094 23 6.

Joan G Salb, *Retail image and graphic identity*, Retail Reporting Corporation, New York, 1995, ISBN 0 934590 62 1.

Akiko Busch, *'Print' casebooks 10: The best in environmental graphics*, RC Publications, Rockville, 1994, ISBN 0 915734 90 7.

Internal signage

Wall, floor and ceiling signage has architectural impact and implications for lighting, cleaning, wear and tear, and sightlines. Booths and counters, corridors and doors, lift wells and stairwells all have labelling requirements that need to be in keeping with the corporate identity. They will probably use one of the corporate typefaces and possibly incorporate the identifiers and colour scheme.

Floors might have logos or directional information woven into carpets, detailed in marquetry or tiled into mosaic. Walls may be adorned with neon tubing, sculpted reliefs, tapestries, painted murals or lighting effects. Ceilings may have backlit signs, neon directional lighting in colour codes, wrought iron type ... even windows may have information stuck to them or sandblasted and sculpted into their glass. In all surfaces, objects and frames can be embedded or attached for display, information purposes or even storage.

When selecting materials for signage, remember the impact of lighting and shadows, reflections, people obscuring the view and extreme viewing angles on the clarity of the sign.

External signage

External signage has two roles: identification on the sides of buildings and at street level, and directional signage in car parks, on walkways and on fences. It can be simply painting a logo onto the building or its front door but, at the other end of the scale, it can become a major sculptural and architectural feat.

The main considerations, beyond clarity and efficiency in communication, are materials that will weather and how the signage will enhance the image of the organisation. The materials must also be able to be cleaned efficiently and perhaps consideration should be given to discouraging vandalism and defacement. Materials will shrink and enlarge in different weather conditions and temperatures, so sign companies know the amount of stress a material can handle and how to accommodate these changes in the design of external signage.

The image issue has implications for lighting systems and the shadows they throw, as well as the shadows thrown throughout the day by sunlight as it moves across the signage – and its seasonal variation.

Clarity from a distance is an issue and each approach to the building needs to be considered. Look closely at highway signage; you will find that the typography features lower-case letters, widely spaced or loosely tracked. This enables our eyes to identify the letterforms by their shape from a distance and read the sign earlier.

Equally, the needs of each person arriving on site need to be considered. For example, the height of signage in the car park will be lower for a driver than the height for signage on walkways for pedestrians.

External signage also includes flags and banners that might be used for a limited time.

Vehicles

Buses, trucks, vans, trains, aeroplanes, pantechnicons, tractors, helicopters, cars, carts, horse-drawn coaches, trams, motorbikes, bicycles and even rickshaws are all vehicles which are used by various businesses to carry corporate livery.

For some businesses, a magnetic-backed printed logo on the car door is sufficient. For others, a fully detailed, total surface design is worthwhile to make a moving corporate statement.

From taxi and bus advertising to total surface design of the vehicles, an organisation wants its statement to be simple and memorable as it whizzes by its audience. Some logos that will be seen predominantly on moving vehicles should be given readability tests at speed to see if they can be accurately identified.

Creatively combining the corporate palette and identifiers, you should create impact for the vehicle that will enhance the corporate image. Consider the appropriateness of coloured reflectors within the design for night impact.

Although slogans, website URLs and positioning statements might be appropriate, phone numbers are less so. Unless a phone number is particularly memorable, it should probably be left off a vehicle. (And you should probably leave the cute, backward type on vehicle fronts for reading in rear-view mirrors to ambulances and emergency vehicles.)

Exhibitions, trade shows and conferences

For particular events or promotions, banners, flags, free-standing units and projection techniques can be used to create an effective but quickly demountable display. In trade shows, standardised booths are transformed by banners, posters and samples, often just secured by Velcro dots so they are quickly set up and dismantled. Such portable environments require a series of freestanding or hanging graphics that can divide off your stand from others while distinguishing it. You may also have to accommodate furniture, plants, stores of pamphlets and giveaways.

At trade fairs, work out the approaches most visitors will make to your organisation's stand and design for those sightlines. Unfortunately, you have no control of the displays around you but you can make some assumptions of people movement through the show.

While they are related, exhibits are often more complex to design.

There are three distinct levels of signage at exhibits: the titling and entry area of the exhibition which might have its own logo; the signage that is seen from a distance that moves people through the exhibition and identifies the thematic areas of interest; and the detailed captioning of displays. In this way, the signposting is used as a technique of guiding visitors by placement and attraction, so they anticipate what's next and do not create bottlenecks, clogging the exhibition.

Exhibition designers must take into account this movement pattern of visitors through the area. There will be fast points where people are moving to the next significant area of the exhibit. There will be slow points where people will congregate, reading and viewing specific displays of interest. These need to have larger floor areas for congregation.

Disney theme parks have developed people movement to an art form. Each surface, even in queuing areas, is considered a part of the whole experience and supports the theme, making queuing almost a pleasure.

Exhibits and trade show stands – and even conferences – are often themed or have thematic events. The development of the theme is often achieved through a combination of artefacts and graphics. Using stage design techniques – including costume design for attendants – environments are recreated as time capsules for the visitor to experience. The theme experience heightens the involvement of the audience with the exhibit. A creative combination of authentic material and recreated material will often help to control costs. Use modern reproduction methods on fabrics, banners and posters to quickly create screens and

CHECKLIST
Exhibitions

Print

- ☐ Labels
- ☐ Brochures
- ☐ Exhibition map
- ☐ Educational materials
- ☐ Teachers' notes
- ☐ Catalogue
- ☐ Souvenir book
- ☐ Advertising
- ☐ Products/souvenirs

Installation

- ☐ Photographs
- ☐ Illustrations and diagrams
- ☐ Curated objects
- ☐ Models
- ☐ Dioramas
- ☐ Interactive objects
- ☐ Lighting

Web or CD components

- ☐ Multimedia
- ☐ Touchscreens
- ☐ Website
- ☐ Animations
- ☐ Virtual tour

Soundscape

- ☐ Sound tour (multilingual?)

Staff uniforms

- ☐ Guides
  - shop attendants
  - ticket sellers

Assembly and packing plans

(particularly for travelling exhibitions)

Exhibition design process

Each stage in the process requires research, development, review and updating as necessary until sign-off.

- ☐ Concept
  - – exhibition
  - – video and multimedia elements
  - – publications
- ☐ Sketches
- ☐ Storyboard
- ☐ Scale drawings
- ☐ Cardboard mock-ups
- ☐ Computer rendering/virtual reality
- ☐ Construction
- ☐ Installation

Giles Velarde in *Designing Exhibitions* has these reminders, among others, for exhibition designers:

- ☐ Do remember people's eyesight varies.
- ☐ Remember:
  - – bifocals
  - – short-sighted people
  - – short people
  - – tall people
  - – disabled people
  - – people who want to touch things.
- ☐ Do remember people have noses and ears as well as eyes.
- ☐ Do remember people have needs:
  - – to sit down
  - – to quench their thirst
  - – to go to the toilet
  - – to hang up their coats
  - – to protect their valuables.

dividers for the space. The more thorough the references to the theme, the more effective the whole event will be.

Lighting of 3-D graphics can be controlled to a much greater extent indoors, and you can also mostly control the angles from which material is seen, though you cannot entirely control how visitors will propel themselves through the space. You can, however, design spaces in your movement plan where you can conceal lighting, hide projectors and install computer units.

Also be aware of reflections from other exhibits and realise that visitors will obscure parts of the exhibit as well.

The exhibition design team can include: exhibition designers, graphic designers, industrial designers, interior designers, photo researchers, curators, archivists, scholars, editors, historians, writers, illustrators, storyboarders, photographers, film-makers, composers, musicians, sound recordists, animators, directors, actors, builders, fabricators, sculptors, conservators, lighting and sound designers and technicians, signwriters and makers.

READ MORE ABOUT IT

Giles Velarde, *Designing exhibitions*, Design Council, London, 1988, ISBN 0 85072 223 3.

Ken Cato & Leigh Cato (eds), *Graphics in the third dimension*, Graphic-Sha Publishing, Tokyo, 1992, ISBN 4 7661 0678 4.

Conway Lloyd Morgan, *Expo: Trade fair stand design*, RotoVision SA, Crans-Pres-Celigny, Switzerland, 1997, ISBN 2 88046 263 0.

Rob Carter, John De Mao & Sandy Wheeler, *Working with type 5: Exhibitions*, RotoVision SA, Crans-Pres-Celigny, Switzerland, 2000, ISBN 2 88046 437 4.

Gail Deibler Finke, *Festival graphics*, Madison Square Press, New York, 1999, ISBN 0 942604 60 0.

Edward K Carpenter, *'Print' casebooks 10: The best in exhibition design*, RC Publications, Rockville, MD, 1994, ISBN 0 915734 91 5.

Screen-based media

If it's on-screen, it must move. It should use colour and sound. If it's on the web, not only can it move, be colourful and be heard, but it should also be interactive and have hypertext layers and links.

All the usual rules of attracting an audience and keeping their attention apply to screen-based media.

Television and film graphics have trained your audience; their moving image literacy is at a high level of sophistication and visual comprehension. They also receive and process moving images and sound very fast, making the connections between scenes very quickly and even having the ability to 'read' video on fast-forward or rewind.

Watching television and film is instructive to the screen-based designer, particularly when layering type and images for titling or credit sequences.

A film title designer needs to consider what will happen to the film title when it transfers to DVD, as it inevitably will. The film screen is often wider than a television screen, so the edges will be lost or the film will be distorted and squeezed or it will be reduced even further and bands of black added top and bottom to create the letterbox effect. Nuance in colour and detail can be lost. A good designer recognises these limitations and sees them, rather, as challenges.

In-house, promotional and instructional videos, whether used for training or corporate communications, are competing with mainstream media for space in the audience member's head. It must be worthwhile watching or production money will be thrown away.

The speed with which the program moves needs to consider viewers' and users' attention span and reading ability. If there are sequenced text screens, for example, ensure you have left enough time for people to read the text. It is preferable to give them the controls for changing the screens in multimedia and websites. In television graphics,

Inclusivity

Representation reflects the cultural diversity of the marketplace, so be inclusive of different ages, body shapes, sexes, races, sexual preferences and lifestyles. Many government and commercial ads – and programs for that matter – now recognise and celebrate a broader definition of families, and are more inclusive in their representation of people of different races and beliefs. Although stereotypes still exist, we are fortunately embracing more dimensional and complex characters in mainstream media. If they feel they are included, viewers can relate better to the imagery.

you need to test the timings with a few viewers from your intended audience.

READ MORE ABOUT IT

Steve Curran, *Motion graphics: Graphic design for broadcast and film*, Rockport Publishers, Gloucester, Mass., 2000, ISBN 1 56496 646 1.

Multimedia

People in training or educational industries who are considering multimedia as part of a flexible delivery package, or in the information kiosk business, or in the technologically assisted sales area need to consider the full variety of media available. Some modes achieve more than others – something need not be described if it can be shown or heard. Some have drawbacks – often showing or hearing is more expensive to develop than describing in writing.

To effectively use multimedia techniques, assess which media are most appropriate for which roles and deploy them to their greatest effect. Many of these basic considerations apply equally to website design and multimedia project design.

In both, avoid the overuse of media. Too many media going at once – even too many media options on one page – can be confusing and distracting for the reader. Consider the appropriate placement of media within the project and build the reader's experience through the project's structure.

Whereas in a website you scroll, in a multimedia production you click on navigation tools and jump to continuations and other parts of the product in hypertext screens. In multimedia products, most screens are produced at 1024×728 pixels and black the rest of the screen; however, you need to discuss the desired screen area with your client. For multimedia web-parts in an intranet, for example, you might only use a half-screen window so that other screen content can be viewed concurrently.

Much of the content discussed in developing website content, graphical user interfaces and navigation – and even forms design – is relevant to multimedia projects.

Instructional multimedia

When developing instructional multimedia products, used in the training and educational industries, a number of techniques will influence the success of the product for both learners and their supervisors or training organisations.

You will need to discuss how it will be delivered: on CD-ROM, DVD, online (web-delivered) or through a Learning Management System (LMS).

Instructional multimedia products too can incorporate text, graphics, print files, audio, video, animation and web links. They can even incorporate some social media components that involve interactive, multiplayer learning.

Also you might consider tracking indicators that provide learners with a system that enables them to know whether they have opened, viewed or completed content. This could also include the familiar thermometer style of indicator that lets the learner know how much of the learning module they have completed and how much is left to go.

Tests and quizzes will often require a certain score before a learner can move on to the next part of the training product. Such score logic systems need to be developed carefully to ensure that essential learnings – for example, safety procedures – are weighted to ensure a learner cannot progress until they have successfully responded. There might be, say, an 80% pass rate determined for other knowledge that is tested.

In many large organisations, the staff learning and development program is managed through a Learning Management System. Essentially a database, the LMS manages enrolment in learning modules and records student progress. The way to ensure your product seamlessly integrates with the LMS requirements is to test it comprehensively.

Audio

There are three sorts of sound you might consider: speech or dialogue, music and sound effects. Sound editing and design is a specialised discipline where an audience is often unaware of the layering of the sound they are hearing.

To make sounds in a home sound more natural, an empty house is recorded to mix over the dialogue track in a studio. In that way, you'll hear kids in the park down the street, cars going by, a radio in the house next door, doors slamming and sprinklers going in the neighbourhood, and the usual house settling sounds such as a fridge or air-conditioning system whirring. If an audience doesn't hear these ambient sounds, something will feel strange and unreal about the domestic scene you're presenting.

DOING IT SMARTER

Interactive tests

In instructional multimedia design, you may be writing or preparing interactive tests or creating lists of choices. For example, you may ask questions on what your readers have just learnt, so they can be sure they can move on to the next section. There are three standard ways of coding the responses:

☐ true/false

☐ alphabetic options: a, b, c, d

☐ numeric options: 1, 2, 3.

Create feedback for each selection for correct, partly correct and incorrect answers. The feedback could be linked back to the section that discusses that topic in the preceding training material.

Plant an 'Easter egg'

For people who are obsessed with multimedia and web publications, some creators plant little moments of delight or surprises in the final document. They will often only be found by running a video clip in slow motion, for example, where a text message may have been embedded. Or there might be a pixel in the wrong colour in an image or a video frame that, when clicked, links to new content. These challenges or treats are sought out by digital natives.

From Ted Page, 'How to create effective band-driven entertainment content for the web', MarketingProfs.com, 18 July 2006

Sound can be used in more psychological ways by layering music tracks and sound effects with the dialogue. When a character screams, you might layer an elephant trumpeting underneath the scream to heighten the effect.

A sound file can distract a reader from a text block. You know it's true – how can you concentrate on a book with the *Grease* megamix going? Spoken or sung words can distract readers from the text. However, instrumental or wordless music and sound effects are unlikely to have the same level of distraction.

Get professional advice about the levels at which you record and play your sound files. You do not want distortion, crackling or 'white noise' to draw your listener's attention from the content of the product.

Avoid looped sounds where a sound file is continuously repeated. If you loop something, give the reader the option of turning it off, and provide a volume control.

It is wise to give a control panel for all sound and moving image files.

Video

Video footage timing is expressed in an eight-digit code, thus: 00:00:00:00 where the first two digits are hours, the second two are minutes, the third two are seconds, and the last two are the number of the frame. In film there are 24 frames per second, but in video there are 30 frames per second.

The moving image with sound is one of the most powerful tools available because it involves more than one of the five senses. The moving image is also something that makes multimedia 'not a book'. You are not using multimedia to its full effect if there is no movement.

Your options for video are documentary footage which is perceived as 'real', live action as distinct from animation, dramatisation that is 'staged', and demonstrations that are either simulated 'live' action or animation.

Talking heads are one of the sad clichés of multimedia – a dead giveaway that the boss wants to be seen in cyberspace. Sound files in most cases are more effective than the talking head – unless it does something funny or unusual.

Staging through dramatisations can be very expensive – just look at feature film costs – whereas documentary footage is often cheaper. You may even find a clip available through a video or film stock library that saves you shooting the footage yourself. To save wasted footage, you should script and storyboard your video before shooting it.

If you expect people to download video from a website, you should give them an indication of the file size. You might limit the amount of video in multimedia products if they are delivered across the web, though if they are CD-ROM or DVD products, this is unnecessary.

Television directors know what to avoid in video: fine patterns in clothing such as neckties and jackets can create moiré patterns on-screen where the patterns appear to move, and venetian blinds in backgrounds should be avoided for the same reason. White in costumes and backgrounds flares with lighting.

There are also certain tones – often lower or darker tones – that don't compress well in web video. You might also consider using a less complex or detailed background.

Graphics

There are many types of graphics to consider in multimedia: photographs, illustrations, charts, diagrams, maps, graphs, icons, symbols and navigation tools. Many of the most powerful graphics will also exhibit a unifying feature that enables the screens within the document to look like they belong together.

A custom colour palette deploys colour in a similar way throughout a project – maybe coding particular levels of information with text or background colours; or even just producing illustrations, photographs and diagrams in a limited spectrum of colours, which can be as simple as just black, white and grey!

There is often a level of stylisation imposed on a document to achieve a unified effect. The stylisation may be in the technique used for the drawn graphics – hard, loose, soft. In the same way, there might be a particular treatment applied to photographs following scanning, even though they may have come from different photographers or photo libraries. This could be a feathering of their edges or a particular border treatment; it could be cropping in a similar way – maybe consistently zooming in on details or always tilting the horizon at lurching angles. These techniques can build the graphic 'attitude' of a document.

READ MORE ABOUT IT

Nicholas V Iuppa, *Designing interactive digital media*, Focal Press, Butterworth-Heinemann, Boston, 1998, ISBN 0 240 80287 X.

Roy McKelvey, *Hypergraphics*, RotoVision SA, Crans-Pres-Celigny, Switzerland, 1998, ISBN 2 88046 313 0.

Bob Cotton & Richard Oliver, *Understanding hypermedia 2.000: Multimedia origins, internet futures*, Phaidon, London, 1997, ISBN 0 7148 36575.

Lisa Lopuck, *Designing multimedia: A visual guide to multimedia and online*

Screen formats

With televisions and computer screens, jumbo screens and information kiosks, it is wise to prepare your screen-based material for output in different formats.

When presenting widescreen formats (16:9) on television screens (4:3), there are two alternatives:

Letterbox

The full screen area of 16:9 is reduced to fit the width of the 4:3 screen with black bars placed top and bottom.

Centre cut

Only the central area of the 16:9 original appears at the full height of the 4:3 screen with the rest of the image on both sides cropped off-screen.

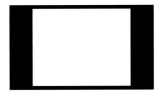

Pillar box

When presenting television formats (4:3) on widescreen, the technique used is similar to the letterbox technique where the 4:3 screen area appears at its full height and is centred in the wide screen with black bars placed left and right.

graphic design, Peachpit Press, Berkeley, 1996, ISBN 0 201 88398 8.

Susan Fowler, *GUI design handbook*, McGraw-Hill, New York, 1998,
    ISBN 0 07 059274 8.

Apple Computer, *Human interface guidelines: The Apple desktop interface*,
    Addison-Wesley, Reading, Massachusetts, 1987, ISBN 0 201 17753 6.

Ron Goldberg, *Multimedia producer's bible*, IDG Books Worldwide, Foster City,
    California, 1996, ISBN 0 7645 3002 X.

Andrew Bonime & Ken C Pohlmann, *Writing for new media: The essential guide
    to writing for interactive media, CD-ROMs and the web*, John Wiley & Sons,
    New York, 1998, ISBN 0 471 17030 5.

Peter Fenrich, *Practical guidelines for creating instructional multimedia
    applications*, Dryden Press, Harcourt Brace College Publishers, Orlando, 1997,
    ISBN 0 03 009264 7.

Bob Cotton & Richard Oliver, *The cyberspace lexicon: An illustrated dictionary
    of terms from multimedia to virtual reality*, Phaidon, London, 1994,
    ISBN 0 7148 2826 2.

Lisa Baggerman, *Design for interaction: User friendly graphics*, Rockport
    Publishers, Gloucester, Mass., 2000, ISBN 1 56496 652 6.

Storyboarding

A storyboard is a series of frames showing changes in the imagery seen on-screen, with a script beneath that describes the action and any sound effects in greater detail and includes all dialogue and references to sound effects and music. You can superimpose text, graphics or animation as required. These graphics, too, can move.

Storyboarding was developed at the Disney Studios in the 1920s and 1930s by Webb Smith, one of Walt Disney's animators, and has since been used extensively for animation and films, even stage shows and theme park rides.

A storyboard should accurately describe the imagery you intend the audience to see; the storyboard is given to a director or production company to shoot. Storyboards are now also being created in multimedia and website design to show what the program or site will look like before going into the final costly production phase. Location finders, set decorators, costumiers, composers, editors and casting agents also use storyboards to guide their part of the process and to estimate costs.

To sell your idea to a client, the storyboard may be turned into an *animatic* – where the storyboard frames are filmed in real time and a soundtrack added – to give an impression of the final piece of film. Comic books use similar techniques to tell a story, but comic artists have a variable frame size and page layout issues, which you do not have with a film, television or computer screen. Create the images of your storyboard through illustration, rough sketching, photocopying, collage or any combination of these.

The techniques of sequential imagery are relatively simple – we look at one picture, look at the next and note the differences. The differences through a series of images compound and we understand the movement that is being implied in the sequence. With most sequential imagery, you need a set of three frames to define movement accurately: the beginning, the middle and end of the movement. In this way, an object can enter, travel through and leave the sequence quite clearly.

Objects can move forward or backwards, towards or away from us; move to the left or right, up or down; move behind or in front of other objects; or they can turn or spin. The action can be fast or slow depending on how many frames it takes to accomplish the movement. You use cuts in the action to move the sequence on, to enhance the atmosphere and to increase the pace.

Animation

Inanimate objects and drawings have the appearance of coming to life with animation techniques. As well as its traditional uses in cartoons, television and movie screen advertising, and special effects, animation is used to create moving logos, icons and advertising for websites and multimedia interfaces. Many special effects are now achieved with a combination of live action and animation.

2-D animation
There are two techniques of 2-D animation: traditional frame-by-frame animation or programmed movement of objects within the frame.

The more traditional form of animation is based on a series of 2-D pictures that are drawn as a set of *key frames*, with the necessary multiple drawing of the movement between them, originally called *in-betweening*. In-betweening is mostly now generated by computer, once the key frames have been identified and rendered.

With film animation there are 24 fps (frames per second), but computer animation uses the video frame convention of 30 fps.

The 12 principles of animation

1 Squash and stretch
2 Appeal
3 Exaggeration
4 Arcs
5 Straight ahead and pose to pose animation
6 Follow through and overlapping action
7 Slow-out and slow-in
8 Staging
9 Secondary action
10 Timing
11 Anticipation
12 Solid drawing

Terry Dentry and Steve Piscopo quote early Disney animation instructor Don Graham in 'Arcs of motion', *Desktop*, 240, July 2008

Animated GIFs

Animated GIFs are the computer equivalent of the flip
book, where a sequence of slightly different still images
is viewed in time and appears to move. So a set of GIF
files is timed to appear in a sequence that effectively
animates their subject. To speed the processing of
GIFs, you might animate just a small portion of your
image. Despite the jerkiness of the movement and its
clumsiness in comparison to what we have come to
expect from television and film animation, we forgive
this low resolution on the computer screen as a trade-off
for the speed of its loading. Like any video loaded online,
although it takes time to load, it is still the fastest way to
take advantage of one of screen-based media's greatest
opportunities – to incorporate movement into otherwise
static information.

Once loaded, the animated GIF sequence can be looped,
creating a continuous repeating sequence. But give the
viewer the opportunity to stop the looping; it is visual
distraction that very quickly aggravates.

Programmed animation

Some animation software is based on programming the
movements for multiple elements within a frame. This is
the basis of Adobe's Flash animation software. Such objects
or elements can fade in or fade out, grow or reduce, enter
and exit the frame in a programmed period of time and on
a defined plane. Characters or objects may move between or
through planes. There can be multiple layers of action that
all work together in the final staged animation.

This is often the style of animation used for moving
typography. Whenever text and content is presented in
animation, be sure to provide a text-based alternative format
for people who are using assistive technologies to 'read'
your product.

3-D animation

3-D animation describes that in which characters or
subjects and the space in which they move are first
modelled. This has been achieved with puppets, plasticine
(*claymation*) and paper cut-outs in cartoons and training
films but, in most cases, this now involves creating a
wireframe skeleton in a 3-D computer-modelling program.
The wireframe creates a pattern of polygons. Each resulting

subdivision of the shape is then individually rendered with techniques such as texture mapping.

An alternative technique is 'lofting', 'loafing' or 'skinning', which is a technique that utilises detailed cross-sections of the shape that are defined like the topological lines on maps. The name refers to slices of bread – a loaf.

The shape can also be given transparency, reflection or refraction attributes. Lighting is then played on the shape, often with multiple light sources of differing intensities. Then the movement of the object or character and the movement of the point of view and light sources are specified. Most computer games and special effects for movies are created in this way. Think Disney–Pixar's *Toy Story*.

When creating movement, animators have observed natural movement and determined a number of techniques that help them to bring 'life' to their creations. One of these techniques is an *arced* path between two points, instead of a straight line. 'No matter how large or small the movement, if it's a living object, chances are it will be moving in an arc of motion', note Terri Dentry and Steve Piscopo ('Arcs of motion', *Desktop*, 240, July 2008). They go on to clarify that while *tweening* may mathematically prepare the staged movements between A and B, *in-betweening* will often create the arc – by defining some of the intermediate stages at points between A and B. Tweening then smoothly completes the motion rendering, the combination lending your animation a heightened sense of reality. Arcing can also contribute to the perceived weight of a character.

Rather than needing to specify the movement, actors can be recorded in 'mocap' ('motion capture') suits. These suits are wired and record the changes of position of the limbs and features of the body. When the same points are identified on the 3-D rendered object in the computer and the movement record for each point crunched, the object moves in similar ways to the actor. Think Golum in the *Lord of the Rings* movies.

There are programs available that enable such complex animation to be quickly generated using programmed movement. Such a program could, for example, be synchronised to voice files to enable a static face to be animated – by keying parts of the face to the movement file.

Early animators closely studied photographic records of movement, particularly the works of Edward Muybridge

Video gaming

'I always want that first reaction to be emotion, to be positive – to give a sense of satisfaction, glee. Certain obstacles may temporarily raise feelings of suspense, competition, even frustration. But we always want that final result, that final emotion, to be a positive one.'

Shigeru Miyamoto, creator of the Super Mario Brothers and *The Legend of Zelda*, 9 March 2007

Film techniques in storyboard form

MOVIE SCREEN

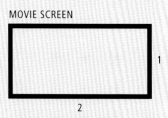

1

2

TELEVISION SCREEN

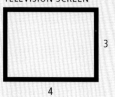

3

4

Movement

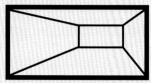

Zoom in or out

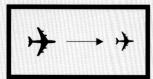

Pan up or down

Pan L–R or R–L

□ *Storyboard frames* are 90 × 180 mm (in ratio 1:2) for a movie screen and for 9:16 plasma television screen; though they were traditionally 90 × 120 mm landscape (in ratio 4:3) for a television screen. A text block beneath the frame contains the accompanying dialogue or voiceover (VO) and describes the soundtrack (music and effects). It also describes any action, details or visual effects that are not clearly visible from the frame.

□ *Movement within the frame* is shown by arrows. For example, in a chase sequence, a character may run through a particular scene and appear twice or more in the same storyboard frame to save redrawing the background. The arrow between the two drawings will indicate where the person has moved within the frame.

□ An *establishing shot* orientates the viewer, giving a context for the location where the action takes place.

□ A *long shot* shows a full scene.

□ A *medium shot* moves closer to the scene.

□ A *close-up* (CU) is shown by drawing the character or object larger in the frame.

□ An *extreme close-up* (ECU) is a tight shot, often of a facial feature, and is drawn as close as desired.

□ A *cut-away shot* is a quick edit that shows another scene, often what the character you've been watching to that point is viewing or giving you an alternative view that puts their predicament in context.

□ A *reverse shot* is used in interviews where they show a shot back to the interviewer.

□ A *composite shot* is where two images have been blended together. The background may have been shot separately and then the foreground action added. It is one of the stalwarts of special effects films.

□ A *zoom in* or *zoom out* is shown by drawing a miniature frame in the same dimensions as the outer frame and connecting the corners with fine lines. In the text block below the frame you define whether the zoom is a 'ZOOM IN' or a 'ZOOM OUT'.

□ *Panning* is where a stationary camera turns or tilts from right to left, left to right, up or down. It is shown in a storyboard by stretching the frame in the direction of the pan. In the text block beneath you define the direction of the pan, e.g. 'PAN L–R' or 'PAN DOWN'.

Cross-fade

Wipe

□ *Tracking* is where the camera physically moves to follow
the action. Also called dollying. It can be drawn the same
way as panning with the instruction to 'TRACK'.

□ A *fade* or *dissolve* is where an image fades on to or off the screen.
You can 'FADE TO WHITE' (also called a 'wash') or 'FADE TO BLACK'
and then 'FADE IN FROM WHITE' or 'FADE IN FROM BLACK'.

□ A *cross-fade* or *cross-dissolve* is a technique of dissolving one image
into another. As one scene fades out, the next scene is faded in over it.
It is indicated in a storyboard by a cross connecting the two frames.

□ A *wipe* is where one scene enters over the top of another scene
and is literally wiped across the previous screen image.

□ *Morphing* is a special effect where one character or object turns into
another by animation. In a storyboard it can be shown as before-
and-after frames with a cross-fade connecting them. The text block
below would simply state the character/object was morphing.

□ A *split screen* is where two or more moving images are sharing the
same screen. It might be the classic split down the middle showing
two people across the world talking to each other on the phone or
it could be a bird's-eye view of the action with a close-up of a race.
You just show the split screen as it would appear in the frame.

□ When *layering* or *sandwiching* film with film or film and graphics, you
create the resulting image in the storyboard frame and explain below.

□ *Special effects* (FX) can be shown in the frame and explained
in the text block below it. 'SFX' indicates 'sound effects'.

□ *Action and title safe regions* define the central area within a screen
format where it is recommended that titles and type appear, so they will
not be trimmed off when the format is varied for different output. Because
these were not considered in old films, you often see title sequences
distorted to fit the information on-screen and occasionally cannot see
action that happened off to the far edge of screen, as it has been cropped
for the 4:3 television format. They now also include provision for other
graphics to be added to the screen, like station identification or subtitles.

□ *SMPTE bars* are provided before film in much the same way as colour bars
on the edge of printing. They are a standardised set of hues and tones that
will give the most real colour effect if the colour output is calibrated to them.

Split screen

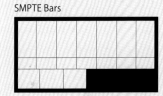

Action and title safe regions

A   T

SMPTE Bars

Machinima

A term joining the words 'machine' and 'cinema', *machinima* refers to short movies that are partially created using the virtual environments of computer games. It often involves using backgrounds and characters from the games and editing in avatars of the creators or live footage to create new characters and stories. The live footage uses conventional video capture as well as mobile phone video and animations, layering them over the other material using blue-screen techniques. A soundtrack is added, creating a movie experience. High schools are using this technique to re-engage senior students in creative writing.

Rotating a 3-D model

When you have a 3-D object or virtual reality environment, you need to give your user a tool in order to move around the object or space. One such tool is a square with arrows indicating left, right, top and bottom as selection points for rotating the object or proceeding through the space. Be sure to give zoom controls if there is greater detail to be seen.

– famous for photographs of animals and nude humans against a white background with a grid drawn on it – which were the first photographs to prove that all four legs of horses actually left the ground when at a gallop.

In virtual reality (VR) environments online or in computer games, users can play existing characters or sometimes create 'avatars' of themselves – fictitious cartoon or illustrative versions of themselves that can operate in the environment. The avatars are defined by a set of physical attributes that are selected from a menu of alternative body parts and features and named, making them a unique representation of that user.

These alternative worlds are referred to as the 'metaverse'. Your avatar can inhabit the metaverse and interact with other avatars in virtual hotels, shops, restaurants, and so on.

Animating logos and other 2-D graphics

There are some basic moves that will animate even a two-dimensional form. It can simply enter and exit a frame; it can grow or shrink; it can spin and stop. You can close on a very fine detail in an extreme zoom, and pull out to the full logo in frame. You might tilt the horizon rather than the logo to imply movement. Simply condensing the logo can have the appearance of falling forward or backwards if condensed from top to bottom, or turning sideways if condensed from left to right.

But with digital publishing applications such as websites and multimedia, you must consider three-dimensional form, time and movement within space, and combine them with sound effects and music to use the media effectively. You could be titling television and video programs, even in-house or training videos; or preparing interactive graphics for websites, games software and multimedia packages; or creating a corporate signature for film, television and Internet advertising; or creating a virtual reality space.

Sometimes you will be working with graphic materials such as symbols and logos that work in two dimensions – and still need to work in their two-dimensional forms – that also must work in these new contexts. You might also be working with something that is well established in print materials and you do not always have the luxury of designing for the new forms.

**Basic 2-D movement
strategies**

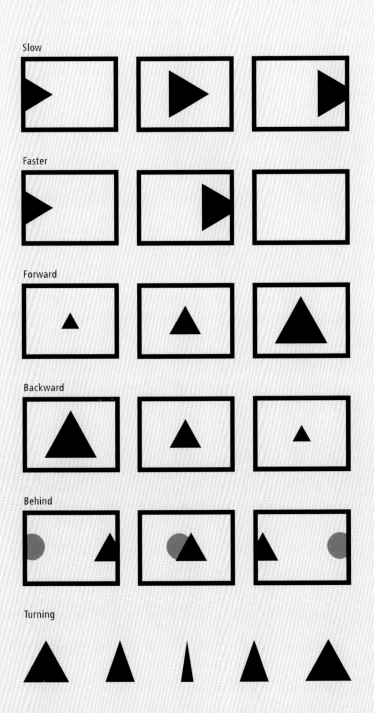

Slow

Faster

Forward

Backward

Behind

Turning

One of the easiest ways to approach animation of a two-dimensional form is to give it a third dimension. Then, moving in space around the three-dimensional form, you have more options for interesting moves. Adding the third dimension can be simply imagining the form is cut out of a slab. Better than this, though, is to look at a triangle and see a cone or half cone; or look at a circle and see a sphere; or look at two concentric circles and see a car tyre or even a sphere with a crater; or look at a line and see a piece of

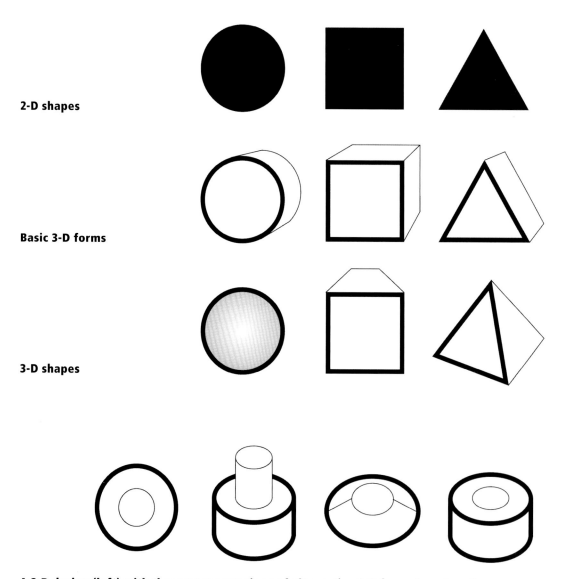

2-D shapes

Basic 3-D forms

3-D shapes

A 2-D design (left) with three representations of alternative 3-D forms based on it

wire lurching through space or a thin plane like we imagine Saturn's rings to be!

Once the third dimension is added, you can explode it into its components. You can then assemble them or move them around until they are all in the right position to read the logo. This assembly might be read accurately from one viewpoint but look quite odd from other views. It could be an optical illusion that obscures the logo (say, starting from behind the logo and moving to the front). You might move through as if it's transparent.

Also, since you now have the third dimension, your light source can become dynamic – that is, the light source or multiple light sources can move about your shape, casting shadows that enable its dimensionality to be seen. Similarly, as your viewpoint changes, the shadows alter.

Light intensity also alters colour perception, so your light source intensity may vary in order to play different colour effects across your 3-D form. As a simple example, you will probably recognise the clichéd logo bathed in the warmth of a sunset that deepens into evening with occasional flashes from passing shooting stars!

You might also texture-map each piece. Like gift wrapping, texture mapping applies a veneer to a three-dimensional rendering. It might be applying wood grain or a chrome finish. With chrome, glass and other reflective finishes, you can distort your backgrounds in your logo. You can then project this shape in perspective from a given viewpoint. Simply altering the viewpoint progressively sets up an animated sequence. You can approach it in a zoom in or move away from it in a zoom out; you can maintain a set distance from it but slowly move around it in a pan; you can follow it as it moves through space in a tracking shot. If you take a low viewpoint, your logo will look monumental, or you could fly over it for a bird's-eye view.

It can fade in or fade out. It can cross-fade where, as it fades out, another image fades in. It can morph as a smooth transition into something else or from something else. You might ripple or melt the logo or wave it like a flag. Any number of distortion filters can produce interesting effects.

READ MORE ABOUT IT

Kit Laybourne, *The animation book: A complete guide to animated film-making – from flip-books to sound cartoons to 3-D animation*, Three Rivers Press, New York, 1998, ISBN 0 517 88602 2.

Mark Wigan, *Basics illustration: Sequential images*, AVA Publishing SA, Lausanne, Switzerland, 2007, ISBN 978-2-940373-60-4.

Martin Lambie-Nairn, *Brand identity for television: With knobs on*, Phaidon, London, 1997, ISBN 0 7148 3447 5.

Websites

A website, like all graphic design, should be user-focused. Through talking with people most likely to be interested in the product and imagining how the expected user will respond to the design, you develop a user focus. Is it going to scare them off? Is it using language that is comfortable and understandable for them? Does it have a logical flow for someone with their level of knowledge about the product or information? Once they are interested, is there an ease – or speed – of movement through the information? Is there a consistent application of layout, colour usage and informational hierarchy throughout the site?

Frustration factors in websites abound. It may be slow to load because it is graphics-heavy. It might have annoying details like looped animations or sounds or flashing buttons. It might be content-listed in an organisation-based hierarchy rather than a user-based needs hierarchy. Or it might just have too many levels to navigate successfully. Maybe its links are not flexible enough and visitors cannot get where they wish to go next without many backward steps.

Try to give the reader only three clicks to the information they need. This has site-plan implications – how do you create a hierarchy that enables you to explain the increasing complexity of the information but still retain only four levels of site? Three clicks beyond the home page is the fourth level.

Scrolling to the right can be cool. Scrolling down is ubiquitous. But scrolling both ways on the one page is incredibly frustrating. Plan it better.

Screen sizes are measured in pixels and the standard web screen is recommended to be 1024 × 728 pixels to accommodate the hardware, often older equipment, of the majority of users. However, while this may be the screen area, it is not all usable area due to browser borders and navigation bars – so users could be thankful for a smaller active screen area on the site. Using a screen area of 950 × 500 pixels – or even the earlier 800 × 600 pixels – should work in most browsers.

'One way to attract attention to your Web site, ad, or product is by making the message venue personally relevant, pleasant and surprising. These three things enhance consumers' motivation to look at and think about things ... Here are three things you need to consider to make your content easy to process: prominence, contrast and competition with other information.'

Debbie MacInnis, MarketingProfs.com, 27 April 2005

'But over time I've come to think that what really counts is not the number of clicks it takes me to get to what I want (although there are limits), but rather how *hard* each click is – the amount of thought required, and the amount of uncertainty about whether I'm making the right choice.'

Steve Krug in *Don't Make Me Think*

Keep the site fast, both in the site loading time and the time it takes to navigate. Spare the scrolling in early pages! Site navigation options should appear at both the top and the bottom of each page if vertical scrolling is necessary. If you have large image or sound files, tell viewers how large and give them the option to load them or not.

Use live graphics and hot text links that jump the reader to other parts of the site. This can avoid opening layer upon layer.

When creating the structure for the contents, think about what the intended audience might want to know, not about how it is most convenient to get the information from sections of the organisation or how you can rejig last year's annual report and product brochures.

Do not lead off with a profile of the managing director if that is not the most important piece of information readers need to know. Too many times, a website reflects internal organisational structures and politics, rather than catering for most external visitors' needs. Having a home page for each section of the organisation is not necessarily the most appropriate solution for the site visitor.

Almost certainly, the most important information will not fit an alphabetical or even a chronological hierarchy.

Sections can be identified by different colours. Choose a palette of colours that look consistent in intensity when seen together on the home page. The colour can be a live graphic that transports the reader to the next section with a click. The colour is then repeated at the head of that page. Colour coding can mean the next visit to the site will be faster, once regular users like staff have broken the code.

Keep navigational icons intuitive. This will enable quick responses and propel your reader through the site. Make the entry sequence and home pages both attractive and fast to load. A reader's decision to stick with the site can be made by this attraction alone. Does the site look worth entering? Put the best contents forward and imply how easy it is to get to them. This is the reception desk – make it welcoming and appropriate.

Use corporate identification – colours and logos should be used that relate the site to all other manifestations of the corporate identity in the marketplace, from printed communications such as letterheads, brochures or annual reports to the television identity. Consistency of image is important. The corporate logo is often in the top left corner

In *Hypergraphics*, Roy McKelvey discusses well-designed sites: 'Well-designed web sites have several things in common. First, they have a clear understanding of their audience. They are designed to provide specific information to users in an efficient and appropriate manner. Second, they focus on using web technologies not for their own sake, but for their power to improve the site's message and service. Well-designed sites are simple in conception and consistent in their organization and interaction. Third, they are designed to accommodate change and growth. Web sites are, almost by definition, evolutionary documents.'

According to Jakob Nielsen in *Designing Web Usability: The Practice of Simplicity*, the four criteria that are the foundation of good web design, based on things users most want, are:
H high-quality content
O often updated
M minimal download time
E ease of use.
If you can provide these four elements, users will be happy and you will have a good site. But it is not enough to simply give users what they want. You need to go beyond the four basics to have a truly stellar site. To move from HOME design to a HOME RUN design, add the three extras:
R relevant to users' needs
U unique to the online medium
N net-centric corporate culture.

of both the home page and all other pages within the site. Almost as often, it is a live link back to the home page from every page in the site.

Sometimes people confuse consistent with inflexible or, worse, boring. Consistency of application means that the intended market receives non-conflicting messages. With a cutting-edge print and television identity, a boring website is not the way to go. Equally, with a restrained, subtle and distinctive print identity and refined product brochures, a website that is a visual fireworks display with wild type and blinking graphics will not be very appropriate.

Avoid blinking or flashing graphics and looped animations and sounds, or at least make them stoppable. Flashing and movement set up a distraction that constantly drags readers' eyes to that point of the page and away from other important information. It can certainly highlight that single aspect to which you're drawing attention – but so effectively that you won't communicate anything else without creating a frustration factor. People will have to be determined to ignore or read through the distraction. Similarly, continuous sound can become a frustration factor.

Backgrounds can also create confusion if they begin to impose themselves onto the text. Readability can suffer. Text and background colour need to be separated by sufficient tonal contrast (dark against light). Any variation in the background must maintain the tonal level of the background, otherwise it starts to interfere with the legibility of the letterforms in the foreground. If the background has an image or a pattern, ensure it is subtle and 'ghosted' sufficiently for the text to be read unhindered.

Use email links and links to other sites as a service to readers, but try not to lose readers to other sites too early. Internal links are more important upfront to get readers further into the site. Hot-linked icons and images are a fast way of propelling readers through a website or multimedia program.

Computer users are accustomed to visual representation of concepts through icons – thanks mostly to the Apple Macintosh interface that was pioneered at Xerox and is also the basis of Windows. The system of icons created to navigate programs, from selecting programs from the desktop, to selecting tools from toolboxes and selecting text attributes from rulers and menus, have currency and relevance to readers of screen-based material. Because the web and multimedia are read on computer screens, it is safe to assume readers are familiar with screen-based icon systems. Do not lose the familiarity by creating a series of new symbols for them to learn. Rather, use that familiarity to create hybrid symbols that individualise your document but retain the readability and instant recognition that classic icons have.

All decisions should be made by asking: What will readers do now? What will they want to know? What will keep them interested?

Additionally, don't frustrate your regular or repeat users.

Developing your information architecture

Sometimes you will prepare the information architecture of a website or multimedia product but, in the case of a complex or vast site, you may employ specialist information architects to create the structure of the site. Whoever prepares this structure will consider all the current information that the client wants to include in light of their intended audience's needs and expectations. They will also identify potential gaps in the information, as well as areas for future development.

So the information architecture is the structure of the content, how it is labelled and indexed, and how you will move around it (navigation).

Card sorting

Consider all the content you want your website to have and write each topic on a separate card. Sort the cards into logical piles, ordering or numbering the content, and then add different coloured cards as title cards and to identify different content types or levels.

You can pin the cards up on boards or tape them to windows and ask potential site users to navigate their way through the cards. By asking questions as they work with the cards, you can clarify the categories, the language you've used in titling and understand the expectations users have of the content that follows particular headings.

Site maps and wireframes

Once the content subdivisions have been determined and the optimal structure for the site's potential users has been approved for development, you will convert the site map into a set of master page wireframes.

Jeffrey Veen, in *Hot Wired Style*, describes the two extremes of web document structure: 'On the one hand, some sites are a vast sea of information, organized rigidly with a strong sense of hierarchy: they're all about function. Others are a pure expression of artistry, with sparse information presented through a strong aesthetic sense: these are all about form.

'Think of the two extremes as the library and the gallery.

'The library has a vast collection of information available in numerous formats. It isn't concerned with the display of the information, just the method of organization. It expects that you know what kind of info you want, so its main goal is a clear, organized system to help you find what you want as quickly as possible. It doesn't necessarily put the best books closest to the front door; it doesn't open their pages to give you a peek.

'Conversely, the gallery offers a controlled presentation of its artwork. It is a carefully orchestrated space designed to give every visitor the same, meticulously curated aesthetic experience ...

'Being clear on where your project fits on the library–gallery continuum is the first step toward successfully navigating the maze of compromises and tough questions that working on the Web will demand of you. The goal is to balance pure information with an aesthetic that not only complements the message but also becomes a part of the voice.'

The site map is like a flow chart or diagram that identifies particularly the top structure of a site, starting from the home page and showing all the paths to different pages with connectors and also banded so you can read how many 'clicks' or levels your user will need to get to a particular page.

The wireframes are created for the top pages – usually the home page and the two levels below that. Usually created on a horizontal or landscape page format in a word-processing program, they consist of different page divisions that identify the different zones required (top and left navigation zones, content, links, etc.) and each zone contains the actual content intended for those pages. In this way, the wireframes can give clients a good idea of the information architecture of the site before the detailed site design and construction begins.

For large websites where the client has commissioned an information architect to prepare the structure, this is the point at which the website designer will start working on the look and feel of the site: with the wireframes and a detailed chart of the content levels to guide them.

Wire frame

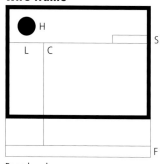

Page header
Search
Left navigation
Content area
Page footer

Web 2.0

The first websites relied on largely passive content delivery, but what is now called 'Web 2.0' describes websites and multimedia products that encourage collaboration and community content creation. Web 2.0 encourages less text-driven content and simpler web pages. It is usually in formats that can be accessed through computers, mobile phones and personal digital assistants (PDAs).

Such 'social media' innovations have included:
- blogs, 'web logs' or online diaries or journals, regularly updated by individuals or small groups
- podcasts of downloadable sound recordings, sometimes 'webcast' or 'audioblog'
- vodcasts of downloadable video clips, sometimes 'videocast'
- streaming content, usually video, broadcast live to the web
- RSS feeds ('Really Simple Sindication') where users subscribe to a feed that could automatically download or send them a link to the download without them needing to return to the source

DOING IT CHEAPER
Interactivity testing

Before you start producing your final website, you can run tests on your content, the planned links, and identify any gaps in the site. You can link a series of draft word-processed pages in a PDF by embedding the planned links to the other pages at every link point. These links enable you to either publish the draft website to a CD and distribute it or email the PDF to your assessors and approvers (even if – or especially if – they are distributed nationally or even globally).

Ask them to identify gaps in expected information, terminology that leads to different or unexpected content, where the logic of the staging of information was uneven, or just where they wished they had a link to another page.

You can then assess the feedback and rejig the site content and architecture with little outlay.

DOING IT SMARTER
Sound loops

Sound files can play once and stop, play a defined number of times and stop, or be looped to play continuously. If you wish the website you're designing to have a distinguishing sound, create a background sound that is on an infinite loop. For sanity's sake, keep it to a low volume. Better still, with all sound files, give the viewer the control to change the volume or stop the sound altogether.

DOING IT SMARTER
Logos on background colours

When you want logos and other graphics to sit comfortably on the background of the site page, apply the transparent option to the background area of the logo or image GIF to blend it into the site background. Alternatively, if the background is a flat colour, simply make sure the GIF background has that exact hexadecimal colour description of the site background.

Site testing

Test your site in a number of browsers. Observe how the pages look as each browser converts the HTML tags, and check how quickly the various files load. Get someone who is unfamiliar with the site to surf it with you, and make any changes to improve or streamline the site. Check it in the browsers again, not just the current versions but also the last two versions of those browsers. Most surfers do not upgrade their browsers on every release.

Navigation

'If the page [somewhere deep in the bowels of a website] is well designed … you should be able to answer these questions without hesitation:

- ☐ What site is this? (Site ID)
- ☐ What page am I on? (Page name)
- ☐ What are the major sections of this site? (Sections)
- ☐ What are my options at this level? (Local navigation)
- ☐ Where am I in the scheme of things? ("You are here" indicators)
- ☐ How can I search?'

Steve Krug in *Don't Make Me Think*

'A world that puts the "me" into media and the "I" in iPod ... For the first time, the full potential of the internet as an interactive medium is being realised in what has been called Web 2.0. More than a third of Australians have traded content on the internet, and it is a safe bet that the numbers will surge here and worldwide.'

> Peter Roberts in *Business Review Weekly*, vol. 28, no. 35, 7 September 2006

Understanding web design

'Web design is the creation of digital environments that facilitate and encourage human activity; reflect or adapt to individual voices and content; and change gracefully over time while always retaining their identity ...'

The experienced web designer accepts that many projects will have headers and columns and footers. Do not whine about emerging commonalities but 'use them to create pages that are distinctive, natural, brand-appropriate, subtly memorable, and quietly but unmistakably engaging'.

> Jeffrey Veldman, AListApart.com, 20 November 2007

- intranets, an organisation's internal information resources
- collaborative working spaces
- wikis, collaborative information sources that encourage users to add, edit, extend or correct content – the word comes from the Hawaiian word for 'quick'
- forums that are mediated discussion spaces including bulletin boards, message boards and discussion boards
- 3-D or virtual reality web environments.

READ MORE ABOUT IT

David Siegel, *Creating killer web sites: The art of third-generation site design*, 2nd edn, Hayden Books, Indianapolis, 1997, ISBN 1 56830 433 1.

Jeffrey Veen, *Hot Wired style: Principles for building smart web sites*, Wired Books, San Francisco, 1997, ISBN 1 888869 09 7.

Jakob Nielsen, *Designing web usability: The practice of simplicity*, New Riders Publishing, Indianapolis, 2000, ISBN 1 56205 810 X.

Steve Krug, *Don't make me think: A common sense approach to web usability*, 2nd edn, New Riders Publishing, Berkeley, California, 2006, ISBN 0-321-34475-8.

Andy Clarke, *Transcending CSS: The fine art of web design*, New Riders Press, Berkeley, California, 2006, ISBN 0321410971.

Craig Grannell, *Web designer's reference: An integrated approach to web design with XHTML and CSS*, Friends of ED, USA, 2005, ISBN 1-59059-430-4.

David Siegel, *Secrets of successful web sites: Project management on the world wide web*, Hayden Books, Indianapolis, 1997, ISBN 1 56830382 3.

Vincent Flanders & Michael Willis, *Web pages that suck: Learn good design by looking at bad design*, Sybex, Alameda, California, 1996, ISBN 0 7821 2187 X.

Roger Black with Sean Elder, *Web sites that work*, Adobe Press, San Jose, California, 1997, ISBN 1 5680 346 7.

Robin Williams & John Tollett, *The non-designer's web book*, Peachpit Press, Berkeley, 1998, ISBN 0 201 68859 X.

Roger Pring, *www.type: Effective typographic design for the world wide web*, Weidenfeld & Nicolson, London, 1999, ISBN 0 297 82539 9.

Anne T McKenna, *Digital portfolio: 26 design portfolios unzipped*, Rockport Publishers, Gloucester, Mass., 2000, ISBN 1 56496 467 1.

B Martin Pederson (ed.), *Graphis: New media*, Graphis Press, Zurich, 1996, ISBN 1 880001 06 2.

Molly Holzschlag, *Web by design: The complete guide*, Sybex, Alameda, California, ISBN 0 7821 2201 9.

Jennifer Niederst, *Web design in a nutshell*, O'Reilly, Sebastopol, California, 1999, ISBN 1 56592 515 7.

Laurie McCanna, *Creating great web graphics*, 2nd edn, MIS Press, New York, 1997, ISBN 1 55828 550 4.

Ken Coupland (ed.), *WebWorks: Navigation*, Rockport Publishers, Gloucester, Mass., 2000, ISBN 1 56496 662 3.

Marc Phillips, *Behind Australia's most successful websites*, Bookman, Melbourne, 1997, ISBN 1 86395 280 2.

Andy Shafran, *Creating your own web pages*, 2nd edn, Que Corporation, Indianapolis, 1997, ISBN 0 7897 1232 6.

Paul McFedries, *The complete idiot's guide to creating an HTML web page*, Que Corporation, Indianapolis, 1996, ISBN 0 7897 0722 5.

Geekgirl [Rosie Cross], *The friendly grrls guide to getting on the internet*, Geekgirl, Sydney, 1997, ISBN 0 646 27793 6.

Graphical user interface (GUI)

Before websites and multimedia, a graphical user interface (called GUI – 'gooey') was a rare project.

You need to keep the interface intuitive. If the icons or screen layout maintain a certain familiarity or ease-and-speed-of-recognition factor, the interface should be successful. As in many design projects, good use of visual metaphors will enable the user to employ previously learned modes of information retrieval.

To work out how a design can be recognised intuitively, we need to consider the number of interfaces we encounter daily. There is your microwave, but most microwaves use a word-based, rather than an icon-based, interface. Word-based interface is fine but has limitations – it is more time-consuming and is language-dependent, but it is faster to load.

Consider the road user interface – signs, lights, road markings and services; and the car's internal interface – petrol gauge, speedometer and dashboard system. These systems give us red warnings, flashing lights for attracting attention, various sirens, the red octagon stop symbol, the give-way triangle, the broken lines for crossing if you need to pass, the green, amber and red circles that indicate go, caution and stop respectively, and the gauges that fill or empty (which are akin to the file transmission gauges that fill when the file is complete). The system is rich in icons – or graphical user interface.

On a similar tack, mapping is rich in symbolism that may be appropriate to consider as a part of the interface design primer: the symbols for farms (cows, corn), historical sites (little castles) and industrial areas (little factories); information counters or booths (i); highways (shields with numbers in them), surfaced and unsurfaced roads (lines of different weights); and others.

What about much older interface systems? There are the systems used for star signs in horoscopes (not the illustrations, or pictograms, but the streamlined versions of them that create almost abstract symbols), the Christian cross (which can also symbolise death due to its use in

> Intuitive user interfaces often use metaphor as an effective 'vehicle of exploration', according to David Siegel in *Creating Killer Web Sites*. His examples of metaphors include: 'galleries, comic strips, television channels, TV remote controls, magazines, tabloids, store environments, museums, postcard racks, amusement parks, going inside things (computers, human body, buildings, ant farm, and so on), safaris, cities, and cupboards.'

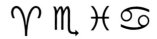

Horoscope symbols

Website

[square brackets indicate option]

[Entry sequence]

- ☐ Splash screen or front door (keep it fast)
- ☐ Animated sequence to open (keep it fast)
- ☐ Entry tunnel (keep it interesting, interactive and fast)
- ☐ Counter to track hits
- ☐ 'Skip intro' button that instantly links to the home page

The principle behind the entry sequence is that it introduces the site while the rest of the site is being loaded and gives an instant response to the user when they get to the home page. Keep it graphically interesting, but condense the files as far as they can go and then some. This is an opportunity to reveal a part of the corporate identity but not necessarily the whole – hold back something for the home page! You could consider having a set of interchangeable splash pages that will give a different look to the site over a few visits. Also you *must* provide a clear option to 'skip intro' because many users don't like splash pages.

Possible lures for entry

- ☐ Free stuff
- ☐ Gimmicks
- ☐ News
- ☐ Deals
- ☐ Games
- ☐ Club membership
- ☐ Survey

Home page

- ☐ Header and site identification
- ☐ Search box for searching the content of the site
- ☐ [Global link bar which links to related websites – often your organisation's other sites]
- ☐ Navigation bar for internal content
- ☐ Quick links/shortcuts to major content areas (usually left navigation)
- ☐ First level of breadcrumb bar: Home >
- ☐ Start of site content or registration page before starting content
- ☐ News and announcements
- ☐ Site map (hyperlinked to the content)
- ☐ Pictures
- ☐ Pull-quotes that link to latest content
- ☐ New features
- ☐ [Banner ads and 'landing pages' that register the user's interest and are often the first page after clicking from a banner ad]
- ☐ Legal statements as required, including copyright and privacy statements
- ☐ Last update so users know the currency of the site content
- ☐ Contact us

Some of the most effective home pages have attractive graphic banners but, as it is still just a person looking at a screen, size is not so important but consistent corporate identification is. The home page is like a contents list and visitors want everything active. They do not want to have to click into a secondary contents list because the graphics or the dot points or the words were not links.

Content of the site with internal and external links (local and remote)

- ☐ About us
- ☐ News and regular updating
- ☐ Help
- ☐ Frequently asked questions (FAQs)
- ☐ Catalogue
- ☐ Shopping cart
- ☐ Advertisements
- ☐ Personalisation (like Amazon.com's 'Last time you bought ...' and 'Other readers also bought ...')
- ☐ Publications in multiple formats (usually HTML, RTF and PDF, each linked and indicating the download size)
- ☐ Media resources with: media releases and product fact sheets; recent speeches, testimonials or 'backgrounders'; a library of downloadable images of people, products or logos; executive or staff biographies ('bios'); video news releases (VNRs) of advertising footage packaged and provided for free to television and other news organisations; product reviews and multilingual resources.
- ☐ Firewalls that make secure site areas for registered user access only
- ☐ Security system for e-commerce, confidentiality and privacy
- ☐ Invisible site content or site administration area for editing and creation of new content and approval

Graphic interface

- Banners including a logo or top left link back to the home page
- Consistent colour palette and text styles
- Links or hyperlinks for active, visited and hover states
- Clickable image links
- Image maps and text option
- Images, graphs and charts with text alternatives ('alt text' or 'longdesc')
- 360° sewn images
- Warnings for large file sizes (audio/ video/image)
- Optional downloading of large images
- Interlaced images (a low-resolution image loads first and is gradually upgraded to higher resolution)
- Preloading image files
- Tables with text alternatives ('alt text' or 'longdesc')
- Logos and icon systems related to content subdivisions
- Backgrounds
- Video clips with play, pause, stop and volume controls
- Audio clips or sound bites with play, pause, stop and volume controls
- Games
- Animation with play, pause, stop and volume controls
- Virtual reality and 3-D environments
- Rollovers
- Text levels and colours
- Three heading levels within the content area of the page
- Two dot point levels
- One text paragraph styling
- One quote paragraph styling
- One reference or source paragraph styling
- Full table specification including: table heading, column headings, row headings, row text, total lines, reference or source text

- Links and active links
- Hover links
- Pull-quotes
- A print style sheet or printer-friendly version of site content
- Navigational aids
- Page header, often a bar of clickable 'tabs' (like ring-binder folder dividers) with submenu lists under each tab
- Breadcrumb bar to allow a reader on any page of your site to know where they are and how they got there
- 'Tab navigation' which helps people with low vision navigate the page elements by using the tab key on their keyboard to jump between navigation elements
- Scroll bars
- Quick links, usually left navigation
- Buttons
- Navigational icons
- [Frames]
- Search capability for the site
- 'Anchor tags' or links to content further down the same page (like a linked content list that saves scrolling)
- Back and next links or other inline navigation that allows users to continue moving about the site without scrolling back up the page to the top navigation
- Page footer (include last updates, copyright information and other legal status, contact details and navigational links)

Exit sequence

- Response form
- Order form
- Blog, chat line, forum, or guest book
- Email feedback link or mailto commands

cemeteries) and fish, the male and female signs (not the little man and woman pictograms used to label public toilets, but the circles with, respectively, a diagonal arrow and a downward cross).

The symbol for returning to the home page on most browsers is the classic five-sided house made from a square with a triangle on top. The letterbox pictogram is used in email systems. These are virtually instinctive symbols. If you asked a child to create a symbol for home or letterbox, those simple shapes are probably close to what they would create. Somewhere inside our heads we respond to these shapes as having these meanings. This is good interface design.

Other signs that seem to be instinctively understood are the heart for love, the ear, speaker or music note for sound, the eye for vision or picture, the old-fashioned movie projector or camera – even the clapper boards with the black and white diagonals – for moving image. These are handy for multimedia selection.

Then there is the sound system. Like a microwave, it relies for some information on words. But the important element here is the symbol (or icon) language used in the cassette deck and CD deck buttons. The forward triangle, rewind triangle, fast-forward double triangle, stop square and pause double lines constitute one of the most influential symbol systems recently developed. You will also have noticed how we use them instinctively in multimedia productions. Although the symbols started with cassette tape players, they have moved through CD players, video and DVD players into multimedia, websites and information kiosks.

Another daily interface we encounter is the computer screen, which features windows, icons, rulers, menus and toolboxes. The symbols that have been developed to speed our use of this interface are well refined and, due to the fact that readers of screen-based information are sitting at a computer, it is a safe assumption that the interface can incorporate some conventions from computer interface design.

Do not stray too far from symbols that work in an effort to create a new interface. If a reader must learn the new system before using the product you design, you will lose a number of potential users. As Jeffrey Veen asks in *Hot Wired Style*, 'What would television be like if every show had a different remote control?' It is commonsense to use a familiar navigation system in your interface design.

You might create a version of an existing symbol that stylistically fits your design. Use a colour palette that fits the site backgrounds and images, and a texture or illustration style that sits comfortably with the display type and site metaphor. But be careful not to obscure the clarity of the navigation system with style for the sake of style.

The best icon systems use an interface that weds recognisable pictorial, symbolic, sound and moving elements in a layout that streamlines selection process. Users don't want to have to dart all over the screen with the mouse or scroll up and down the page to find the options. The nature of the system you develop should have ease of use at its core with minimal explanation needed for the interface. That way, the reader can concentrate on the content and message, rather than how they will extract the message.

Intranets

The needs of most organisations and offices include a set of online resources and applications, including all office information systems. These are collected into a secure web environment for staff, called an 'intranet'.

An intranet collects and archives business information that can include:

- news and announcements (usually on the home page)
- links to the organisation's external-facing websites
- calendar of events (which may include meetings, public events and public holidays)
- directory of contact details for all staff, including live email links
- online staff magazine and special interest areas (which may include a bulletin board and different social forums)
- archive of business documentation (which may include product fact sheets, systems training documentation, policy guidelines and forms)
- collaborative workspaces (which allow small teams or committees to store their meeting agendas, minutes and resources or to work remotely on the same project)
- individual staff pages (with personal resources including regularly visited links and documents).

Design for an intranet is often easier because the organisation has control of the output through purchasing

David Siegel, in *Creating Killer Web Sites*, describes his restaurant model for websites:

'I use a restaurant metaphor when thinking about sites. You hear about a restaurant from an advertisement or friend, or discover it while passing by. You check out the daily specials chalked on a board out front and smell the aroma in the doorway.

'Once through the door, you make a quick stay-or-bail decision. In a popular restaurant, you might have to wait for a table. If you stay, someone shows you to a table and hands you the menu. You make your selection.

'When the food arrives, you have no urge to rearrange the various items on the plate. The food and presentation are the creations of the chef. You sample the various items, skipping among them, mixing flavors and textures.

'When you are finished, you have dessert, ask for the bill, and pay. You leave a tip, pick up the card next to the cashier, and maybe exchange a few pleasant words with the owner. Later, when you are hungry again, you return or you don't, based on the quality of that first experience.'

File types

The file types you are most likely to encounter in website and multimedia design are:

Text, page and site description files

HTML	Hypertext Markup Language
SGML	Standard Generic Markup Language
DSSSL	Document Semantic Style Specification Language
XML	Extensible Markup Language (subset of SGML)
RSS	Really Simple Sindication (subset of XML)
CSS	Cascading Style Sheets
AJAX	Asynchronous JavaScript and XML (Google maps use it – a combination of JavaScript and data storage)
EPS	Adobe's Encapsulated PostScript
PDF	Adobe's Portable Document Format (which in 2008 became a new ISO International Standard, ISO 32000-1)
RTF	Rich Text Format

Image files

PICT	Picture
TIFF	Tagged Image File Format
GIF	Graphical Interchange Format ('giff' not 'jiff')
JPEG	Joint Photographic Experts Group ('jay-peg')
PNG	Portable Network Graphics ('ping')
Wavelets	

Video and animation files

MPEG	Moving Picture Experts Group ('em-peg')
QTV	Apple's QuickTime Video
AVI	Audio Video Interleave
SWF	Adobe's ShockWave File
M-JPEG	Motion JPEG (from the Joint Photographic Experts Group) ('em-jay-peg')
MNG	Multiple-image Network Graphics (PNG animation) ('ming')

Audio files

MIDI	Musical Instrument Digital Interface ('middy')

RealAudio

QTV	QuickTime Video can carry audio layer only
AIFF	Audio Interchange File Format
WAV	Waveform Audio File Format
SND	Sound
MP3	MPEG audio layer
WMF	Windows Media File

Three-dimensional site description files

VRML	Virtual Reality Modelling Language
QTVR	QuickTime Virtual Reality (seamless 360° pix)

Site transfer – how computers 'talk' to each other

FTP	File Transfer Protocol
HTTP	Hypertext Transfer Protocol
WAP	Wireless Application Protocol (for hand-held and wireless devices)
VoIP	Voice Over Internet Protocol
SMS	Short Message Service
MMS	Multimedia Messaging Server

Other

DITA	Darwin Information Typing Architecture
DTD	Document Type Description
GUI	Graphical User Interface ('gooey')
SEO	Search Engine Optimisation
CMS	Content Management System
JDF	Job Definition Format (integrates business and production planning applications in print management)
JMF	Job Messaging Format (receives real-time production updates from machines in the print process)
SCORM	Sharable Content Object Reference Model (web-based e-learning standards)
CD	Compact Disk
DVD	Digital Versatile Disk
URL	Universal Resource Locator

standard hardware. This means you can design the intranet site for a specific screen size and resolution and design each page to minimise scrolling.

Intranets have many of the same design requirements as other websites. They may have some limitations placed on them by the organisation's commitment to a content management system or applications that drive internal services that are delivered through the intranet.

Using Hypertext Markup Language (HTML)

If you are designing text for the Internet, you will use HTML to define your content and its attributes.

Type attributes

HTML type attributes give you the option of bolding, italicising or underlining text; you have a number of heading sizes; and you can capitalise. You can create lists and use indent levels.

Stress within text in print is normally created using italics because they do not interrupt the line. Italics can make a sentence read differently – compare 'It was *really* excellent' with 'It was really *excellent*' and even 'It *was* really excellent'. The only limitation of italics in website design is their low screen resolution, which often makes them a little confusing to read for any length of time. A single word or phrase is mostly fine. Extensive use of italics is not recommended for web documents.

But note it is better to use the 'emphasis' tag <em>, rather than the italic tag <i>, so that the role of the italics is understood. Electronic screen-reading software will also correctly interpret this tag and make a suitable vocal difference.

Similarly, instead of the bold tag <b>, you should use the 'strong' tag <strong>.

If you are signalling the hypertext (linked text behind the textual reference), colour variation and underlining are used for the link. Readers will assume they can jump to another part of the document by clicking on this piece of information. This is the only excuse for underlining – which limits readability by striking through and confusing the pattern recognition of the descending characters of the letterforms. Colour variation by itself should be enough to signal the link.

Underlining also interrupts the flow of the text and signals the reader to read what is underlined out of context.

Tags

HTML relies on a series of tags. Each specification has a set of tags: the opening and closing tags. For example, the opening tag for a paragraph is <p> and its closing tag is </p>.

Tags can also have attributes that modify display and, like the boxes that enclose them, the tags can be 'nested' – that is, tags within tags.

The style sheet then addresses each content element and makes a declaration of the properties or values within a set of brackets, like this:

p {
color:#0000ff;
}

which translates as 'paragraph in blue (defined in hexadecimal colour description)'. Note the colon separation and the semicolon ending the specification.

'Class selectors' are descriptors that you will use throughout your style sheet for a number of elements – and you may use them to create microformats that identify particular content elements or subdivisions of your content within existing classes.

'Grouped selectors' take a set of tags and define them at the same time:

h1,h2,h3 {
color:#ff0000;
}

will display the first three heading levels in red.

Semantic markup uses the <title> </title> tags instead of heading one <h1> </h1> tags. The print style sheet might then specify that the font-size for the title will be 240% of the text size – meaning that, if the text size was 10 pt, the heading size would be 24 pt.

For different output devices, rather than specifying such a size change, you might use the <big> </big> or <small> </small> tags instead. They will interpret the size difference for the output.

Leading or linespacing is called *lineheight*.

While tags are not case-sensitive, they are preferred in lower case.

That is, the underlines are seen before the paragraph is
read, so the reader often reads the type that is underlined
first and then returns to the beginning of the paragraph.
This means the reference is then out of context, but
this speed of scanning is what hypertext is all about, so
underlines are used. But as far as possible, avoid the
<u> tag.

Bold type is usually reserved for headings, so avoid using
paragraphs of bold – or strong – text. Changing a word to
bold/strong mid-sentence is the same as underlining it – do
it only if you want it to stand out for some reason.

Most Internet documents ignore the possibility of
capitalising headings. Remember one point about the use
of capitals – capitals slow down reading, so use them only
for short headings – one- or two-word headings are fine. For
the same reason, never type a paragraph in full capitals.

In print, horizontal rules are used for separation. Use
the <hr> tag sparingly and avoid decorative and animated
rules. Do not use the horizontal rule as an underline to a
heading, otherwise it separates the heading from the text
that logically follows it. Rather, use it as a cut-off line for a
section. But, as far as possible, avoid using horizontal rules
– they just increase the scrolling the reader has to do – and
instead use border controls (defining the bottom border
of a text content box in pixel width and padding the box to
separate the border from the text).

Cascading style sheets (CSS)

The principles on which CSS is based are greater
typographic and page layout control, more akin to the
production of style sheets for a print document. CSS is
more concerned with accurate content description than the
physical presentation, though it also defines the output for
different formats, by embedding different style sheets for
different outputs – for example, you may create a print style
sheet that defines the look of output from a printer and a
'hand-held' style sheet that defines the output for hand-held
devices.

The style sheet is loaded first and contains all the content
tags and their corresponding typeface and font attributes
and layout requirements, including spacing and colour
specification. These become the 'rules' for application when
the document requires a particular tag.

However, you are reliant on the font set that is installed

on the user's machine. This is one of the most significant limitations of CSS. If users don't have the font you have defined, a font will be substituted from their font set. This is why some fonts like Verdana were created and freely distributed – in an attempt to get some guaranteed fonts across systems.

There are two methods of applying the cascading style sheet. You can create the style sheet (which might be named '.../style sheet.css') as a separate document that all the other text documents in the site are linked to. In this way, any change that is required need only be made to the style sheet and it will automatically flow through the rest of the site. The second way of applying the style sheet is to import it at the beginning of each text file. This allows more than one style sheet for a particular document.

The style sheet will then 'cascade' into any elements until the style is overridden by another style.

As far as layout issues are concerned, measurements on-screen can be defined in the style sheet by number of pixels, points and picas, ems and x-heights (variable measures that depend on typeface selection), millimetres and centimetres, and inches.

CSS uses page divisions and box formatting. Each element on-screen is considered to be in a box and you position the boxes by defining, in order, *padding* (the equivalent of runaround), borders, margins and other display attributes. 'Sidebars' in the side margin and 'boxouts' of side content (contained in a box) float an element to the left or right of page content, which then 'wraps' around the element.

Liquid and fixed design

Many designers who work in print are used to defining the exact look of their text – defining font sizes and text widths, page depths and spacing between elements – what you could call 'fixed' design. However, in web design, there are so many output devices with different screen sizes and using different software to interpret the input content, that you can only be sure of the display by checking it in different devices with different programs.

What emerged from this was the idea of content description and 'liquid' or 'fluid' design that stretches or shrinks to fit the available screen area. While maintaining the defined content relationships, usually expressed in a

Fluid design

'Ratios are just the job for constructing adaptive grid systems because they are independent of any unit of measurement. They are just a ratio to the whole, whatever the whole may be. This whole, be [it] a browser window or whatever, can change and therefore so does the ratio or the grid.'

MarkBoulton.co.uk

ratio where the main content area is the larger element, the output will not necessarily look the same in each format or device.

Email newsletters, e-books and e-zines

With the capacity for email content to be defined in HTML, email newsletters or e-zines now appear as fully designed publications. They have mastheads, text and images. They are also often like an annotated contents list designed to attract the reader's interest and then link to full articles contained in web pages.

One of the most important considerations is that they fit in the preview pane of the user's email software – 600 pixels wide and text starts within the first 350 pixels of depth. Because the software default or the users will have disallowed the automatic downloading of images, your newsletter's early text needs to attract the reader or they may trash the email unopened. Minimise the graphics to let the content attract them. Email newsletters are often designed with table-based positioning rather than CSS but, as with all online products, you should test the output on various versions of the software your readers are likely to use.

Users will possibly have subscribed to the newsletter from your website or may have responded to a 'permission pass' – an initial email offering a subscription which may be made to an existing client list or to a purchased mailing list. Give them an easy option to 'unsubscribe' on each mailing.

There is sometimes legislation governing what you need to include in an email newsletter. This often includes the requirement for an unsubscribe option and even a physical address or post office box number, rather than purely online contact details.

E-zines may be prepared as a PDF for printing, but they should also consider how many readers may just read them on-screen and use the horizontal or landscape orientation of a screen, to avoid the reader needing to scroll through the pages. They should be able to read each page in one screen and click through to the next page, instead of scrolling.

For printed publications that will be distributed online, in a vertical or portrait format, it is often better to use a single column format to avoid the frustration of scrolling that multicolumn formats have on-screen.

'Unless you're emailing something of personal relevance or urgency to your client, you have only three and a half seconds to be interesting. Fail, and you're deleted.'

Gary Levitt and Rob Lubow, 'Simplicity is the nature of great emails', MarketingProfs.com, 10 June 2008

Nesting

An important web concept is that of *nesting*. In box elements you can 'nest' other smaller boxes of content. In a dot point list, the second subdivision is called a 'nested list'.

Links

There are a number of link types that are usually indicated by colour change:

☐ link <link> describes the usually underlined link that readers recognise can be clicked (or a link without action)

☐ active link <alink> is the selected state of the link

☐ visited link <vlink> lets a reader know they have previously visited that link when they return to the page

☐ hover link <hlink> describes the 'hover state' where the cursor is hovering over the link but it is not yet selected (sometimes also called a 'mouseover').

Netiquette?

Type in all capitals is considered to be 'shouting' in email and websites. Although it may be considered good etiquette to avoid all capitals in digital publishing, avoiding capitals is more accurately – and valuably – aiding readability.

Mash-ups

To create new website possibilities, you might combine two existing technologies to create a new user experience. The resulting *mash-up* often combines a third party product with your specific information to create a hybrid product. An example is Google Earth, which combines satellite imagery with directory content and global positioning systems (GPS).

Personalised output

Some users set the preferences on their browsers to increase the size of the text or to switch off all images so the text content appears faster. CSS and content description ensures that the correct relationships are maintained in content when they vary its presentation.

Other users prefer to personalise the interface for all their applications and recreate or even revise the structure and look of the software. This is called *skinning*.

Advertising and marketing

'Advertising' covers reserved space in a publication or air time on radio, movie screen, television or website that is paid for. Unpaid time or space is generated by 'publicity' and is called 'news', 'free listings', 'community service announcements' or 'sponsorship'. 'Marketing' is really the over-arching discipline for all advertising, sales generation and brand management.

Advertising has a lead time; there is a production schedule to accommodate. In the case of newspapers, a week or preferably two is required to book space, and a few days before publication for provision of artwork or electronic file lodgment; in the case of newsletters and magazines, two months is usual.

Advertising agencies will often employ market researchers; a creative team of writers, art directors, film directors and production staff; account management people; and strategists. This service comes at a price, so many people decide to do it all themselves. Although this can save money, it can limit success. Effective advertising more than pays for itself – it generates brand awareness and sales that increase profit. If it is not doing this, it is not working.

However, another problem here is that a single ad placement will not necessarily generate that profit. An organisation needs to create enough awareness and keep the product in the mind of their consumers by advertising regularly. It has been found that consumers need to encounter a product a number of times before they are confident enough to purchase.

Advertising needs to convey information about the benefits of a product or service to the users and purchasers of that product or service. It also needs to provide differentiation from competitors – other sellers or service providers.

An advertisement can give information that leads to a purchase decision, but the deciding factor is rarely from

Jim Alexander, in *How to Create and Evaluate Advertising that Sells*, defines advertising as 'professional salesmanship multiplied by media'.

The eight greatest lies you'll ever be told, according to Jim Aitchison in *Cutting Edge Advertising*, are:
1 You must have a unique selling proposition.
2 You must offer a rational benefit.
3 Humour doesn't sell.
4 You must have a memorable slogan.
5 You must have a logo in the ad.
6 You must show the product in the ad.
7 Every ad in the campaign must look the same.
8 Creative ads don't sell.
The one creative truth is:
Every ad must have an idea in it.

According to Gallup & Robinson and Readex, two US research organisations, the six principles of creating print ads that work are:

1 Be specific in promoting the benefit for the consumer.
2 Make the product the big benefit.
3 Keep your advertisement simple.
4 Use large spaces to emphasise the benefit.
5 Personalise the benefit.
6 Don't obscure the benefit – being catchy and cute don't always work.

As described by John Machado in *Creating Desire*

Roy Grace, a US creative director, has a checklist for creative ideas:

☐ Is it the kind of idea that's never ever been done before by anyone else in the product category?
☐ Is it an idea you can do many variations on, enabling it to last many years?
☐ Is it not only informative but entertaining as well? Does the message move you?
☐ Does it make people think? Are people actually involved in the selling premise so they participate in the ad?
☐ Do you like it – not because it's correct, or clever, or powerful – but genuinely like it? Because if you do, the chances are your audience will like the product.

Cited by John Machado in *Creating Desire*

a logical progression of analysis of the data presented – it is nearly always influenced by an emotional response to the product, service or the company offering it. So organisations establish credibility and recall through what is called *brand advertising*. An organisation can create distinction in the marketplace by associating its brand with particular traits that consumers will find attractive. Organisations establish attitude through their advertising, or associate with a particular mood or create an atmosphere around their product range.

There will also be different audiences that an advertiser needs to attract. So the advertisements might have different messages that emphasise different product attributes for those different audiences. In that way, the purchasing information needed can be focused on particular audience needs and placed in appropriate media.

If there is the likelihood that advertising to one audience might alienate another, there is a choice to be made. Often, advertisements that are not aimed at certain people are ignored or filtered anyway, so this alienation may not manifest itself.

Media selection is based on that media's 'reach', which is why ratings, circulation and readership figures are gathered. If a magazine knows that a majority of its readers are young professional women, advertisers can be confident that their message will get to the right audience by advertising in that magazine.

In a study of 200 highly regarded ads, 89% were found to fit these six categories:

• Pictorial analogy: extreme analogies shown
• Extreme consequences: unexpected consequences of a product attribute
• Extreme situations: product performing under unusual circumstances or exaggerated attribute
• Competition: comparing one product with another
• Interactive experiments
• Dimensionality alteration: a time leap showing long-term implications.

The study, 'The Fundamental Templates of Quality Ads', was devised by Jacob Goldenberg, David Mazursky and Sorin Solomon, originally published in *Marketing Science*, 18 and cited in Chip and Dan Heath's *Made to Stick*.

Sometimes an organisation will use advertising not so much to attract consumers but to appeal to their staff.

Marketing terminology

- *Media reach:* how many people get at least one view of the advertising message
- *Effective frequency:* how many times the message is encountered
- *Recency:* when the purchaser last saw an advertising message and how close it was to the purchasing decision time
- *Experiential marketing:* started with sampling and expo pavilions and has become branded environments and experiences
- *'Above the line' media:* 'traditional' media like television and radio, newspapers and magazines
- *'Below the line' media:* promotions, events, public relations and direct marketing
- *FMCG:* Fast Moving Consumer Goods
- *ROI:* Return On Investment
- *VOC:* Voice Of Customer
- *B2B:* Business to Business
- *B2C:* Business to Consumer
- *CRM:* Customer Relationship Marketing
- *DIGA:* Dynamic In-Game Advertising which describes product placement in online games and virtual environments
- *STV:* Subscription Television or 'pay TV'
- *FTA:* Free To Air television
- *Roadblock ad:* booking the same ad in the same timeslot on a number of commercial free-to-air television channels so viewers cannot avoid it when channel-surfing
- *Viral advertising:* creating short video and possibly audio files that are sent to, say, 1000 'influencers' who email it to their friends, avoiding spam filters and giving greater credibility to messages
- *WOM:* Word Of Mouth
- *Touchpoints:* each point where a brand is experienced, including 'pre-purchase' points (websites, word of mouth, direct mail, research, sponsorships, public relations, publicity, advertising), purchase or usage points (sales, stores, sales staff, demonstrations) or 'post-purchase' points (loyalty programs, customer satisfaction surveys, warranty and repairs, rebates, how the product performs over time) (Some of these touchpoints from Ray George, 'Tapping into brand touchpoints', MarketingProfs.com, 16 September 2003.)

CHECKLIST

Marketing mix

- Print advertising:
  - newspapers
  - magazines
  - classifieds
  - directories
- Television spots
- Radio spots
- Cinema ads
- Direct mail:
  - letterbox drop
  - addressed mail
  - catalogues
  - parcels and packages
- Packaging
- Point-of-sale displays
- Promotional CD-ROMs or DVDs
- Product placement:
  - TV programs
  - movies
  - video games
  - virtual environments
- Information kiosks
- Brochures and fact sheets
- Promotions and sampling
- Demonstrations
- Websites
- Email newsletters
- Blogs
- Podcasts
- Online video
- Events
  - exhibitions
  - tradeshows
  - expos
  - festivals
  - markets
  - workshops
  - seminars
  - conferences
  - breakfasts
  - dinners
  - balls
- Sponsorship

CHECKLIST
Advertisements
Might include:
- ☐ Free offer
- ☐ Announcement
- ☐ Trial or sample
- ☐ Story
- ☐ Gift
- ☐ Coupon
- ☐ Comparison
- ☐ Innovation
- ☐ New feature
- ☐ Example
- ☐ Directions
- ☐ Price
- ☐ Country of origin
- ☐ Imported
- ☐ Endorsements
- ☐ Case study
- ☐ Client list
- ☐ Product list
- ☐ Sponsorship
- ☐ Location/map
- ☐ Logo
- ☐ Slogan
- ☐ Jingle
- ☐ Contact information
  - – phone
  - – fax
  - – mobile
  - – website URL
  - – email address.

This level of *image advertising* can help staff see their organisation in a favourable light and develop pride in it. Image advertising can also help when an organisation has some public challenges to face, such as a product recall or a chemical spill. If a strong image is established and the crisis is managed well, an organisation can come back stronger than before.

READ MORE ABOUT IT

David Ogilvy, *Ogilvy on advertising*, Pan Books, London, 1983, ISBN 0 330 26985 2.

John Machado, *Creating desire*, Sympress, Kuala Lumpur, 1996, ISBN 983 99149 0 1.

Jim Aitchison, *Cutting edge advertising: How to create the world's best print for brands in the 21st century*, Prentice-Hall, Singapore, 1999, ISBN 0 13 012897 X.

Max Sutherland & Alice K Sylvester, *Advertising and the mind of the consumer: What works, what doesn't, and why*, 2nd edn, Allen & Unwin, Sydney, 2000, ISBN 1 86508 231 7.

The Designers and Art Directors Association of the United Kingdom, *The copy book: How 32 of the world's best advertising writers write their advertising*, RotoVision SA, Crans-Pres-Celigny, Switzerland, 1995, ISBN 2 88046 258 4.

Herschell Gordon Lewis, *On the art of writing copy*, 2nd edn, Amacom, New York, 2000, ISBN 0 8144 7031 9.

Chip & Dan Heath, *Made to stick: Why some ideas take hold and others come unstuck*, Random House, London, 2007, ISBN 9781905211562.

Bob Pritchard, *Marketing success stories*, Milner Books, Burra Creek, NSW, 1997, ISBN 1 86351 201 2.

Ian Oshlack, *Advertising without agencies: A guide to successful advertising for small business*, The Business Library, Information Australia, Melbourne, n.d., ISBN 1 86350 093 6.

Superbrands Pty Ltd, *Superbrands: An insight into 65 of Australia's superbrands*, vol. 1, Superbrands, Sydney, 1997, ISBN 0 646 32253 2.

Superbrands Pty Ltd, *Superbrands: An insight into more than 80 of Australia's superbrands*, vol. 2, Superbrands, Sydney, 1999, ISBN 0 0577000 0 8.

Torin Douglas, *The complete guide to advertising*, Macmillan, London, 1984, ISBN 0 333 38639 6.

Jim Alexander, *How to create and evaluate advertising that sells*, Newspaper Advertising Bureau of Australia, n.d.

Posters

The usual mistake people make with posters is information overload. A poster will be most effective with a dominant image and with a minimal text area, often in a strip down the right-hand side or across the bottom. Posters herald the existence of something and inspire, interest or engage the viewer.

Remember where the poster will be seen. If it will be on a hoarding, design it so it looks good in multiples and creates a pattern at its joins. If it will be in-store, it should contrast with the store's walls and roof colours to stand out. If it will be in the window at the local shops or on the community noticeboard at the shopping centre, it should be A4 or smaller and in full colour to contrast with the photocopied and handwritten signs. These are all separation techniques – your poster needs to stand out from others.

People need to know what the event is, and when and where it is. They are the determinants of interest and need to be the most obvious. Include the organisation's symbol, school badge or church logo. Although relevant, because people want to know who they are supporting, the symbol can be small because it's not as important as getting people interested in the product or event. Concentrate on the benefits to the viewer of purchasing or attending.

Do something with additional text that gives the information clearly but doesn't clutter the poster. Usually it can be very small in a block or a column. The poster needs to attract attention (and mostly the image and colour are what will achieve this), so minimise the text area to maximise the image area. Sometimes you can put all the details on the back of the poster so the front can concentrate on attracting attention and increasing awareness.

List sponsors and include any other necessary information – a map of where to find the outlet or event, times of opening and closing, ticket prices, and a phone number to contact for further information. These can be quite small, because you've gained people's attention by now.

Postcards

There are a number of reasons that make the postcard or mini-poster an attractive marketing and advertising form – it's personal, collectable, and cheap to produce and distribute. It's also easy to update and keep fashionable. An organisation's image won't become stale if it is reinvented regularly and with creativity.

People seem to respond well to postcards. They are small enough to keep and display, as distinct from posters, which are often too intrusive on our personal environments.

'But the real essence of a poster, rather than an artwork, I think, is the invisible but palpable contract between a designer, the commissioning institution, organization or company that funds a poster's distribution, and the viewing public who engages with it. The designer agrees to make something to promote this product, advance this cause, project this message because he believes in it and, because of that, often makes it more beautiful than it needs to be. The client promises to produce as many copies of the poster as she can afford to and to circulate them in the most strategic ways she knows. Lastly, it is understood that if the passerby is persuaded and seduced by the poster, they will carry out whatever action it calls for. It is this unseen tripartite contract, and all the conflict it brings with it that gives the poster its urgency and reason for being. Without that tension, the poster ends at the wall.'

Alice Twemlow, DesignObserver. com, 3 July 2007

CHECKLIST
Event posters
- ☐ Presenters of event
- ☐ Name of event
- ☐ Positioning statement/advertising line
- ☐ Date/s (include year for historical purposes)
- ☐ Time/s
- ☐ Venue/s
- ☐ Cost/s (not always given)
- ☐ Ticketing information (often just phone number or web URL of booking agency)
- ☐ Featured items or performers
- ☐ Legal and copyright requirements as necessary
- ☐ Logos of event sponsors

A sequence of mailings can be produced at the same time for little extra cost if it is a series of postcards. Greater interest can be added to the mailing sequence if there is a teaser mailing, where the full intent becomes clear after a few have been received. Postcards are great inclusions with letter mailings, too. They become miniature full-colour posters to retain even if the letter goes into the bin.

Some organisations are creating such a great series of images that they can repackage them into a gift set, enabling even greater marketing opportunities and cost recovery if sold.

There are two sides to this particular story. The front is, of course, the main event – it is best to have a single message and an arresting image. But the back is the opportunity to enhance it, with details and credits, to continue the visual message using graphic style that supports the front and perhaps creating a dynamism of its own.

On the right-hand side, you might use the stamp area at the top, which is often just defined by a rectangle (25 × 20 mm), as an opportunity for a company logo or a new graphic, illustration or copy-line. You can continue the character of a hand-drawn graphic with hand-drawn lines for the address instead of the ordinary fine ruled ones or just a blank area.

You may choose to have details about a product on the left-hand side or leave it blank to encourage someone to use the card, thereby communicating with two people, the sender and the receiver. If the information fills the back, there will be only one receiver – the person who picked up the card.

Sympathetic typography that reflects the typographic treatment on the front keeps the card operating effectively. There should be some level of front–back interaction – the message can start on the front with the punchline or an ironic twist on the back.

Flyers, information sheets and handbills

With flyers and handbills, consider the distribution method. Many are handed out to people at shopping centres or in foyers at trade shows, conferences or theatres; many are home-delivered as a letterbox drop; some are stuffed under windscreen wipers in car parks, or pinned on work bulletin boards and community noticeboards at shopping centres, or inserted into magazines or newsletters.

Consider how they will be received. People feel frustration and inconvenience with these particular forms of communication, but they can deliver information appropriately. Much of the print run is wasted, but assuming that is known by the organisation, they can generate more value from their outlay.

A simple idea is to print on both sides of the sheet, since a two-sided flyer increases the communication value of the piece. How many times have you thrown out stuff from your letterbox without opening it up to see what was advertised inside the folded one-sided flyer? Flyers and handbills can be considered mini-posters – with the bonus option of giving extra information on the back, such as duplicates of advertisements that are running in magazines or newspapers. Some magazines offer this as a service to their advertisers anyway. When the reprint is received, the local copy shop or printer can print extra information on the back which might localise the ad for a particular region, introduce local staff, or include a special deal or coupon.

Small-space press ads

These are time-consuming, little, and they usually have to include *War and Peace*! Small-space ads are getting smaller, too. With the rising cost of advertising space in newspapers, magazines and the *Yellow Pages*, and the diminishing marketing dollar, many organisations have reduced the physical size of their advertising.

If competitors are booking long, skinny, one-column ads, you should book a wide, squat, three-column ad. If all the ads around yours are white with black type, be the one that is black with white type.

Delete all repeat references in the copy so you can display the name once only, but make it bigger – to encourage recognition of the logo. Consider the material carefully and give helpful suggestions about what might be deleted and why – clients will usually respond positively. Does the copy include a postal and a street address when a phone number alone would do? Would just a street address be sufficient? Other deletions could include unnecessary punctuation – '29 November 2002' could become '29 Nov 2002', saving

Piggyback marketing

Two parties can creatively join forces to jointly market each other. You can see this when Disney releases a film and McDonald's has movie tie-in merchandise available in-store, thereby marketing the film and the fast food for the same advertising outlay.

At a suburban level, if there's a regular letterbox drop by a local store or organisation, another organisation could piggyback its message. Sometimes a business might give a school or other community group a mention in their ad or let them use the back of their flyer in return for contributing to the costs or a sponsorship line.

quite a few letters. Dates can be expressed numerically also, e.g. '29/11/2002' or '29/11/02' (or '29.11.02'), but note in the United States this would become '11/29/02'. By saving spaces you can save lines and dramatically reduce the area devoted to copy.

In a small-space ad, you need to retain legibility. You can fit more lower-case letters than capitals in a line – and lower case is easier to read anyway!

Sans serif typefaces that are slightly horizontally scaled will reproduce best. They reduce well and are quite readable at small sizes – even at 4 point! Look at the telephone book and newspaper classified ad sections to see how well they can be set. One tip here is to set the tracking looser for a small-space ad. Small type will read better if it is tracked wider.

Avoid slab serifs which, although they reproduce well enough, have serifs that take extra room on the line so it will set wide. Serif type like Times Roman gets too fine and spindly in small-space ads, causing the type to break (where the fine lines do not reproduce at all) or fill in (where the small white spaces within letters like *a*, *g* and *e* can't hold out against the tide of ink). Serif types also don't reverse well. When you use bold type, you increase the area you need – so use it sparingly but effectively.

Include an image – even just a single character from a picture or symbol font – in the smallest ad, as a picture or symbol can attract attention. If you were a travel agency, you could use a little plane to lead in to the text. This is another good reason for reducing the area devoted to copy. A little breathing space in an ad is also a positive thing. Try to discourage your client from filling it with more product information.

Use a border, but don't cramp the type. Leave some breathing space between the type and the border, even in the smallest ad.

READ MORE ABOUT IT
Cheryl Dangel Cullen, *Small graphics: Design innovation for limited spaces*, Rockport Publishers, Gloucester, Mass., 2000, ISBN 1 56496 693 3.

Classified ads

Establishing a corporate presence in the classified pages can attract people to ads with very little effort on their part, as they will want to find what the organisation is offering, such as a job, tenders, public notices, competition winners or items for sale. An organisation does not want to pay an exorbitant amount of money for this identification, so it must not take up much room in the area of the ad. The options come down to:

- borders
- banners
- attitude.

An effective way to stand out in the classifieds is with large type, because everything is small, or space (but this is expensive blank area and likely to be difficult to justify, particularly to a committee who will see it as wasteful). Bold or reversed type also stands out in that sea of grey. Unusual angles and curves – or an unusual colour combination – in a border stand out because so many people use every square millimetre in the allocated or purchased ad area. Handwriting always provides a noticeable contrast.

Magazine and display ads

Magazine advertising can be very seductive with its colour, comfortable size, or full-page bleeds. Consequently, text-heavy advertising can be very successful in this format. If advertising is read like the articles, that's okay, and is probably preferable. This is where ads in lifestyle magazines feature products with recipes in the ad. Advertisers can even create the effect of a feature article by buying a set of pages.

In magazines, there are options of one-column, half-page and full-page ads, double-page spreads, and multipage advertising features. In newspapers, column widths are bought by the centimetre, and half pages, full pages and double-page spreads. In both magazines and newspapers, a premium is paid for guaranteed placement, which most agree is worth it if it guarantees a right-hand page or a specific section or, in magazines, the back cover and inside front and back covers.

The back cover of a magazine can be expensive. A very cute trick that some advertisers have used well is to buy the back cover, the inside back cover and the last page. They've turned the magazine upside-down and effectively created their own magazine. Busy newsagents will sometimes even put it out separately on the shelf. When

Tom Patty, in *Design for Response* by
Leslie Sherr and David Katz, says that
in order to figure out the means of
persuasion in each particular case, one
must:

□ understand the elements of
persuasion (including the
physiology of persuasion)
□ determine the purchase process for
the given product or service
□ determine the persuasion task for
each stage in the purchase process
□ determine the credibility of the
brand or speaker
□ determine the personality of the
brand or speaker
□ develop a fully integrated
persuasion plan.

Leslie Sherr and David Katz in *Design
for Response* wrote: 'Designs
should reflect the visions, tastes and
aspirations of the target audience. This
not only ensures that the recipient pays
attention to the mailer, but also, when
multiple components are part of the
package, that the reader's attention
is transferred from one element to
the next. Tactile additions, such as
perforations or unusual materials,
create interesting shifts that invite
the recipient to explore every piece
mailed.'

you open it, their advertising continues on the inside
spread and then the whole magazine goes upside-down.
Magazines will sometimes use that technique themselves
for a special feature or supplement, maybe even using half
the available pages.

The price for magazine advertising is usually justified
on readership statistics (who buys, who reads, in what
localities, and what percentage of the marketplace they
deliver), the amount of time a magazine is kept and the
number of people likely to see each copy. In doctors'
surgeries and waiting rooms, on coffee tables at home and
in aeroplanes, a magazine has a greater 'reach' than, say,
a newspaper ad. Newspapers are immediate, but thrown
away at the end of each day. Magazines are often kept until
the next issue arrives and sometimes they are used much
longer or collected.

Coupons or competitions in an ad generate leads that
enable an organisation to gauge the effectiveness of the
ad and give a database so they can direct-market to likely
prospects. Ads that feature a full-page or double-page
spread image and are text-sparse can be a great rest place
in busy magazines and newspapers. Type doesn't need to
be large in magazines, so a single line of well-chosen
text below can hold the attention after the attraction of
the graphic.

Some advertisers have created some interesting sets of
ads by buying the same space on two or more consecutive
right-hand pages. This allows them to ask a question on the
first page and answer it on the second or create a flip-book
style of attraction.

READ MORE ABOUT IT
Dave Saunders, *20th century advertising*, Carlton Books, London, 1999,
ISBN 1 85868 520 6.
Bryan Holme, *Advertising: Reflections of a century*, William Heinemann, London,
1982.
Allyn Salomon, *Advertising photography*, Thames & Hudson, London, 1982,
ISBN 0 500 54081 0.

Direct-mail advertising

In direct mail, more information is good and more
involvement is good. Short words and sentences are quick
and easy to read and therefore reach more people. The
design should be kept lively and feature many headings

and self-contained text units. Format variation will keep the mailer interesting.

This is one-to-one selling so it needs to be written in a conversational and even intimate tone. The message should be individualised so the recipient can feel a relationship developing with the advertiser through the material. Customising is made that much easier with high-quality digital printing technology.

The mailer needs to entertain and involve the person who receives it. Some involvement tricks are taste tests, samples, free gifts, CDs, videos, boxes, assembling things, scratchies, and folding, licking and sticking stamps onto reply coupons. The more relevant and involving these gimmicks – even to sophisticated markets – the more effect will be created.

A series of mailings is sometimes used to build interest. There can be a teaser mailer that simply says something interesting will be arriving in the mailbox in two days time.

Direct marketing is sometimes referred to as Customer Relationship Marketing (CRM) and often involves direct mail as well as other techniques like telemarketing and email marketing.

READ MORE ABOUT IT

Vin Jenkins, *Direct mail advertising in Australia: A handbook in 6 volumes*, Australia Post, Melbourne, 1984, ISBN 0 642 89539 2 (set).

Malcolm Auld, *Direct marketing made easy*, Harper Business, Sydney, 1997, ISBN 0 7322 5676 3.

Leslie H Sherr & David J Katz, *Design for response: Creative direct marketing that works*, Rockport Publishers, Gloucester, Mass., 1999, ISBN 1 56496 380 2.

Sheree Clark & Wendy Lyons, *Creative direct mail design: The guide and showcase*, Rockport Publishers, Gloucester, Mass., 1995, ISBN 1 56496 143 5.

Ian Kennedy & Bryce Courtenay, *The power of one-to-one*, Margaret Gee Publishing, Sydney, 1995.

Packaging

Packaging design can attract people to purchase a product, even if they were not in the market for that product when they entered the store, walked the aisle or stopped at the shelf. It can distract a purchaser's eye from a competing product.

So packaging design needs to be distinctive. It needs to have a high on-shelf presence that distinguishes it from the competition beside, below or above it. This is where

CHECKLIST
Direct mail

Envelope

- ☐ 'Teaser' copy that encourages the receiver to enthusiastically open the letter
- ☐ Stamp
- ☐ Personalised

Letter

- ☐ Personalised
- ☐ Text highlights benefits to customer
- ☐ Headline at the top of the text
- ☐ Letterhead with company name, logo, address, phone numbers, website URL, email address
- ☐ Signature
- ☐ PS
- ☐ Special offer or time limit

Brochure or catalogue

- ☐ Text that highlights benefits to consumer
- ☐ Picture/s of product/s
- ☐ Endorsement/s, awards
- ☐ Product description: size, colour range, price

Order form with freepost envelope or card

- ☐ Optional purchase methods
- ☐ Company name, logo, address, phone numbers, website URL, email address
- ☐ Guarantee
- ☐ 'Involving' devices like stickers, scratchies, pop-ups

the concepts of 'separation' design need to be maximised. Your brand needs to 'own' your corporate colour in the category so that a consumer reaches for it without thinking.

It also needs to be recognisable, consistent and uniform – so that the strengths of your existing brand are capitalised on.

Don't ignore category conventions, like bright colours for washing powders.

Also ensure that your labelling includes all the legal requirements for the category, particularly in pharmaceuticals, food and beverage packaging. These may include ingredient lists, nutritional information boxes, recommended intake guidelines and warnings.

Then there is the design consideration of how multiple products will look when on a shelf together – and how they will be correctly identified if the shelf-packers don't display them as intended. For example, it was believed that cans needed three 'sides' in order for a brand to be clearly identified if it was turned as it was shelved.

Equally, you need to consider the ability of the package to be stacked. What are the implications for your design if the package contents settle during shipping? How resilient is the boxing of the packages – will distribution have scuffed or crushed them? How can a better pack design avoid such damage? What will be the impact of refrigeration or freezing on your pack and its contents?

There is also the possibility of 'on-product' advertising where, for example, wine companies put competition details in a miniature brochure that is secured around the neck of the wine bottle by either a die-cut circle in the brochure or an elastic band. Clothing racks have clothes that are festooned with 'swing tags' or the familiar jeans pocket labels that are sometimes sewn in to avoid staples damaging the denim. One company developed a label for water bottles that, when torn along perforations on the right side of the label, became a miniature magazine.

You might also consider 'on-shelf advertising' like hanging tags and how their design stands out against the background of your stacked products.

There are also legal requirements in packaging that define typeface size (the alcoholic content in wine packaging) or require a certain standard content description

'The average supermarket stocks 25,000 products – yet the average purchase is only seven items in a trolley.'

Grant Simpson in *AdNews*, Pack Design Special, April 2007

'Nowadays, packaging needs to work harder than ever, as in many instances it is the only form of "advertising" that a brand receives.'

Sue Knox in *AdNews*, Pack Design Special, April 2007

'You're presented with a client who has a product they wish to transport, display and sell, so as a designer you have to make them a "box" that conforms to all these standards, so that it's value for money, provides features that are somehow unique for that client and works within their budget.'

Roy Riuc, quoted by Hugh Edwards in 'Eat me, drink me', *Desktop*, 240, July 2008

'Preventing contaminants such as ink, varnish and substrate toxicity, is a major consideration. There is a lot of legislation that needs to be addressed on packaging design, this can take up a lot of valuable space (nutrition info, disclaimers, bar-codes, etc.).'

Nick Price, quoted by Hugh Edwards in 'Eat me, drink me', *Desktop*, 240, July 2008 (nutrition panels in food packaging) or other production requirements. In Europe, pharmaceutical packaging must carry braille identification of the product and its recommended dosage for different ages.

CHECKLIST

Packaging

- ☐ Raw or unpackaged
- ☐ Stacking
- ☐ Hanging
- ☐ Boxed
- ☐ Wrapped
- ☐ Bottled
- ☐ Canned
- ☐ Shrink-wrapped
- ☐ Bagged
- ☐ Tamper-proofing

Materials

- ☐ Paper/cardboard
- ☐ Glass
- ☐ Plastic
- ☐ Fabric
- ☐ Netting
- ☐ Tin
- ☐ Aluminium
- ☐ Foil
- ☐ Moulded foam

Inclusions

- ☐ Fastener
- ☐ Seals
- ☐ Hooks
- ☐ Handles
- ☐ Drawstring
- ☐ Window
- ☐ Tags
- ☐ Labels
- ☐ Stickers
- ☐ Bands/belly bands
- ☐ Zipper
- ☐ Ziploc seal
- ☐ Flap

Labelling

- ☐ Brand mark
- ☐ Product name
- ☐ Size and recommended serving size
- ☐ Nutritional information
- ☐ Ingredient list
- ☐ Country of origin
- ☐ Company details
- ☐ Website URL
- ☐ Legal requirements
- ☐ Bar code
- ☐ Product code
- ☐ Use-by date
- ☐ Positioning line
- ☐ Description
- ☐ Instructions
- ☐ Serving suggestions
- ☐ Warnings

READ MORE ABOUT IT

Stafford Cliff, *50 trade secrets of great design: Packaging*, Quintet/Rockport Publishing, Gloucester, Mass., 1999, ISBN 1-56496-599-6.

Roberto Carra, Oliviero Toscani & Tamotsu Yagi, *Esprit's graphic work 1984–1986*, Esprit De Corp, San Francisco, 1987, ISBN 0-9614437-2-3.

Douglas Tompkins, *Esprit: The comprehensive design principle*, Robundo/Esprit De Corp, San Francisco, 1989, ISBN 4-947613-20-3.

Capsule, *Design Matters: Packaging 01: An essential primer for today's competitive market*, Rockport Publishers, Beverly, Mass., 2008, ISBN 978-1-59253-342-8.

Production

Layout

A layout is really a piece of abstract art. You're fiddling with basic shapes in different tones and trying to get them to sit comfortably, logically and interestingly together in order to tell a story and impart information clearly. As with any abstract composition, the aim is to lead the viewer's eye around the piece, and entertain it with repetition (patterns and texture), contrast (scale, tone and colour), and direction (created through the interaction of shapes and lines).

If you can reduce text and photos, headlines and subtitles, pull-quotes, captions and logos (these are all called 'elements') to their basic shapes, and the tone or colour that those shapes have, it is easier to create an effective layout. The interaction of the basic tones and shapes (including their unity – or similarity to each other – and their proximity or positioning in relation to each other) is what creates the 'layout'.

But page design is not an accident determined by how the text is given to you, what photographs or illustrations the author has supplied or considered appropriate, and how you put it together in an abstract composition. The 'accident' needs to be arranged to lead a reader through it, so a good designer relates pieces of the puzzle to one another until the connections are visually communicated as well as being textually discussed.

Errors of alignment can occur when the designer has not read and understood the text. For example, pictures might be scaled to sizes that distort their logical relationship and confuse the reader. If elements are grouped together without a logical relationship, the reader will seek to relate them to one another and possibly distort the message that was intended. Ensure that you group elements in a page design appropriately. While accidental cross-readings can be fashionable, intriguing and diverting, they tend to limit communication clarity.

In layout, you make choices about the positioning of the elements (imagery, text and space) of the design. The variables are then brought into play.

Images can be square-cut, free-form or soft-edged. Text can be *display text* such as titles and featured type; *body copy*, which is the bulk of the textual content; or short text bursts such as headings, captions and pull-quotes. Space can be placed in bands, e.g. margins around the perimeter of the page, gutters that run between columns, or text drops where an invisible line runs across the layout from which text is hung. Space can also be free-form.

You make decisions at each stop of the way about specific placement and details such as colour, weight and size. But it can be a bit hit and miss. The quick way to make these sorts of decisions – to work every time – is to look underneath it all, behind the actual to the implied. There is an invisible layout structure that enables some layouts to succeed better than others.

Many people are too concerned with getting the obvious correct, concentrating on text details such as punctuation, the positioning of picture credits and colour balance in images. But these do not of themselves create a good layout. The details need to be correct but not at the expense of the success of the piece – after all, if people don't notice the piece, they don't get the opportunity to admire the detail!

The relationship between certain elements should be maintained throughout a layout. For example, you should treat and place captions in the same way throughout and keep spacing around headings constant. This consistency will help readers to decode the message without distraction.

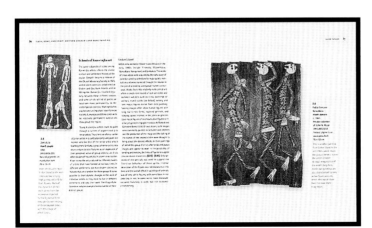

The subtle distortions of the text blocks in this layout reiterate the shapes of the illustrations, creating a relationship between the text and images that brings unity and logic to the composition.
Client: University of Virginia
Publication: *Art from the Land: Dialogues with the Kluge–Ruhe Collection of Australian Aboriginal Art* edited by Howard Morphy and Margo Smith Boles
Design: Maureen MacKenzie-Taylor
Studio: Msquared Research Assisted Design

Hanging your text from a chosen line – like washing – also achieves this. It is better that the relationships between elements (that you have decided will best suit the reader's requirements) are maintained, than that the columns fall to the same depth, for example.

And don't forget the underlying layer – the layout is the abstract composition that is the aesthetic basis of your design. There are potential distractions in this 'invisible' layer, too.

To demonstrate the implications of even simple decisions, take a blank A4 sheet of paper and type a line of text in the centre of the page. This line of text creates a number of implied or invisible lines and shapes within the page:

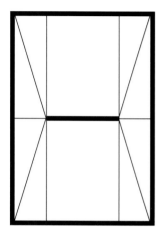

- An invisible line runs through the text to the left-hand edge of the page and similarly from the end of the text to the right-hand edge of the page, dividing the page into two segments.
- Those two segments are two implied rectangles.
- At the beginning of the text is an implied vertical line connecting the first letter of the text to the top and bottom edges of the page.
- Similarly, at the end of the text there is another implied vertical, which connects the top and bottom edges of the page through the last letter.
- These verticals further divide the page area into invisible shapes – you now have six rectangles implied.

Part of the reason that these verticals and horizontals are so strong is that the edges of the page create vertical and horizontal stress or at least conform to it; in a different shape, the implications may be different. There is an even more subtle tension that can be a further complication to exploit in your layout – the diagonals connecting the beginning and end points of the text line to the two corners closest to them.

So the placement of one line of text can create this amount of clutter! Can you see why playing about with many elements becomes so difficult?

One way to ease the resulting angst is to limit the numbers of implied lines and shapes, by using the same ones many times, instead of creating new ones at each introduction of a new element. This strengthens the layout.

The secret formula to successful layout – particularly in poster and cover design – is to limit the number of vertical

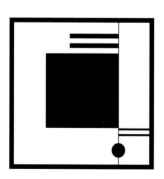

One vertical division can perform many roles

and horizontal divisions of the space. Let the same line do a few jobs. It could:

- be the edge of the title block
- be a picture's border
- be where the author's name runs from
- point to the publisher's logo at the foot of the page.

The last point here also introduces the concept of implied direction. Lines can be said to direct us or 'move' to the right and down, due to our understanding of standard eye flow.

Eye flow

It may seem obvious, but, in the West, we sometimes forget that we read from top to bottom and from left to right. Therefore, at whatever point we enter a layout, we automatically continue to the right and down.

In the East, there is reading from top to bottom and right to left.

In either the West or the East, it is a contrary movement to go 'backwards'.

In the West, backwards is either reading up from the bottom to the top or backwards from the right to the left. This is why captions are expected to be at the bottom or to the right of photographs or illustrations.

That is not to say that our eyes are not tempted back to other areas of the layout. But be careful to avoid too many 'backward' moves in a layout.

In Western double-page spreads, it is understood that the eye travels in a parabolic arc from the top right-hand corner (where the eye follows the double page as revealed by the turning action), across to the far left and back to the exit point at the bottom right. It is suggested, then, that there should be something on the left-hand page that drags your eye fully across the spread. In many magazine feature stories, the left-hand page is a full-page illustration and the title, and the start of the story is on the right-hand page. This follows the standard understanding of hierarchy – the large picture has the most attraction value and, from there, eye flow leads into the headline. It also explains the marketing wisdom that insists that advertisers pay the premium for right-hand page advertising space in magazines and newspapers, because the reader's attention may never get to the left page!

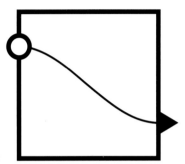

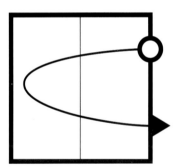

Parabolic curve of entry/exit for double-page spread

In Japanese books, for example, this is exactly the opposite as they are bound on the right and open to read from right to left, so the arc is reversed.

READ MORE ABOUT IT

Colin Wheildon, *Type and layout: How typography and design can get your message across – or get in the way*, Strathmoor Press, Berkeley, 1995, ISBN 0 9624891 5 8.

Timothy Samara, *Design elements: A graphic style manual: Understanding the rules and knowing when to break them*, Rockport Publishing, Beverly, Mass., 2007, ISBN 978-1-59253-261-2.

Backward movement

How often do you read backwards? That is, how often do your eyes travel against the assumed eye flow? All the time. As layout designers, harnessing eye flow and understanding how each layout decision you make will affect it is actually what layout 'is', the positioning of elements within a space for impact and effective communication in order.

Understanding that backward movement is natural but contrary to the standard flow enables you to use it more effectively. It is recommended that you limit the amount of backward movement required in a layout, because too much will confuse readers and they'll leave the layout without finishing, missing the communication your client expects them to receive.

On a printout of a layout, draw a line of the journey the reader's eye will make around it. Watch people's eyes as they are reading your work and get an idea where they are looking. Note down the pattern of their glances and see if you can reconstruct it when you are back at your desk with the layout.

Jumping through a layout, the eye goes in order through the pictures from largest to smallest, from most colourful to least colourful, and eventually to the text. You can help this landing on the text by leading the eye in a simple curve – if eye movement continues in the same trajectory, it will hit the start of the text once it has left the smallest image.

Of course, the eye gets interested in an image as well and takes a stroll through the focal points and textures within it. It leaps from flashes of intense colour to a brief exploration of shadow areas, so understanding the interest areas within an image is also necessary. A number of introductory art books will deconstruct an image and the eye flow through it in a discussion of its composition.

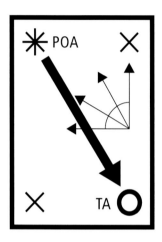

The Gutenberg diagram

Based on the diagram devised by Edmund Arnold, a US typographer, who described the basic eye flow (shown by the solid arrow) as the Axis of Orientation. The entry point is coded as the Primary Optical Area and the exit point as the Terminal Anchor. Arnold identified two fallow corners with crosses as being dead spots in a layout. Fine arrows in an arc represent the angles within the page that are considered to be backward movements that the eye avoids.

The skimming of the reader continues through a layout from elements to elements in a hierarchy and a path. If you are in doubt as you get further down the hierarchy, assume the eye flow from any point to be to the right and down.

This phenomenon is how text can be lost or hidden in plain view. Particular placements can mean the eye will simply not get back to the areas of the layout that are called the 'fallow' areas, unless something extreme is done to attract them there.

Eye flow is one of the difficulties for layered image/text techniques because the eye is not only reading through the imagery, but also reading foreground and background. In many cases, the eye is expected to wander over the same area twice, focusing differently to catch the juxtaposed message (because the image will register first).

If you need to correct eye flow, change the size relationships of your images and alter their alignment. If there is a lot of backward reading, sometimes a mirror image of the layout will correct it – in the same placement relationships, just swap everything on the right to the left.

Spatial relationships

There are numerous compositional concepts to understand, with their own language. They mostly describe opposites. There is the foreground's interaction with the background, called figure/ground and sometimes object/space interaction. Further than this there is the implied dimensionality of foreground, middle ground and background.

There is the interaction of positive and negative or light and dark. Further to them are the mid-tones that can also imply dimensionality (things fade as they recede into the distance).

The language of composition also includes dots, lines and planes.

A dot is considered the smallest possible object but also a focal point, so a circular photograph can be a dot within a layout.

Lines are directional and can have numerous qualities, textures and even be implied or created by joining a series of dots. A line's direction is usually moving out from the centre of a page though a horizontal line, due to eye flow, is usually moving to the right. Backward movement along

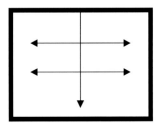

Reading on-screen

Readers scan a screen, reading down the centre with a left–right scanning motion. In this way, they can quickly access needed information from short paragraphs, dot point lists, headings, links and graphics.

Four critical relationships in type and image interaction

1 Separation (they are independent of each other)
2 Fusion (they merge into one entity)
3 Fragmentation (they displace, disturb or disrupt each other)
4 Inversion (they trade places – where type takes on pictorial properties or image takes on typographic qualities).

Nancy Skolos and Tom Wedell in *Type, Image, Message: A Graphic Design Layout Workshop*

Some of Timothy Samara's 20 excellent rules for making good design:

- ☐ Have a concept.
- ☐ Communicate – don't decorate.
- ☐ Speak with one visual voice.
- ☐ If you can do it with less, then do it.
- ☐ Move it! Static equals dull.
- ☐ Look to history, but don't repeat it.
- ☐ Be decisive. Do it on purpose – or don't do it at all.

'Rules exist – especially the ones set forth here – as guidelines, based on accumulated experience from many sources. As such, all rules come with exceptions and can be broken at any time, but not without a consequence. The consequence of breaking one rule might mean reinforcing another, and it might mean true innovation ...'

Timothy Samara in *Design Elements: A Graphic Style Manual*

DOING IT SMARTER
Faces
People pictures are most important. Faces are even more important. And the eyes have it! Think of mass-market magazine covers – usually a face with text crowded around it. In extreme close-ups, the eyes are the most beguiling features of the cover.

Even implied faces have attraction. Think about your car: the headlights are the eyes, the grille is a nose and the bumper is the mouth. Does your car smile at you? In layout terms, this subliminal smiling 'face' creation can make strong designs.

a line is possible if it is moving from the dominant focal point to a less dominant focal point.

Planes are created by giving a line dimension. They are also called shapes. The planes can be flat, shaded, textured and can also exist in foreground, middle ground or background.

Dominance

Pictures dominate a layout – and coloured pictures assume more importance than black-and-white ones. If there is a picture in a layout, readers will look at it first. So that's where they land in your layout and their eye flow starts. If it is on a right-hand page, you may have just lost the left-hand page, unless you somehow drag the reader's attention back to the left (in a backward motion). Be aware of the eye's movement through your design: What will it see first and where on the page is it? Does it move logically – using standard eye flow – to the next place or is the eye rushing around awkwardly? Does the eye have a resting spot or somewhere to concentrate for an extended period? Has the eye moved around the page so much that it longs to get out? Has it stopped at all the information points? Does the reader remember what the major pieces of information were? Is the reader enjoying the contrast of details and the overall form?

There are very few examples of designs where pictures do not overpower type. This is the reasoning behind the classic advertising format: a picture at the top, a headline underneath, followed by the body copy, and usually finished with a logo or coupon in the bottom right-hand corner. If the headline was placed above the picture, it may not be noticed because the reader's attention is already further down the page (on the picture).

Simplicity

The value of a 'simple' layout is its strength. This is often a comparative value, because a majority of layouts do not have this simplicity and absolute logic that is achieved through both vertical and horizontal simplicity in the layout. For example, extensive indenting can have the effect of complicating your layout vertically. Review your indents and limit them. The persistence of any element – even a 5 mm paragraph indent – quickly establishes another 'invisible' vertical line, complicating your layout. Each tab has the same effect.

In newsletters, the layout is often complicated horizontally where stories finish at different depths in different columns. Try to have fewer of these 'invisible' lines of breaks running across your layout.

The most striking layouts also tend to rely on recognition of basic shapes, such as square, triangle, circle ... These basic shapes need not be obvious. Disguise them through an understanding of implied line and shape. Strengthen the layout by using the standard or pure geometric shapes: circles rather than ovals; squares rather than rectangles or rhombuses; equilateral rather than isosceles triangles.

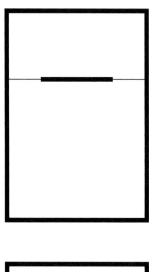

There is another consideration here. The audience will perceive curves and rounded shapes as friendlier than sharp points and crisp lines, which can be seen as harsh. And curves turning upwards at both ends are 'subliminal' happy faces.

Let's go back to our previous example, the placement of one line of text on an A4 page. If you now place that line about one-third of the way down the page, you create an implied rectangle above the line and an implied square below the line. This is a stronger layout option, because the square is a more pure shape than a rectangle.

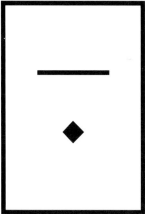

Then if you placed a logo shaped like a diamond centred about two-thirds of the way down the page, you would create an implied triangle where the logo is connected by invisible threads to the beginning and end of the line of text below. If you then work the spacing between the two elements to create an implied equilateral triangle, you create a stronger layout statement. The diamond-shaped logo would also give you the point of the triangle – super-strength!

But the structural lines within a layout do not have to be parallel only – or even straight! Many successful layouts use irregular shapes and curves, using fewer structural lines and placing elements in harmony with existing curves. Usually, this recognition that you can use an existing structural line instead of creating a new one will improve a layout.

There are meanings implied by design decisions that are purely visually communicated. If you use a design technique thinking it's simply good to look at without understanding the visual conventions you have used and what they are saying, you may be communicating incorrect meanings to the reader.

For example, if you bleed something off the page or crop in close to something, you are implying that the image is moving off the page or too large to be contained by the 'frame'. This can be very dramatic.

Graphing conventions used in picture layout will imply the simultaneity of events, creating hybrid visual form of a graphed storyboard. This technique is used in the layouts for snowboarding, surfing and skating magazines to capture some of the spirit and dynamism of those sports, effectively capturing the fourth dimension (time) in the two-dimensional space of a page.

Snowboarder magazine uses graphing and storyboarding techniques to capture the dynamism of snowboarding in a layout style they call a 'sequence pictorial'.
Publisher: Morrison Media Services
Publication: *Snowboarder*
Art director: Graeme Murdoch

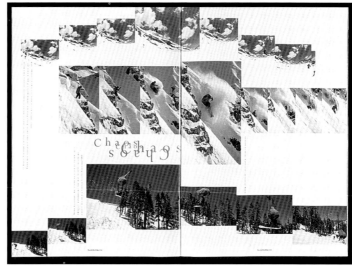

Similarly to the implied simultaneity or concurrence of photo layouts using graphing techniques, if you were to run a series of photographs that describe steps in a process, in either a long string across the top of a layout or in a clockwise direction around a layout, they'd better be in the correct order of the process – as the reader will link them. Remember that readers read proximity as having a relationship – either a connection or a juxtaposition of ideas.

For example, in an agricultural magazine, you might illustrate the process of a product from planting, growing, harvesting; to its packing, branding, distribution; and its appearance in-store, preparation in the kitchen and on the table at home ready to eat. Positioning the captions can be an interesting dilemma, too! Often they will be run together, rather than under each photograph. The caption will start with 'L–R:' meaning 'reading left to right', 'Clockwise from left:' or sometimes have a miniature graphic of the set of images individually numbered.

Type over an image limits its ability to be perceived as a window showing reality. The type anchors the image into the page, limiting its effectiveness. However, you can balance this 'con' with the 'pro' that type over an image also gives greater penetration to the text message.

If type starts small and gets larger and darker throughout a line of text, it is akin to musical notation, and the effect is that of a crescendo (getting louder). The opposite is also true – if type gets smaller and fades away, it is mimicking a diminuendo. This can be a volume thing or a 3-D thing – the type could also be seen to be advancing or receding into the distance.

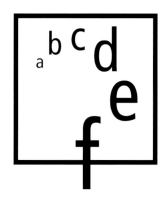

Size and colour also have an impact on where in the visual space we see type and images. If something is smaller, muted or paler, it recedes. If something is larger or brighter, it advances. Anything that overlaps something else implies it is 'forward'.

Another layout technique that is recommended for photo layouts is that of implied storytelling akin to storyboarding.

READ MORE ABOUT IT

Robin Williams, *The non-designer's design book: Design and typographic principles for the visual novice*, Peachpit Press, Berkeley, 1994, ISBN 1 56609 159 4.

Lori Siebert & Lisa Ballard, *Making a good layout*, North Light Books, Cincinnati, 1992, ISBN 0 89134 423 3.

John Bowers, *Introduction to two-dimensional design: Understanding form and function*, John Wiley & Sons, New York, 1999, ISBN 0 471 29224 9.

Bryan L Peterson, *Using design basics to get creative results*, North Light Books, Cincinnati, 1996, ISBN 0 89134 651 1.

Alistair Campbell, *The designer's lexicon: The essential illustrated dictionary of design, print, and computer terms*, Cassell & Co., London, 2000, ISBN 0 940087 20 0.

Roger C Parker, *Looking good in print*, 4th edn, Coriolis, Scottsdale, Arizona, 1998, ISBN 1 56604 8956 7.

Marcelle Lapow Toor, *Graphic design on the desktop: A guide for the non-designer*, 2nd edn, John Wiley & Sons, New York, 1998, ISBN 0 471 29307 5.

DOING IT SMARTER

Dummy text

For rough layouts, use actual headings and possibly the first words in an opening paragraph, but replace the real text with 'dummy' text. Dummy text is just gobbledegook that looks like text, but it encourages clients to consider the design effect of the type without being distracted by the content. Your client or boss will then focus on the design and not the minutiae of spelling and proofreading detail.

Unity

What is 'unity' in graphic design terms? Unity is in the details. It is relationships that drive decision making. For example, when choosing rules to place between lines of text or to surround photographs, there is a good technique that subtly brings unity to a design. If you choose the stroke thickness of the crossbar of a capital A in the typeface that appears closest to the rules, it means your underlines or photo borders relate to the typeface they are seen with, bringing a 'unity' to those elements. Consistency in captioning style, heading style and text placement in relation to images all help to create a harmonious layout.

Unity is in type selection. You can save time by using a few typefaces consistently – and, by doing so, also achieve unity. They look like they belong together because you set up the expectation that they will recur. In multipage layouts in brochures and feature articles, this type consistency means establishing the fonts throughout the piece, not just using them once. The title face may come back in pull-quotes or drop capitals or photo captions, but it doesn't have to come back in the same weight. It might just come back in the italic version or the bold version or small capitals.

Unity is in image-editing. Crop photographs in a range of similar sizes (say, only three: a square, a vertical rectangle and a horizontal rectangle) so there is a visual rhythm created in the layout or the whole publication that also reinforces that the photographs belong. There might be a photographic attitude too: photojournalism, studio set-ups, detail photography – these styles might create sets of images that imply a consistent image selection and editing approach.

Unity is in space. 'White' space can have a unifying effect on disparate elements. Of course, space does not need to be white – it can be any area of colour that doesn't have a pattern, image or text in it. Similarity in the way you choose to structure space into your layouts can bring unity to a multipage project. Do you normally put space around the edges or just at the bottom of the layout?

Unity is in colour selection. There can be a colour 'attitude' to a piece, where you try to achieve a colour balance between the images and the text. In book covers and posters where there is a colour photograph, it is often a

'All visual form is made up of three categories of components: elements, characteristics and interactions. Visual elements are dots, lines, planes and volumes, and each element possesses characteristics of size, shape, texture and color. These elements and characteristics are directed by principles of visual interaction, which are position, direction and space.'

John Bowers in *Introduction to Two-Dimensional Design: Understanding Form and Function*

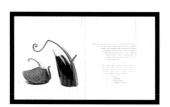

Unity is achieved in this catalogue through repetition in the text block shape of curves taken from the images.
Client: Australian Exhibitions Touring Agency
Publication: *Contemporary Silversmithing: Connections across National Boundaries*
Designer: Maureen MacKenzie-Taylor
Studio: Msquared Research Assisted Design

unifying decision to select colours for the type, background, border and any symbols or single-colour graphics that come from somewhere in the image, thereby unifying image and type. Subliminally, we feel the text and layout elements belong with the photograph. In photo selection, discard photographs that do not have a similar colour palette to your main photograph and instead use photographs that complement its colours.

Unity is in proximity or alignment. When you align elements of a layout, the grouping that results may operate as a single entity. So the positioning of four square-cut photographs, in an aligned stack of two on two, creates a larger square within the layout. Even with a group of different sized and shaped elements, close proximity can generate a 'group shape' that may become the foreground element in your layout. Viewers will find connections and assume connections when objects are aligned, juxtaposed or positioned in close proximity.

While it does not have to be too rigid, remember there are benefits to unity. In magazines, the benefit is that you can find the articles between the advertisements. In feature articles or an ad campaign, the identification of like characteristics signals the continuation of the story. In a website, similarity of navigation elements and content presentation enables users to move about easily. In corporate identity programs, the similarities signal a unified organisation and enable you to rely on a level of branding that means you are jumping off with the new story – a whole slew of information is already known about the organisation and doesn't need repeating.

Graphic detailing

A visual logic system can operate in a design that makes it an 'entity'. This logic system involves consistent application of styling and appropriate decision making on text and image hierarchies and font selection, but also an individualising – and unifying – component that could be termed 'graphic detailing'.

You will need to create a unified design entity for each client and often for each project. If your project is a website, a publication, an advertisement, a corporate identity or a film title, creating a unique visual system will help it achieve a stand-out quality, and make it harder for your competitors to duplicate. It is creating a 'house style'

CHECKLIST
Design dynamics
To vary your layouts:
- Balance:
  - symmetry/centring
  - asymmetry
- Line (and implied line)
- Shape (including the shape of text)
- Colour and tone (dark/light values)
- Scale (relative size of elements)
- Contrast (big/small, dark/light)
- Texture, pattern and repetition
- Unity and alignment
- Space

In *Using Design Basics to Get Creative Results*, Bryan L Peterson discusses design dynamics in this set:
- Format
- Elements:
  - line
  - type
  - shape
  - texture
- Structure:
  - balance
  - contrast
  - unity
  - value (tone)
  - colour.

DOING IT FASTER
Dingbats

If you want a circle, equilateral triangle or square, consider using the Zapf Dingbats font instead of the drawing tools in your program. Because they operate as a font, you must be sure you have removed general font variations such as baseline shift, italicising or horizontal scaling because they will affect the draw of the character. (*Hint:* You can use horizontal scaling to create an oval out of a circle dingbat, an acute-angled isosceles triangle out of an equilateral triangle dingbat, and a rectangle out of a square dingbat. You can then italicise them for fun – and even rotate the text block.)

In many cases, it is faster to resize a typeface than to redraw, enlarge or reduce a redrawn element. You can alter the position of dingbats minutely because they operate as a font, so alignment can be fine-tuned using leading, baseline shift, tracking and kerning controls.

A letterform might be used as the basis for a layout

for layout and design decision making that reflects the uniqueness of that project.

Graphic detailing entails using visual references to unique characteristics of your project. It also involves subtle repetition of those references. It is seeing a chance for individualisation in the smallest details or seemingly most mundane aspects of a design. It saves time because you do not need to create new graphic devices to enliven your layout; simply use the ones you already have. But more importantly, it gives an inner strength to your layout because of the resonances that subtle reiteration can have.

You will be surprised how effective this technique can be. It is often a design ingredient that you don't actually notice until it's pointed out, but you respond to the design and wonder why some designs don't work as 'logically'.

Finding the 'unique' characteristics of the job can be as simple as looking at the letters in the title. If you choose one of the more interesting letterforms in the title and then convert your chosen letterform to paths in your illustration package, select maybe just a curve or angle from the top or bottom of the character. Depending on how you then scale that feature and where you place it in the layout, it might give you a path to which you can snap a title or headline. It could give you a unique shape with which you could crop a photograph. It could become a curved or angled margin that your column of text could contour down. It could become the dividing line between two fields of colour in the background. You could step and repeat it, and then colour between each, to create a pattern of coloured stripes down your page. All of these possibilities can arise simply from a feature of a letterform from the title!

The fact that a tiny detail like this can provide a rich variety of graphic options means you do not need to create new graphic devices. Simply recognise and use the ones you've already chosen.

Within images, too, there are details that can be recropped and featured elsewhere or used for backgrounds. They might be ghosted to provide a pale but related background for the layout. They might be repeated and distorted into a pattern or texture. You might use the negative version. There are colours that can be duplicated for display text. There are infinite possibilities.

But let's assume you decided that all the photographs in your report would be cropped into squares. The square becomes a graphic device within that layout as a result of that decision. So reiterate it. How? Use squares instead of bullets in dot-point lists. You could also put all pull-quotes or chapter headings into a square. Your folios could be contained in a fine ruled square placed equidistant from the top and outer trim, creating an even more subtle square of blank space. In bar charts, the bars could be a stack of squares instead of a rectangle. Your colour codings would have square samples of colour in the key. You could justify your text and fill square text blocks. In a sans serif title, you could customise the letter *i* by replacing its circular dot with a little square. Okay, these really are the details – but they have resonance.

Part of effective corporate identity design involves this type of detailing, using pieces of your existing corporate symbols, logos and colour palette. Maybe you can use stripes that mimic a diagonal line in your symbol to fill borders and strips of colour in the backgrounds of brochure covers and other corporate paraphernalia. In a series of report covers, you could use enlargements of details taken from the symbol to create the base layout.

It can be as simple as a slight colour variation in the background that subtly reinforces the symbol. This reinforcing is the layout secret. If you then incorporate a band of, for example, diagonal stripes that reinforce the diagonal from the symbol, you are creating a design ground that is 'exclusive'; to your organisation. Another client could use those same graphic devices (diagonals and subtle details) because they are not, of themselves, exclusive. But their use elsewhere will not have the same resonance that they will have if you use them. Worse still, if accidentally used by a competitor, their material may be perceived as emanating from your organisation.

Balance

Balance is achieved when the elements in a layout are comfortably related to one another and the different weight of the elements has been distributed evenly across the area of the page. Imagine an adult and a child on a seesaw. For balance to be achieved, you must place the adult and the child carefully at different distances from the fulcrum.

An element's size, shape, colour and tone determine weight in a layout.

BEFORE
detail
AFTER
detail

Subtle refinements like a dot on the *i* can reiterate a chosen theme: in this case, the use of squares. Also note the altered alignment.

DOING IT SMARTER
Edge detail
Fine trimming and registration slows the job on press and finishing processes – avoid complexity and detail on the trim edges of your designs. Avoid lines, rules or borders that run parallel and very close to the trim edges, because if the trim is slightly out, the parallels will look wrong.

A symmetrical layout will always be balanced unless you add a rogue element. In asymmetrical layouts, balance is much more complicated and you use other dynamics to achieve it.

To simplify some of the complexities, you can select a group of elements (often title, author and a small illustration or symbol) and centre them off-centre. That is, you can centre them to balance their relationships but then place their centre line anywhere on the layout – often to the right of a full-page illustration balancing a character or object on the left.

Symmetry

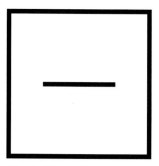

Physical centre

Designed around a central axis, symmetry will always balance, but it can be too predictable. For 'predictable', read 'boring'. This traditional Western design style always creates a balanced design because the elements are reflected around a central axis, meaning the 'weight' of each element is evenly balanced on either side of the centre line. The symmetrical layout is static. It will always look neat – and is a good default design if you're running short of time – but is just a bit boring or bland. This is the result of the main structural interest being a downward centre line.

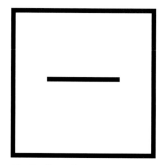

Optical centre

Vertical centring
Try to remember to lift the elements to 'optical centre' – which is slightly above physical centre. This is achieved easily by putting a larger margin measurement at the bottom of the layout than at the top. It avoids the feeling that the text block or print area might have 'slipped' down the page. This is also the reason that title pages normally have the title placed in the top half of the page.

Asymmetry

Asymmetry is inspired by Eastern design traditions. Asymmetrical layouts are much more involving for the viewer than symmetrical ones. The response to an asymmetrical design is a physiological response as well as an aesthetic one. Asymmetrical designs are interesting designs for your eyes. Your eye responds by travelling to and fro across the layout. This eye movement is a physical involvement and is part of our perception of increased dynamism within these layouts.

For balance within asymmetrical arrangement, the Japanese have developed a modular approach to layout in architecture with their arrangement of *tatami* mats, which is also used in screens for room division. The *tatami* mat is a rectangle created from two squares. In combination, *tatami* mats will create balanced patterns that are not necessarily symmetrical.

Asymmetry fascinated Piet Mondrian (among others) in the early 20th century. Using the methods explored by Mondrian can create a strong interrelated layout.

Balance is complicated in asymmetrical layouts because the relationships between the elements are dynamic. There is 'tension and movement' created by positioning. For example, a large black-and-white photograph at the top left of a page might be balanced by a small red logo at the bottom right of the page. The weight distribution here is not only to do with size but also to do with the comparative 'weight' of the elements' attraction value – the red has stronger attraction value and is therefore 'heavier' than its size alone indicates.

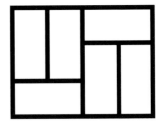

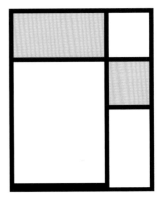

Piet Mondrian's work with areas of flat colour (*above*) demonstrates clear techniques for creating balanced layouts (*below*).

Freestyle layout

'Organic' or 'free-form' layout is mostly used on posters, packaging and advertisements. Often you'll sketch a layout and keep sketching until you can see the completed design in the scribbles you have made. Then, sitting at the keyboard with trusty mouse or graphics tablet with stylus at the ready, you convert the scribbles into your final piece. This is the ideal working method – establish what you want each element of the design to achieve and then translate that, massaging text and image to fit your idea. Details, of course, are not worked out so much in the sketching phase.

Free-form design might answer a particular project more effectively than the often rigid grid structure that many designers adopt. For brochures, pamphlets, handbills, packaging, stationery, covers and posters, consider using freestyle or free-form design.

With freestyle, you can size and place images and text according to their level of importance and their image quality, and interrelate them by juxtaposition or layering. Remember that the viewer or audience will need to get some information from your design, so don't disguise the information or hide it. Help the viewer to understand.

A small element can dominate or balance a larger element in asymmetrical layout.

Having the maximum flexibility that free-form offers allows you to place pictures directly where the text refers to them. You also have the ultimate inflexibility for text massaging. You can vary line lengths and leading according to what is most readable for your chosen typefaces, without the limiting structures of modules or grid-based column widths. Pictures, too, can be whatever size is most logical or interesting for the image without having to conform to column widths or modules. Free-form implies an asymmetrical layout.

In most designs, there are places where small changes could be made to improve the accurate retrieval of information. With free-form design, there is the flexibility to do some fine-tuning of type and image sizing and placement, all the while maintaining an interesting design that follows the logical flow of information, rather than a pre-ordained presentation system like a grid.

There are drawbacks to free-form design. It is so flexible that some people find it hard to start. And you don't want to make decisions that allow yourself or others to procrastinate any longer. That flexibility can also make it hard to stop (there is always a little more tweaking you could do). Unfortunately, computers encourage this, regardless of the layout style you choose.

In order to use this technique successfully, you need to have decision and experimentation time – and sometimes that is just too hard to find.

Free-form layout can work in publication design but is rarely used. Grids are faster for production of multipage documents and usually make it easier to control the layout for consistency and general flow through the document. Magazines, however, sometimes use free-form layout in a feature section.

Grids

To bind elements within a layout and to achieve a visual consistency over a series of layouts, designers often use a grid. A grid is an invisible structure that underlies a layout. Elements such as pictures, text, headings and logos are positioned in the layout in relation to the grid. Nearly all publications, and many advertisements, use a grid.

There are sound financial reasons for using a grid scheme too, because a grid simplifies a number of decisions and controls production. This is why it is important to develop a grid that enables, rather than a grid that disables. You need a grid that will give you the flexibility of application that you will need in future applications of that grid, not just the initial task.

At its simplest, a grid can just be the four margins surrounding a text area. Don't forget that the bottom margin should be larger than the top margin to accommodate the optical centre.

Pages are designed to be read together, so always create a double-page grid. The page layout will usually be reflected on the spine, though left-hand and right-hand page layout can differ according to the type of publication. Avoid numerous indents, as each indent creates a new text element.

A grid system strives to achieve unity. However, we have become so used to breaking the grid that we often break it before it's been established. This will often weaken a publication.

Some grid systems actually work against unity because they are too flexible. The grid systems that allow two, three, four, six or eight column widths on any page tend to make it difficult to establish unity within all but the largest publications where there is a chance that the diversity will be appreciated.

Grid systems often are created by determining column possibilities across the page size. However, to further enhance the structure and bring greater unity to the publication, a series of horizontal page divisions is often created. These give particular points on the page for pictures, captions or headings to hang from. They bring a strength to the publication. They are sometimes called 'flow lines'.

At their simplest, they can be a mathematical division of the column depth, a series of cross-rules placed at regular intervals. This option tends to be used for newsletters and newspapers where the variety of material is wide.

They can be modular for ease of placement of photographs, diagrams, logos and text. Headings can be devised to work in a particular size of module. Then it is simply a case of playing with a jigsaw – fit all the pieces into the page using leftover space for alignment.

For brochures and books, though, the cross-rules are often customised for the particular publication, and there may only be a few well-placed cross-rules that perform specific tasks in the publication.

According to André Jute in *Grids: The Structure of Graphic Design*, there are three purposes of a grid:

- Repeatability, particularly important in:
  - multipage documents
  - a series of documents
  - corporate identity
- Composition
  - to blend linear text with illustration
  - to arrange size, shape and balance of elements
- Communication
  - finding given elements in the same place
  - as a guide to important elements.

DOING IT SMARTER
Breaking a grid

Grids need not be followed slavishly. Indeed, it can be very dynamic to 'break the grid'. It is important to remember that you are breaking something, so it needs to be established before a break can have its full impact.

You can break a grid by bleeding a picture – it is said to 'bleed' if it continues off the page – or having a contoured picture break into a margin. You can also break a grid by contouring type around an illustration, creating a runaround. Give a comfortable zone around the illustration (in most cases, 3–5 mm is 'comfortable') so the type does not limit the illustration.

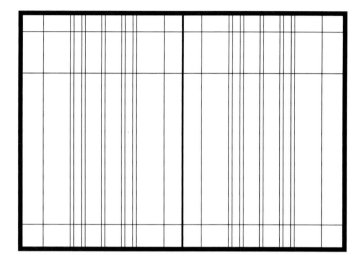

Mixed column grids

On the same template, this grid will accommodate two, three and four columns.

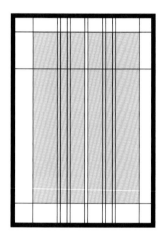

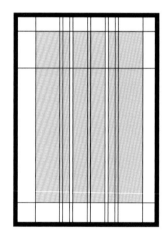

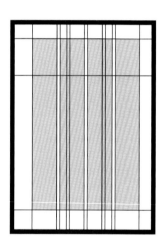

Picture box and rule sizing in unjustified text setting

When your text is unjustified it has an optical width narrower than the maximum text width. To take account of this in picture layouts, the column width of picture boxes is narrower by 5–7 mm in order for the picture to sit more comfortably in the unjustified text.

Similarly, if you are placing rules below or above headings or captions in unjustified text, use the optical column width for the width of the rule, not the full column width. Rules will also be 5–7 mm shorter.

READ MORE ABOUT IT

Allen Hurlburt, *The grid: A modular system for the design and production of newspapers, magazines and books*, Van Nostrand Reinhold, New York, 1978, ISBN 0 422 23598 4.

Allen Hurlburt, *Layout: The design of the printed page*, Watson-Guptill Publications, New York, 1977, ISBN 0 214 20674 2.

André Jute, *Grids: The structure of graphic design*, RotoVision SA, Crans-Pres-Celigny, Switzerland, 1996, ISBN 2 88046 277 0.

Gavin Ambrose & Paul Harris, *The layout book*, AVA Publishing SA, 2007, ISBN 978-2-940373-53-6.

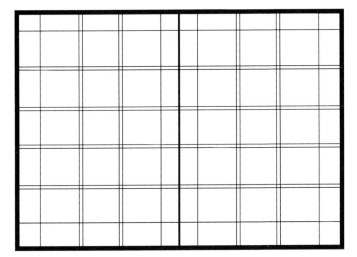

A modular grid
created by regular mathematical subdivisions of the columns

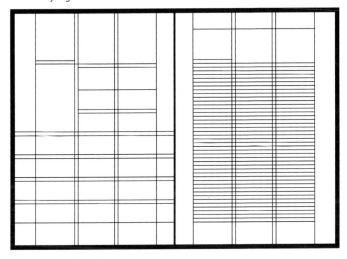

Customised divisions
designed to accommodate publication-specific content blocks

Corporate grid relationships
You might decide that, for your corporate identification to be consistent across all materials, a coloured band will appear in the top quarter of any shape. So whether it is a badge, the website or the letterhead, the top quarter of each shape will be coloured and contain the corporate identification.

Further from this, alignment of logos or symbols is often detailed by measurements taken from the symbol itself. Usually this ensures that the logo is not crammed into spaces that are too small for it. Often it is a placement issue where a particular measure, which could be half its width, is placed above and to the left of the symbol. A quarter of its width might be placed to its right before any type is set.

Using relationships with your elements like this can create a coherence that is simple to maintain across varying sizes, formats and requirements.

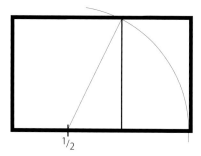

$^1/_2$

The Golden Section

is constructed by taking a square, using its centre point on one edge and creating an arc from the opposite corner to create the depth. This point gives the relationship of the sides of the rectangle 1:1.618 ... or 8:13.

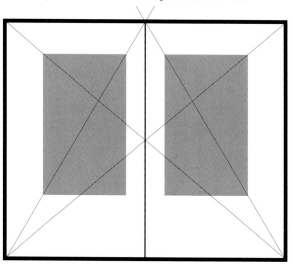

The Golden Section's classic subdivisions

are generated by diagonals within a format based on the page dimensions of the Golden Section. These enable you to position text in the classical or Renaissance format.

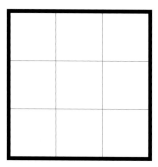

The rule of thirds

divides any given format into nine equal areas. These divisions are used in photography to determine the positioning of focal points or objects of interest in the frame. They are also used in illustrations and page layouts. You could, for example, subdivide the text area defined by a grid into the nine equal areas.

Formats

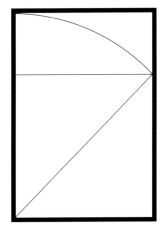 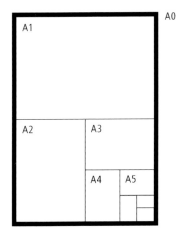 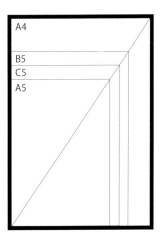

Relationship between A, B and C sizes

International paper sizes are based on the ratio 1:√2 or about 1:1.4 (*left*).

There are three series, called the A, B and C series (*right*).

The base sheet for the A series is A0, which has a total area equal to one square metre.

The sheets divide proportionally into their smaller sizes (*centre*).

International Standards Organization (ISO) series A, B and C series, DL

Note: These are all given with height first then width, as per Australian, United Kingdom and Far East practice. American and European practice is to lead with width first then depth.

2A0	1682 × 1189 mm				
A0	1189 × 841 mm	B0	1414 × 1000 mm	C0	1297 × 917 mm
SRA0	1280 × 900 mm*				
A1	841 × 594 mm	B1	1000 × 707 mm	C1	917 × 648 mm
SRA1	900 × 640 mm*				
A2	594 × 420 mm	B2	707 × 500 mm	C2	648 × 458 mm
SRA2	640 × 450 mm*				
A3	420 × 297 mm	B3	500 × 353 mm	C3*e*	458 × 324 mm
A3+	457 × 305 mm*				
SRA3	450 × 320 mm*				
A4	297 × 210 mm	B4*e*	353 × 250 mm	C4	324 × 229 mm
A5	210 × 148 mm	B5*e*	250 × 176 mm	C5*e*	229 × 162 mm
A6	148 × 105 mm	B6*e*	176 × 125 mm	C6*e*	162 × 114 mm
1/3 A4	210 × 99 mm	B6/C4*e*	125 × 324 mm	C7*e*	114 × 81 mm
DL*e*	110 × 220 mm	B7	125 × 88 mm	C7/6*e*	81 × 162 mm

*   Each allows bleed and colour bars for trimming back to size
e   Envelope sizes

Imperial paper sizes

A range of paper sizes from the United Kingdom and also used in the United States has different sized sets of at least three related sizes. A *folio* is halved and called a *quarto* (4to), which is halved again and called an *octavo* (8vo), and so on through 16mo, 24mo and 32mo sizes. Some of the sets are called Crown, Demy, Medium, Foolscap, Royal, Super Royal and Imperial. For example:

Crown folio	254 × 381 mm	Demy folio	286 × 445 mm	Foolscap quarto	171 × 216 mm
Crown quarto	191 × 254 mm	Demy quarto	222 × 286 mm	Foolscap octavo	108 × 171 mm
Crown octavo	127 × 191 mm	Demy octavo	143 × 222 mm		

Other product measures

CDs and DVDs	124 mm diameter
CD jewel cases	
Back cover i.e. 6 mm + 137 + 6 mm (2 spines)	118 × 149 mm
Booklet	121 × 121 mm
CD label	118 print diameter with 40.5 mm diameter central void
DVD cover	125 × 175 mm
Spine	14 mm
Slimline spine	7 mm
DVD label	118 print diameter with 17.5 mm diameter central void
CD and DVD wallet	125 × 124.5 mm
Mini-CD	85 mm diameter
Mini-CD label	79 mm diameter with 18 mm diameter central void
Video covers	115 × 196 mm
Spine	28 mm
Movie posters	
Single sheet	1008 × 688 mm
Day bills	650 × 330 mm
Bus shelter posters	1.8 × 1.2 m
A ream	500 sheets

Other stationery and publication measures

Foolscap	337 × 206 mm
Quarto	260 × 206 mm
American quarto	279 × 216 mm
Also called US Imperial	
In half	140 × 216 mm
In thirds	93 × 216 mm
American foolscap	330 × 216 mm
Magazines	270 × 207 mm
Paperbacks	198 × 128 mm
	178 × 110 mm
Large format	234 × 153 mm
Business cards	55 × 85 mm
	50 × 90 mm
	45 × 90 mm
	51 × 76 mm
	(2″ × 3″)

Japanese Industrial Standard (JIS) B sizes

Note: The JIS A series is the same as the ISO A series.

JIS B0	1456 × 1030 mm
JIS B1	1030 × 728 mm
JIS B2	728 × 515 mm
JIS B3	515 × 364 mm
JIS B4	364 × 257 mm
JIS B5	257 × 182 mm
JIS B6	182 × 128 mm
JIS B7	128 × 91 mm
JIS B8	91 × 64 mm

READ MORE ABOUT IT
Poppy Evans, *Forms, folds and sizes: All the details graphic designers need to know but can never find*, Rockport Publishers, Gloucester, Mass., 2004, ISBN 978-1-59253-054-0.

Measurement preferences

Page measurements, margins, picture boxes and text area are now often expressed in millimetres. Text area always used to be expressed in picas and points. A pica is 12 points or approximately 3.5 mm. This option is still usually available to you in your 'preferences' set-up. But because of the advent of computers and desktop publishing, page divisions are now often expressed in millimetres. However, type measurements, leading and the space measurements within a text block are still expressed in points. Text indents and tabs though, which were previously specified in picas or points, are now often expressed in millimetres, in order to fit with the page divisions.

While you can select any measurement system online, usually it is best to create your measures in pixels.

Margins

Generous margins make a book feel easy to read. Traditionally, the *inside margin* (called the *back margin* in traditional book terminology) is about the same as the *top margin* (the *head*); the *outside margin* (the *fore edge*) is slightly larger; and the *bottom margin* (the *foot*) is the largest. This is based on the Renaissance page dimensions gleaned from the Golden Section.

The inner margins are smaller than the outer margins so the text areas in a double-page spread are seen to be more evenly spaced. If they are specified as half the outer margin, the inner margins create a band of space equal to the outer margin. But there is an optical illusion created by the folding of paper at the spine, so the inner margins are usually two-thirds to three-quarters the specification of the outer margin. Of course, inner margins will need to be larger to accommodate binding techniques like ring-binding, side-stapling and perfect binding.

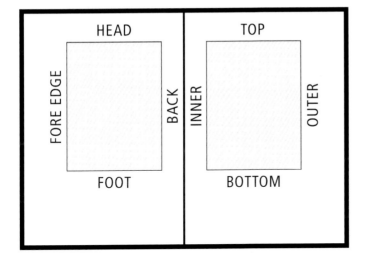

DOING IT FASTER
Formats

Reuse icons, style sheets and templates. If you have created icons for one document, keep them in a library or drag them between documents. Do not recreate them each time you need them.

Likewise, if you have created a new template for a page size different from your usual, save it somewhere where you can access the template when you need it again.

Saving just a short period of time, such as that used to create the page margins and column guides, can speed your production. You've done it once, don't waste it.

You may find it handy to have an A4 landscape page and an A4 portrait page at the ready ... and a few other standard sizes:
- a six-panel, 1/3 A4 pamphlet template
- a four-page, three-column newsletter template
- an A4 template for correspondence
- invoice
- orders
- other regularly used forms.

Columns and gutters

Columns are usually set with 5 mm gutters between. Use more space if the column is justified than if it is unjustified. If space is limited, you might choose to run a fine vertical rule between justified columns in order to separate them appropriately.

Columns within a publication can be of equal width, or unequal as in this book – and this is largely determined by the style of the publication and the information it contains.

DOING IT SMARTER
Making a style book

A style book documents, in one place, all the production and design decisions to date in the production of a book, magazine, newspaper, newsletter, website or larger scale work like a series of publications or a corporate identity. It should include a hard copy or written description of:

☐ typographic style sheets
☐ rules for information architecture
☐ wireframes, templates, grids and master pages
☐ editorial style sheets
☐ colour palettes and swatches
☐ standard graphic elements like rules, picture boxes, symbols and other page furniture
☐ illustration preferences and stylings
☐ paper stock specifications
☐ print specifications
☐ suppliers' names, addresses and phone numbers
☐ sample copies and screen-dumps.

The style book enables easy replication if the file is lost or temporarily unable to be accessed or if a new producer needs to prepare material in the same style.

DOING IT SMARTER
Widows and orphans

An orphan is the first line of a paragraph that has been left at the foot of a column or page by itself. A widow is the last line or, worse, the last word, in a paragraph that has been taken over to start a new page or column by itself.

To avoid these two unfortunate circumstances, a paragraph with three lines or less should be taken over to a new column or page. That is, only a four-or-more-line paragraph can be broken, provided the break takes at least two lines and leaves at least two lines.

A side column can be useful for commenting on the main text, incorporating headings and images, or summarising and drawing attention to the main content. If columns are of different widths, in many grid systems they will be related proportionally.

Multicolumn layouts are used if the manuscript is made up mostly of short paragraphs. Long paragraphs in a narrow column measure make the text look daunting to read.

Page depth

There are two choices for page depth. You can keep all the elements on your page consistently spaced or keep the bottom line of your page consistent by altering the spacing throughout the page to maintain it. In both cases, you usually define the maximum page depth by creating the bottom margin in your document set-up. But in the case of variable page depth, you can reduce or extend your text block as required.

Variable page depth

Variable page depth maintains constant spacing between elements but the page finishes on or above its maximum text depth line. The top line of text remains constant and the text hangs from that line like clothes on a clothesline. Variable page depth is a convenient way of avoiding 'widows' and 'orphans' and other awkward page breaks.

Footnotes still sit at the bottom of the grid. It is even more desirable to have variable column depth in publications that have two or more columns, as artificially evened-out columns on the same page usually look peculiar due to the distortion in their vertical space distribution.

Constant page depth

Constant page depth indicates that pages throughout the publication will always start and finish at the same points. This is achieved by artificially stretching the spacing between elements of the page. This means adding or subtracting space around headings, paragraphs, tables, illustrations and, on rare occasions, between lines of text. Unless it is prepared with extreme care, the manipulation of text like this should be avoided; although this is the 'classical' style of page make-up, the fine skills that perfected it are rarer these days.

Avoid your computer's vertical justification operation. If you want your pages to be a constant page depth, make the spacing decisions yourself. It is time-consuming, but will also ensure that the alterations are not too obvious. Your computer is not nearly as considerate.

Imagery

Images should add dimension to the text that cannot be achieved in any other way. The illustration should complement the text and be, at least, relevant, and preferably enhance the reader's understanding.

To decide where images should or could go, read the manuscript and jot down ideas for images in the margins. The positioning of images should also lend pace and variety to the document.

No image is preferred if the only option is a poor image. The quality of any illustrative material will not be improved by reproduction techniques.

It takes planning, and in many cases research, to find an appropriate image with excellent reproduction quality. Photo libraries and archival institutions are good initial sources.

It is advisable to seek the services of a professional illustrator or photographer if the material you require does not exist, is not readily available or would have greater impact if it were consistent and original.

When placing an image into your layout, be aware that images usually create a square or rectangular shape on the page. They also have a tonal level. Even though they will vary in tone, they can be reduced to a basic tonal level which is usually seen if you squint at the image.

They may also be 'contoured', where they make a complex shape on the page because the subject is cut out from its frame. When you squint, this shape will also 'reduce' to a basic form – circle, triangle, oval, rectangle, square or trapezium. This becomes the layout element for balance purposes.

Photographic imagery is one of the strongest elements in a design because, since television brought moving pictures into our homes, our society has become reliant on visual information. Imagery was always the strongest element in a design – even in illuminated manuscripts, the pictures are the first things we notice.

Jason Grant of Inkahoots Design Studio, speaking at *Sydney Design 99*, noted: 'A picture is worth a thousand words – and a thousand words for what it omits.'

Picture selection and text interaction

Seeking imagery to support text is a skill in itself. The interaction of images with text is a complex piece of design manipulation. To practise the technique, choose an image and a word that when seen together make someone laugh, sad, angry, nostalgic. Four concepts. Isolated.

To work with basic interaction of text and image, start with book covers with usually not more than two levels of text – title and author – and select an appropriate image. Posters are also a good starting point. Gradually increase the complexity and the interaction of the different elements.

'We have always known that photographs are not representations of truth. It is impossible to take a photograph that does not have some sort of editing imposed, even if it is simply what one happens to leave out of the frame.'

Wendy Richmond, 'Trust me, trust me not', *Communication Arts*, May/June 2006

CHECKLIST

Images

☐ Photographs
☐ Drawings
☐ Paintings
☐ Photographs of 3-dimensional
   illustrations
☐ Digital illustrations
☐ Cartoons
☐ Symbols
☐ Pictograms
☐ Maps
☐ Diagrams
☐ Graphs
☐ Flow charts
☐ 'Found' material or authentic
   materials such as old letters, faxes,
   telexes, telegrams, tickets (and
   other 'ephemera')

CHECKLIST

Illustration techniques

☐ Drawing
   – pencil
   – cross-hatch
   – pen and wash
   – engraving
☐ Painting
   – oils
   – watercolour
☐ Cut paper
☐ Linocut
☐ Monoprint
☐ Silkscreen print
☐ Photocopy
☐ Collage
☐ Assemblage
☐ Cross-stitch
☐ Embroidery
☐ Quilting
☐ Plasticine/modelling clay
☐ Dimensional illustration
☐ Mixed media
☐ Theatrical lighting
☐ Sand painting
☐ Food sculpture
☐ White on white

It would be foolish to deny the greater attraction of the image over type. So use images carefully and look at what information they are giving. Photographic images have had such power because traditionally they have been 'real' – they were recognisably a slice of reality captured in a single image. However, with image manipulation, the strength of that implied 'reality' has been eroded.

When you analyse a photo, what should you look for? Does the subject stand out from the background? Whatever the subject of a photo, it is usually best for that subject not to compete with its background. It may mean the photographer has chosen a simple background (as in controlled studio portraits – black, white or mottled back cloths) or has separated the subject from the background by focusing carefully so the subject is in focus and the background blurred. In portraits, a photographer will often backlight a person's hair to create this separation from the background.

Is the photo in focus? If not, what part of the photo is in focus? If the subject is moving, sometimes it will have moved just out of focus and there will be a tree in the background perfectly in focus. This is fine if you wanted a photo of a tree, but not necessarily appropriate if you wanted a portrait of an Olympic cyclist.

Does the photo have a full range of tone? In black-and-white photography, are there a solid black and a pure white somewhere in the photo, and a complete range of greys in between? In colour photography, is there a solid black somewhere and a pure white somewhere with a representative colour range between?

Is the photo colour-correct? Does it have a colour 'cast' where there is the unwanted effect of seeing the image as if through a filter of one particular colour? Is there a yellowy tinge like indoor shots taken without flash on outdoor film? Often, colour film will have a predisposition to produce a particular colour cast.

But more than this, when selecting photographs for a project, select ones that will look as if they were specifically created as a set. There should be a certain consistency of subject matter or attitude to the subjects. It can be to do with where the focus is or a specific method of lighting the subject – soft or harsh, dappled or pin-lit, bright or shadowy. There might be a particular point of view. The colour set might be limited in some way or manipulated to have a similar palette. Equally, you might choose photographs that have a particular grain or texture or use a filter that gives them a consistent texture. You might use cropping techniques to help the photographs fit a consistent format.

READ MORE ABOUT IT

Peter Bonnici & Linda Proud, *Designing with photographs*, RotoVision SA, Crans-Pres-Celigny, Switzerland, 1998, ISBN 2 88046 353 X.

Tim Daly, *Digital: photography: A user's guide to creating digital images*, New Burlington Books, London, 2000, ISBN 1 86155 273 4.

Catherine Slade, *The encyclopedia of illustration techniques*, Simon & Schuster, Sydney, 1997, ISBN 0 7318 0599 2.

Terence Dalley (ed.), *The complete guide to illustration and design techniques and materials*, Chartwell Books, Secaucus, New Jersey, 1980, ISBN 0 89009 316 4.

Steven Heller & Teresa Fernandes, *The business of illustration*, Watson Guptill, New York, 1995, ISBN 0 8230 0545 3.

Terry Jones, *Instant design: A manual of graphic techniques*, Architecture Design and Technology Press, London, 1990, ISBN 1 85454 838 7.

Kathleen Ziegler & Nick Green, *Paper sculpture: A step-by-step guide*, Dimensional Illustrators/Rockport Publishers, Gloucester, Mass., 1994, ISBN 1-56496-329-2.

Cropping

Deleting unwanted or distracting areas of an image is called cropping. Cropping can change the shape of an illustration or zoom into a small area of it and refocus attention. This is perhaps the designer's single most effective tool in using photos. It can change a horizontal photo to a vertical one, alter the subject matter of the photo and improve the composition of a poor photo. It can also destroy an excellent photo (and some photographers will not give reproduction clearance for a photo if it will be cropped).

Cropping enables you to delete half the photograph to highlight a particular piece of information. You might want to highlight the office furniture for a catalogue and delete the workers who are in unfashionable clothing. Cropping also enables you to fit a predetermined layout shape, as sometimes the layout is created while you wait for a photo to be supplied. It also means that you can alter the appearance of a photograph by cropping it radically. What might have been an ordinary snap can become a dynamic image by creative cropping. By deleting one element in the foreground, you may be able to alter the visual structure of the image enough to lend it greater drama. Let the reader become involved in the picture.

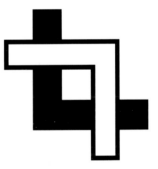

DOING IT SMARTER
The 2-Ls cropping method
Take a sheet of light card about A4 in size (mid-grey is a good colour if you have a choice) and cut out the centre, leaving about a 30 mm frame. Then cut two L-shapes. By overlapping them and sliding them left to right, up and down, you can alter the size and shape of the frame. You can see how a photograph looks in square, vertical or horizontal rectangular formats – just by moving the two Ls.

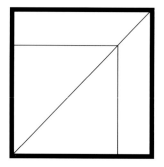

**Enlarging and reducing
on the diagonal**
To scale an image, use its diagonal for
enlargement or reduction calculations.
Where the cropping is known, the
column depth can be determined by
moving along the diagonal until the
column width is reached. Measuring
from that point down will tell you
the depth.

If the final size is known but the
cropping needs to be done, you can
use the same technique.

DOING IT SMARTER
**Calculating percentages for
enlargement or reduction**
To calculate a percentage for either
enlargement or reduction, divide the
measure you want (from your layout)
by the measure you have (from the
original image) and multiply by 100.
You can use either the vertical or
horizontal measure – or the width of a
person's eyes if you want to get faces
looking the same size – as long as you
measure the same part of the image.

With the 2-Ls method, you can see what the photo looks
like when cropped diagonally. Try it with a portrait and
see what happens to the profile of a face when it is tilted
upwards and downwards in the frame – doesn't that begin
to have an effect on how you perceive the person who is
portrayed?

Scaling

Scaling is a technical process where you find out how much
area to leave in your layout for the image you want, or you
have allowed a certain area in your layout for an image and
you need to decide which part of the selected image to use.

Sources of photographs and copyright

If you do not have any, photographs can be accessed
through image libraries. Charges for the use of an image
usually depend on:
- the number of copies that will be reproduced and
  distributed
- the size or area the image takes up in your layout
- whether it is used on the cover or inside the publication.
Photographers may sell images they have shot previously,
or you can commission photographs to be taken
specifically for your project. Make sure you brief the
photographer on what you actually need, and the format
you need it in, such as slide, print, transparency or, most
likely, a digital file.

Ask to see a portfolio of the photographer's work before
commissioning. This is the same for illustrators – make
sure that their style is the style you want before you sign a
contract or a commission.

Remember also that you often purchase the image
only for the specific use you have negotiated. Any further
reproduction from that image without renegotiating rights
is infringing the copyright of the work.

The image belongs to the originator of the image
– the photographer or illustrator – unless they assign
the copyright to you or a third party (such as an image
library) or give you unlimited usage. You will usually pay
more for unlimited usage or copyright purchase – though
many photo libraries package disks of images that, once
purchased, allow you unlimited reproduction rights.

You will also need to include an image credit line (usually
in very small sans serif type up the side of the image or the

Picture cropping

By cropping, you can create four pictures (*below*) from one original image (*left*).

Limit picture scalings

Choose a scaling that will fit the majority of your photographs and then draw one picture box. Multiply it by duplicating, and position the clones. Even if some of the photographs are landscape format, you can rotate the box by 90° from a portrait position to the landscape. By carefully specifying the runaround on the original box, you can place the clones anywhere and the text will consistently wrap around the boxes.

This will save you money, too, because the person who produces your scans can scan a batch of images at once, minimising the time spent on the scanner.

Photo clearances

When commissioning photography of people or works of art, ensure you have the agreement of the people and artists in writing. This is called a 'clearance' and should be checked over by a lawyer before you ask anyone to sign it. You should keep it with your photos to prove you have the reproduction approval of the subject.

You will need to specify the likely uses of the images. If you haven't negotiated further uses, if it was only for one project, you will need to seek further clearance when you want to use the image again.

When organisations commission photo collections, they will insist that the photographer, acting as their agent, obtains this permission in writing and gives them a copy of the form for every person who appears.

page on which it appears). In many publications, image copyrights have a separate listing in the acknowledgments or credits, referring to the image's position on the page and the page number on which the image appears. The credit will usually include both the originator of the image and the name of the image library from which it comes.

Image libraries will limit the number of times an image can be purchased and decide if the resale of that image to the next person who requests it will have adverse effects for the last sale. If so, they will not release the image. However, if the two markets are different enough, and the likelihood of the image being recognised or diminishing the return to either of the purchasing parties is not at risk, they will release the image for other users. For example, if the image is for an annual report that will be released in Australia, the image may also be released for an advertisement in the United States.

This is also the reason you need to be careful using the images you purchase – another studio working for a competitor may have purchased the same image and you will see, for example, two travel agencies using the same image of Paris on promotional material at the same travel show.

Clip art

Many companies release volumes or selections of 'useful', 'standard' illustrations, photographs and backgrounds on CD-ROM or downloadable from the Internet. Unfortunately, the wide availability and widespread use of these illustrations can make them less effective.

Another problem with clip art is the compatibility of one image with another. For example, illustrations will often have conflicting drawing styles, which can sit awkwardly with each other. For unity in an ad campaign or through a publication, you will probably want stylistic continuity.

Alternatively, the most successful thing you can do with clip art is to design your layout and style around a diversity of imagery sources. This can create its own difficulties, since it means you may have to find optional pieces for one spread, because the styles are too similar. Fortunately, with image manipulation programs, you have the capacity to alter images stylistically.

If you use clip art, crop it or combine it to create a 'new' image. In that way, if the studio next door bought the same image, your use of the image will be different from theirs.

In most instances, your purchase of clip art pays the fee for unlimited use of the image. You will often pay a subscription to an image library's website that allows for unlimited downloads. (Note that this is not the case with image libraries where you pay for each use of an image. You may also find an image is not allowed to be cropped.)

Cartoons

Cartoons can enliven text. But check before you commission a cartoonist – does the client organisation really want a hard-hitting 'editorial' cartoon, or does it want simply a funny picture?

If you choose a well-known cartoonist and leave it in their hands to illustrate a particular aspect of the text you have supplied, you can expect to pay them for the image, even if you choose to not use it in the final production. Ascertain how much leeway for interpretation your client is prepared to give. Most cartoonists understand there may be sensitivities, limitations or particular requirements and are happy to comply if adequately briefed.

Diagrams, graphs and charts

Diagrams explain complex processes, phenomena and relationships with an easy-to-understand clarity. By recognising patterns and hierarchies of information, a diagram designer is able to simplify and communicate the hidden or even the abstract.

By taking a lead from techniques such as mapping, a flow chart evolved – where a process becomes the journey. There may be twists and turns in the path. You may have to repeat a particular sequence. There may be sub-processes operating concurrently in the familiar form of a diagram.

When creating a chart, the first requirement is to select the nodes (towns on a map) and then create the links (access routes). Then you might start relating the nodes to each other by differentiating different processes with colour, shape and size (some towns have particular facilities or higher population density). The sorting process attempts to make the clearest, least complicated explanation of the connections and relationships between the nodes.

Tony and Barry Buzan in *The Mindmap Book* list the skills available to all of us that are used in the mapping process they describe (not a bad list to consider when creating diagrams, graphs and charts):

- □ Language
  - words
  - symbols
- □ Number
- □ Logic
  - sequence
  - listing
  - linearity
  - analysis
  - time
  - association
- □ Rhythm
- □ Colour
- □ Imagery
  - daydreaming
  - visualisation
- □ Spatial awareness
  - dimension
  - gestalt (whole picture).

READ MORE ABOUT IT
Tony Buzan with Barry Buzan, *The mindmap book*, rev. edn, BBC Books, London, 1995, ISBN 0 563 37101 3.

As part of this simplification, for example, you may convert a map into a linear diagram that maintains the relationships and connections between the nodes but alters the distances and simplifies the linking lines in order to diagrammatically represent the relationships. The best example of this style of linear diagram is the London Underground map, originally designed by Henry Beck in 1933, and now used as the basis for public transport maps worldwide.

Then there is the choice of diagrammatic representation. Which graphing styles could be used? Which will give the most appropriate understanding? Which will maintain clarity and simplicity and yet be aesthetically pleasing within the final product?

And then there is the unexpected connection. What about an exploded diagram of an organisation instead of an organisation chart? Why not a recipe card for a manufacturing process? What about a map of your brainstorming session (actually, that's a technique called 'mindmapping' by Tony Buzan)?

Graphs are one of the most misused and misunderstood communication techniques. They tend to be used to hide information rather than to clarify it. They can instantly convey a message, but are so easily manipulated that the message conveyed can be quite erroneous. However, graphs and charts in the right hands are a technique for making the complex clear. Graphs should contain accurate information and compare relevant and appropriate data. If you need to prepare a graph, find out what is supposed to be understood after reading the graph. Most graphs start as tables of numbers with multiple columns of statistical information. You may be able to delete whole columns from the table if you know the intention of the author in providing a graph. This will simplify and amplify the graph's message. The audience needs to be able to see accurately in only a glance what the graph is communicating. For example, we do not read area accurately unless it is in rectangles or squares that relate to each other.

A graphing convention that confuses information, despite being a convenient technique for graph drawing purposes, is the use of exponential axes. When you are comparing amounts that are very small with amounts that are very large – as in 'exponential growth' – it is convenient

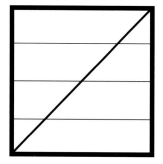

A standard line graph

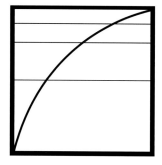

A distorted graph
showing the same information using an exponential scale

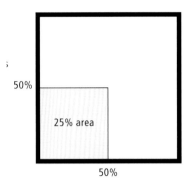

Optical and actual area
It is difficult to read comparative area in graphing. It is easier to read the dimensional variation than the mass variation.

to show this in a sliding scale where the axis divisions get smaller as they increase.

As readers, we do not dwell on graphing and examine detail, so we assume that the axes are evenly divided. If you have huge numbers to compare with tiny numbers, consider showing this in other ways that will enable people to accurately see the magnitude of the difference.

Think about the impression people reading the graph should gain from a glance. Will they see the contrast more clearly by producing a different style of graph?

If you are producing graphs – usually to convert tables into a form more easy to read – choose the appropriate graphing style for the information. For percentages, consider pie charts. For increasing amounts over time, choose a line chart or bar chart. For showing the connections in a process, consider a flow chart.

Line charts
Line charts show quantities over time. The progress of time is conventionally represented from the past on the left to the present on the right. Line charts can compare two or more lines, but the fewer lines the better.

Colour-coding the lines works. In single-colour reproduction, keying the lines works better than tonal variation in the lines. Combining colour coding and line keying can work, but you may get too many levels of information if you need to resort to that.

It can be helpful to run a series of evenly spaced background lines off the left axis to enable more accurate reading of the graphed values.

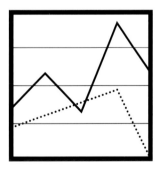

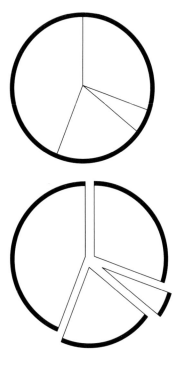

Key lines
(Most important to least important)

1	Bold continuous line
2	Fine continuous line
3	Dashed line
4	Dot-dash dotted line
5	Dotted line

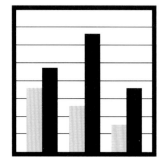

Pie charts

Usually based on figures that have been converted to percentages, a pie chart shows a whole divided into its parts.

In annual reports, there can be a temptation to compare pies of different sizes with the justification: 'This year's pie was smaller than last year's'. It is unwise to compare pies of different sizes, as people do not accurately read the comparative area of circles. In most of those pie charts, the main information to be communicated is based on comparative distribution and, if featured with last year's pie, the difference in distribution, possibly showing a priority shift or even showing maintenance of the status quo.

The comparative size of pies can be compared in a separate figure with a different graphing form, such as a bar chart (where bars show the comparative size variation of the total budget – which could possibly be subdivided by colour coding to show the distribution of the parts).

Consider the size at which the final pie will be reproduced when you decide into how many parts it will be divided. Avoid slices that are too thin – they are difficult to key clearly.

Colour-coding the slices works, or tonally coding the slices in single-colour reproduction. Introducing line and dot patterns into the slices rarely works because the patterns do not have enough area in narrow slices to clearly establish which pattern they are. 'Exploded' pie charts tend to distort sizes and are consequently less accurately read.

Three-dimensional pies tend to confuse information. And combining a pie chart with pieces that are different heights due to a vertical graphing process – effectively bar-charting a pie – is fascinating, but totally confusing for the reader.

Bar charts

Showing comparisons of quantities, bar charts have a high recognition of actual figures – particularly if a few well-chosen rules establish some standard divisions of the numerical axis.

Sometimes it is desirable to read the exact figures, in which case, each bar is labelled, either centred inside the bar at its top, or in the space directly above the bar centred on the width of the bar.

Subdividing a bar into its component parts can work, but can also become confusing. It might show the variation in priorities in funding between different years, but will need some explanation or discussion in the text because the reader will not always accurately read the information.

Colour coding and tonal coding of bars works.

Avoid three-dimensional bar charts, because accurate readability of the actual figures is lost, which is one of the bar chart's strengths.

Variations of bar charts, such as horizontal bar charts and building the height or length of the bar with a pictogram that represents what the bar is graphing, provide opportunities for increasing the visual attraction of the bar chart. For example, when comparing male and female participation rates in sports, you could prepare a horizontal bar chart that moves out from the centre labels with males moving numerically to the left and females moving to the right. This would demonstrate any imbalance visually.

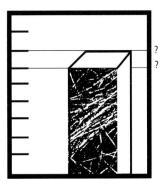

3-D confusion
where your reader is unsure which line gives the correct figure

3-D graphs

In all graphing styles, it is best to avoid three dimensions. The third dimension often only confuses the information. A graph is produced to clarify or put figures into perspective, to give an idea of trends. Bevelled edges and shadows are about as adventurous and intrusive as the third dimension needs to get.

Flow charts and process diagrams

Flow charts show a process in sequence and can be very effective. They can incorporate optional paths and often use straightforward graphic symbols like arrows to propel the reader accurately. Used in manuals and handbooks, they are often more easy to comprehend than narrative text or numbered sequences in text. They do not need to use the original flow-charting coded shapes of diamonds signifying a choice between optional paths, rectangles for answering statements, and circles for completion. They do generally incorporate connecting lines, numbering, arrows and colour coding as required.

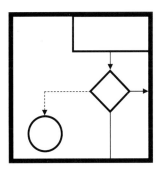

Flow charts are used in the planning of multimedia and use icons and shapes to indicate which media is used in which page in the program. Site plans for websites are also often based on the principles of flow charts.

Often it is advisable to summarise complex processes into a process diagram that introduces the detailed description. In that way, readers have a useful overview of the process rather than trying to comprehend the complexities of the process from text description alone. It is also easier to recall.

Organisation charts and tree diagrams
Hierarchy and connections, lines of authority and areas of responsibility are often shown in organisation charts. They are often based on a simplified flow-chart style. Authority is generally depicted from highest authority at the top to least authority at the bottom.

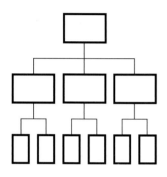

Another option which can be successful – particularly with layered captions, that may indicate a division title, a name, a position title for each person on the chart – is to make the authority move from the highest authority at the left to least authority on the right. This can accommodate alignment of divisions and simplify the fitting of all the people onto the chart when the lower authority levels kick in.

Often, designers will centre the text contained within the blocks of the chart, but there can be problems where there are disproportionate amounts of information in blocks at the same levels of hierarchy, e.g. where you need to accommodate 'Human resource development' and 'Operations'. Always design the block based on the longest heading, but also consider how the shortest heading will look. Will you vertically centre each heading in its box or will you align all top lines? Vertical centring will often make each box look better, but alignment of the lines usually makes the chart as a whole look better.

You might try a variation where, using connecting rules and arrows only, you connect type in columns, avoiding the need to plan the blocks.

In photographic organisation charts, which are increasingly popular, try to keep the scale of all the heads the same and the background colour even. This is easy if all the people portrayed are photographed on the same day, by the same photographer, against the same background, from the same distance. But if you are dealing with photographs supplied by individuals, try to make the distance from the left of the left eye to the right of the right eye the same when scaling all the photographs.

Similar diagrams illustrate genealogical relationships and are referred to as tree diagrams (as in 'family tree'). Though for ease of presentation, they will often be chronological from left to right and continue over many pages.

Sequence diagrams and timelines

Staged sequences can describe the evolution of the world or the creation of a publication or how your client's new product will get to market. Using a numbered sequence of pictures or pictograms that describe each step in the process, a visual representation of the process can clarify a task for a team, educate a novice in the area, or introduce a new skill in a logical manner. The sequence will often have a series of descriptive captions below each of the pictures.

The captioning might also have time frames allocated. Time can be represented by a clock face or a digital clock readout (in the case of, say, a recipe) or by a calendar or seasonal reference for longer processes.

On a larger scale, time can be indicated by decades or centuries in a timeline that can be illustrated or have text descriptions or both.

Sequence diagrams are used in project management. The critical path method is widely used. Time progresses from the left, where a project starts, to the right, where a project ends. Horizontal bars represent each of the stages and can be layered to show concurrent activities.

The program evaluation review technique (PERT) diagram is similar in principle but uses numerically staged events and links them with arrows, indicating where two processes need to culminate before another can begin.

Exploded diagrams, cutaways or cross-sections

Assembly instructions often 'explode' the parts being assembled and show how they connect and interconnect with arrows. The assembly is often numbered in sequence as well. The illustration is often a realistic uncluttered line drawing in either perspective or axonometric projection.

This style of diagram is used to show the floor plans of multilevel buildings and even website plans, as well as its more familiar role in model aeroplane construction.

Sometimes a similar diagramming style is used to show how everything fits together by illustrating a slice through an object.

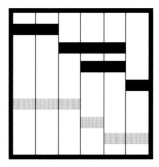

DOING IT SMARTER
Animating or staging diagrams, graphs and charts
In websites, television and multimedia, diagrams, graphs and charts need to move. In bar charts, the bars can grow; in line graphs, the line can travel its course; pie charts can spin. But diagrams and processes often need more attention. The chart will have been broken into stages or sections or modules, so focus on building each module and then integrating in the full chart. In this way, you might have a simple structure that takes you to a further level of detail when you click on an element. Readers can create their own path through the information, much like they do with a site.

Don't forget to use the animation techniques and 2-D movement techniques to help the diagram maintain attention on-screen. You might develop a character that will guide the reader through the information. You might incorporate sounds and video of the process. With virtual reality (VR), readers can be walked through a museum or trade show on-screen without having to read a map in the traditional manner.

READ MORE ABOUT IT

Nigel Holmes, *Designer's guide to creating charts and diagrams*, Watson-Guptill, New York, 1991, ISBN 0 8230 1338 3.

Peter Wildbur, *Information graphics: A survey of typographic, diagrammatic and cartographic communication*, Trefoil Publications, London, 1989, ISBN 0 86294 110 5.

Trevor Bounford, *Digital diagrams: Effective design and presentation of statistical information*, Cassell & Co., London, 2001, ISBN 0304 354074.

Walter Herdeg (ed.), *Graphis diagrams: The graphic visualisation of abstract data*, 4th edn, Graphis Press Corporation, Zurich, 1981, ISBN 3 85709 410 9.

Peter Wildbur & Michael Burke, *Information graphics: Innovative solutions in contemporary design*, Thames & Hudson, London, 1998, ISBN 0 500 01872 3.

Paul Mijksenaar & Piet Westendorp, *Open here: The art of instructional design*, Thames & Hudson, London, 1999, ISBN 0 500 28170 X.

Molly W Joss, *Looking good in presentations*, 3rd edn, Coriolis, Scottsdale, Arizona, 1999, ISBN 1 56604 854 0.

Tim Harrower, *The newspaper designer's handbook*, 4th edn, McGraw-Hill, Blacklick, Ohio, 1998, ISBN 0 697 32720 5.

Harry Mills, *Artful persuasion: How to command attention, change minds and influence people*, MG Press, Sumner Park, Queensland, 1999, ISBN 0 908722 91 5.

Contrast

Contrast can be the most powerful technique used in a layout, particularly contrasting:

- scale (size variation)
- tone (dark against light) and/or colour
- texture.

Contrast is an overriding design element. So much of the success of a layout is to do with effective deployment of contrasts, such as using contrasting typefaces, images and groupings of elements. This is one of the most useful design techniques.

Contrasting scale

A layout with two elements is often made more dynamic by altering their scale (or their size relationship).

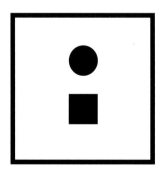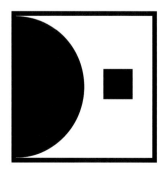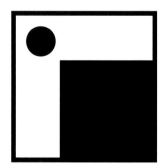

Scale

The interaction of shapes with one another can be dynamic if you contrast the size of various elements. This is the basis of the design principle called 'scale'. The scaling of elements can have a distinct effect on your message.

Contrasting scale is the single most useful technique for improving a layout that is not working. Making one element larger and reducing the other elements to subservient roles will always help a boring layout by adding implied dimensionality.

Tone

Light or dark. Positive or negative. White or black. In black and white (or any other single-colour work – the black is a single colour printed on a white paper), you always have three colour options: the colour of the paper (white); the colour of the ink (black) and tones of the ink colour (greys) created by reducing the solid colour to a halftone or stipple.

To create an interesting tonal layout, identify the tonal average of your photos and text blocks. You do this naturally when you are deciding to reverse a headline or caption out of a photo – or whether you'll just overprint the image. If you can reverse out comfortably, it is a dark photograph; if you will need to overprint, it is a light photograph.

Boring layouts are layouts where everything reduces to a grey soup. You need the interplay of dark areas and light areas to interest the eye. Illustrations and photographs will reduce to an average tonality. Night shots usually have an overall dark tone. Shots of the Sydney Opera House at midday usually have an overall light tone.

But look at an alpine tourist brochure. The snow and sky will probably reduce to light, but the forests will usually reduce to very dark. With such well-defined contrasts in a single photograph, consider the picture area not as a rectangle filled with a mid-grey (an average of those two areas) but as an abstract pattern of light and dark. When you crop the photo, decide how the light and dark areas of the illustration will work in your layout. Do the lights and darks set up directions within the illustration? Can you use the directions they set up to lead to another layout element?

'Design is largely an exercise in creating or suggesting contrasts, which are used to define hierarchy, manipulate certain widely understood relationships, and exploit context to enhance or redefine those relationships … all in an effort to convey meaning. Contrast is important because the meaningful essence of any thing is defined by its value, properties, or quality relative to something else.'

Andy Rutledge, 'Contrast and meaning', AListApart.com, 3 May 2007

Andy Rutledge's primary forms of contrast:

Size

Orientation

Shape

Texture

Color

Position

Typecolour

You can alter the tonal value of type (referred to as its 'typecolour') by creating bolder text or using a chunkier typeface, which gives a darker tone to the text block. Usually body text has a light-grey tone. Leading and tracking also affect typecolour. If there is more space between the lines or the letters, more of the background colour can be seen, which, if it is white, makes the text block appear lighter. You can check their tone by squinting at the elements – the famous 'squint test'.

Contrast the tone of text blocks with the tone of other text blocks or illustration areas.

Typecolour also helps define the shape of a text block. Usually text falls into vertical strips – light-grey rectangles. However, when you contour your type around an illustration or centre the text, you are dealing with different light-grey shapes in your layout.

Repetition, pattern and texture

Repetition creates logic within a design. It is the technique behind the principle of consistency in a publication.

You repeat text attributes to enable clear communication or a hierarchy of information. You might prepare your style sheet in order to consistently present particular information in specified type treatments. You can repeat a style or technique of illustration for unity. You might repeat a particular set of colours or specific textures to bring continuity to the job. Sometimes, repetition of line width around headings or as photograph borders is enough to identify that a particular design has come from a particular company. Even repetition of a particular scale relationship between two pictures in each of a series of advertisements can create a recognisable style.

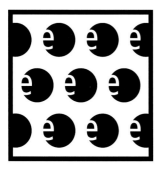

But repetition of a visual element can also create texture and pattern. It can be ordered repetition of recognisable elements creating a pattern or random repetition of an abstract unit creating a texture. In pattern formation, you can create a pattern with photographs, illustration or type. The complexity of the pattern depends on the sequence you develop in order to repeat the original image. You may choose a small element simply duplicated in a line, then duplicate the line and place it underneath, continuing the duplication until the desired pattern exists. You might duplicate and flop or turn the original image to create a more complex sequence.

Direction

Many shapes also imply a direction. For example, triangles tend to point somewhere. Rectangles tend to have a vertical (downward if it's a text block – because we read down) or horizontal (pointing to the right if it's a short text block – because we read across) stress. Only squares and circles are static in themselves.

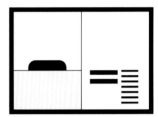

Think of the classic photo of Uluru or Ayers Rock – horizons that seem to stretch forever from the central monolith. This is establishing a really powerful horizontal line within your layout. You can use that line and mimic it with, say, a long thin headline or a number of horizontal layout elements. Alternatively, you can use the contrast of strong vertical elements (text blocks, rules and other illustrations).

Borders and rules

Borders and rules should largely be avoided, as they are text distractions and can break the flow of information. However, they can help establish an old-fashioned feel or help organise material in complex spreads and forms.

There are many decorative and illustrated borders and rules that can recreate the feel of early theatre and 'Wanted' posters, country catalogues and Edwardian concert programs.

When using rules, it is important to remember that they are separation devices, so they will create the impression that material between them is linked. Bold or strong rules are used as section dividers; lighter rules separate with a category. Rules can separate information layers in tables, contents lists, indexes and even in multideck headings, but this separation can be achieved more efficiently with spacing and type attributes.

In lists, rules might be used to separate items, but note that the placement of a bold rule is above a fold heading to visually keep the heading with the text that follows it. When creating the style sheet for this sort of rule, specify the rules as 'rule above' each level of information.

DO	DON'T
Vegetables	**Vegetables**
Asparagus	Asparagus
Broccoli	Broccoli
Carrot	Carrot
Fruit	**Fruit**
Apple	Apple
Banana	Banana
Cherry	Cherry

There is little place for rules in layout – they are more an affectation of styling. Similarly, boxes are more usually achieved with colour change than with borders. Borderless tinted boxes or boxes and photographs with fine (0.25 point) ruled borders are less intrusive.

Space and pace

I'm
the
smallest
type
on
this
page:
bet
I
got
your
attention!

In a layout, balance is determined by placement of design elements within space. Many people are frightened of 'gaping holes' in the layout, but space is an incredibly forgiving design element – it is truly your friend.

If you have been found guilty of leaving space in a layout, you may well have been told that it is 'wasted'. It rarely is. Space is a dynamic layout element. It can guide the reader's eye through a page. Space is essential for accentuating the dynamics of scale and contrast, and provides a resting place within a layout. It can provide an area of calm in a dynamic design, which serves to heighten the dynamism, because you create a greater contrast between the busy and the relaxed, the fast and the slow, the loud and the soft.

Space – an area without a picture or text, but occasionally with a background colour or even a faint texture – can 'balance' a difficult design. Space is used to separate levels of information, highlight and support a heading hierarchy, and as rest area for the eyes.

The more space around a heading, the more importance the heading will assume. It is possible to set a heading in type smaller than the text of a story. If the heading is given a large area of space in which to float, it will be read first. You may have seen a 'blank', full-page newspaper advertisement that has only a small text area like a classified ad floating in the centre. Bet you read it!

In publication design, layouts with generous space provide a marked contrast to layouts where the page is filled with text and images.

In website design, to avoid having the reader scrolling through empty layouts, there is a tendency to fill all the screens, but this can have an adverse effect. Readers can become tired of the site and exit prematurely. Build the experience by pacing its delights. Document design is entertainment design – even more so in electronic documents with sound, movement and interactivity.

Predominantly 'white', or empty, layouts contrast well with busy layouts. This contrast – achieved partly through the distribution of space between stories – is one of the determinants of the 'pace' of the document. Pace in documents is best understood using the metaphor of a stage musical. Start with an overture. In a website, this is the splash screen or entry sequence or the home page. In a book it is the cover, endpapers and maybe a frontispiece.

Audience members might read the program before the show starts. In a website, this is the home page, the site plan and the left navigation bar. In print, this is the contents list.

Then the show starts. It contains a series of big production numbers, separated by smaller numbers, ballads, duets and dialogue scenes that bring a rhythmic structure to the whole. The website, then, has major sections, multimedia-heavy scenes and text-only documents, small specialist sections and brief updates; video, sound, animation, text and graphics. The book has colour sections, heavily illustrated parts and sparsely illustrated parts, appendixes and even inserts; text, images and graphics.

There could be an intermission. In a website, this might be a community forum or blog. In a book, this might be a part title, chapter or part summaries, or a full-bleed, double-page photo.

At the end of the show, there are the curtain calls, leaving the theatre and buying the souvenir T-shirt. In a website, there is the exit sequence, the credits and copyright information, the visitor registration form and the online shop. In a book, there is the conclusion, the colophon that describes the production technicalities, the verso title and acknowledgments that list the production personnel, and sometimes an order form or registration card for catalogues from the publisher in the same subject area.

In theatre, comedy is placed to heighten – or lighten – tragedy. The juxtaposition of contrasting elements is equally effective as an entertainer or 'pacer' in document design, too. In magazines, the 'songs, scenes and choruses' are replaced with regular columns, news items and feature articles respectively; articles can be light or serious, text or picture spreads. Feature articles often use different layout devices to achieve an identity of their own, and the deployment of space is one of those devices.

'White space, sometimes referred to as negative space, is the conspicuously open space found between other design elements or objects within the borders of an ad. It is typically used to convey elegance, power, leadership, honesty, trustworthiness, a modern nature, and a refined taste associated with the upper social strata ... In short, by considering the "nothing" of white space, we actually see a lot ... we see why "nothing" now means "something".'

John W Pracejus, G Douglas Olsen and Thomas C O'Quinn, 'How nothing became something: White space, rhetoric, history, and meaning', *Journal of Consumer Research*, vol. 33, June 2006

'Build a book like a body moving in space and time, like a dynamic relief in which every page is a surface carrying shapes, and every turn of a page a new crossing to a new stage of a single structure.'

El Lissitsky, quoted by Lewis Blackwell in *20th Century Type: Remix*

According to Karel van der Waarde in *Visual Information for Everyday Use*, readers assume relationships between different graphic components based on their:

- □ Proximity
  - – Physical proximity implies an informational connection.
  - – Physical separation implies an informational separation.
- □ Similarity
  - – Similarity implies a functional connection.
  - – Difference implies a functional differentiation.
- □ Prominence
  - – Prominence differences imply hierarchical (status) differences.
- □ Sequence
  - – The visual sequence implies the sequence of information.

In some publications, margins and chapter breaks are the only rest area. In novels, this is fine. In newspapers, it is probably fine. In magazines, it is unwise. Rest areas, as they are on highways, exist for a reason. If you are tired – and you can be visually tired – you should stop and rest. Advertisers and publishers do not want you to close the magazine; they want you to continue on your journey – so rest areas should be provided. Some articles provide this service. Sometimes, full-page or double-spread, full-bleed pictures can do it. Sometimes, just having a bit of extra space in a layout is enough.

If in doubt, rely on space – large, empty, clean space. It can bind disparate elements together and help stylistically different combinations sit comfortably within reach of each other. Space also contrasts texturally and tonally with the elements of your layout because it is usually white and gives your layout the highlight area for that important tonal range. So do not underestimate the importance of some 'empty' areas in a layout.

Knowing when to place a picture and a pull-quote or how and when to present tabular information can make a difference between losing a reader and retaining them. You need to consider not only the author's intent but the reader's motivation for reading.

You are essentially building in ways to keep invigorating your reader:

- give them moments to pause (usually white space or pictures)
- give them moments of delight or attraction (usually images, coloured headings or patterns of information)
- give them tempting chunks of information (spacing can make it look easier to read another paragraph)
- give them interruptions to the pattern (a video or sound file maybe; or a picture that takes a full double-page spread or an interactive component like a self-test).

Much of this is provided by the 'natural rhythm' of the content. You just need to analyse the content to discover it. You are looking for patterns:

- Which heading level occurs the most?
- Which occurs the least?
- Are there heading levels that always appear together?
- What is the longest and shortest heading in each level?
- What are the best references for illustrating?

- What concepts could do with a diagram or chart to help the reader?
- Can you think of an image for each major heading?

Knowing all these answers allows you to cluster styles to interrupt the text in a visual rhythm of fonts, sizes, alignments, colours and images that follows the natural rhythm of the content.

Traditional and modern layouts

Most text designs will fall into either the traditional or modern categories. Traditional layouts can be traced back to the Italian Renaissance, and even farther back to hand-prepared illuminated manuscripts – before movable type. For 'traditional', read 'classical', as it is the style based on Italian book and type design from the 1600s. It has been the dominant styling used for books since and can lend an old-world atmosphere to advertising and posters.

'Modern' in this sense is not 'fashionable', 'trendy' or even 'contemporary', but a specific styling from the mid-20th century. Greatly influenced by the Russian Constructivist and the Dutch *De Stijl* designers early in the century, Bauhaus teachers in Germany taught it, and it was refined by the Swiss. It became the dominant international corporate style.

Both styles are used for annual reports because they give particular visual clues to how an organisation wishes to be seen.

The modern style says an organisation is forward thinking, at the cutting edge, a bit of a risk-taker, even casual or brash. But it can sometimes be stark and harsh. Most manuals, magazines and reports, all forms, and nearly all websites and corporate identity programs are based on the modern format.

The traditional style, by contrast, implies the organisation has roots and a solid foundation, it values where it has been and can be trusted and respected. Be careful to avoid being seen as pompous or, worse, backward. Most books, some manuals and nearly all wedding invitations are based on the traditional format.

Although it seems bizarre to say designs fall into these two categories, you will find that they are fairly easy to spot once you know the styles. But to create a uniquely flavoured design, substitute ingredients: mix in serifs or scripts

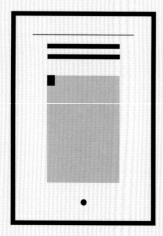

Traditional layout

Create substantial margins that relate to each other, from smallest to largest: the top, the inside, the outside and the bottom margin. The margins should look generous. The page number should be centred on the text block and roughly central in the bottom margin.

Choose a good, strong serif typeface (Bembo, Garamond, Times, Baskerville, Palatino or another classic font), and prepare your text with italics for stress when necessary. Indent paragraphs by about 5 mm, with no extra space between them.

Justify the type and specify generous leading.

Loose-tracked capitals and small capitals can be used for centred headings.

Initial drop capitals on chapter opening pages and printer's flowers or dingbats centred at the end of the chapter will add a traditional touch. A few fine line rules and lots of capital letters for headings and first lines will also help. If you can get ligatured character pairs and swash characters, which are sometimes available in a 'specialist' set, it will add to the traditional detailing.

Place the text in your page layout to fill each page to a constant page depth – the bottom line as defined by your bottom margin. Put some extra space around your headings. Remember that more space above a heading than below it will keep the heading with its text.

Images, in the classic form, are on separate pages with centred captions in tracked small capitals below the image. You can, of course, vary this – and hang small pictures in the centre of the text block or maybe the top left corner, ensuring that the text wraps but is still justified.

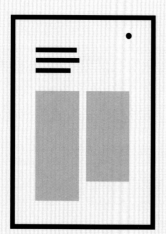

Modern layout

Create light margins, keeping the top margin and side margins much the same. The bottom margin should be slightly larger. Then divide the text block into two or three even columns, each separated by a narrow gutter.

Prepare your text in a sans serif typeface with an extensive font family (Helvetica, Univers, Frutiger, Gill Sans or Futura will have the range of light, medium, bold, extrabold and italics that are required). Type should be formatted flush left unjustified, avoiding hyphenation as far as possible, and leaded generously to separate the sans serif lines for easy readability.

Use blocked paragraphs – not indented – and separate them with half to one line space. (This is now usually reinterpreted to be 5 mm indented paragraphs with no indent in the first line after a heading.)

Be creative with your headings, carefully avoiding the use of capitals, but being generous with the use of different point sizes and weights. Headings often hang from the top margin line and are separated from the text by a space, which creates a text drop line further down the page. The headings will mostly be bolder than the text and italics are usually avoided, except for stress within text. Sometimes you might use the occasional line rule or bar in association with a heading, often taking it to optical column measure and placing it above the heading.

Fill each column comfortably to a logical paragraph break, but don't fill to the bottom, just let the text hang. Images should also hang from the text drop line. Images will probably conform to one- or two-column standard scalings and might be positioned according to a strict grid for placement. Captions are often in italics the same size and leading as the text.

where sans serifs are specified; or add more line rules and typefaces to spice up the layout; use contemporary typefaces in traditional layouts; use old typefaces in modern layouts.

Contemporary designers do not follow these styles as rigid rules, more as guides. They usually create a distinct hybrid. You usually want classic but not dated; contemporary but not fashionable.

READ MORE ABOUT IT
Suzanne West, *Working with style*, Watson-Guptill Publications, New York, 1990, ISBN 0 8230 5872 7.

In Jan Tschichold's first manifesto in *Kulturschau*, Heft 4, Spring 1925, he gives his first description of *Die neue typographie*:

- Typography, in the sense of new design, is construction with the most suitable materials
    1   in the simplest form
    2   with the minimum means
- according to the function of the kind of communication to be achieved.
- The exclusive materials of New Typography are those given by the task: the letters and rules in the typecase. Ornament of even the simplest form (shaded rules!) is superfluous, impermissible.
- The simplest and therefore only persuasive form of European script is the block (sanserif) type.
- The strongest differentiation can be formed through the use of bold and light weights and different type-sizes.

    Translation in Christopher Burke's *Active Literature: Jan Tschichold and New Typography*, Hyphen Press, London, 2007

Four ways to save a failing design

There are times when your design – like your hair – simply looks dull, boring and lifeless. On such design bad-hair-days, don't throw out all that work and start again. Do a bit of judicious design teasing and moussing. Look at the design with a new set of eyes. Imagine someone else did the design and you have the job of fixing it up.

There are four good techniques for fixing an ailing design, which are relatively quick and work wonders. But note that if you are working on a publication or website and it's looking boring, you don't have to enliven every page – occasional breaks are sufficient. Every page does not have to be dynamic and new.

Increase tonal contrast

A design that looks grey can be very boring. Text blocks reduce to grey tone if you squint at them. The 'squint test' is the clincher – if it is boring to squint at, then it's boring to look at. What the squint test shows you is the interaction of the tones in the layout.

Fix your tonal contrast. Get some dark and light areas happening in that grey base. For dark, choose a darker typeface for some headings (such as an extrabold). Perhaps use a reverse – where the type is white on a black block. Use a dark stripe somewhere (off the side of the page or down the side of photographs). Then add some light – some large white type can be reversed out of a photograph, or a logo could be reversed out of a dark stripe, or simply keep a larger area of white space below the main heading or create bigger margins or gutters.

Redistribute space

Many people are scared of leaving a blank area in a design, fearing that it makes them look inept because they couldn't fill the page neatly and their layout looks like something's missing. On the contrary – this area is called *space* or *white space* (even if it's black) and can have a wonderful effect on the liveliness and vibrancy of a layout, partly because space has the effect of increasing the tonal variety, but also because it becomes a layout element that interacts with picture blocks and text blocks. So manipulate space.

Space can be added to a margin to increase the layout's feeling of space. This can be done by hanging type and pictures from an invisible line across the top part of the page and letting the columns fall to a natural length, leaving the space at the foot of the page. Even in a web page where you don't want to increase the scrolling, you can have a main column that is pretty full and side columns which have text hanging short, in order to get some of this precious space into your layout without sacrificing the usability.

If a printed page is full and it looks like there is no space to redistribute, try altering the setting from justified to unjustified – it will immediately open up the page. Also, you can reduce the size of the pictures to get some space. You can reduce a heading size but keep the space around it the same, giving the illusion of more space.

Alter scale relationships

One of the best fixes is to alter scale (the size relationships within the layout). Basically, the contrast of little with big is dynamic and interesting.

If there are three pictures in a layout, make one picture big and the others very little. Not just little – very little. The one that is big might be so big that it fills the layout, forcing you to place the little ones somewhere on top of it.

Don't forget that type can work that way, too. What about an enormous title that has little tiny pictures floating in it? What about large body copy (the main body of text) with a tiny heading? (It can work, but it's tricky.)

Repeat something

You can enliven a layout simply by repeating some of its existing elements – logos, images, even type. When you repeat them, you can create a pattern. Or you can alter their sizes and use scale variation. This works well with logos and photographs, particularly if you use a technique called ghosting where you fade the logo or image until it's like a shadow. It can then float behind the text or the solid version of itself. This effect of different layers gives dimension to the design, which is why it works as a fix. You need to be careful that you maintain easy readability of any text that runs over the ghosted image by retaining sufficient contrast.

Typography

Handling type is the special skill of the typographer. It is sensitivity to the forms of the alphabet and numerals that other mortals use carelessly every day in handwritten memos and even in email. It is a tradition that goes back to the scribes who were the official carers for our fledgling letterforms.

The difference between a good piece of design and a great one is often the level of expertise in the selection and use of type. Type must be appropriate to its subject, its message and the illustrations that surround it – and the reader's experience of type.

Typefaces can have many associations for a reader. There are typefaces we read as a child; those that recall a bygone era; those that feel traditional and others that feel modern, type that says, 'This is news'; type that is romantic; faces that are quirky and others that are serious. The 'personality' of a typeface can be related to historical or emotional associations, or simply a reflection of our experience of type.

One of the exciting things about the personal computer and desktop publishing (DTP) is the discovery that there is a whole new world of 'typography' out there – something experienced from our earliest years, so often taken for granted, but also misunderstood. Although it is exciting, it is also a concern because we soon find that using type is not as easy or as intuitive as we expect.

Typing for publication has always had more refinements than simply keying in text, because typeface designers had many more characters available to them in a type case or on a computer than would fit on the typewriter keyboard.

As a result, people are much more critical of draft text that is in typography. If a politician handwrote, or even typed in the Courier typeface, a letter that had a spelling error, no one would mind. In Times Roman, that same mistake simply confirms our suspicions and demonstrates

'Type is about much more than questions of legibility or readability. Fashions and technological change are just part of the backdrop. What makes typography fascinating, and an essential enquiry for anybody involved in design, is that this activity is a manifestation of our search for greater efficiency and greater power in the written word. It reveals personalities, politics, and economic factors, along with advances in science. It is a celebration of humanity, and a vital and subtle indicator of values.'

Lewis Blackwell in *20th Century Type: Remix*

Mechanical spacing & constant character width

Typewriting
Mechanical spacing and constant character width are aspects of typewriter fonts like Courier.

DOING IT SMARTER
Spell-checks and proofreading
Use spell-checks regularly, particularly as you are typing and before you transfer the text file into a page layout program. But don't forget to fully proofread the final text. A spell-check is better than nothing, but it is not as accurate as a good proofread.

DOING IT FASTER
Keyboard shortcuts
Use as many keyboard (and extended keyboard) shortcuts as you can remember. Selecting from a menu every time is time-consuming. Using rulers and toolboxes also helps, but the keyboard shortcuts really streamline document production.

the sender's incompetence. And if they're this incompetent just getting a letter right, how much more incompetence is hidden from our view? Don't throw away that Courier font just yet – it can save you.

If the text has the appearance of a published document, it should exhibit all the other hallmarks of typesetting. If it doesn't, readers may perceive it as unprofessional and sloppy. There are a number of areas where you can establish a professional styling within text:

- punctuation styling is different between typing and typesetting
- italics are used for stress within text instead of underlining
- heading handling is different because with typesetting and DTP there are options which were not available in typing
- by using columns, rules, colour, boxes, variable spacing and other graphic elements.

With the vast capabilities many word-processing, DTP and page layout programs contain, many people are tempted to use a number of techniques that were previously used sparingly. Now it is so easy to click on the menu or key in the command that some users are no longer considering the wisdom of using techniques such as drop-shadows, type set around a circle, outlined type, contoured text (or wrapping text), boxed text and even justification.

All these capabilities are needed on occasion, but not as regularly as they are being used. It is just like the smorgasbord of typefaces that are available which are there to give variety and flexibility to typography. They were never intended to be used in the same document at the same time.

READ MORE ABOUT IT
Robin Williams, *The Mac is not a typewriter*, Peachpit Press, Berkeley, 1990, ISBN 0 938151 31 2.
Robin Williams, *Beyond the Mac is not a typewriter*, Peachpit Press, Berkeley, 1996, ISBN 1 201 88598 0.
Erik Spiekermann & EM Ginger, *Stop stealing sheep: And find out how type works*, Adobe Press, Mountain View, California, 1993, ISBN 0 672 48543 5.
Karen A Schriver, *Dynamics in document design: Creating text for readers*, John Wiley & Sons, New York, 1997, ISBN 0471-30636-3.
Lakshmi Bhaskaran, *Size matters: Effective graphic design for large amounts of information*, RotoVision SA, Mies, Switzerland, 2004, ISBN 2-88046-705-5.
Andreu Balius, *Type at work: The use of type in editorial design*, BIS Publishers, Amsterdam, 2003, ISBN 90-6369-041-X.

Jeff Bellantoni & Matt Woolman, *Type in motion: Innovations in digital graphics*, Thames & Hudson, London, 1999, ISBN 0 500 01914 2.

Stefan Rögener, Albert-Jan Pool, Ursula Packhäuser & EM Ginger (eds), *Branding with type: How type sells*, Adobe Press, Mountain View, California, 1995, ISBN 1 56830 248 7.

John Miles, *Design for desktop publishing: A guide to layout and typography on the personal computer*, Imprint Publishers, Sydney, 1987, ISBN 1 875132 00 7.

Jan V White, *Graphic design for the electronic age: The manual for traditional and desktop publishing*, Xerox Press, Watson-Guptill Publications, New York, 1988, ISBN 0 8230 2122 X.

Jill Yelland, *Typo survival kit: For all type emergencies*, 2nd edn, Press for Success, Perth, 2000, ISBN 0 646 28070 8.

Kate Clair, *A typographic workbook: A primer to history, techniques, and artistry*, John Wiley & Sons, New York, 1999, ISBN 0 471 29237 0.

Robin Williams, *The non-designer's type book: Insights and techniques for creating professional-level type*, Peachpit Press, Berkeley, 1998, ISBN 0 201 35367 9.

Considering the manuscript

How will the document be used?

Will it be scanned or read continuously? Is the reader tired or alert, relaxed or stressed?

Does the reader want to read it?

Is the reader motivated or reluctant?

Is it information?

Are there enough headings to indicate specific areas of interest?

Is it instruction?

Can it be read in order and followed clearly? Will it be translated into multiple languages? Is there enough room for the increased text area of many other languages? What production requirements does its use imply? (For example, you may need a printed surface that can be wiped clean in a kitchen or a garage.)

Is it reference material?

Are specific areas of interest clearly labelled and logically ordered?

Is it entertainment?

Will the reader be unnecessarily distracted from a sustained read?

Is it familiar?

Has it a recognisable form to streamline usability like that of a dictionary, a TV guide or a novel?

How many types of headings are there?

Are there enough subheadings for readers to find what they need when skimming? What is the longest and shortest of each heading level? How many headings appear together, without text between them? Does that always happen or only sometimes?

Does the text have references, links or footnotes?

Has information that will not interest all readers been 'contained' elsewhere? Will there be a single area for endnotes or will they appear at the end of sections?

What parts of the text could be presented differently?

Where are there references to nouns and procedures that might benefit from photographs, symbols or illustrations? Where are there complex paragraphs explaining sets of numbers that might benefit from being turned into graphs or tables? Does the content tell a story or contain dialogue or direct quotes from people that could benefit from sound files or video?

Type categories

It helps to have an appropriate language to talk about type. Type falls into five main categories: serif type, sans serif type, scripts, specialty or display typefaces, and symbol or picture fonts.

READ MORE ABOUT IT

Christopher Perfect, *The complete typographer: A manual for designing with type*, Quarto Publishing, London, 1992, ISBN 0 316 90326 4.

Gordon Rookledge & Christopher Perfect, *Rookledge's international typefinder: The essential handbook of typeface recognition and selection*, Laurence King Publishing, London, 2004, ISBN 978 1 85669 406 3.

Timothy Samara, *Type style finder: The busy designer's guide to choosing type*, Rockport Publishers, Gloucester, Mass., 2006, ISBN 978-1-59253-190-5.

Philip B Meggs & Roy McKelvey, *Revival of the fittest: Digital versions of classic typefaces*, RC Publications, New York, 2000, ISBN 1 883915 08 2.

Robin Dodd, *From Gutenberg to open type: An illustrated history of type from the earliest letterforms to the latest digital fonts*, Ilex, Cambridge, UK, 2006, ISBN 1-904705-77-4.

Ken Garland, *Illustrated graphics glossary: Of terms used in printing, publishing, photography and other fields of interest to graphic designers, their clients and their suppliers*, Barrie & Jenkins, London, 1980, ISBN 0 09 141511 X.

Stanley Morison, *A tally of types*, Cambridge University Press, Cambridge, 1973, ISBN 0 521 20043 1.

Eric Gill, *An essay on typography*, 5th edn, Lund Humphries, London, 1988, ISBN 085331 509 4.

Christopher Burke, *Active literature: Jan Tschichold and new typography*, Hyphen Press, London, 2007, ISBN 978-0-907259-32-9.

Jan Tschichold (trans. Ruari McLean), *The new typography: The first English translation of the revolutionary 1928 document*, University of California Press, Los Angeles, 1998, ISBN 0 520 07147 6.

Alexander Lawson, *Anatomy of a typeface*, Hamish Hamilton, London, 1990, ISBN 0 241 13267 3.

Hermann Zapf, *About alphabets: Some marginal notes on type design*, The MIT Press, Cambridge, Mass., 1970, ISBN 0 262 24010 6.

Allan Haley, *Alphabet: The history, evolution and design of the letters we use today*, Thames & Hudson, London, 1995, ISBN 0 500 27835 0.

Allan Haley, *Typographic milestones*, Van Nostrand Reinhold, New York, 1992, ISBN 0 442 23642 5.

Friedrich Friedl, Nicolaus Ott & Bernard Stein, *Typography: When, who, how*, Könemann Verlagsgesellschaft mbH, Cologne, 1998, ISBN 3 89508 473 5.

Allan Haley, *Type: Hot designers make cool fonts*, Rockport, Gloucester, Mass., 1998, ISBN 1 56496 317 9.

Leslie Cabarga, *The logo, font and lettering bible*, North Light Books, Cincinnati, 2004, ISBN 978-1581804362.

Sebastian Carter, *Twentieth century type designers*, Trefoil, London, 1987, ISBN 0 86294 076 1.

Lewis Blackwell, *20th century type: Remix*, Laurence King Publishing, London, 1998, ISBN 1 85669 116 0.

Spencer Drate & Jütka Salavetz, *Extreme fonts: Digital faces of the future*, Madison Square Press, New York, 1999, ISBN 0 942604 74 1.

Rob Carter, *American typography today*, Van Nostrand Reinhold, New York, 1989, ISBN 0 442 22106 1.

Steven Heller & Louise Fili, *Typology: Type design from the Victorian era to the digital age*, Chronicle Books, San Francisco, 1999, ISBN 0 8118 2308 3.

Wolfgang Weingart, *My way to typography: Retrospective in ten sections*, Lars Müller Publishers, Baden, 2000, ISBN 3 907044 86 X.

Serif typefaces

Serif type has 'little feet', like the type you're reading at the moment. If you were drawing the letters by hand, the individual movements of a calligraphy pen that make up a letterform are called strokes. Serifs are the flicks – mostly small horizontal strokes – at the start or the end of each character stroke.

Serif type is believed to be the most readable type for continuous text, which is why many magazines, books and newspapers use serif type for body copy. For extended reading, it is more comfortable, which explains why fiction paperbacks – motivated, narrative reading with few headings or other interruptions – are always in a serif typeface.

Serif typefaces are often associated with tradition and can lend an air of authority to text. Many of the 'big name' classical serifs like Bembo, Times, Baskerville and Garamond have been around for centuries and immediately conjure up a feeling of tradition, which is exactly what many companies want to project, particularly at annual report time in a recession.

Serif types usually have strokes of different widths. Look at a capital A – the left stroke is thin, the right stroke is thick and the crossbar is thin. This is because typeface designs were based on the writing of scribes which was produced with nibbed pens.

The problem with variable stroke thickness is that it can make small type and reversed type a problem. The fine lines might drop away when they are printed. Avoid using serif typefaces on gloss paper, in reverse, or at very small sizes because their serifs and thin strokes can disappear.

Note: Slab serif typefaces can usually be used in a manner similar to the use of sans serif typefaces, because of their apparently even stroke thickness – even their serifs are as thick as the strokes.

Variable stroke thickness

Times new roman

Original fonts

Why spend money on original fonts? Why not use the many lookalike font clones that are available in cheap font sets? This is not font piracy (where you copy a font that someone else has paid for). This is where a new font is released and becomes so popular that other font companies create lookalike fonts in order to keep their customers from changing to a new supplier. But they don't pay the original font designer or buy the original drawings from the original font producer – they redraw their own version. It happened with Helvetica, which is available as Megaron, Helvetia and Geneva. Arial is based on it as well. It happened with Palatino, which is available as Palatio, Palladium and Andover.

It's happening still, although there is a new twist in the legal definition. In a 1998 US case, it was upheld that although the designer still can't copyright the font design itself, the software program that defines the font can be copyrighted.

But what's wrong with it, aside from dubious ethics and dodgy principles? Why is it worth the money to get the original?

Most designers would acknowledge that the original font contains nuances that most redraw copyists appear to have been unaware of or ignore. These nuances are most often found in optical correction. The designer of a font will often draw a geometrically and measurement-correct letterform only to find through tests and close observation that, when our eyes see that character, we perceive it incorrectly. We may thicken one part of it or see an oval where a circle is desired. Optical correction of a font means that capital letters are different measured heights even though they appear the same height. An *O* or a *W* are actually taller by measuring than an *H*. An *A* is somewhere between the two. This is to

do with the alignment of characters on the baseline where, for example, the points of a *W* actually sit below the line to ensure that the letterform appears to sit comfortably. Similarly, the curve of the *O* sits below the line. The *H*, having no curves or points, sits on the exact baseline.

In font design, there is also optical correction of stroke thicknesses. Particularly in *S*, but also surprisingly in *I*, and any straight strokes, the actual shape of the stroke is full of nuance. Rarely, even in the most deceptively geometrically constructed sans serif font, is there a straight line, due to optical correction. Most straights are, in fact, subtle curves that come in at the waist of the straight stroke and fan out at the top and bottom.

The mistake made by many font redrawers was to trust their eyes!

So you will miss the nuances, but who cares as long as it looks okay? And it probably will look okay at text sizes up to about 12 point. But when won't it look okay?

This is where the digital font revolution has really made an impact. All those original nuances become obvious in enlargement. But so do any of the font redrawers' shortcuts. If you've tried to enlarge a poor font, you will know the problem – it looks ugly, ungainly and lumpy. Points are often not sharp and smooth curves can have an unsightly kink in them.

This is often an indicator that they were scanned and redrawn from a printed character that had gained thickness due to inking in the printing process. It also means that the originally finely tuned contrast between the medium and bold versions of a face can also be lost.

Also font designers often drew slightly different draws of the same weight of a font in different sizes. The smaller a font is reproduced, for example, the comparably thicker thin strokes are needed so they reproduce;

but if they were that thick at large or 'titling' sizes, they'd look too thick and heavy. The inter-character spacing at smaller sizes is defined slightly wider; for larger titling sizes, it will be reduced. (Often with DTP, we don't have these nuances as font companies produce a 'generic' font – which is why it is recommended that you track small type slightly looser.) These finely tuned fonts for different-sized reproduction are called a different 'draw' of the weight.

The other testing that an original font designer will do concerns how particular character pairs set and the overall texture of the new font in text setting. This is all to do with interletter spacing and character kerning.

The redrawer will not have spent the same amount of time as the originator in the detailing of those combinations and the testing of the setting, so often uneven setting results with a redrawn font. This is okay if you are prepared to do the kerning and letterspacing yourself, but how much actually gets done that should?

Originators of a font will also spend more time creating the full font requirements for high-end publishing – they will often create an expert set and sometimes foreign language font sets to match.

Serif typefaces

ABCDE abcdefg 12345

Century schoolbook Morris Fuller Benton 1924

ABCDE abcdefg 12345

Garamond Claude Garamond 1530

ABCDEFGHIJ 12345

Trajan Carol Twombly 1989

ABCDE abcdefg 12345

Baskerville John Baskerville 1754

ABCDE abcdefg 12345

Goudy old style Frederic Goudy 1915

ABCDE abcdefg 12345

Times new roman Stanley Morison 1931

ABCDE abcdefg 12345

Bodoni Giambattista Bodoni 1798

ABCDE abcdefg 12345

Palatino Hermann Zapf 1949
Optional names for *Palatino: Palladium, Elegante, Andover,
Paladio, Patina, Malibu*

ABCDE abcdefgh 12345

Bembo Francesco Griffo 1495

ABCDE abcdefg 12345

Galliard Matthew Carter 1978

ABCDE abcdefg 12345

Cheltenham Bertram Goodhue 1896

ABCDEFGH abcdefgh 12345

Matrix Zuzana Licko 1986

All typeface examples are shown in 18 point.

System or 'default' fonts

It can be useful to have a number of similar fonts when specifying cascading style sheets for website production. You can specify alternative fonts that the style sheet can use if the font you originally designed the site for is unavailable on the user's machine.

These fonts are often called 'system fonts' – that is, most systems will have them installed. The usual set is: Times Roman, Arial, Helvetica, Verdana.

If you don't specify these alternatives, Times New Roman may go to a default font (let's say Courier) instead of Times Roman, for example.

Fonts for different uses

Fonts are devised for all manner of uses. There are fonts designed for maximum readability in signage systems. There are others that maximise the number of letters and numbers in a narrow column and the number of lines in a column for directory listings.

Numerous fonts have been developed specifically for display on-screen or on hand-held devices like mobile phones.

Serifs

Bracketed serif

I

Times new roman

Modern serif

I

Modern no. 20

Slab serif

I

Rockwell

This is Rod.
This is Janette.
See Rod and
Janette run.

Futura

DOING IT SMARTER
Tiny type
Sans serif type remains quite readable
at even 3 or 4 point. You should use
wider letterspacing at such small sizes.

Constant stroke thickness

Transit

Slab serif typefaces

ABCDE abcdefg 12345

Rockwell Inland Typefoundry 1910
Optional names for *Rockwell: Stymie, Memphis, Cairo*

ABCDE abcdef 12345

Clarendon English Fann Street Foundry 1845

ABCDE abcdefgh 12345

Italia Colin Brignall 1975

Sans serif typefaces

'Sans serif' is a French term, which means 'without serif'. Sans serif types used to be called 'grotesques' and that's the way some people prefer to think of them.

Though sans serif type is considered to be less readable than serif type, it is the most legible type. When you learn the alphabet, you are taught sans serif shapes because they are the basic or 'pure' forms of the symbols, and therefore the most legible or easiest to recognise letterforms. You were probably taught to read using sans serif type.

Its greater legibility is one of the reasons that sans serif type is used for headlines, billboard advertising and numberplates, and for signage on highways, at hospitals, in airport terminals and car parks.

However, as typefaces for text setting, they are considered 'modern', like the architecture of Le Corbusier. If you want a futuristic or contemporary look, sans serif type can help. This is probably because the 'big name' sans serifs like Futura, Helvetica and Univers were developed in the mid-20th century and sat comfortably with Art Deco's geometric designs and its development into streamlining and, later, the international style.

Sans serif can look more informal or 'friendly' than serif type, although some perceive the 'clarity' of a geometric sans serif to be 'clinical' or 'distant'.

Sans serif type also has the appearance of constant stroke thickness. If you look at the capital **A**, all strokes appear to be the same width. Because of this, they work at very small sizes and in reverse – good news for people who need to put photographers' credits up the sides of photos, write

Sans serif typefaces

ABCDE abcdefg 12345

Helvetica Max Miedinger 1957
Optional names for *Helvetica: Newton, Triumvirate, Helios, Swiss, Geneva, Megaron, Claro, Vega*

ABCDE abcdefg 12345

Univers Adrian Frutiger 1957

ABCDE abcdefg 12345

Frutiger Adrian Frutiger 1975

ABCDE abcdefgh 12345

Meta Erik Spiekermann 1991

ABCDEF abcdefgh 12345

Gill sans Eric Gill 1929

ABCDE abcdefg 12345

Optima Hermann Zapf 1958
Optional names for *Optima: Chelmsford, Optimist, Musica, Oracle, Zenith*

ABCDEFGHIJ 12345

Lithos Carol Twombly 1989

ABCDE abcdefgh 1234

Franklin Gothic Morris Fuller Benton 1905

ABCDE abcdefg 12345

Friz quadrata Ernst Friz 1965 (a hybrid serif font, used as sans serif)

ABCDE abcdefg 12345

Futura Paul Renner 1927

ABCDE abcdefgh 12345

Template gothic Barry Deck 1990

ABCDEFGHIJKL 12345

Avant garde Herb Lubalin 1970 CAPS ONLY

'Registered trade mark' under a logo, or use other fine print.

They also work more successfully when pixelated for on-screen reproduction, so they are recommended for websites, multimedia and hand-held devices. There have even been fonts developed for such small reproduction like QC Sans.

These bitmap fonts have been designed for hand-held devices and have a larger x-height and larger counters for ease of readability with a slightly condensed form so there can be a bit more space between letters. These requirements are similar to the constraints for typefaces used in printed directories and classified ads.

Serif vs sans serif
Arguments rage about which style of type is superior. Some people like to quote readability tests and all sorts of statistics to back up their claims. But the fault with much of the testing is that it starts from the assumption that serif and sans serif types are interchangeable – that you can set up your type specifications (which include the size of type, the leading and the length of each line) and simply change the typeface and run the test again. But you don't specify a holiday based on your car's limitations, and then change to an airline booking, without altering your schedule and costing.

Each typeface category has tasks it performs well – and there will be some tasks it will not perform well. It is not usually the typeface at fault, but more what the user does with it.

Readers do tend to prefer serif for fiction and sans serif for directions, information and facts.

Scripts

Script typefaces tend to mimic hand-drawn or calligraphic type. The letters are often linked to each other, hence the self-explanatory subdivisions of script called *connecting scripts* and *non-connecting scripts*. There is also a subset called *blackletter* based on Gothic pen letterforms which was the form of the movable type Johannes Gutenberg invented for his Bible published in 1455.

In nearly every case, script typefaces should be used only in lower case with initial capital letters.

A mistake often made with wedding invitations and other traditional uses of script faces is to choose a swirling

Compare a serif typeface with a sans serif
Notice the serifs at the end of the stroke and compare the thickness and stress of the strokes.

So
Times new roman

So
Transit

Script typefaces

ABCDEFG abcdefghi 12345

Zapf chancery Hermann Zapf 1974

ABCDE abcdefgh 12345

Snell roundhand Matthew Carter 1965

ABCDEFG abcdefghij 12345

Kaufmann Max R. Kaufmann 1936

ABCDE abcde 12345

Brush script Robert E. Smith 1942

ABCDE abcdefg 12345

Mistral Roger Excoffon 1955

ABCDE abcdefg 12345

Sassoon primary Rosemary Sassoon 1990

ABC abcde 1234

American uncial Eisner and Flake

ABCDEFGHI abcdefghijklmno 123456

Erikrighthand Erik van Blokland 1991

ABCDEFGH abcdefghijklm 12345

Justlefthand Just van Rossum 1991

Blackletter typefaces

Old English Morris Fuller Benton 1901

Fette fraktur Wagner and Schmidt 1875

Wilhelm Klingspor gotisch Rudolf Koch 1925

copperplate script typeface, which is often difficult to
read. Script typefaces can be used effectively but usually
need to be larger than 14 point and used for titles, and
headings such as 'The Wedding of Jennifer and Matthew',
'The Signing of the Register', 'The Exchange of Rings'. But
when it comes to readability, consider pairing them with a
classical serif which often works well with the traditional
scripts and blackletter fonts associated with weddings.

Contemporary scripts and casual scripts usually work
better with sans serif typefaces.

Specialty and display typefaces

Specialty typefaces can have letterforms that have been
adorned in some way. They are usually relegated to titling
and can lend atmosphere to a piece of text.

Avoid clichéd typeface choices in this category, such as
using letterforms with icicles on them for refrigeration
contractors and flame letterforms for 'red hot' sales – the
novelty has worn off and is less than successful.

Many decorative typefaces do not have a complete font
set. They may have only capitals, numbers and selected
punctuation marks. Often they aren't extended into a family,
so you will rarely find an italic or a bold.

Symbol or picture fonts

There have always been dingbat fonts. They haven't always
been called that, because it's the American word used to
describe a font of symbols. Europeans used to call them *pi
fonts* (after the mathematical symbol *pi* – π), *symbol fonts* or
fleurons (or, in England, *printer's flowers*). But what do they
do? Whatever you call them, they come in handy for:
· dressing up a pull-quote
· setting mathematical equations or formulae
· creating a border
· making some interesting bullets for a series of dot points
· decorating a title page
· producing a piece of feature typography.
On forms, tick boxes are outlined squares. On business
cards and in *Yellow Pages* advertisements, instead of using
the word 'telephone', telephone symbols are often used.
On coupons, the scissors along the broken line are found
in dingbat fonts. There are many pointing tools (hands,
arrows, aeroplanes) that are used on pamphlets to highlight
product features and prices. In magazine and newsletter

Specialty or display typefaces, symbol or picture fonts

A B C D a b c d e 1 2 3 4
Broadway engraved Morris Fuller Benton 1929

ABCDEFGHIJ abcdefghijklmn 12345
Playbill R. Harling 1938

ABCDEFGHIJK 12345
Neuland Rudolf Koch 1923

A B C D A B C D 1 2 3 4
Copperplate gothic Frederic Goudy 1901

ABCDE ABCDEFG 12345
Typeface six Neville Brody 1986

ABCDE ABCDEFG 12345
Typeface seven Neville Brody 1986

A B C D E a b c d e f g 1 2 3 4 5
Fur extra rounded Paul Sahre 1993

ABCDEFGHIJ abcdefghijklmnopqrs 12345890
Industria inline Neville Brody 1990

ABCDE abcdefg 12345
Beowolf 23 Erik van Blokland and Just van Rossum 1990
This random font will construct a slightly different letterform each time.

Specialty or display typefaces, symbol or picture fonts

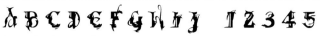

Osprey Stephen Farrell 1993

ABCDE abcdef 12345

Verdana Matthew Carter 1996
This font was developed as a free-to-air font for the World Wide Web.

Zapf Dingbats Hermann Zapf

ABXΔE αβχδεφγ ≤°∞ℑ♠

Symbol font

Decorated initials

pull-quotes, chunky opening and closing quotes are sometimes dingbats.

There are some other uses you can put them to – particularly as they are now installed on your computer and can be used as you would use any other font. They can be italicised, outlined, reversed, tracked and kerned, enlarged or reduced, overlapped (horizontally by tracking, vertically by changing leading, or, with even greater freedom, by layering different text blocks), condensed or expanded (using horizontal scaling), and their baseline can shift.

If you need an angled oval, you can condense a circle by slimming it down with horizontal scale, then italicising it and, if necessary, rotating the text block to the desired angle. However, it's quicker and easier to do that with a drawing tool.

Picture fonts have been released by some font producers and are able to be distorted with type commands in the same way. Picture fonts compete with clip art.

With these symbols and pictures available as a font, they have the attributes of any computerised font – they are much more flexible than dingbats used to be.

Typefaces, families and fonts

The naming conventions of typefaces are similar to how we name one another – there is a family name and given names to distinguish each of the family members. In type nomenclature, the family name comes first. That is the name of the typeface – Helvetica, Palatino, Garamond, Frutiger. This is followed by the name of the family member or *font* (or the English preference, *fount*) – bold, medium, light, italic, etc. A 'font' is one set of capitals, lower case, numbers, punctuation marks, symbols and special characters.

Often, many fonts will exist within one typeface design. The typeface is developed like a family – there is a set of characteristics (based on the genetic make-up or the type equivalent of the DNA of the originally drawn version) that the resulting family members share. It might be a geometric detail, a particular shape of serif, a particular method of generating a stroke or a more complex curve that recurs.

Each of the fonts is then given a name that describes its difference from the original. If it leans to the right, it is called *italic* or *oblique*. If it is slimmed down, it is called

DOING IT SMARTER
Type families
Develop your awareness of the capabilities of a type family by using only one typeface and its variants. That is, don't rely on different faces to create a hierarchy of information. Insist that only one typeface (and its family members) be used.

DOING IT SMARTER
Readable text type
Develop awareness of readability requirements for text setting by setting short pieces of fiction. Effort is not expended on selecting heading attributes, but focuses on the details of creating good text – type selection, leading, tracking, justification, line length, etc.

Unicode
Unicode is the standard coding system that describes all characters in a font set. It allocates a unique identifier, made up of four characters, that distinguishes each font element. For example, here is a selection of the forms that the letter *A* can take:
A = 0041 (capital)
a = 0061 (lower case)
ᴀ = F761 (small capital)
æ = 00E6 (diphthong)
Ä = 00C4 (umlaut)
α = 03B1 (Greek *alpha*)

condensed or *narrow* or *compressed*. If it gets wider, it is called *expanded*. If its strokes get thicker and it looks darker, it is called *bold*. If the strokes get even thicker, it is called *extrabold* or *black*. If its strokes get thinner, it is called *light*. If its strokes get even thinner, it is called *extralight* or *thin* or *fine*. There are other variants, often self-explanatory, such as *outline*, *inline* and *shadow*.

With all these variants taking the family name as well, the original face is often given a font title – it could be called *medium* or *roman*. If there is a font drawn between the medium and the bold, it might be called *demi* or *book*.

When you first start to use type, the safest thing to do is to stick with a good strong type family. Usually a text typeface will have a set of four variants; that is, the type nuclear family – the original typeface, the bold, the italic and the bold italic. With this basic family, you can create cohesive type layouts because the letterforms will work comfortably together because of their similar design attributes.

When type was made of little metal characters that were placed together in lines by hand, each size of the typeface had to be cast in metal – so 'font' described one set of characters at a specified size. Unlimited, digital sizings were not available: only sets or 'fonts' of 6, 8, 10, 12, 18 and 24 point sizes and a limited range of larger sizes were available. Now, due to digital scaling, size is not an issue, so a font has come to mean the particular collection of characters that makes up a type family member.

Type size

Type sizes are described in *points* (abbreviated as *pt*). There are 72 Anglo-American points to an inch, or roughly 3.5 Anglo-American points to a millimetre. In Australia,

Type nomenclature

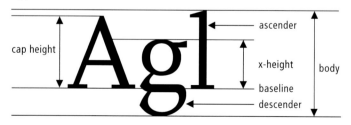

A font
Scala Martin Majoor 1990–98

ABCDEFGHIJKLMNOPQ
RSTUVWXYZ
Capitals/upper case/majuscules

abcdefghijklmnopqrstuv
wxyz
Lower case/minuscules

ABCDEFGHIJKLMNOPQRST
UVWXYZ
Small capitals

1234567890   1234567890
Oldstyle/text/non-lining numbers   Lining/display numbers

-	—	—	•	&	#
Hyphen	En rule	Em rule	Bullet	Ampersand	Hash

Æ æ Œ œ	fi fl	ß	$	¢	£	¥	€
Dipthongs	Ligatures	Eszett	Dollar	Cent	Pound	Yen	Euro

ç ñ å ä â á à ˘ ‾ ·	ı	@	©	®	™
Diacritical marks/accents (L–R: cedilla, tilde, ring, umlaut, circumflex, acute, grave, breve, macron, dot)	Dotless i	Commercial 'at'	Copyright mark	Registered mark	Trade mark

+ = < > − ÷ ≠ √	¼ ½	%	°	π	Σ Ω Δ μ
Mathematical symbols	Fractions	Per cent	Degree	Pi	Greek symbols

:	;	?	¿	!	¡	\	/	/
Colon	Semicolon	Question	Opening question	Exclamation	Opening exclamation	Backslash	Fraction bar	Solidus/slash

,	.	…	*	†	‡	§	¶	‖
Comma	Full stop/period (US)	Ellipsis	Asterisk	Dagger	Double dagger	Section marker	Paragraph marker	Parallel lines

' '	" "	‹ ›	« »	„	' "	( )	[ ]	{ }
Single quotes	Double quotes	Single guillemets	Double guillemets	Base quotes	Foot and inch	Parentheses	Square brackets	Braces

Expanded font sets
A specialist set or expert set will mostly include:

- small capitals that are slightly thicker and stockier than the capitals so that they are the same optical weight and spacing as the lower-case characters
- titling capitals that are slightly slimmer and narrower than the normal capitals
- an old-style number set as an alternative to the normal aligning numbers
- full set of diacritical marks for foreign language setting
- more ligatured character combinations
- 'true' fractions
- optional swash capitals for display setting
- optional ampersands
- a selection of dingbats in the style of the font.

A serif type family

Roman
Times new roman

Italic
Times italic

Bold
Times bold

Bold italic
Times bold italic

Ampersands

Times new roman

Goudy

Scala italic

&
Palatino italic

A sans serif type family

ABCDE abcdefg 12345
Frutiger light Adrian Frutiger 1975

ABCDE abcdefg 12345
Frutiger light italic Adrian Frutiger 1975

ABCDE abcdefg 12345
Frutiger roman Adrian Frutiger 1975

ABCDE abcdefg 12345
Frutiger italic Adrian Frutiger 1975

ABCDE abcdef 12345
Frutiger bold Adrian Frutiger 1975

ABCDE abcdef 12345
Frutiger bold italic Adrian Frutiger 1975

ABCDE abcdef 12345
Frutiger black Adrian Frutiger 1975

ABCDE abcdef 12345
Frutiger black italic Adrian Frutiger 1975

ABCD abcde 12345
Frutiger ultrablack Adrian Frutiger 1975

ABCDEF abcdefghijk 12345
Frutiger light condensed Adrian Frutiger 1975

ABCDEF abcdefghijk 12345
Frutiger condensed Adrian Frutiger 1975

ABCDE abcdefghi 12345
Frutiger bold condensed Adrian Frutiger 1975

ABCDE abcdefghi 12345
Frutiger black condensed Adrian Frutiger 1975

Measurement systems

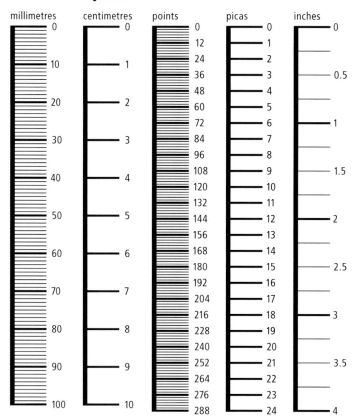

the French–European Didot point system is not used to measure type.

The 'point size' is the body size of the type measured from the top of the ascender to the bottom of the descender. In some typefaces there is a distinct difference between the height of the ascender and the usually smaller cap height, so type is mostly measured from the ascender line rather than the cap height.

On-screen, while 11 point type can be quite comfortable to read, often the letterforms at 11 point are distorted by pixelation and it is easier to read the default 12 point font. It is worth noting that measuring fonts by pixels means the output size of the fonts will vary due to the different screen resolutions that are now available – and this means that the higher the screen resolution, the smaller the letterform, due to the smaller pixel.

x-height comparison
Each *x* is from the
48 point font

Times new roman

Transit

NuptialScript

DOING IT SMARTER
Type selection
Develop your typography skills by
excluding illustration (or photography)
from your design. Illustration has such
a dominant effect in a design that it
can be a crutch for a poor designer.
Take away the illustration to extend
your typographic skills.

Most people can comfortably read printed text type in
sizes from 9 point to 12 point, with the most popular being
10 point and 11 point. For children's books or material
for the aged, text size should be larger and start at about
14 point.

Usually, a sans serif font can be set a point size smaller
than a serif font. It is all to do with the *x-height* (the height
of the lower-case *x*) and its relation to the ascending and
descending characters that surround it. A serif *x* will mostly
be smaller than a corresponding sans serif *x*.

On a narrow measure, 9 point might be necessary, but
on a wide measure, it is best to increase the size to 12 point.
These choices will determine the number of characters on
the line.

All other type decisions are made following text font
selection and the text size and text leading decisions.

Type selection

One of the safest ways to produce a cohesive text treatment
is to select a type family and use its variants exclusively.
One family member – usually the original version – is
chosen to be the basic font. Its designer determined that
this font is best for text setting. It usually is.

All decisions on text width, leading, spacing, indenting
and headings are made based on that selection. It should be
legible and easy to read, which often means it is free from
decoration and unusual letterforms.

Often an organisation will choose a typeface that
becomes its 'corporate' typeface – all materials produced by
the organisation are effectively identified by the use of that
type family.

There are even families designed with matching sans
serif and serif typefaces. Using such extended families gives

The Stone family includes:

Sans
Stone sans Sumner Stone 1987

Informal
Stone informal Sumner Stone 1987

Serif
Stone serif Sumner Stone 1987

a 'corporate' cohesion to text and, because of the similarity in curves, weight and stroke thickness, removes the difficulty of finding compatible typefaces.

Compatible typefaces

To avoid the 'ordinary' or 'boring' look of a single typeface used through a publication, you can add interest by adding a second 'special' typeface. It works best when the second face is used sparingly. This retains the interest in it on the occasions when it is used, possibly for headings, running heads, pull-quotes or captions.

Think of one face as the 'special' and the other – probably the text typeface – as the working face. You can then use variants of both families for various tasks within the text.

The secret of successful combination of typefaces seems to be the ability to maintain several contrasts between them. It is best to use at least two of those contrasts when selecting your 'special' and your 'worker'. The stronger the contrast, the more effective the combination will be. You can contrast:

- their form – serif, sans serif, script or decorative
- their weight or typecolour – reversed, bold, medium or light
- their scale – large or small
- their spacing – wide or narrow
- their direction – roman or italic
- their shape – condensed, normal or expanded
- their case – capitals or lower case.

Another guide here is to choose typefaces from different type categories, with no more than one face from any one category on a page. Use their variants, but maintain a minimum of two contrasts between each combination. This gives not only compatibility but also flexibility.

But there are times when the contrast might be too great or the differences may be in conflict. For example, it is often unwise to use an italic serif font with a script typeface because their letterforms will clash. Also consider the effect that one typeface – and its associations – will have on another. For example, contemporary script faces are often too 'casual' to sit comfortably with traditional serif typefaces because their associations are different and there is a lack of logic in their proximity to each other.

CHECKLIST
Type compatibility

The most successful technique for selecting two types that will complement each other is to use at least two contrasts between them:

- **Form**
  SERIF vs SANS SERIF
  Decorative vs Normal
- **Weight**
  LIGHT vs **BOLD** vs `REVERSE`
- **Size**
  LARGE vs SMALL
- **Spacing**
  W I D E vs NARROW
- **Direction**
  Italic vs roman
- **Shape**
  CONDENSED vs NORMAL vs EXPANDED
- **Case**
  CAPITALS/UPPER CASE vs lower case

Legibility and readability

We read best what we are used to reading. It's best to avoid idiosyncratic typographic features, because they can be unwelcome distractions to a reader. Due to pixelation, for example, serifs on-screen can appear lumpy and uneven and distort lettershapes at small sizes, so they are best avoided in websites. It is also the reason decorative and script typefaces are avoided for long body copy – the complex shapes that give them their character can slow readability in long text. Don't make long text documents harder to read – it's difficult enough as it is to get people to read them.

Because people have a finite amount of time to spend reading, there is an emphasis on the speed and accuracy of their comprehension. This puts great importance on the ability to achieve clarity of letterforms and to maintain correct emphasis within the text. What you do with your chosen typeface to enable the reader to find and understand the material being presented is paramount.

A major inhibitor to smooth reading is inconsistency. Be consistent in:

- headings, once you have established an appropriate hierarchy
- the style for references and cross-references
- spelling
- punctuation
- the structure of information.

READ MORE ABOUT IT

Rolf Rehe, *Typography: How to make it most legible*, Design Research International, Carmel, Indiana, 1984.

Colin Wheildon, *Communicating or just making pretty shapes*, 3rd edn, Newspaper Advertising Bureau of Australia, Sydney, 1990.

Line length

Optimum line length, on-screen or in print, is generally considered to be between 1.5 and three alphabets or, given the alphabet contains 26 letters, 39–78 characters (which is sometimes rounded up to 40–80 characters) or, for people who prefer a single figure to a range, 60 characters.

The range is more useful than the absolute. The number of characters per line in various typefaces and formats will change, so you will not be able to achieve the absolute of 60 in every setting, and that does not necessarily mean that

DOING IT FASTER

Measuring optimum line length

In order to quickly decide how wide your columns could be without counting, find a type catalogue that presents settings of the lower-case alphabet of each font in different sizes. Simply measure the setting of the lower-case alphabet in the size you intend using and multiply it from 1.5 to 3 times to determine the range for optimum line length. Then consider whether your format or grid allows a line length within that range.

DOING IT SMARTER

A personalised type catalogue

Create your own type catalogue by typing up the alphabet in all caps and then in lower case, a set of numbers and punctuation marks. Caption it with font and size information. Duplicate it numerous times, selecting the size options you are most likely to use, remembering to revise the caption. Print it out. Then select the whole page and allocate a different typeface and print it out, too. Do this for all the typefaces you have and generate new pages when you invest in a new face.

your readability is compromised. A range also implies that, if you go beyond that range, you are entering potentially difficult areas.

In any case, line lengths that are near the upper limit will need more leading than those near the lower. This enables readers' eyes to accurately and consistently drop to the starting point of the next line without doubling (where you read the same line twice or even three times).

In narrow columns, there are a few standard techniques to increase the number of characters to a comfortable reading level:

- Reduce the point size of your type.
- Select a condensed or narrow typeface.
- Use the italic font, which will mostly set narrower.

Another consideration is the written style of the text. If the manuscript has many long words, such as a scientific or technical paper, and long sentences and paragraphs, it does not lend itself to narrow, multicolumn setting; if it has short paragraphs and lists, or dot points with short entries, it will.

Leading/linespacing

When printers used metal type, they inserted thin strips of lead between the lines of type to separate them. The term *leading* (pronounced 'ledding') refers to the space between lines of type. This space is generally measured from the baseline of one line to the baseline of the next, so it is nearly always larger than the point size of the typeface.

If there is no leading between the lines, the text is 'set solid'. Solid setting has the potential for the descenders of one line to touch the ascenders of the next, which upsets the word shape and inhibits readability. You need some leading in all cases where readability is paramount, particularly in text setting.

Auto-leading refers to a default setting that places an extra 20% of space between the lines – if your text is set in 10 point Times Roman, the auto-leading is 12 points (which means there are 12 points from one baseline to the next).

It often helps to imagine how this was achieved with metal type. Type is measured from the top of the ascending characters – like *d*, *h* and *k* – to the bottom of the descending characters – like *g*, *y* and *j*. Using the same example, you would have a line of Times that was 10 points

Leading between
LEAD
lines of type

Minimum leading

As a general guide, the minimum requirement is an x-and-a-half between lines of x-height in both serif and sans serif type – or 2.5 times the height of an x.

Minimum
leading

deep with a 2 point wide piece of lead between it and the next line of 10 point Times.

Leading is now measured in points from baseline to baseline (which is the sum of the body size of the type and the width of the imaginary lead strip between the lines). It is then expressed as the size of the body 'on' the measurement from baseline to baseline.

The amount of leading required is determined by the interrelationship between the x-height and the number of characters that fit in the measure. The longer the line, the more leading it will require. Conversely, with short lines, less leading will be required.

Sans serif type usually requires more leading than serif type. This is related to the x-height of the letterforms – usually sans serif typefaces have a larger x-height than serif typefaces.

As a rule of thumb, you should be able to fit a minimum of an x-and-a-half space between your x-heights.

With a serif face, the minimum recommended leading is one extra point on the size of the face. For example, 10 point Times with 1 point of space between the lines is called '10 on 11 point Times' and written as '10/11 pt Times'. The leading is entered as '11 points' even though, in the past, it would have been a 1-point lead strip placed between the lines. As a rule, leading for a serif font will be between 1 and 4 points on the size of the font – using 4 on a long line. Using the same example, if you had 60 characters in a line, the appropriate specification might be 10/13 pt Times. If closer to 80 characters, it may be 10/14 pt Times.

With a sans serif face, the minimum recommended leading is 2 extra points on the size of the face. Leading for sans serif will vary from 2 to 6 extra points on the size of the font, again using more on a longer line.

If you do not feel confident enough to make leading decisions, auto-leading is a good guide, but not infallible, as it is also mostly based on the appropriate leading for a serif face.

As a further example, if you set 10 point Times Roman with 12 point leading and then changed the typeface to the sans serif Helvetica, you could alter the size to 9 point Helvetica but keep the 12 point leading (which is greater than the auto-leading for 9 point, at a comparative leading of 133%).

If you apply leading more generously, you create a lighter looking text block, which can be a useful technique to remember for varying the tonal arrangement within a layout.

Extreme leading

You might leave a line space or more between lines, e.g. '10/24 pt Times'. As a display setting style for advertisements or annual reports, it can be quite effective. Some designers interweave headings, footnotes, even other paragraphs or a second column of text through the wide linespacing.

It can be a most effective technique but has drawbacks; it relies on a reader being able to identify the typeface variation. Maximising the contrast seems to be the easiest way to ensure that both levels of information are read. This is best done with colour, weight of font, or an entirely different typeface.

Negative leading

In display lines that are set in capitals, a negative leading is often allocated, i.e. leading that is smaller than the body size of the type, e.g. '10/8 pt Times caps'.

This is done to avoid the distance that occurs when there are no descenders to fill the gap. Without the descenders, the space between the lines can separate the lines too much, particularly if the second line is a continuation of the first and not a separate heading.

In extreme cases, you may want the lines of capitals to touch. Trial and error is the best way to determine the amount of negative leading for this, but ensure you zoom in on the text on-screen – at least 200% but preferably even larger – so you can see how it will appear.

You can use this technique to make a cohesive heading shape with lower case as well. It is often used when centring two- or three-line headings in an oval shape. Ensure that descenders from above don't crash into ascenders from below. You may need to massage the line breaks in order to avoid a crash or even use optional characters (the dotless i [ı] is sometimes useful to avoid a descender from the line above). You might also 'interpret' your centring, creating a more asymmetrical arrangement of the lines to avoid any clashes.

When using extreme leading,
Extreme
you may offset headings and other
leading
text elements like footnotes, cross-
creates
references or links by placing them
cross-readings
between the lines of the main text.

Capitals set solid in 18/18 pt Scala are changed to 18/15 pt Scala to better shape the three-line title.

BEFORE   THE   —
             DAY'S   —
             END   —

AFTER   THE   —
             DAY'S   —
             END   —

A title set solid in 18/18 pt Scala looks uneven in this three-line setting due to the descending *y*, capital *E* and ascending *d* that fill the second linespace – creating an optical illusion of those lines being closer. While the second line has a capital *D*, the first line has no descending characters so the leading between the first and second lines was reduced by 2 points to 18/16 pt Scala to optically correct the title.

BEFORE

The
Day's
End

AFTER

The
Day's
End

DOING IT FASTER
Kerning
Don't fiddle with kerning at rough or draft stage – if at all.

Uneven leading within a heading

In a multiple-line heading set in lower case, such as those that sometimes appear on narrow pamphlets, you will need to alter the leading for each line of the heading so that it will look optically even. The optical distortion usually occurs when there is a line that has no descenders. The space between it and the next line will often look inordinately large, so you need to move the next line up a few points until it looks even.

For this to work, make sure that each line break is established with a line return, otherwise any leading change will flow through the entire heading.

Letterspacing

Letterspacing is usually achieved by a combination of optical and mechanical spacing. Optical spacing achieves the look of there being similar space between characters but takes account of the letterforms and their counter-spaces. You can use a combination of techniques to achieve this. For instance, imagine a number of jellybeans that neatly fit between each letter so the black area or white space takes the same number of jellybeans, despite their odd distribution around some lettershapes. Another technique is to determine the optical edge of the letterforms and then mechanically space them.

Mechanical spacing puts exactly the same amount of space between letters, but it is measured from the right of the first letter to the left of the following letter, regardless of the letterform. This means some letter combinations will look further away than others.

Letterspacing controls are at your fingertips in most page layout programs, and the terms most often used to describe letterspacing techniques are 'tracking' and 'kerning'. They are not interchangeable terms – in most programs you will encounter both because they have different functions.

Kerning

Letters are usually spaced so there is the appearance of even space between them, but in some combinations of letters, the spacing remains awkward. *Kerning* is the respacing of the specific pairs of letters that are causing uneven spacing within a word. Although this does not usually need to be used in text setting, it is often worth the trouble for titles, logotypes and headings. Kerning is usually required in setting where there are capitals such as T, A, V, W and L.

Kerning alters the space between any combination of two characters, i.e. how the first letter relates to the second letter. Place the cursor between the two letters and reduce or enlarge the space with the kerning controls until it is optically correct. It is usually best to do this having zoomed to at least 200%.

Most fonts include specified kerning pairs that are automatically applied to particular character combinations, according to the font designer's wishes. These usually include problem letters and how they will set with each other and any lower-case letters that follow. For example, will the *a* sit under the crossbar of the *T* in *Table*? In capitals setting, will the L sit neatly under the T in ALTER? Will the A and V overlap in AV?

You should bother with kerning only in display type, because it is time-consuming and few clients can afford the time it takes you to tweak it. But consider editing your fonts so your kerning preferences are saved and automatically applied.

Tracking

The mechanical method of letterspacing is called tracking, which evenly distributes more or less space between each letter. Some text designers have a preference for tightly spaced characters; others prefer 'open' or 'loose' spacing.

As a general rule, the larger the type, the tighter you can track. Many programs do this automatically. However, tracking capabilities are occasionally handy for respacing a headline, logotype or title.

Tracking alters the amount of space between each letter in the whole word, heading or text block. Select the word or line and go to tracking commands. Less space between the characters makes the word narrower and is called 'tight'; more space between the characters makes the word wider and is called 'loose'.

Often, tracking decisions are aesthetic, but there are readability issues here. As type gets smaller, there needs to be more space between the individual letters – the spacing cannot be mathematically reduced like the characters themselves. There needs to be slightly wider tracking as the word shrinks.

DOING IT FASTER
Kerning preferences
If possible, edit the kerning pairs in each of your fonts to suit your personal preferences. Save them and they will be applied automatically.

This problem is often highlighted in logos where they are fine on cover designs but do not work in running heads, or they may be fine on a letterhead but hard to read on the side of a building – the spacing may be at fault. Some organisations have logo artwork for reproduction at different sizes, so those readability and reproduction problems are resolved.

You will often need to use looser tracking when you set a word or some text in small capitals. To approximate the same grey as the text block, tracking of small capitals usually needs to be looser than the surrounding text.

Very loose tracking is sometimes used in all-capitals setting as a display technique. Rarely do we wide-track lower-case letterforms, although it is becoming more accepted through occasional use.

If there is very wide spacing in a heading and the heading spills onto the following line, the 'rule' is to have at least the same amount of space between each letter as between the lines, so increase the leading.

If you loose-track bold type, you alter its weight on the page. If loose tracking erodes that importance, the page looks duller (because of lack of contrast) and the relative importance can be lost.

If you tight-track bold type, the letterforms will often overlap, which can create legibility problems. Used in large sizes, overlapped letterforms can create interesting hybrid shapes, but you have to be sure your audience can be bothered trying to decipher the message.

Street signage – or better still, highway signage – contains some valuable lessons when it comes to readability. You can apply them to shop signs, posters, or even Saturday morning garage sale signs.

If you analyse a highway sign at close quarters, you'll find that there is a very significant amount of letterspacing in road signage. This is for precisely the same reason that you use very loose tracking on 4 point type – when type is small, you need exponentially more space between the letters, and at the distance from which you start reading a highway sign, it is very small type.

If readers will be across the room or down the road, extra letterspacing will help them read the message.

Capitals tracked wide in 18/18 pt Scala are changed to 18/28 pt Scala to better shape the three-line title and avoid vertical groupings. Also note the kerning of the apostrophe.

Using type variation

To show relative importance within text, there are a number of standard type variations that can be used. Each decision will have an impact on a reader's comprehension of the text, as type variations imply a particular level of importance due to their traditional role in typography.

Bold type

Bold type is 'heavier' in *weight* than text fonts. This is achieved by thickening the strokes of the original font's letterforms. Thickening makes bold fonts appear darker. The level of relative darkness of a font is referred to as its *weight* and how it is set on a page determines its typecolour or tonal variance to the other type around it.

Weight variation is often used to add life to a page layout or to help define levels of information contained within text. Darker text tends to jump out of a page of ordinary text and grab the reader's attention (which makes it perfect for indicating the location of specific information, as a heading does, or for warnings). The choice of a body font is all to do with the resulting patterns of tone that are created on a page by the areas of type.

In a heading hierarchy, bold type is the strongest (with the exception of a reversed block of text) – and is therefore reserved for the most important information. Bold headings within a text area will stand out because of the contrast between bold type at its heavier weight and the lighter text type. It is easier for readers to find the section they want to read.

Because bold type is a thickened version of the typeface, the counters (i.e. the enclosed space within letters such as the loop of the *e*) are correspondingly smaller. This can make the letters a bit difficult to distinguish, so it is wise to track bold type a little looser – but only fractionally, because the more space you put between the letters, the lighter the typecolour will appear to be, and you must not lose the benefit of the weight change.

Similarly, if you select a heading level to appear in colour, you may want to bold it at the same time to counter the visual weight loss that the colour creates.

Typefaces like Helvetica, Frutiger, Gill and Univers (notice they are all sans serif) mostly come with an extrabold or black weight. This weight is particularly handy

DOING IT SMARTER
Typeface associations
Create 12 layouts that show type contrasts for the pairs of words listed below. Each layout should be in a 60 mm square (but can be any size you want). Select a typeface for each word and choose the way you set it: In capitals? What spacing? In bold or italic? On an angle or upside down? Reversed out of black to white? Tracked? What size? Not only should these design decisions help to convey the meaning of each word, they should also depict the difference between the two words.

This is not just a type selection exercise. Use layout to help communicate the difference in meaning as well. Use repetition, reversing, centring and other formatting options. Run one word through the other or explore other forms of dynamic placements in an asymmetrical layout.

To increase the complexity of this exercise, use a typeface only once. This means that for the 12 examples, 24 typefaces must be chosen. If you have used Helvetica extrabold, don't use Helvetica again – find another sans serif type that will work as you want.

This is a great exercise if you are working on book titles and advertising headlines, or feature articles in newsletters, magazines, websites or e-zines.

The words to be contrasted are:
- big/little
- fat/thin
- dark/light
- happy/sad
- out/in
- old/young
- rich/poor
- up/down
- fast/slow
- east/west
- beautiful/ugly
- powerful/meek.

– its contrast is very sudden when compared with the text weights and can be impressive.

If overused, bold type can be too distracting and can inhibit reading. Judiciously used, it can enhance meaning by giving appropriate importance and it can add the dark tones to a page that help the page to live.

Reversed type

When you change the colour of type to white on a black background, it is called reverse. It is like a text negative.

It is better to reverse a bold font. This helps the type when it is printed as well as on-screen. You may have noticed that black type tends to thicken slightly when it is printed; when it is reversed, the black background is thickened, making the white type spindly and more difficult to read. If you use reversed bolder type, it will often look like the same weight as the text because of this optical illusion.

It is also better to reverse a sans serif typeface. The same slight thickening of the background of a reversed area tends to make the narrow strokes of serif type and the serifs themselves thinner – and, in some cases, they disappear altogether – which makes the type more difficult to read. To avoid this problem, type that is reversed out of black, a solid colour or a photograph should be sans serif.

It is better to track reversed type a little wider (or 'looser') than if it were not reversed. This too helps the definition of the individual letters and aids readability.

Italics

Aldus Manutius, a Venetian printer and publisher of the Renaissance, first used italics in 1501. He developed them to fit more words into the small page of his pocket editions of classical literature – and you can still usually fit more words to a line if you set italics, because the characters are often narrower than the roman font. Francesco Griffo, the typeface designer in Aldus's studio, based his italic design on a popular slanted handwriting style of the day.

Physically, italics lean to the right and are a redraw of the roman font to which their name corresponds. When comparing a roman serif typeface with its italic version, you will notice that some letterforms are different, particularly the lower-case g/*g* and a/*a*. The italics are often

Comparing italic forms

a

Scala regular

a

Scala italic is an italic form

a

Helvetica

a

Helvetica italic is an oblique form

more calligraphic in appearance, which makes them a logical choice for headings with a difference.

In sans serif typefaces, the italics are often just an *oblique* version of the roman font, i.e. they are the same character shapes slanted.

Because of the awkwardness of the pixelation and the furriness of the anti-aliassing required of italic letterforms on-screen, it is advisable to minimise their use for websites and publications that will be viewed on-screen.

Italics should have the same weight (or the same tone on the page when you squint at them) as the roman font. Because of this, the use of italics through text does not interrupt the texture of the page, which means they are perfect for stress within a text block.

Avoid setting italics in all capitals. In fact, when Aldus used them in 1501, all the text was set in italics except the headings which were set in roman capitals, and the first letter of each line, which was a roman capital letter – there were no italic capitals.

The readability of the text is not sacrificed when you use italics. In testing, there has been no significant difference in the speed and accuracy with which people read italics when compared with the readability of roman letters.

Quoted material used to be cited in italics and still can be if desired. Italics are regularly used for the captions to photographs or diagrams and for cross-references. They are also traditionally used for specific text functions.

When you are quoting titles of magazines, newspapers, books, films, plays, long poems, operas, musical works (those with specific non-musical titles only), ballets, shows, paintings and television programs, it is customary to use italics, thus: *Australian MacWorld* magazine; *The New York Times* newspaper; Sally Morgan's novel, *My Place*; George Miller's film, *Happy Feet*; Noël Coward's play, *Blithe Spirit*; AB 'Banjo' Paterson's poem, *The Man from Snowy River*; Peggy Glanville-Hicks's opera, *Nausicaa*; Peter Sculthorpe's *Kakadu*, but Peter Sculthorpe's Piano Concerto; Graeme Murphy's ballet, *Tivoli*; Mel Brooks's musical, *The Producers*; Leonardo da Vinci's *Mona Lisa*; and TV's *Neighbours* and *Friends*.

However, when citing an article, episode of a television program, short poem or song title, it is customary to use quote marks, not italics, thus: 'Makeover', a column from *Desktop*; *Bananas in Pyjamas* 'The Big Parade' episode;

CHECKLIST
Titles or names
that are set in italics:
- ☐ Books
- ☐ Magazines
- ☐ Newspapers
- ☐ Plays
- ☐ Operas
- ☐ Films
- ☐ Television programs
- ☐ Long poems
- ☐ Musical works
- ☐ Paintings
- ☐ Sculptures
- ☐ Artworks
- ☐ Acts of Parliament and Regulations (when full title, including date; shortened forms are in roman) but not Bills
- ☐ Legal documents
- ☐ Ships
- ☐ Trains
- ☐ Aircraft
- ☐ Genus
- ☐ Species
- ☐ Subspecies
- ☐ Varieties

Judith Wright's poem 'Bora Ring'; 'Solid Rock' from Goanna's album, *Spirit of Place*. Also note public service preferences for citations: Hansard but *Commonwealth of Australia Gazette*.

On the occasions that you need to quote the name of a vehicle, usually a ship or an aircraft, it is a convention to use italics for the name of the vessel. For example, HMAS *Success* or the *Queen Mary*; Kingsford Smith's *Southern Cross* or Charles Lindberg's *Spirit of St Louis*; or even the starship USS *Enterprise* from *Star Trek*, but note the TARDIS from *Dr Who* (which is an acronym for Time And Relative Dimensions In Space).

Foreign words which are not regarded as anglicised are set in italic, but use them sparingly. Many expressions are considered to have entered English, such as café, consommé, cliché or résumé (note the acutes so the word 'résumé' is not confused with the word 'resume'). Australia's *Macquarie Dictionary* will not italicise any foreign words or phrases that it lists, which means they can be considered part of Australian English and need not be italicised. If it doesn't appear in the *Macquarie*, use italics.

Scientific names like *Acacia flavescens* (yellow wattle) are italicised.

In military histories, the enemy's formations are cited in italics.

Note the following details of plurals and punctuation for italic usage:

- She handed me a few *Sydney Morning Herald*s. (roman *s* for plural form)
- Have you read the Melbourne *Age*'s book review yet? (roman apostrophe, roman *s*)
- Have you seen Tom Roberts's painting, *Bailed up*? (roman question mark)

Italics can be used as a separate voice in text and are sometimes used in fiction works for thoughts or a second narrative. They are often used in interview transcripts to distinguish the interviewer's questions from the interviewee's answers. In the same way, they can be used for editorial notes to the reader [*like this one*] because they separate the voice of the information from the main voice of the text – a sort of ancient hypertext.

Capitals/upper case

When the Romans conquered Greece, they took what they liked and improved on it. And that's exactly what they did with the Greek alphabet. The Romans refined the letterforms to a point where the alphabet looked very much like it does today. But all this development was only in that part of the alphabet that we call 'capital' letters or 'upper case'.

Now, if you think of gods like Zeus and Jupiter, goddesses like Athena and Minerva, think of ancient buildings like the Parthenon and the Pantheon. 'Capital' is an architectural term, which describes the decorative top of a column. Atop the capitals is a strip of marble that is inscribed with the name of the god or goddess to whom the building is dedicated, and these are literally 'capital' letters. Stonemasons cut them to precise specifications, so that each letter would have its correct width in comparison to the others.

The relative widths of capitals were defined as part of their essential character for optimum shape recognition, so the M and O were wide, the S and V were medium, and the I was very narrow.

That is why typefaces with letterforms that do not follow these width interrelationships are often less legible; correct character relationships enable recognition.

Of course, now we use a 'double alphabet' – capitals and lower case – or, if you prefer the correct Latin terminology, majuscules and minuscules.

The concept of big and little letters really came from the monks who were scribbling copies of the Bible and got bored. They started embellishing the first word of a section with large initial letters and similarly with the first letter in important names. But, skipping a fairly long and involved story that would take us from Greece and Rome to Ireland (where a heap of monks toiled, developing an alphabet called 'semi-uncials' which was like our little letters), France (where the lower case we know today was developed at the court of Charlemagne and, incidentally, named 'Carolingian minuscules'), and Germany (where two gentlemen put the alphabets together and put serifs on the little letters so they'd match the capitals), we find that, at the end, we have developed a code of use for capitals and lower case and a fairly complicated code called 'punctuation'. Both codes help us to communicate in written form.

Proper nouns

that take an initial capital letter:

- □ Names
  - – people
  - – organisations
  - – products
  - – places
- □ Titles
  - – publications
  - – stage shows
  - – films
  - – musical works
  - – visual arts works
- □ Public service preferences
  - – specific references capitalised
  - – generic references in lower case.

For example: Note the capitals in Department of Foreign Affairs, but no capitals when simply referring to 'the department'.

CAPITALS SHOULD BE AVOIDED IN CONTINUOUS TEXT BECAUSE THEY SLOW THE READER DOWN. THIS IS BECAUSE CAPITAL LETTERS CREATE WORDS THAT HAVE A RECTANGULAR SHAPE AND WE CANNOT RECOGNISE THE SHAPE OF THE WORDS AS DISTINCTLY AS WE CAN WITH lower-case words, which have a more quickly identified individual shape due to their particular combination of ascenders and descenders. This helps us to read lower-case words more quickly.

Capital letters are used to signify a proper noun – 'naming' words such as Australia, *The Design Manual* and Whitbread.

You might also have noticed how capitals in a paragraph jump out. Capitals appear to be more important so they can be used for information that needs to be brought to the reader's attention urgently. But there are other techniques that achieve the same result. Bold or italic fonts are often better suited than capitals.

Capitals are usually reserved for short pieces of information such as titles, headings and logotypes.

These days, although it is preferred to set headings in lower case with an initial capital, titles on covers are often set in full capitals to make the title a solid block – a rectangle is often an easier shape to use in a layout. That's why we often relegate capitals to what we call display setting, where the shape of the letters and words is more important for its design implications than its readability. After all, the difference in the time it takes to read one word in capitals and the time it takes to read the same word in lower case is negligible.

Often, a heading in capitals can be reduced in size, but sometimes this leaves the heading looking squashed. To counter this, use looser tracking with headings set in all capitals.

All-capitals headings also work well reversed to white in black boxes. That still needs a bit of loose tracking and normally a bolder typeface for easy printability. This creates one of the strongest heading styles, because the black box has such a powerful impact on the layout. Usually, as a result of this, the reversed heading is not used for headings that occur quickly after one another – that can chop up the page too much.

Because of their clear shapes and defined widths, capitals are more easily recognised forms and considered to be more legible. Lower-case letters are often based

In full-capitals feature headings, sometimes each word is given a line of its own and increased in size until they are the same length. Sometimes it is worth using different weights of the font to better balance the heading. In the 'before', each line is set in the medium weight, creating a most uneven setting. In the 'after', the top line is set in light, the second line in heavy and the last line in medium, which creates the illusion of the heading being the same weight.

BEFORE

AFTER

THE ENCYCLO PÆDIA   THE ENCYCLO PÆDIA

on a circular stroke that inhibits that recognition factor. Compare A with a and *a*: the triangular capital letterform is more distinct in a grouping. But lower-case letterforms are considered more readable because the distinguishing character of ascender and descender combinations enables us to recognise the word shape more quickly.

Minimal and maximal capitalisation/sentence and title case
Minimal capitalisation is where only the first word and proper nouns in a title take an initial capital. This is also called *sentence case.*

Maximal capitalisation is where all major words in a title take an initial capital. This is called *title case.* It is problematic because of the definition of 'major words' and the resulting uneven look to the text. All main words in a title or a heading used to be capitalised:

> The Namatjira Works on Paper
> *For the Term of His Natural Life*
> An Analysis of Sculthorpe's Symphonic Works

But with minimal capitalisation, only the first word and any proper nouns in a title or heading will be capitalised. So the above examples would reduce to:

> The Namatjira works on paper
> *For the term of his natural life*
> An analysis of Sculthorpe's symphonic works

Although it is optional how much capitalisation you use, the trend towards less punctuation implies dropping capitals to lower case where possible. This book uses minimal punctuation in its further reading reference lists, for example, but note that in text, titles take maximal capitalisation. The Vancouver referencing system also uses minimal capitalisation.

Typographically, capitals break up text passages by disturbing the even texture of lower-case text. This is also the reason for typing only one space after a full stop in a paragraph – the capital that starts the next sentence is easy to find, so doesn't need the extra space.

Small capitals
In a specialist set, small capitals are a redraw of the font where the small capital height is slightly higher than the x-height of the face and the small capitals are close to the same width of the lower-case letters.

Maximal capitalisation has been used in the title of this book. Note how the title has then been detailed: auto-leading has been altered to negative leading to better group the lines; and the capitals have been optically aligned, with the crossbar of the *T* allowed to 'hang' in the margin.

BEFORE

The
Design
Manual

AFTER

The
Design
Manual

In packages where small capitals are drawn from the font matrix for standard capital letters, you should set the height or vertical scaling to about 66% and the width or horizontal scaling to about 85%. This will create small capitals that are scaled closer to the dimensions of a true small capital font – where the small caps are a squat version of the real caps.

In display type, where you might be using capitals beside small capitals, it is often worth playing with the weight of the fonts. A true small capital font will have a comparatively thicker stroke that matches the standard font stroke thickness. If you are scaling your small capitals, you might try using the demibold font or bold font to match the character width of the initial capital. Alternatively, use a lighter font for the initial capitals.

It is preferable to use small capitals in text setting where you want to set a word or phrase in full capitals. This will not interrupt the text flow or 'jump out of the page'.

Small capitals may even be used for all-capital abbreviations such as personnel position references, post-nominals, and state, department, organisation and company names that appear in text: CEO, PA, MBA, VC, ACT, NSW, USA, UK, EU, ASEAN, UN, UNSW, NRMA, IBM.

Some fonts also now have 'petite' capitals which are the same height as the x-height.

Raised and drop caps

Care should be taken that unintentional cross-readings do not occur, as readers notice the featured letters in order of their dominance: in this case spelling 'RIR'.

Raised and drop capitals

Sometimes in a layout the positioning of some graphic elements requires that a text block go in a position that does not follow a logical reading flow. A raised or dropped cap is a graphic device where something is needed to drag the reader's attention back to the text, particularly if there is a picture or heading to the right of the text block.

A raised initial capital.

IN ORDER to redirect the reader's attention to the text block, we use a device of colouring and/or making a graphic element of the initial letter of a text block. It is usually quite low in the hierarchy on the page: we see pictures, headlines and then drop or raised capitals. They are used to lead us into the text.

A two-line drop capital aligned with the cap height of the first word and the baseline of the second line.

Raised capitals are certainly the easiest to use – they have the same effect, but you simply change the size and font of the capital as desired and the text then flows on using the same baseline. The increased height needs to be taken into account by adding more space above the paragraph.

A three-line drop capital aligned with the x-height of the first line and the baseline of the third line.

Drop capitals can have a two- or three-line drop. Their size is determined by the size of text and its leading. Usually the drop cap aligns with the x-height of the top line of text and sits on the baseline of either the second or third line of the paragraph.

Sometimes the rest of the first word of the paragraph is set in capitals to ease the reader into the smaller size, in which case the drop cap is set to align with the cap height. You will probably need to track the first word a little looser and kern it carefully into the initial drop cap so it runs smoothly into the word.

Drop caps might also have text set to run around them rather than leaving a white block of space for them to sit in.

Some designers overuse the technique and can come unstuck. You might spell presumably unintentional words across a layout or down a layout with strong random initials. They also tend to cancel each other out, becoming just a decoration and losing their importance in redirecting the reader's gaze.

READ MORE ABOUT IT

Department of Finance and Administration (rev. Snooks & Co.), *Style manual for authors, editors and printers*, 6th edn, John Wiley & Sons, Brisbane, 2002, ISBN 0 7016 3648 3.

Geoffrey Rogers, *Editing for print*, Macdonald & Co., London, 1985, ISBN 0 356 10787 6.

Baden Eunson, *Writing at work*, John Wiley & Sons, Brisbane, 1996, ISBN 0 471 33564 9.

George Stern, *Choosing your mark: A guide to good expression and punctuation*, AGPS, Canberra, 1995, ISBN 0 644 42663 2.

Constance Hale (ed.), *Wired style: Principles of English usage in the digital age*, HardWired, San Francisco, 1996, ISBN 1 888869 01 1.

Punctuation

The accurate detailing of punctuation is a part of professionally presented text. If it is inconsistent or incorrect, it makes your client or organisation look incompetent or, worse, inept.

The rule of thumb for editorial correction is that, while you may have personal preferences, many options are acceptable, provided that they are consistently applied.

The current practice is leaning towards minimal punctuation, minimal capitalisation and minimal text interference. That said, you would again find personal preferences often win out. But readability and understandability are the main determinants of how much punctuation to use.

Spacing punctuation marks

Punctuation marks nearly always immediately follow or precede that which they punctuate.

Question and exclamation marks, commas and full stops, semi-colons and colons do not have a space before them, and they only have one space after them – never two.

Apostrophes have no space either side, unless they follow a plural (e.g. 'She could never remember her uncles' birthdays.' – the birthdays of several uncles) or unless they indicate that the beginning or ending of a word is missing (''Allo, 'allo, what's goin' on 'ere, then?').

Opening quotes are preceded by one space, but no space follows them. Closing quotes do not have a preceding space, but are followed by a single space.

If punctuation marks were spaced, they would leave gaps within the texture of the type and interrupt the typecolour.

Minimal and maximal punctuation

These two addresses demonstrate one of the most important principles to remember about modern punctuation: reduce it to bare essentials. Compare:

Mr DW Whitbread	Mr D. W. Whitbread,
PO Box 3127	P. O. Box 3127,
Weston Creek ACT 2611	Weston Creek, A. C. T., 2611.

Note that it is also acceptable to space initials if desired:

D W Whitbread

Excluding sentences and poetry, do not put punctuation at the ends of lines because the line return is enough to make the distinction. However, in text where you might run the address within a paragraph, you would punctuate it like this: Mr DW Whitbread, PO Box 3127, Weston Creek ACT 2611.

Street names do not include possessive punctuation – so 'King Georges Terrace' is not punctuated to 'King George's Terrace'. This is also becoming the case in titles, headings and advertising, where punctuation is reduced or removed from display text.

Also recognise the modern practice for referring to states and territories without full stops: NSW, WA, SA, NT and

Different spaces

There are spaces achieved in lines of text with indents and tabs – either preset or customised. And either tracking or kerning can customise spacing between letters. However, there are other spacing options.

The normal space bar is pressed once for a space between words. It will vary in width in justified settings and also allows lines to be broken at that point. But there are times when you do not want a line broken at that point, e.g. in the middle of a phone number, code or number, or after initials in a name. In these instances, use a *non-breaking space*, which is a different keystroke.

In web usage, this is inadvisable. On websites, delete spaces in phone numbers and add commas to numbers higher than three digits.

In listings, you sometimes want to space some text slightly further away from an entry, such as prices in menus or page numbers in contents lists. You can use an *em space* or an *en space* (which are the same widths respectively as the em and en rules).

A *fixed space* or *thin space* (called a *punctuation space* in America) is the width of a comma and often used instead of a comma in numbers. Because it is a 'fixed' space, it will not increase or reduce in size when used in justification.

ACT. This is largely because postal computers do not like punctuation in the final line of addresses, which always includes the reference to the state. So 'VIC' is preferred to 'Vic.' for Victoria; 'TAS' is preferred to 'Tas.' for Tasmania; and 'QLD' is preferred to 'Qld' for Queensland.

Acronyms and initialisms

Like states, in acronyms and initialisms we delete full stops: UNSW, UCLA, NYU, MIT, WHO, NAB, BHP, CSR, ALP, USA, UK, OHS, ASIO, CIA, FBI.

Note the following exceptions, which, although they are acronyms, are set with an initial capital only: Qantas, Anzac, Unesco.

Full stop/full point/period

Full stops appear at the end of sentences, immediately following the last word. Only one space follows them and then the next sentence starts. 'Period' is the US term.

Full stops should not appear in logos, no matter how strongly an advertising agency argues the case. They should rarely appear in headlines, and if they do on the occasion that the headline is a sentence, they should be reduced in size and kerned to make minimal impact on the text. A full stop on a headline has been found to be a disincentive to continue reading the body text that follows it.

Full stops should be used in lists when the dot points are in sentence structure, and on the last point when the list is a continuation of a lead-in phrase.

Full stops are used to divide the parts of a web URL and to signal abbreviations but are not used in contractions.

On the occasions where you are tempted to key three full stops, replace them with a single keystroke called the 'points of ellipsis'.

Contractions/abbreviations

Where the last letter of a contraction is the final letter of the word that has been contracted, the contraction does not have a full stop. Note these examples:

• 'Pty' for 'Proprietary'
• 'Ltd' for 'Limited'
• 'Bros' for 'Brothers'
• 'St' for 'Saint' or 'Street'
• 'Ave' for 'Avenue'
• 'Rd' for 'Road'

In display setting, punctuation marks will sometimes be reduced – which, in the case of apostrophes and quote marks, will also require them to be repositioned. They are then kerned and 'hung' in the margin for an improved optical alignment of the text block.

BEFORE

'Okay,'
he said.

AFTER

'Okay,'
he said.

Punctuation to watch

☐ Use open (') and close (') quotes
☐ Single quotes preferred to double
☐ Only one space typed after a full stop
☐ No space typed before: % ? ! : ; /)]
☐ No space typed after: $ / (['
☐ No space before or after: -
☐ No punctuation in:
   – addresses
   – dates: 18 November 1989 (but note: Saturday, November 18, 1989 which is US usage)
☐ No full stops in:
   – logos or headings
   – post-nominals: BEd, PhD, MSc, BA(Hons)
   – abbreviations in capitals: GPO, AGDA, AIGA
   – metric symbols: km, g, L, mm

- 'Mr' for 'Mister'
- 'Mrs' for 'Missus'
- 'Miss' for 'Mistress'
- 'Dr' for 'Doctor'

but note 'no.' for 'number', which is a contraction of the Italian word 'numero', but takes a full stop to avoid ambiguity.

Abbreviations take a full stop when their final letter is a letter partway through the word, thus:

- 'Inc.' for 'Incorporated'
- 'Dr.' for 'Drive'
- 'Cl.' for 'Close'
- 'Pl.' for 'Place'
- 'Prof.' for 'Professor'
- 'Uni.' for 'University'
- 'Co.' for 'Company'
- 'Cor.' for 'Corinthians'.

There is also a software titling convention that has become a standard naming convention, which is often playful or gimmicky and usually incorporates contraction, particularly of spacing and punctuation, but retains capitals within a hybrid term, thus: QuarkXPress, InDesign, PhotoShop. But note: Westpac (for 'Western Pacific').

Comma

If the text is understandable without punctuation, i.e. it is unambiguous and reads logically, then don't interrupt it with punctuation. To this end, we do not use as many commas as may have been used in the past. Commas rarely appear in headlines or display text. We also avoid them if line breaks separate ideas, so the idea that every line in an address or poem finishes with a comma has been superseded.

They do appear in numbers as the separators of thousands and millions. While this was achieved by using a fixed space or punctuation space in many style preferences for numerical expression, due to web limitations, it is often safer to use commas:

    1,000 instead of 1000 or 1 000
    2,000,000 instead of 2 000 000.

Quotes/inverted commas

In dialogue or quoted text, the preference is for single quotes for a first-level quotation and double quotes within a quote. This is probably exactly the opposite of what you were taught at school. Thus, bearing in mind that less is best:

> The Professor asked, 'Why is it so?'
> 'Then she said, "I'm 18, okay?" and I admitted her,' the attendant explained.

However, note this is different in the United States, where it is the opposite: double quotes first and single quotes within. Also note some preferences in journalism for direct speech to be in double quotes. Provided there is consistency throughout your document, it is a case of selecting your preferred practice and defining it in a house style.

Slash/solidus/slant

The slash or solidus usually stands between two options, hence 'and/or' and even 'him/her'. This is why it is incorrect to use the solidus to express a financial year: '2009/10' implies 2009 'or' 2010. The slash is used to separate elements within web URLs:

> http://www.unswpress.com.au/designmanual/

It can also be used in the expression of dates: 09/01/94. Note that the use of double figures in this method of expression creates a more even look than 9/1/94. Also be aware that this date as expressed is understood in Australia as 9 January 1994 but in the United States would be understood to be 1 September 1994. For websites and other international communications, it might be more appropriate to use a spelt-out date for clarity. In forms it is becoming more widely recognised that a coding specifying the sequence is required: 'DD/MM/YYYY' for Australia and 'MM/DD/YYYY' for the American preference.

Note also that the standard date and time expression in computing is 'YYYY/MM/DD/HH:MM:SS' incorporating year/month/day/hour:minute:second.

Hyphen

The hyphen is a single keystroke and is used in compound words like blue-green algae.

It has also been used between double vowels when the vowel sound needs to change as in 'co-operate', so you don't read 'coop' as in chickens, but this detail is now passing out

Real quotes

'   Opening single quote

'   Closing single quote

"   Opening double quote

"   Closing double quote

The symbols for imperial measures for inches and feet

'   Foot mark

"   Inch mark

Smart quotes

Many programs have a preset default that will automatically replace typed inch and foot marks with opening and closing quotes. The ability of the program to do this is based on accurate preparation of the spaces around the marks. If a space precedes the mark, it assumes you want an opening quote. If a space follows the mark, it assumes you need a closing quote. It will also assume you want a double quote if you type the inch mark and a single quote if you type a foot mark. This has its problems when it comes to wanting apostrophes to start a word, because the default wants to give you an opening quote mark, not an apostrophe.

Compare:

'Tis the season
Apostrophe

'Tis the season
Opening quote

of usage, successfully argued by proponents of minimal punctuation, so 'cooperate' is now preferred.

When you break a word at the end of a line to continue it on the next, as in most justification programs, a hyphen is used.

For display setting
There are a few finer details of their use you might like to consider:

- In large headings, punctuation marks (including hyphens) are often reduced so they are not so intrusive. If they are smaller though, they are raised to correct position for the type using baseline shift.
- Between words set in all capitals you need to raise the hyphen to the centre of the capital letters, because the hyphen is set at the centre of the lower-case x-height.

Compare:

Hyphen   -

En rule   –

Em rule   —

Double em rule   ⸺

En rule

An en rule is about double the length of a hyphen and is used in compound terms and stands for the words 'and' or 'to'. Therefore the Sydney–Brisbane grand final takes an en rule for Sydney 'and' Brisbane. The Melbourne–Perth rail link takes an en rule for from Melbourne 'to' Perth.

The 2009–10 financial year has an en rule meaning 2009 'to' 2010. The solidus is often incorrectly used in this form (i.e. not 2009/10, as there is no sense of option or 'per').

Spaced en rule
The spaced en rule (space, en rule, space) should be used with compound terms that are compounded. Therefore, the United States – United Kingdom match is the compound of two compounds and should take a spaced en rule. The Australia – New Zealand agreement is a compound term because New Zealand is two words. So the rule is: When one or both the terms have a space within the term, there should be a space either side of the en rule.

Another example of this is in date spans: the weekend of 30 September – 1 October, or 1 July 2009 – 30 June 2010.

In text setting, the spaced en rule is also used in websites, as it is in this book, instead of an unspaced em rule. This is a preference that has the practical result of allowing text to break either side of the dash, which does not happen automatically with an unspaced em rule, creating unsightly line turnovers and requiring an intervention by the designer. You don't always have the time – and a spaced en rule will suffice.

For display setting
- In large headings, punctuation marks are often reduced so they are not so intrusive. You would also probably avoid the spaced en rule in headings.
- In titles, you may like to replace the en rule with a circle or diamond to make the setting more interesting.
- In all-capitals setting, you need to raise the en rule to the centre of the capital letters because the en rule is set at the centre of the lower-case x-height.

Em rule/dash

An em rule is double the length of an en rule. It may or may not have a space either side but, if it falls at the end of a line, the line can be broken either before or after the em rule.

Most justification programs will not separate two words that are connected with an em rule unless there is a space. Consequently, most magazines, websites and publishers have a policy of using a spaced en rule (space, en rule, space) instead, as in this book, so the rule will break at the end or beginning of a line.

The em rule is not like a hyphen, which appears only at the end of a line in a broken term. The em rule can appear at the beginning of the next line if it does not fit on the previous line.

But when should it be used? There are arguments that the em rule can be replaced by other punctuation marks, specifically commas or parentheses (these round brackets). Often, em rules are used in sets of two—though not exclusively—for a parenthetical statement. If you reread the previous sentence, it could read 'Often, em rules are used in sets of two (though not exclusively) for a parenthetical statement' or even 'Often, em rules are used in sets of two, though not exclusively, for a parenthetical statement'.

For display setting
- In headings and titles, where possible, em rules are avoided and other punctuation marks, such as commas and parentheses, are used instead.

- In all-capitals setting, you need to raise the em rule to the centre of the capital letters, because the em rule is set at the centre of the lower-case x-height.

Double-em rule

A double-em rule is used in bibliographies and references. It is used in lists of publications where an author or authors may have written more than one book listed in the bibliography. List the author/s for the first entry and then, instead of repeating the author/s for the subsequent entries, use a double-em rule to indicate that they are the same as the previous entry:

Meggs, Philip B. *A History of Graphic Design*. New York: Van Nostrand Reinhold, 1983.
——. *Type and Image: The Language of Graphic Design*. New York: Van Nostrand Reinhold, 1989.

Colon

Colons introduce quotations, summaries and lists, either in catalogue form or in continuous prose. They are also used to indicate a ratio (1:2) and to separate chapter and verse in references to the Bible (Deut. 4:26).

In computing, film and video referencing, they are also used in the expression of time to separate minutes from hours: 12:00 (but note that this is not the practice in general text).

Semicolon

Semicolons can be used between entries in listings where commas would not be clear enough or the entry has numerous parts that already contain commas. A semicolon is thus a separation device. In sentence structures, they are sometimes used in place of conjunctions (words which join two related statements).

Parentheses/square brackets/braces/brackets

Parentheses are the curved 'brackets' that separate ideas from main text (like these).

Square brackets [like these] are often used for editorial asides within text – they indicate another voice. They are also used as the secondary level of bracketing within parentheses in mathematical setting. In display setting, they often work better than parentheses with sans serif and slab serif typefaces.

Braces are the wriggly ones {like these} and are mostly used in mathematics to join two elements of an equation. They are handy for display setting at times as they sit more decoratively with script and traditional serif typefaces.

Citing the Bible

The punctuation of Bible references is standard: 'John 3:16' cites an individual verse and means a reading from the Gospel of Saint John, chapter 3, verse 16. The colon follows the chapter number and the verse number follows with no space. 'I Corinthians 13:1–13' cites a chapter and means a reading from Paul's first letter to the Corinthians, chapter 13, starting at verse 1 and finishing at verse 13. The first letter is denoted by using the Roman numeral for 'one' which is a capital *i*. Paul's second letter to the Corinthians would be cited: 'II Corinthians'. The colon follows the chapter number, then comes the starting verse number, followed by an en rule and the closing verse number, with no space either side of the en rule.

To abbreviate the Bible sources, the same citation could read: I Cor. 13:1–13. Since verse 13 is the final verse of that chapter, you could also cite this reference, without specifying the verse, as: I Cor. 13.

Some Bibles will give a preferred abbreviation guide in the contents listing at the front.

Other sacred texts have similar citation systems.

Text formatting

There are five text formatting options available to you, but really only two that are practical for continuous reading. The other three are suitable for display text setting and some specific purposes, but need to be used with care.

Unjustified text

If the lines in a text block remain uneven in length, it is called *ragged right, range left* or, more often, *flush left unjustified*.

The left side of the text is set at a regular point which aids the return of the eye to the next line, and the right side of the text is uneven, ensuring the texture of the type is even. Text that is set flush left unjustified has an even typecolour because the spacing between words is constant.

Spell-checks and proofreading

Nothing beats the proofread for fixing errors. Spell-checks can only go so far. A spell-check will not recognise such typos as the miskeying of 'from' to 'form' or 'for' to 'fro'. Although a spell-check will identify words it doesn't recognise, and this enables you to catch most typos, there is a need for someone to do a proofread for sense and style following the spell-check.

Proofreading marks

There is a margin mark to draw
attention to the error and a text mark
that defines exactly where it occurs.
At the end of each margin mark there
is a solidus or slash to separate it
from the next mark if one occurs in
the same line.

Margin mark	Text mark	Correction as it would appear
r/	Inse t	Insert
#/	Insert space	Insert space
i /	My stake	Mistake
sp. out/	&	and
⌐/	Delete	Delete
⌐/	Delete and close up	Delete and close up
STET/	Leave as is	Leave as is
CAP/	capitalise	Capitalise
c.+s.c./	Capitals and small caps	Capitals and small caps
l.c./ l.c./	lower case	lower case
itals/	Italicise	*Italicise*
bold/	Make bold	**Make bold**
rom./	Make roman	Make roman
w.f./ w.f./	Wrong font	Wrong font
sup/sup./	degree o footnote I	degree° footnote [1]
sub./sub./sub./	x a + y b = z c	$x_a + y_b = z_c$
trs/	Transpose	Transpose
c.u./	Close up	Close up
align/	Align	Align
align/	Align	Align
align/	Correct alignment	Correct alignment
run on/	Run on	Run on
⊙/ ⊙/ ⊙/	colon semi-colon full stop	colon: semi-colon; full stop.
?/ !/	question exclamation	question? exclamation!
⅋/ ⅋/ ⅋/ ⅋/ ⅋/	single double comma	'single' "double" comma,
s.q./ s.q./	Single quotes	'Single quotes'
en/ ⊘/	Hyphenate	Hyphen-ate
⊘/	2000/01 Sydney Canberra	2000–01 Sydney–Canberra
⊘/	You you're kidding?	You—you're kidding?

It leaves that extra space at the end of the line, which gives it the ragged look, hence its alternative title 'ragged right'. It even usually avoids the cross-patterning of 'rivers'.

Unjustified text also looks a bit more modern – it was considered an essential ingredient in the Swiss styling that dominated design in the mid-20th century. Other ingredients of that 'modern' style were sans serif type, a multicolumn grid and a generous use of white space.

If text is set in narrow columns, it should be set flush left unjustified to avoid the uneven spacing and hyphenation that justification causes but also to give extra 'optical' separation between the columns. The actual measure of unjustified columns is wider than their optical width, due to the space (which would be distributed between the words if the setting was altered to justified) being placed on the right-hand side of the text. The optical width of the column gives the impression of a wider gutter between columns.

However, when people are asked their preference, unjustified text is often disliked because it looks so 'untidy'. So don't ask – they will often not notice until it is pointed out.

To make unjustified text more even down the ragged right side, you can introduce limited hyphenation either by using judicious hyphenation as a manual process by the editor or designer, or by using a *rag zone*. By setting a minimum line length, any word that sets beyond that length is hyphenated according to the program's hyphenation dictionary.

Flush right and centred settings
There are two other options to consider when choosing unjustified text format: *ragged left, range right* or *flush right unjustified*; and *centred*. These are self-explanatory and, interestingly, best used in a similar manner.

Due to the difficulty of extended reading of either centred or flush right unjustified text, use those styles only for brief, self-contained pieces of information, such as pieces used in posters, titles or invitations: headlines, titles, names, dates, times, places, addresses. Each line break should be logical.

It is believed that the difficulty of reading these two styles stems from the fact that the left side of the text is uneven. When reading justified or flush left text, the left side is constant, giving our eyes a standard point to which they can return. This is believed to be essential for comfortable, extended reading.

Flush left unjustified

or

ranged left

or

ragged right

Flush right unjustified

or

ranged right

or

ragged left

Asymmetrical/free-form text

There is a free-form text styling that is sometimes used by poets to create a random or unstructured text layout. You may use a set of standard indents for alternate lines of text and allow short and long lines to fall as they will. Asymmetrical text has grown from modern poetry layout and has become a popular option for dynamic display type: magazine article headings, advertising and cover titles.

There is a readability issue. Being able to find the start of the next line has been shown to be a reading aid – that is why flush right and centred text formats have been found to be unfriendly to readers. It also explains the ease with which we read flush left unjustified and justified text formats – the eye can return consistently to the same starting point for the following lines.

So asymmetrical type layouts are best when made up of self-contained lines of text. But for occasional titles and short bursts of information, such as those in websites and advertising, asymmetrical text formatting can be a fresh and dynamic option.

Always consider the overall shape of the text block you have created.

Justified text

Justification is achieved by spreading the space left at the end of a line evenly through the line so that all lines become the same length. Usually this means the word-spacing varies; though in extreme cases the letterspacing varies as well. Basically, it is this extra spacing and the unevenness it creates that are disturbing to the typographer. Justification often interrupts the typecolour of the text – the uneven spacing can make the text block look blotchy when you squint at it. However, justification does lend a traditional feel to a layout, and is almost essential if you want centred headings because it firmly establishes the width on which you are centring the heading.

When text is justified, the left and right sides of each column of type are parallel. If the words and spaces were left to fall naturally, the end of each line would occur at a different point.

So why bother? Many people assume that justified type is 'professional' type. They refer to the traditions built up over centuries of book and newspaper design – but let's face it, those old newspapers were hardly reader-friendly.

Rivers

A 'river' of white space running contrary to horizontal reading rhythm can subliminally distract your reader. It is more likely to occur in justified text – due to the extra space distributed through the lines to justify them. An example is marked.

In fact, it is only when specifically asked that people even notice the difference between justified and unjustified text – and then they state their preference for justified text because it 'looks neater'. It makes no difference to how effectively they read the text.

Books are another matter. If you need to feel like a part of the continuum, justify your text. But do so with an understanding of the craft of justification. It is this craft, a finely honed sensibility to type and its readability, that has largely been lost since the development of computer-generated type (including computer typesetting here as well, not just DTP).

When type was justified by hand, the person setting the type made decisions at the end of every line: Will the line have too much space distributed through it if I don't hyphenate? Will a hyphen be needed? If so, where will it best go in the next word to avoid misreadings? Can I squeeze the letterspacing of a few well-chosen words to accommodate an extra word in the line?

Hyphenation
It is essentially the process of justification that has necessitated the development of hyphenation programs. It is very convenient, if you choose to have your text justified, to be able to fit a bit of the next word onto a short line. Because of this, justified text will usually save a few lines in column depth over an article or a chapter.

However, a worst-case scenario is the possibility of a connect-the-hyphens game down the right-hand side of a paragraph. This can be the result of either a poor hyphenation program or a text width that is too narrow for justification.

Once text has been justified automatically, do a quick scan down the right side to seek out strange or overused hyphenation. In most cases, a wise decision to force-hyphenate (typing in a hyphen that sends part of a word back to the previous line) can fix a paragraph.

Sometimes a punctuation mark that is not spaced, such as an en rule, will be ignored as a logical breaking point. If you type in a space on one side of the en rule, it will split the term over the line break. This is also why, with default line-breaking rules as they are, people often use a spaced en rule instead.

In many cases, ugly justification or hyphenation can

be fixed editorially – a skilful editor or copywriter will occasionally find a shorter adjective or add a word to 'fix' a line on request.

Paragraph styling

The distinction between paragraphs is traditionally made as a selection from two options. However, there are often many paragraph stylings contained within the one document. So although you may think your decision is just whether to indent or to block and space your paragraphs, you will have further paragraphing decisions to make.

Indented paragraphs

The most widely used form is the paragraph indent. Simply set a first line indent of 5 mm or as small as 1 em (or the width of the typeface: in 10 point text, this becomes a 10 point indent).

As a layout element, this creates an irregular pattern of white blocks down the side of the grey block. You might choose to introduce more paragraph divisions to keep the pattern more regular. Discuss this with the author or editor.

You might maximise the effect of the random paragraph indents by featuring them: decorative indenting is simply achieved. For example, in justified text, you might do a half-line paragraph indent, which with centred headings reasserts the central axis. In unjustified text in a pamphlet or a press ad, you might do a 30 mm indent that creates a pattern like piano keys down the side of the text block. Sometimes an author or editor will help you to achieve a specific pattern.

Maximising paragraph indents by using them for the indents in lists and as the line used for photo borders reinforces the grid line established by a paragraph indent.

It is better to delete or override the paragraph indent with contoured text or runarounds (so that the runaround doesn't have an unsightly bump where the paragraph indent occurs).

Blocked paragraphs

Reasonably popular with letter presentation and a good one to remember if you have a short letter on your letterhead, the blocked paragraph has no indent and is separated from the other paragraphs by space. This spacing is often achieved with an extra line return, but that is a poor

DOING IT SMARTER
The squint test
Graphic designers don't necessarily have bad eyesight when they squint at a layout! You can check the tonal arrangement on the page if you look through your eyelashes. The type and pictures recede and appear to become rectangular blocks or free-form areas of grey tone. These areas, some of which will be light and some dark, create patterns, which are like a piece of abstract art.

method. The preferred method (because it allows greater options for your text beyond the initial use) is to use the spacing-before-or-after section of a style sheet and allocate a specific space.

The full line return, which in text set 10/12 allocates 12 points of space between the paragraphs, is too much. A half-line return is better: a 6 point space. Even a 3 point space can succeed – anything less can look accidental.

As a layout element, spaced full blocking can create a disjointed page due to the horizontal white stripes that appear randomly through the grey text block. For this reason, it almost never works in multicolumn setting.

First paragraphs

As a layout consideration, the first paragraph after headings is blocked; that is, with no paragraph indent. Consider using this blocked paragraph even after indented lists to avoid the look of the paragraph continuing the final dot point.

It is easy to create this first paragraph styling in a style sheet as 'based on' normal text but with the indent deleted.

This is both a typography and a layout issue. Typographically, the indent serves to separate a paragraph from other paragraphs, but we signify the difference between paragraphs and headings with at least a font variation and often a spacing variation, so an indent is unnecessary. As a layout issue, the text block is strengthened if the corner is established in the top left, making a sharp rectangular grey block, rather than a dulled one, which an indent would create.

Consider using a first paragraph styling if a paragraph falls at the top of a column to strengthen the text block on that page. A paragraph that is broken in the middle has the correct effect because it simply continues across into the next column or page with no indent.

Hanging indents

In lists, you specify a hanging indent but do not show it because you set a tab position to the point at which the continuing lines 'hang'. So this odd indent (where the first line is the full width and the second and continuing lines are indented) is rarely used in other text setting. Some people use it to give an unusual and attention-getting effect in pamphlets and brochures, like a backward paragraph indent. It has been used in the 'Read more about it' lists in this book.

Lists

Lists provide a helpful technique to break up text, particularly for presentation of text on-screen. If lists in the text are indented:

- use bullets and align them with the left margin
- align the text entry with the paragraph indent
- do not justify the text.

In legal documents, the lists are numbered and subdivided alphabetically and further subdivided with roman numerals, thus:

1   Recommendation
   (a) First point
   (b) Second point
      i) First subdivision
      ii) Second subdivision
      iii) Third subdivision
   (c) Third point
2   Second recommendation

In technical reports, the subdivisions will be numerically coded with paragraph numbering:

1   First chapter
   1.1 First point
   1.2 Second point
      1.2.1 First subdivision
      1.2.2 Second subdivision
      1.2.3 Third subdivision
   1.3 Third point
2   Second chapter

You should as far as possible use dot points for subdivision of text, unless you are describing a process where the sequence – and therefore sequential numbering – is important, such as the steps within a recipe or a description of the process for how to get a refund.

1   Describe step one.
2   Describe step two.

Dot points

Avoid more than two levels of dot points if possible.

Use bullet first then en dash and align as shown to reduce the number of indents/tabs:

• Bullet or symbol on margin; text aligned with paragraph indent
    – dash or secondary bullet on paragraph indent; text indented one more step.

Many people prepare lists with indented dot points like this:

Our products include:
• Apples
    – Golden delicious
    – Granny Smith
    – Fuji
• Oranges
    – Valencia
    – Navel

In the following examples, the layout is instantly improved and, incidentally, stronger because of the reinforcement of the margin and avoidance of secondary tab levels:

Our products include:
• Apples
    – Golden delicious
    – Granny Smith
    – Fuji
• Oranges
    – Valencia
    – Navel

Our products include:
■ Apples
    □ Golden delicious
    □ Granny Smith
    □ Fuji
■ Oranges
    □ Valencia
    □ Navel

You can use bullets or any combination of appropriate dingbats as markers.

Tabs

All a tab can do is align text. Tabs control the horizontal placement of text within a line. They are mostly used in producing tables or lists. When used to position headings or the starting line of text, we normally call them 'indents'.

Indenting

Too many indents can make a page look really ugly. Some people go indent-crazy, choosing to tab successive levels of information without using some of the other techniques available to them for establishing levels of importance (altering fonts from medium to bold, for instance). It often happens in contents lists.

Punctuation options for lists

There are three alternatives in the setting of lists.

In lists with full sentences (like this one):
□ Start each sentence with a capital letter.
□ Finish each sentence with a full stop.

In lists with a lead-in phrase, long dot clauses and subsets (like this one) you should:
□ start each entry in the list with lower case unless it is a proper noun;
□ use a dash
    – for a subset of a dot point
    – to indicate a list within a dot point;
□ use a semicolon at the end of each entry, except for the last point which takes a full stop.

In lists with a lead-in phrase and dot points (like this one), use:
□ lower case
□ no punctuation
□ a full stop at the end.

Consult a style manual for more detail on capitalisation and punctuation options for lists.

Compare: with: or:

Title	**Title**	**Title**
Subtitle	Subtitle	Subtitle
Author's name	Author's name	*Author's name*

Tables

In tables and lists it can get much more complex. Take a simple table with some standard tabbing errors:

Product	Sales ($)	Sales (% of stock)
Apple	114	54.4
Orange	255	61.75
Lettuce	12	9.5

or worse, the same table with each column centred:

Product	Sales ($)	Sales (% of stock)
Apple	114	54.4
Orange	255	61.75
Lettuce	12	9.5

Ugly. Even worse, though, is the same table with rules separating the columns:

Product	Sales ($)	Sales (% of stock)
Apple	114	54.4
Orange	255	61.75
Lettuce	12	9.5

Vertical rules in a table may link the wrong information: horizontal rules relate the appropriate information string.

Now, reset the table with correct tabs set (which will align the $ sales on the right, so that the figures align correctly – units above units, tens above tens, and the percentages will be aligned on the decimal point) and a slight improvement in the definition of levels of information (the use of italics for the column headings). The column headings will be tabbed differently from the content of the columns – so there are two tab sets defined because of the third column heading not having a decimal point in it.

Product	Sales $	Sales % of stock
Apple	114	54.4
Orange	255	61.75
Lettuce	12	9.5

The following table uses the now familiar 'zebra striping' for every second row of content that enables readers to follow entries across the table. Note the solid bar of colour with reversed bold text used for the column headings.

Product	Sales $	Sales % of stock
Apple	114	54.4
Orange	255	61.75
Lettuce	12	9.5

In both cases, greatly – and simply – improved.

Get to know what your tabbing commands mean. Usually you have left-align, right-align, centre-align and decimal-point-align tab options.

And don't fall into the trap of using only preset tabs (they are usually evenly spaced, left-aligned tabs at regular intervals across your column measure). Preset tabs can be a problem when you import from a word-processing program to your page layout program.

Even in spreadsheet programs output and tabular web content, turn off most of the column borders and use type variation, colours and tints, and spacing to make the tabular material easier to read.

Footnotes/references/bibliographies

Footnotes appear at the foot of the column or page on which a text reference occurs but can be set beside the text reference in margins or a side column or, in text with generous leading, footnotes can sit between the lines at the point where the reference is made.

Endnotes are set like footnotes but occur in a list at the end of the chapter or the end of the publication or document.

Reference systems vary but there are a few common stylings. (For further information and extensive examples, consult the relevant style manuals.)

Note too the different use of commas and colons. Also, there are no full stops at the end of cited URLs unless they are part of the URL.

Article referencing

When referencing articles from publications like magazines or journals, the article title will often be cited in inverted commas and separated from the title of the source document by a comma (except in the APA and Vancouver systems). A date reference or volume and number references will usually follow the title of the source. For full details, you should consult a style manual.

Website referencing

Following the same form as a book reference as far as possible, Internet references include a reference to the medium in which it was published, a carefully checked, full URL and the date on which the reference was sourced by the person making the citation.

Traditional footnotes

In text: Use these symbols in order, starting anew on each page: * (asterisk), † (dagger), ‡ (double dagger), § (section marker), ‖ (parallel mark), ¶ (paragraph marker).

In text, it has become more usual to use the superior number instead of the symbols. There are three options for numbering: consecutively through the page, consecutively through the chapter or consecutively through the book or document.

At the foot of the page: The footnote is usually set in the same font but two point sizes smaller than the text size, mostly unjustified even if the text is justified. Sometimes a fine rule (0.18 mm) of about 15 mm in length is used above them to set footnotes apart from the text. The number corresponding with the text superior appears at the left and then a tab, usually set at the paragraph indent of the main text, then the note follows, starting with a capital letter and finishing with a full stop. The number of the footnote need not be a superior figure.

Some people use Latin terms such as 'ibid.', 'op. cit.' and 'loc. cit.', but not everyone understands their meanings fully so it is best to avoid them.

Author–date style

The author–date style is based on the Harvard referencing system. Another variant is the American Psychological Association (APA) system.

In text: The text reference is in parentheses and immediately follows a quote or a reference to a particular work. It refers to a bibliography or reference list that contains the full reference to the citation.

> One commentator suggested that the world is flat (Brown 1996, p. 43).

> Widening the paragraph in this way (Samara 2007) results in …

OR

> Samara (2007) believes that widening the paragraph in this way …

Note the punctuation and the positioning of spaces.

At the end of the chapter or the document: The bibliography or reference list is organised alphabetically according to the author's family name and the date of the publication:

> Brown, J 1996, *History of the world*, 2nd edn, West Books, Sydney.
> Samara, T 2007, *Design elements: a graphic style manual: understanding the rules and knowing when to break them*, Rockport Publishers, Beverly.

Note the punctuation and spacing – no full stop after the author's initial, commas between elements after author and date, italics for titles, colons and lower case for subtitles.

In the author–date system the website reference extension will read:

> Retrieved [day] [month] [year], [full URL]

American Psychological Association (APA) system

In text: Exactly the same as the author–date system.

At the end of the chapter or the document: The bibliography or reference list is organised alphabetically according to the author's family name and the date of the publication:

> Brown, J. (1996) *History of the world*, 2nd edn. Sydney: West Books.
> Samara, T. (2007) *Design elements: a graphic style manual:*

understanding the rules and knowing when to break them. Beverly: Rockport Publishers.

Note the punctuation and spacing differences – a full stop after the author's initial, parentheses around the date, elements are separated by full stops and colons.

In the APA system, the website reference extension will read:

Retrieved (or 'viewed') [month] [day], [year], from [full URL]

OR

Available: [full URL]

Documentary note system

The documentary note system codes the references according to their occurrence in the text. Each reference is coded by number and the reference is either a footnote or an endnote. A variation is the Vancouver referencing system which consolidates the reference list at the end of the document.

In text: The text reference refers to a reference list that contains the full reference to the citation.

One commentator suggested that the world is flat.[1]

Widening the paragraph in this way results in an optimal number of characters and words.[2]

At the end of the document: The reference list is organised numerically according to the reference:

1   J Brown, *History of the world*, 2nd edn, West Books, Sydney, 1996, p. 43.
2   T Samara, *Design elements: a graphic style manual: understanding the rules and knowing when to break them*, Rockport Publishers, Beverly, 2007, p. 135.

Note the order of the elements, their punctuation and spacing – the author's initial precedes the family name, elements are separated by commas.

The Vancouver system

Very similar to the documentary note system, the Vancouver system is preferred particularly by the medical profession but also scientific publications generally. The numerical code becomes the code for all references from that same source throughout the document.

In text: Exactly the same as the documentary note system, the text reference refers to a reference list.

> One commentator suggested that the world is flat.[1]

> Widening the paragraph in this way results in an optimal number of characters and words.[2]

At the end of the document: The Vancouver system is slightly different to the documentary note system in order and punctuation:

1   J Brown, History of the world, 2nd edn. Sydney: West Books, 1996;43.
2   T Samara, Design elements: a graphic style manual: understanding the rules and knowing when to break them. Beverly: Rockport Publishers, 2007;135.

Note the revised order of the elements, their different punctuation and spacing – the title is not in italics; elements are separated by full stops, colons and semi-colons; page numbers are the final reference without a page abbreviation, nor a space.

Boxed text

Boxing text separates it from the rest of the text. It should be done for a reason – either it is more important, it is a distinct, self-contained subject, or it adds dimension to the text that surrounds it. When boxing text, do not crowd it. Make the box fit the grid and indent your text on all sides. The box becomes the dominant visual element in the layout, not the text width.

Beware of giving relatively unimportant pieces of text great importance in the page layout due to being boxed. Also avoid using too many boxes, because each competes for the reader's attention.

Therefore the correct text to place in a box is text with importance and text that stands alone (i.e. it does not need the context of the story to be understood).

You can also box a section of information that is on a tangent to the main article – as you often see in magazines or in websites. In an article on the arrival of the 'First Fleet' to Australian shores, there might be a boxed section on 'The Eora People' and their Indigenous lifestyle and culture.

When boxing dot-point material, always include the lead-in phrase or write a heading so the boxed list stands alone. This applies to the headings of boxed tables and graphs as well.

Positioning text boxes in a column

A common mistake is for the text block to be left as it is (same width as the rest of the text and same spacing between paragraphs) and a box superimposed over the section that is to be highlighted. This means the box bursts into the margins and is squeezed between the surrounding paragraphs. The strongest layout element is the box, not the text inside the box, so the box should align with the columns and the text should be indented on both sides. The box will then align with the margins, and the text inside the box will be indented in comparison to the text outside the box. As here.

If you use text in ovals and boxes on the same page, the text that is more important should be in the oval. The oval will be seen as a more important element than the box.

Consider the colouring of boxed text. Readability tests have shown that, for text, you can have any colour as long as it's black – and this on-screen as well! So let's assume black text. They've also shown that background colours can limit readability, but background colours have an attraction value, which is not to be easily dismissed, so limit the background to 5% or 10% of a colour. Certainly, if you are using tones of black (light grey), don't go heavier than 10%.

A large amount of reversed, boxed text is very tiring to read. If you have a black box and reversed text, remember the text should be sans serif, preferably bold, and it should also be the most important information on the page. Do not reverse a full story, just the first paragraph. You might have a two-tone box where the heading reverses out of a black band and the rest of the box is tinted with black text.

Page furniture

A page pretty much designs itself but, to be distinctive, there are a few page components that can establish a designer's presence:
- heading style and typeface selection
  - chapter openings and part titles
- captions to illustrations and photographs
- folios (page numbers) and running headings
- footnotes.

In books, reports and other long documents, the way you

furnish a page determines the success of the design. The pieces of text interact with each other and with illustrations and basic page requirements such as folios to create the overall look of each double-page spread. Those spreads combine to create an interesting document.

So that it remains interesting, build in design features that occasionally appear. They could be decorative chapter openings or title pages for different sections.

You must create design interest in the page furniture because the body text (the bulk of the content) must be kept typographically simple – it needs to be legible and, more importantly, readable.

Captions

As the use of images has increased, in print and on-screen, the power of the photograph caption has increased exponentially. It is now one of the most important pieces of text in a design. As a consequence of this, captions are getting longer and, instead of simply defining the subject of a photo, they now offer opinions and express concepts that previously would have been discussed in the body of the text. Caption wisely.

Captions are usually unjustified even if text is justified. They are sometimes set in italics, a point size smaller than the text. However, captions can be designed in many different ways and may appear differently within the same publication to fit the various photograph or illustration formats used. There is a readability value in having them consistently fall to the bottom and/or the right of their corresponding image.

Folios and running heads

One of the key design features of a page can be the placement of the folio. It is usually at either the bottom or the top on the outer margin or fore edge, or sometimes centred at the bottom.

The reader, who has used either the contents or the index to find a particular reference and is flicking through to find the folio, must be able to find it easily. Although it is acceptable to delete the folio on full illustration or advertisement pages and chapter openings, it is well to remember that the folio helps people to locate the text they seek. Multiple pages in a sequence with folios obscured by pictures or advertising can be most frustrating.

DOING IT FASTER
Duplicate

Many people will draw rules above each heading in their document. They end up drawing the rule and going to a menu to specify its width every time that heading occurs.

That's what duplicating is for. You create it once, duplicate (usually a keyboard command once you have selected the item) and then you just have to drag the clone to the correct position in the document.

You might find it faster to create a complex rule and heading arrangement if the heading is a separate text block to the body copy. In that way, you can group the heading and the rule and any other graphic elements and duplicate them. When you have placed the duplicate in position, you can alter the heading to the new text.

In the same way, don't draw text and picture boxes each time – duplicate the first and drag the duplicates into position.

Better still, some programs will allow you to do it all within the style sheets so you need only apply the style. This is even faster.

DOING IT FASTER
Copy and paste

Using the copy and paste functions can help you to duplicate complicated heading stylings. Remember to choose the space that precedes the heading and the space that follows it, so that the spacing of elements is consistent. Complex type treatments then need to be created only once, so that you simply select and overtype the new text.

This works for the set-up for tables and any regularly occurring text feature.

It can even be faster to copy and paste a grouping of styles than to use the style sheets.

DOING IT FASTER
Heading hierarchy presets

If you have created style sheets of complex heading treatments, keep them in a style sheet that you can duplicate when you start a new document.

If you have a favourite hierarchy of headings, create it using the 'based on' feature that many style sheets have. Then, for each document change the 'normal' typeface that the style sheets were based on and insert the typeface for the new job. If your 'based on' commands were worked correctly in the original style sheets, all the headings will automatically change to the new desired font, retaining the characteristics (size, capitalisation, bolding, italicising and tracking) that your style sheet had allocated to each level of heading.

When there is a running head, which is usually the name of the book, the chapter or a subject identifier for the page, it is usually designed to sit with the folio. Called a running head because it was traditionally placed at the top of a page, it can be a running foot (at the bottom) or even run down the outer margin. The running head might be the document title on the left-hand page and a changing subject category or chapter title on the right-hand page. In some documents such as proposals and magazines, the title, security information and date appear on each page.

The combination of folio and running head can help to create a distinctive page layout if designed wisely. Because it will be a feature of every page of the book, it can help establish a typographic theme and may feature rules, flourishes, borders or even logos and symbols.

Heading hierarchy

The creative use of type contrast makes interesting layouts.

Remembering that people use headings to skim text to find the information they need, headings must jump out of the grey body copy. We tend to use bolder type or a different typeface. Just enlarging type can be enough to establish a different level of importance. Each of these techniques can be helped by the amount of space placed above and below the heading. The more space around a heading the more important it is perceived to be, even if it is in tiny type.

Try to keep the heading linked to the text that follows it. Putting more space above the heading than below can do this. If you are using rules to separate sections, the rule should go above the heading rather than below. If there are rules above and below a heading, the rule below is often lighter (thinner or finer) than the one above.

Consider the number of times that a particular heading will be seen – if it is too prevalent, large sizes or blocks of white space may start to look clumsy (a bit like an ugly chequerboard).

You must create different levels of importance – the 'heading hierarchy'. Determine which headings are most important and least important; place all other headings between them, in order. Then create a style for each, where – by using variations in size, typeface, weight, tracking, formatting, indenting and capitalisation – you show the reader these levels of importance.

To be 'reader-friendly', you need to consider levels of information within text and indicate their comparative importance to the reader correctly.

Importance is determined by differences in size, weight and capitalisation. Something can be set in a light type at a large size and it will have more emphasis than something small and extrabold on the same page.

When type is the same size, emphasis is determined (in order) by:
- capitalisation
- weight
- direction (whether it is roman or italic).

A capitalised heading at the same size as the text is more important than a heading set in bold or italics.

The larger a design element, the more dominance in the layout it assumes. But a page is not a billboard: your reader is reading at arm's length, not across the room. So headings do not have to be enormous, just comparatively larger than the text type.

In larger headings, there need not be extra leading between lines. Tracking is tighter as size increases.

Weight in order of importance is determined by colour on the page: reversed text and extrabold text attract because by comparison with the text block mid-grey, they are very black. Headings and titles usually rely on their size to attract attention, but often it's not the size that counts – it's what you do with it. If it's bold or extrabold, it can assume more importance than its size suggests.

Although capitals imply an extra level of importance, they should be avoided when there are very long headings.

Lower-case headings should be consistent in what is capitalised and what is not.

Hierarchy clarity
Headings and headlines should not have full stops, even if they are in sentence structure.

When deciding what should be bold or italicised, think about the level of importance to the reader.

For example, in a theatre program's actor profiles, a character's name is less important than the name of the person playing that character. However, in the cast list, the character's name helps us to identify the actor, which explains why the first column is usually the character's name. Similarly, in orchestral listings, the musician is

DOING IT SMARTER
Learning heading hierarchy
If you want to learn about the ability of spacing and formatting to create a basic hierarchy, limit the project to one type font (that is, a typeface without using any other family members) and one point size. Then set a piece of text with three levels of heading to be determined – with only that one font and one size! It forces you to use spacing and layout tools to indicate the relative importance of the headings. This enables you to isolate formatting options (centring, spacing and leading) and type options (capitalisation and tracking) and learn how to use them more effectively.

identified according to the instrument listing. Production personnel can be listed either way, because some people may identify them by their role, but many people will be none the wiser, so you can list them much like an acknowledgments listing – with their name first.

In the profiles, you usually give prominence to the actor's name in bold, capitals or larger-than-text size, or any combination of these. This is followed by a minor reference to the character played or, in the case of production personnel who are profiled, their production role, which could be in small capitals, italics or just smaller than the name. The text then follows in a comfortable size for reading with appropriate leading. This text often includes the titles of other productions and production companies, so it is mostly in the regular weight of a font, and italics identify other production credits.

If you have a heading or paragraph in italics that cites a title that would normally be italicised, simply reverse the practice: set the title in roman type in italic text setting.

Display type

Often when you are designing a pamphlet or a book, an advertisement or a poster, an article heading in a magazine or a section title page in a manual, the information or subject matter does not lend itself to imagery, either photographic or illustrative. This is the moment when display type is seized as the design concept. But how do you start and what techniques really work with titles and headlines?

Don't let anyone tell you size doesn't matter: in design, contrast of scale (the relative size of design elements) is often the success factor. One of the main techniques is to use type confidently. That is, big.

Of course, you don't have to use all the type in your headline at an equal size – maybe only the first letter will be huge; maybe only the main word that defines your subject will be large; maybe a great letterform (like an optional f: f, or the ampersand: &) will be highlighted; maybe each word will be a different size.

But the argument that it's not the size but what you do with it is equally strong. For example, a well-placed rule will add that little bit of structure to your layout, but will also fill any unsightly gaps or give a sense of unity to the letterforms.

Two rules might spice up the action, particularly if they are of different widths.

Typographers also look for a pattern of letterforms that can be highlighted or structured to create an interesting pattern in the display type treatment. For example, in a pamphlet on road safety, you might try to find three of the letter *o* in the title (or even edit the title to create this, so you could stack them in three lines and colour them red, amber and green. If there were only two letter *o*s, but there was an *a* in another line, don't forget you could use a typeface where the form of the letter *a* is a circle with a side stroke, to create the pattern required.

The pattern could be similar letterforms or a pattern of strokes, maybe the verticals. Try to balance curves and straight strokes through the type. This means you need to consider the capital letterforms, the lower-case letterforms and any optional letterforms. You may need to use the roundness of a lower-case *a*, instead of the triangular capital A. In display type, the mixing of letterforms is a design decision that should be made to improve the look of a particular combination of letters.

You could also change the attributes of individual letters. So who says you can't have an italic lower-case *a* in the centre of an all-roman word? You will often see this technique used to lend individuality or uniqueness to titles and logotypes. Sometimes this is done most effectively with the vowels. To create a visual liveliness, maybe the letter 'i' will be altered to italic. This can create a rhythm through a title if there are a few 'i's and the title is spread over a few lines. The italic pattern that is created runs through the roman text. If you can introduce a colour change as well, the text becomes quite decorative in what is a very simple technique that doesn't hinder readability.

Double letters are particularly useful for this treatment. Double *ff* in italics should be tracked so the crossbar in the centre overlaps slightly and you create almost a new hybrid letterform. The same can be done with double capital TT.

Have a look in your specialist sets of typefaces – they will often contain a number of interesting ligatured characters. These hybrid characters lend individuality to a heading treatment and are regularly used in logotypes.

DOING IT SMARTER
The squint test
Look at a page of text. Blur it by squinting (or removing your glasses). The page will be reduced to its layout elements and each will appear as a tonal block. The light grey blocks are usually body copy. A bold introductory paragraph will have a darker tone. Dark or black spots in a largely light or grey page are going to be the layout elements that attract most attention.

Your computer will save you the trouble of squinting at every page. Just reduce your page on-screen and, at the lower resolution, it will often have a similar effect.

DOING IT SMARTER
Rules with type
Sometimes a good way to judge how thick a horizontal rule should be is to look at the crossbar of the capital A or the horizontal stroke of the capital L of the typeface and match the thickness. Subliminally, the horizontal rules will then look as if they belong to the typeface and create a more cohesive display.

DOING IT SMARTER
Learning display setting

Practise display setting by choosing
a calendar quote (those one- or two-
sentence quotes by famous people on
desk calendars) and creating a display
setting of it. This means creating
an interpretive piece of typography
that adds an extra dimension to the
meaning or the way we read the quote
because of the way in which it has
been set using a combination of type
characteristics. Do not use illustration;
just let the type say it.

This project can be extended into a
series of posters or a book by selecting
the full text of a speech (Martin Luther
King's 'I have a dream' speech is
excellent) or some religious writings.
Abstract concepts allow you to
interpret typographically, rather than
resorting to pictorial representation
where, for example, in a fairytale you
might consider making a forest out of
tangled letters and words. Abstract
text allows you to develop themes and
rhythms based on the recurring words
and concepts, allowing the design to
be led by the text.

DOING IT SMARTER
Two-line and three-line headings

Regardless of the chosen alignment
(centred, flush left or flush right), two-
line headings should have a longer
top line.

In three-line headings, the middle
line should not be the shortest, so the
sequence should be either:

- short, long, short
- short, medium, long
- long, medium, short.

A swash character is also sometimes available in a specialist set. The swash is an extension of a character stroke (often the tails of capitals R and Q or the arm and tail of capital K are extended, for example). Often you will find you can use a swash character or a ligature from a different typeface if your selected typeface does not have that character. Alternatively, you can create the character in your font by taking the letters into an illustration program or font creation program and creating the desired character.

And what's to stop you from making every second word in the line extrabold and completely deleting the word spaces?

In fact, it is often desirable to avoid gaps in logotypes, particularly, by deleting the word space entirely and allowing the capitals to indicate the second word. Certainly, the word spacing of display type can be very narrow.

Type selection can influence your success rate with display type. There are so many faces available in so many fonts, and who says you can't mix and match them? Again, confidence and a certain panache are called for – you can combine stocky, bold young sans serifs with refined, genteel serifs past their prime.

Display type can also be a bit like a jigsaw puzzle – which piece goes where? There are so many weights and variations in most type families that you can successfully create a splendid piece of display type just by positioning the family members well.

Structuring the type, try to create a simple shape. Based on the geometric shapes of triangle, circle or square, choose line breaks to create the most effective shape.

Chapter openings and title pages, feature article titles, logotypes and website title banners are the main points for establishing the separation between you and your competition.

Altering the position of multiple headings or pieces of information in relation to each other can also add an interesting liveliness to a layout – overlap them or have them sitting on each other. If one is large enough, the other can run through it.

You might have them run-on (where the typeface changes to a new level of information in a different typeface midway through a line).

Beware of giving undue emphasis to the least important words. In book titles, see how many times the words 'and', 'is', 'with', 'the' and 'of' are enlarged to fill out a line, giving undue emphasis to the least important words for attraction to the book and definition of the intended audience and content. These words are the ones that should not be in bold or fluorescent ink or foil. They should be relegated to the background, minimised and cleverly handled within the typography to recede.

READ MORE ABOUT IT

Brody Neuenschwander, *Letterwork: Creative letterforms in graphic design*, Phaidon, London, 1993, ISBN 0 7148 2801 7.

Marion March, *Creative typography*, Phaidon, Oxford, 1988, ISBN 0 7148 2559 X.

Maggie Gordon & Eugenie Dodd, *Decorative typography*, Phaidon, Oxford, 1990, ISBN 0 7148 2601 4.

Rob Carter, *Working with computer type 4: Experimental typography*, RotoVision SA, Crans-Pres-Celigny, Switzerland, 1997, ISBN 2 88046 279 7.

Teal Triggs, *The typographic experiment: Radical innovation in contemporary type design*, Thames & Hudson, London, 2003, ISBN 0-500-51143-8.

Type Directors Club, *Typography: The annual of the Type Directors Club*, Watson-Guptill Publications, New York, 1980–, ISSN 0275 6870.

John Langdon, *Wordplay: The philosophy, art, and science of ambigrams*, Broadway Books, New York, 2005, ISBN 0-7679-2075-9.

Style sheets

Whenever a magazine or book is created, the designer devises extensive style notes for the publication.

The designer incorporates all the type features into a list that defines the possible uses to which the text will be put. These are contained in a job file so that the designer can refer to them whenever similar usage surfaces, e.g. a revised edition of the book, the next issue of the magazine, another book in the series.

If material is designed by an outside designer and then formatted in-house, the outside designer should be commissioned to prepare and install the style sheets and master pages in the program being used.

If you are designing a newsletter, book, magazine or website and are responsible for its future production, create style sheets that document the entire publication.

If you're not using style sheets, you should be. Once you have set up your master pages or grid, style sheets really streamline production.

It is easiest to work out all the style tags from what can be called the 'Normal' text. As the majority of text content – the body copy – falls into this category, it deserves careful

A
TOWN
LIKE ALICE
OR
Neville Shute's
A Town like
Alice
❧

BEFORE   AFTER

POWER
AND
GLORY

POWER
&
GLORY

Type specification

The traditional specification of a style was: the size of the type over the leading (expressed as a fraction) or the size of type followed by the word 'on' and then the leading; the measurement system – usually points ('pt') or pixels ('px'); the name of the typeface and the font weight; the capitalisation; the format ('flush left unjustified'); 'to'; the measure/width of the text block; 'indented to'; any indention desired; the space desired expressed in points or pixels then 'space above'; the desired space expressed in points, pixels or millimetres (in cases where text is hung at a chapter opening, for example) then 'space below'.

For example: '10 on 12 pt Times bold caps, flush left unjustified to 70 mm, indented to 5 mm, 9 pts space above, 3 pts space below.'

DOING IT SMARTER
Idea file

Keep a file of interesting type treatments and use some of the great ideas you find. Photocopy or scan them from magazines, books and catalogues or print them off a website. Try to work out how it was done, and any special techniques that might be necessary to reproduce it, and maybe even identify the typefaces by using a type catalogue.

attention. Define the typeface, the weight and size that will be most readable in the measure (which is the column width you have already established in creating your master pages). Determine the amount of leading most appropriate to the average number of characters across that measure.

Set the indent for the first line if you intend having one. If you intend to block the paragraphs and leave space between them, define that as 'space below' each 'Normal' paragraph. About half the leading (equivalent to a half-line space) is recommended. Save this into your style sheet as 'Normal' and, if you have the option, give it a keyboard command for easy application.

'Normal 1' would be 'based on' 'Normal', which means that it would maintain all the attributes of 'Normal' but would be, in this case, distinguished by no indent in the first line. This is used for the first paragraph following a heading, hence calling it 'Normal 1'.

If your text has dot points, you could create a style called 'Dot point' or 'List' or call it 'Normal 2'. This is because it usually has all the same attributes for its type as 'Normal', so it is easy to use the 'based on' feature and then set the tab for the first line and the hanging indent for continuation lines.

The beauty of using the 'based on' feature is that if you decide to alter the specification for 'Normal' text, that alteration will flow through, avoiding the need to respecify all your tags. It also means you can save the style sheets and use them as the basis for another publication by simply inserting a new typeface and leading.

Create a series of heading styles, which can be given titles such as 'Heading 1' or 'A head' for most important, 'Heading 2' or 'B head' for next most important, and so on; or 'Title', 'Subtitle', 'Chapter title', 'Heading', 'Subhead', 'By-line' and 'Author'.

You should also add any special paragraph stylings required – such as 'Abstract', 'Continuation line', 'Intro', 'Lead para', 'Quote', 'Quote source' and a set of 'Pull-quote' options (so that your pull-quotes are not all the same).

Follow the same formula for captions, footnotes or endnotes. Create the complete set of type specifications for tables, including 'Table number', 'Table head', 'Table subhead', 'Column head', 'Row head', 'Row entry', 'Spanner head' (which is a heading that spans columns), 'Total' and 'Table source', etc.

Three heading styles 'based on' the 'Normal' text are self-explanatory and optically keep the same size: 'Normal bold', 'Normal italic' and 'Normal caps' (this one will need looser tracking and you may specify small capitals instead). Each will usually come in handy as a heading within text or tables.

You can create as many as you like, defining as you go the size, the leading, the typeface, the weight or font of the typeface, capitalisation, the colour (black, white or any preset colours), format variations (justified, flush left, flush right or centred), the indent, the measure/text width (not always done – in order to allow flexibility without having to redefine the style sheet), and, if possible, any rules that are linked to the heading and the spacing between the rules and the heading as well as the space that separates the element from the surrounding text. The rules would also be defined by their thickness, their form, their colour, and so on.

Test the size and weight relationships and how each level of information works with the text that surrounds it. How do the different levels of heading look if they follow each other? This often happens early in a chapter.

Depending on the results of these tests, refine the spacing and indenting, which are the usual attributes requiring attention, as you will have ironed out most problems with type sizes and weights before creating the style sheets.

Because complications often arise, you may need to create a series of heading options using the 'based on' feature which alters the way headings are spaced when they follow each other or when they break over to a second line. Because the 'space above' one heading is added to the 'space below' the heading line that precedes it, you may find you have a yawning chasm of space. So the new style tag becomes, for example, 'Heading 2 after 1' or 'B head after A' which usually deletes the 'space above' the second level heading and maintains the space below the first level heading. Check the manuscript for the number of heading combinations you may need to consider.

Remember, as far as possible, to use the 'based on' feature for creating style sheets – it enables fast updating and alterations. You need insert only a typeface name in two of your tags and all the rest follow because they are based on those two main specifications. As shown, the easiest is the one tagged 'Normal', but you may also have a heading style (say 'Heading 1' or 'A head') that can become your other main tag.

CHECKLIST

A guide to web typography for print-based designers

- ☐ Always specify alternative fonts in your style sheets, ensuring some are free or system fonts.
- ☐ If you use graphics as headings, ensure the 'alt text' is tagged as a heading and contains the heading text in full.
- ☐ Do not use line returns to force line breaks that will fix widows or orphans as text will display differently, due to browsers, screen size and reader preferences.
- ☐ Do not use line returns or the space bar to create alignment, for the same reason and because different fonts will have different widths.
- ☐ Do not confuse users with coloured text, as they will likely assume it represents a clickable link.
- ☐ Use 'strong' and 'emphasis' tags instead of 'bold' and 'italic' tags when coding in HTML.
- ☐ Limit use of italics to text emphasis and citing titles.
- ☐ Use commas in numbers instead of fixed spaces.
- ☐ Don't use spaces in phone numbers as they will split the phone number across a line break – unless you know the phone number will start the line.
- ☐ Always review how your work displays in a selection of common browsers – and up to two versions earlier than the current (for people who have not updated their software).

CHECKLIST
On-screen document quick fix
- Provide links within the document to other parts of the document or to other websites and documents.
- Edit text length to make text and paragraphs as short as possible.
- Use a horizontal format to help readers avoid scrolling.
- If you use a vertical format, make sure it is single-column and single-page display – and that it automatically opens to full-screen width.
- Remove blank pages from the print document – but be careful not to repaginate if cross-references are to page numbers.
- It is largely meaningless to have Roman-numeral-numbered preliminary pages in an online document. But retain them to avoid repaginating indexes and contents lists.
- Provide text alternatives to all images, charts and process maps.
- Ensure there is sufficient contrast between the text and the background colour.
- Use fonts that are readily available – preferably a sans serif system font designed for screen display.
- Don't create text as an image.
- Avoid background patterns that can distract.
- Reduce image size to ensure readers get the content they expect on each page; maybe give them the option to enlarge an image.
- Provide a print style sheet or a print-friendly version (many people prefer this to be black-and-white, rather than colour).
- While HTML is preferable, ensure the links to other versions of the document (usually a PDF, RTF, sometimes Word files or a print-friendly PDF) indicate the size of the download.

CHECKLIST
A guide to print design for screen-based designers
- Ensure readable type sizes for body text by specifying from 10 points for a serif typeface or 9 points for a sans serif typeface.
- Define the leading required, based on the width of the printed column – do not assume the default setting will be sufficient.
- Text should be mostly in black and ensure that any coloured text will be readable when printed.
- Be careful with coloured text and fine rules – ensure there is a solid colour (with no halftoning) in one of the specifications. Halftoned type is the print equivalent of jaggies on-screen.
- Pictures do not need fine grey borders as they end up halftoned and furry.
- Reduce the tonality of any background patterns to maintain sufficient contrast between type and background.
- Remember that you will see two pages side by side, so design double-page spreads, not individual pages.
- Proofread carefully as, once it is printed, you can't just update it – unless you reprint.
- Ensure image files are sufficient quality for print reproduction without pixelation.
- Avoid fine details – like borders – close to the trim edge of the page.
- Give sufficient colour bleed off the edge of the page for the printer to be able to trim.

THE DESIGN MANUAL

Side text style sheet

A side [*used for 'Read more …' and 'Doing it …' headings*]
7/11 pt Transit Normal flush left unjustified, all capitals, tracked 10, 11 pt space before
B side [*used for side subject headings and some captions*]
9/12 pt Transit Black flush left unjustified
C side [*used for internal side headings*]
8/11 pt Transit bold flush left unjustified, 5 pt space before
Side text
8/11 pt Transit Normal flush left unjustified, 5 mm first line indent
Side text 1 [*used for first paragraphs*]
Based on 'Side text', 0 mm first line indent
Side text 2 [*used for dot points and 'Read more …' listings*]
Based on 'Side text', left indent of 5 mm, first line indent of –5 mm
Side text 3 [*used for dash points*]
Based on 'Side text', left indent of 10 mm, first line indent of –5 mm
[**Tabs** set at 5 mm and 10 mm]

Document design

Style sheets are the fastest way to produce a complex document and speed even the simplest task. Being able to allocate keyboard commands to each tag just makes the manuscript processing even faster. Understand all the options and commands you have available in each tag so you can maximise their capabilities.

If the style sheet has been created using the 'based on' feature as much as possible, you should be able to use it for future documents with just a little tweaking. Often, all you will need to do is change the typeface that is defined in the 'Normal' setting.

Colour

DOING IT SMARTER
Spot colour
Establish a basic colour – often black in text layouts – and use another 'spot' colour only for highlights. This gives greater dynamism to the spot colour – it can be more effective in its attention-getting and interest-arousing roles.

DOING IT SMARTER
Colour images and colour selection
If you want colours in your design to complement the photography or illustration, choose colours that appear somewhere in the photograph or artwork – the most successful choice is often not a dominant colour in the photo or artwork.

To practise this skill, choose a coloured photo and force yourself to come up with three colour variations using only background and border colour variation. Assess the results to determine which presented the photograph most successfully. This helps you to isolate the colours that drain colour from an image from the colours that may enhance it. Note that the impact of 'accent' colours in an image will often be diminished if they are used in a border.

Irrespective of likes or dislikes, the brighter the colour, the greater its attraction. This is a physiological response – the brightness stimulates the eye to a greater extent, which partly explains children's preference for bright colours.

Bright colours, or light colours, by definition have a high reflection value – they look closer and larger and are easier to recognise. As a general rule, they are exciting and good for the mass market. They are brash and friendly. They are good colours for accents and we consider them to be younger, less conservative, extrovert and dynamic, and they are more attractive to men. The light, bright colours are also more popular in sunny climates and seasonally in spring and summer.

Soft, dark and modified colours have an air of dignity and restraint about them and are associated with up-market audiences. They look further away and smaller than bright colours. They reflect tradition and sentiment, and are considered to be older, and they are more attractive to women. They are the colours of the establishment and sophistication. Soft, muted, dark and modified colours are more popular in cloudy climates and seasonally in autumn and winter.

Colour should be used mainly for attraction, not for communication, so use it liberally in images, display text, backgrounds and borders, but be particularly conservative in its use in text. Never compromise the contrast of foreground and background simply to create a colour effect.

Colour terminology uses *hue* to describe the pure form of a colour that enables us to distinguish a yellow from an orange. All colours have a tonal *value* as well as their hue. The tonal value of a colour describes the grey it becomes on a black-and-white monitor or in a black-and-white photograph. Put simply, tonal value can be dark or light.

When choosing a colour palette, select colours of similar tonal value to do a similar job, such as when colour-coding a series of publications or on-screen tabs.

Tints are created when a hue is lightened. *Tones*, using colour parlance, are created when a hue is deepened by the addition of a darker colour, often black.

For a foreground to stand out from a background, the tonal value can be altered. Make the background darker and seemingly further away, hence the standard recommendation that slides in the presentation industry have dark-blue backgrounds with yellow text.

How readers view colour will depend on the lighting conditions where they are reading or their screen setting preferences for material on-screen. Incandescent home lighting gives a yellow cast as distinct from the blue–white of fluorescent lighting and the 'pure white' of daylight. Screens will often have their brightness dimmed and their contrast diminished, and sometimes even have a tinted screen over them to protect the viewer's eyes. All these choices and conditions will affect how the colours you select are seen by the audience.

Colour coding

Colour can identify an organisation or the type of document a reader is perusing or distinguish points of difference between one printed piece and another. Coding enables people to quickly find what they need.

Allocate a colour, or a series of colours, to each variable. The colours, when used consistently, become associated with a particular style of document or information, and effectively code material. It can be a code established for use within one publication or over a range of corporate materials.

Choose a colour to represent each arm of the organisation – the rainbow of colours represents the corporate palette for an organisation. Maybe one overriding colour links them all.

Just remember that once you get beyond about six colours, it gets hard for your audience to remember the code.

When selecting colour for a series, try to maintain a similar tonal value. For example, with a burgundy, steel blue and bottle green, you would not select a bright orange

DOING IT SMARTER
Learning to use colour
To develop your skill in using colour, create a project where you do not allow yourself to include black or white.

To test the psychological effect of colours, try experimenting with a colour portrait using just different border and background colours, but communicate these personality attributes: strength, weakness, coolness, warmth. You can see what can be implied – why isn't this used more in, say, election advertising?

Colour sequencing
In animated films and graphic novels particularly, but in film and comics generally, there is a sequence of colour that is determined as part of the storyboarding phase. This enables particular sequences to be related to each other but also to use the psychological responses to different colour palettes as subliminal enhancers to the storyline.

It works by coding contrasts, like warm/cool or bright/dark to represent good/bad. The colour sequence can be summarised by key frames from the movie.

Achieving colour balance
Consider the colour and tonal arrangement of your elements. Try to reduce your layout to a Mondrian-like composition. It is an effective way to analyse the interrelationship of the colours of your elements.

– tonally the orange would be the odd one out – but you might select a burnt orange or even a terracotta in order for the palette to have parity.

Similarly with pastels, you would not add a charcoal. A more tonally appropriate choice would be a pearl grey. Of course, maybe the charcoal grey could become the standard instead of, for example, black text. It would be softer than black and perhaps sit more comfortably with the pastels.

Also, the charcoal grey – as the bright orange in the previous example – could become the over-arching corporate colour, because of its contrast to the established palette.

Colour reproduction

Colour reproduction is one of the most exasperating and frustrating challenges for the graphic designer who is trying to control colour through all stages of a project, from concept to rough, approval, screen and print output. The computer has not made colour control any easier, though there are many systems attempting to manage it.

READ MORE ABOUT IT
Rob Carter, *Working with computer type 3: Color and type*, RotoVision SA, Crans-Pres-Celigny, Switzerland, 1997, ISBN 2 88046 278 9.
Veruschka Götz, *Color and type for the screen*, RotoVision SA, Crans-Pres-Celigny, Switzerland, 1998, ISBN 2 88046 329 7.
Leatrice Eiseman, *Pantone guide to communicating with color*, Grafix Press, Sarasota, Florida, 2000, ISBN 0 9666383 2 8.
Olga Gutiérrez de la Roza, *An eye for color*, Harper Collins/Collins Design, New York, 2007, ISBN 978-0-06-121006-8.
Ikuyoshi Shibukawa & Yumi Takahashi, *Designer's guide to color*, Angus & Robertson, Sydney, 1984, ISBN 0-207-15023-0. This developed into a series of four.
Shigenobu Kobayashi, *Colorist: A practical handbook for personal and professional use*, Kodansha International, Tokyo, 1998, ISBN 4 7700 2323 5.
Mattias Nyman, *Four colors/one image*, Peachpit Press, Berkeley, 1993, ISBN 1 56609 083 0.
Roger Pring, *www.colour: Effectiveness of colour for web page design*, Cassell & Co., London, 2000, ISBN 0 304 35607 7.

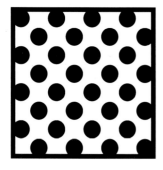

Halftones, stipples, screens and reverses

A *halftone* turns an image into a series of dots of varying size or pixels of varied distribution that, when far enough away, our eyes register as smooth tones of the printed colour. We perceive tone when it is actually patterns of a

Conventional screening

SHOWING ROSETTE

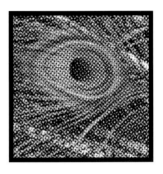

Stochastic screening

SHOWING RANDOM PIXELS

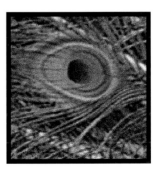

Process colour separation
CONVENTIONAL SCREENING

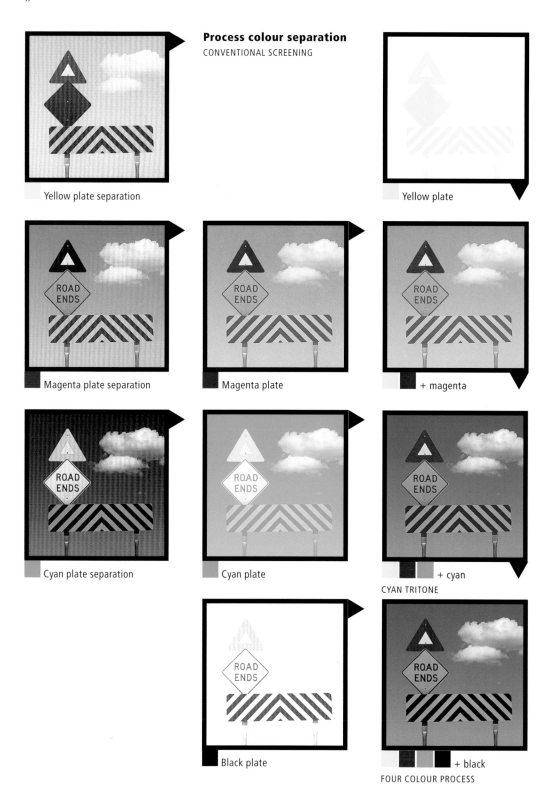

Yellow plate separation

Yellow plate

Magenta plate separation

Magenta plate

+ magenta

Cyan plate separation

Cyan plate

+ cyan

CYAN TRITONE

Black plate

+ black

FOUR COLOUR PROCESS

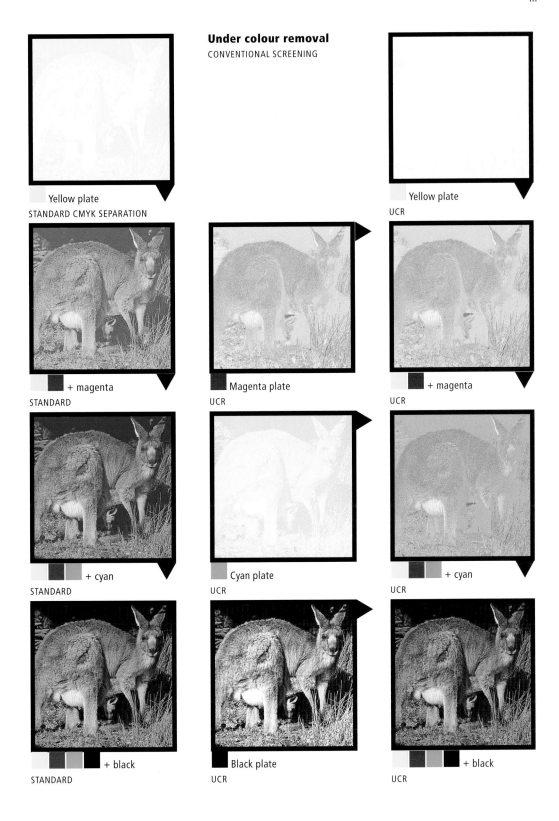

Under colour removal
CONVENTIONAL SCREENING

Yellow plate

STANDARD CMYK SEPARATION

+ magenta

STANDARD

+ cyan

STANDARD

+ black

STANDARD

Magenta plate

UCR

Cyan plate

UCR

Black plate

UCR

Yellow plate

UCR

+ magenta

UCR

+ cyan

UCR

+ black

UCR

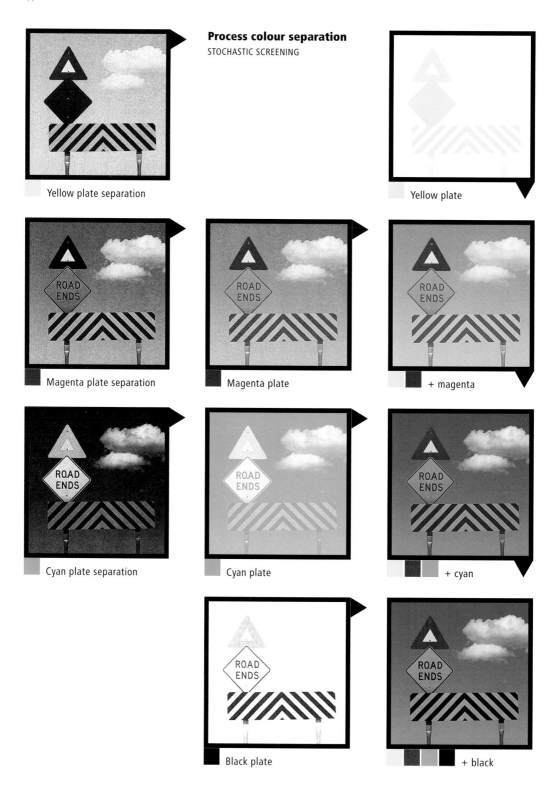

Process colour separation
STOCHASTIC SCREENING

Yellow plate separation

Yellow plate

Magenta plate separation

Magenta plate

+ magenta

Cyan plate separation

Cyan plate

+ cyan

Black plate

+ black

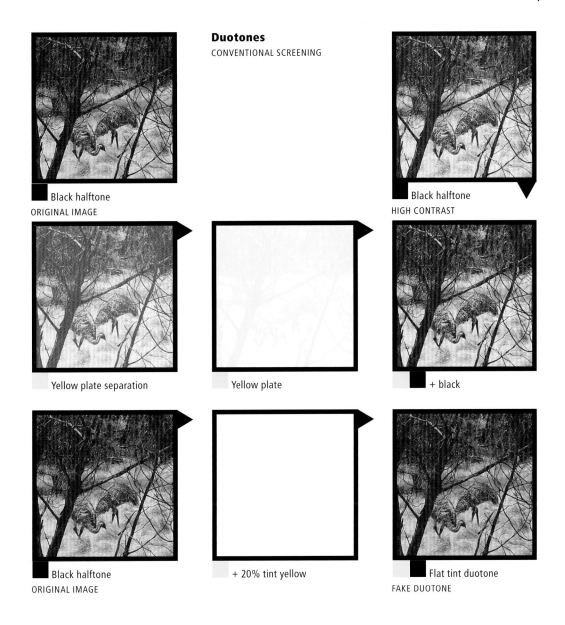

Duotones
CONVENTIONAL SCREENING

Black halftone
ORIGINAL IMAGE

Black halftone
HIGH CONTRAST

Yellow plate separation

Yellow plate

+ black

Black halftone
ORIGINAL IMAGE

+ 20% tint yellow

Flat tint duotone
FAKE DUOTONE

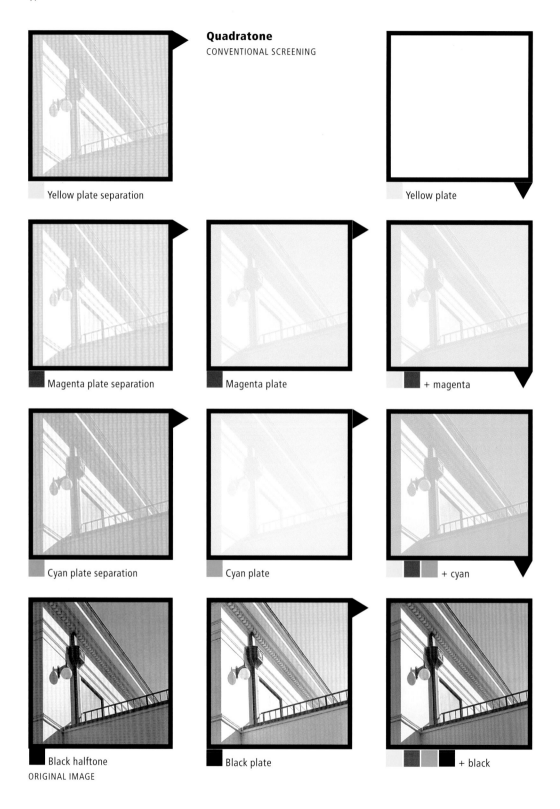

Quadratone
CONVENTIONAL SCREENING

Yellow plate separation

Yellow plate

Magenta plate separation

Magenta plate

+ magenta

Cyan plate separation

Cyan plate

+ cyan

Black halftone
ORIGINAL IMAGE

Black plate

+ black

Halftone with metallic ink
CONVENTIONAL SCREENING

■ Black halftone
ORIGINAL IMAGE

■ Black halftone
SAME AS ORIGINAL IMAGE

■ Metallic plate separation
REVERSE OF BLACK PLATE

■ Metallic plate

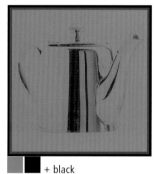

■ ■ + black
METALLIC HALFTONE

Duotone with metallic ink
CONVENTIONAL SCREENING

■ Black halftone
ORIGINAL IMAGE

■ Black plate
MODIFIED HALFTONE

■ Metallic plate separation
VERY LOW CONTRAST

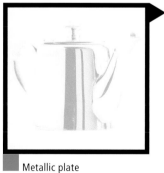

■ Metallic plate

■ ■ + black
METALLIC DUOTONE

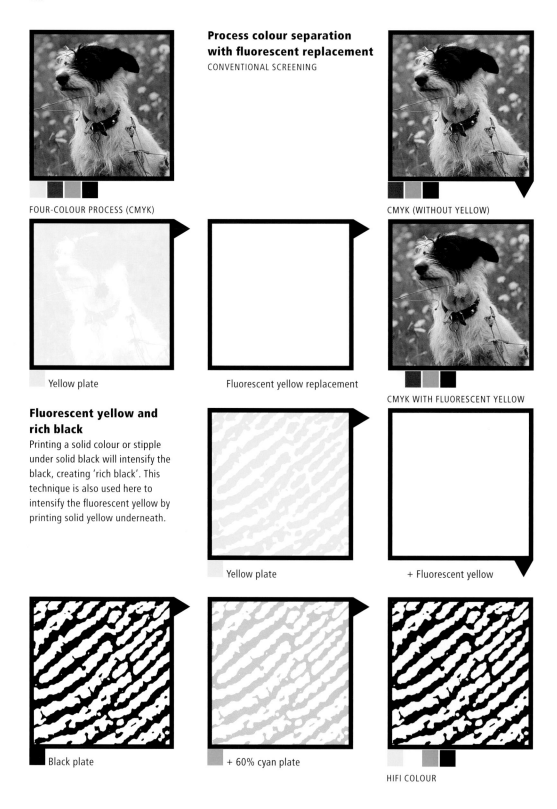

Process colour separation with fluorescent replacement
CONVENTIONAL SCREENING

FOUR-COLOUR PROCESS (CMYK)

CMYK (WITHOUT YELLOW)

Yellow plate

Fluorescent yellow replacement

CMYK WITH FLUORESCENT YELLOW

Fluorescent yellow and rich black

Printing a solid colour or stipple under solid black will intensify the black, creating 'rich black'. This technique is also used here to intensify the fluorescent yellow by printing solid yellow underneath.

Yellow plate

+ Fluorescent yellow

Black plate

+ 60% cyan plate

HIFI COLOUR

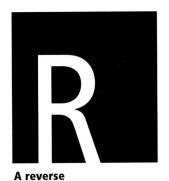

A reverse

Stochastic screening
uses random pixels

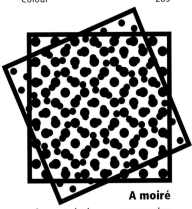

A moiré
is created when screens overlap

solid colour. In this way, we create the effect of a full tonal range in a black-and-white photograph in a newspaper by simply varying the size of the dots of black and allowing the paper to come through. Similarly, we create the effect of a complete spectrum by using only four printed process colours that are halftoned and overlapped.

Stipples are tints of a printed colour achieved in the same way, but they are made up of dots of the same size or pixels in a set pattern. Stipples are always expressed as percentages of a colour where 100% is the solid colour with no dots. Stipples of greater than 50% have a reverse dot within the solid colour; stipples of less than 50% are solid colour dots on the background because more of the background determines the lightness of the colour we see; 10% of a colour means that the dots take up 10% of the page area, allowing 90% of the colour you see to be the paper colour.

The pattern of dots was originally created using a series of screens, hence the term *screening*, which refers to the process of creating halftones.

There are two types of screening: AM and FM. AM (amplitude modulation) screening is conventional halftone screening with a variable-size dot. FM (frequency modulation) screening is more commonly known as *stochastic* screening using a random pixel.

A *reverse* is when a negative image is produced through a solid printed colour, allowing either the paper or another colour to show through.

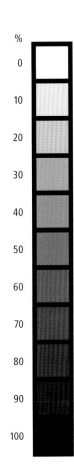

%
0
10
20
30
40
50
60
70
80
90
100

Stochastic screening

In stochastic screening, random pixels (little square 'picture elements' that are all the same size but much smaller than the variable dots used in traditional screening) give the effect of continuous tone.

Limited colour

There are many good reasons to resist the temptation to use full colour, such as to get a cheaper print job, to produce the job faster, and to save on expensive proofing processes.

In limited colour jobs, the attraction value of colour is achieved by using tonal variation when printing colour and by using incidental colour selectively; that is, choosing paper that is coloured in the paper-making process rather than printed specially for the particular job.

To achieve a full range of tone out of one-colour production, consider using the following techniques:

- screens or halftones
- reversed blocks of text or illustrations
- an ink colour other than black (but keep it very dark so it is still easy to read the type and still gives a good tonal range for photographs)
- a coloured and/or textured stock
- contrasting weights of type to give tonal contrast to the page
- some unusual cuts (even pinking shears!) or folds to add interest and create shadows.

If you have a number of items – maybe a stationery range or media kit – use different coloured paper for each item. This will create the effect of a wider use of colour for considerably less money. In publications such as newsletters, use a different coloured paper for an insert or to make the outside pages look like a cover.

To add another colour without the costs of printing another colour, have a rubber stamp made and use a coloured inkpad to add an extra colour by hand.

In two-colour work, you might mix the two colours you have chosen by overlapping them to create a third colour. As a rough guide only: yellow + red = orange; blue + yellow = green; red + blue = purple.

Select one dark colour for type and photographs and one light and/or bright colour to add vibrancy. Do not overuse the light or brighter colour – save it for flashes and splashes.

Two darker colours will often create a black when overlapped, which is handy for type readability but can be a production concern for a printer who will need to register the coloured type exactly.

You can use halftone screens of both colours, but be very careful when overlapping screens of two different colours. You can create moiré patterns that are quite distracting. For the uninitiated, it is best to mix a solid colour with a screen of the other colour.

READ MORE ABOUT IT

Mike Zender, *Getting unlimited impact with limited colour*, North Light Books, Cincinnati, 1994, ISBN 0 89134 568 X.

Gail Deibler Finke, *Fresh ideas for designing with black, white and gray*, North Light Books, Cincinnati, 1996, ISBN 0 89134 700 3.

Supon Design Group, *Great design using 1, 2, and 3 colors*, Madison Square Press, New York, 1992, ISBN 0 89134 502 7; *More great design ...*, 1994, ISBN 0 942604 44 X; *Even more great design ...*, 1997, ISBN 0 942604 54 7.

'Simplify, simplify: Effective two-color design' and 'Graphic alchemy: One-color design magic', two articles by Catherine Fishel in *Step-by-step graphics*, vol. 9, nos 4 and 5, 1993.

Duotones

A duotone is an image created from two overprinted halftones. It usually has the appearance of greater depth. The same image is prepared twice and a different printing plate is generated for each colour. The darker of the two colours to be printed will be a high-contrast version created to deepen the shadow and add crispness to detail areas. The lighter colour to be printed will be a low-contrast version that particularly fills in details in light areas. The dense and quite murky shadow areas in the light colour plate become good bases for the darker colour to create the deeper tones and detailing.

Duotones are often used to reproduce black-and-white photography in calendars and photography books. There is more detail in the highlight areas, more variety in the mid-tones and a deeper black in the darkest areas when you print a duotone in black and a mid-grey. The black plate is effectively a high-contrast plate to allow the grey plate, which is a low-contrast plate, to show through and fill the details.

Duotones can be made with other colours, depending on the subject matter. Buildings often look impressive with

DOING IT FASTER
Fake duotones

Fake duotones, or flat-tint duotones, are simply a standard black halftone reproduced with a 10–20% tint of another colour placed behind. It isn't really fooling anyone because it does not come close to the increased depth of a duotone, but its use speeds the production of presentation roughs. You need not do all the careful tonal variation to create the final duotone; you can simply indicate that it will be a duotone by using this fast process.

blue and black; forests and gardens are often good with green and black; for a fake sepia effect, you can even use yellow and black. Duotones of people work best in grey and black or red and black. In all cases, the black plate is a high-contrast plate and the colour plate is a low-contrast plate.

Tritones

Working on the same principle as duotones, tritones use three differently coloured versions of the same photograph overlapped to create an illusion of greater depth within a halftone photograph. The same principles generate a duotone but tritones use a third plate for increased detail in the lighter areas.

Colour systems

Process colour (CMYK)

The process colours are sometimes referred to as 'full colour' or 'four colour'. There are four process colours: cyan (C, a sky blue), magenta (M, a deep pink), yellow (Y, a pure yellow) and black (the 'key' colour, hence the K). They produce the effect of the 'full' colour spectrum by overlapping four halftones generated from the same full-colour image and printed in each of the four colours.

A separate printing plate is therefore required for each colour and the process of creating these four plates is called *colour separation*.

The standard order for specification is CMYK. When specifying a specific colour mix in CMYK, such as Australian flag red which uses 100% yellow and 100% magenta, it is cited as '100Y.100M'. Australian flag blue is '100C.80M'. There is no reference to the colour channels that are blank or 0%.

Screen angles

In the traditional separation technique, four halftones with dots of variable size have their screen placed at different angles and overprint each other to create a 'rosette' or 'flower'. Based on the same principles of colour that the Impressionist artists were exploring at the end of the 19th century, the colours both overlap and appear side by side. Your eye blends the colours and sees a representation of the full spectrum. The finer the screen, the smoother the image and the harder it is to discern the dot.

Screen angles are different when there are only two colours, like you have in a duotone, so alert your prepress operator when duotones will be used.

Stochastic screening, a digital separation technique, was developed as a response to the difficulty created when computers could not match the screen angles for

DOING IT CHEAPER
'Full-colour' tritone (CMY)

A process-colour tritone, where the black plate is removed and the cyan, magenta and yellow plates only are used, can effectively create the illusion of a complete palette of colours – the shadow areas are a dark brown rather than a black but quite effective for the cost-conscious.

DOING IT SMARTER
Sepia tone in CMYK

Copy a full-tone black-and-white scan into three channels using black, magenta and yellow channels only. There will be no cyan plate. Alter the representation of tone in each channel: (1) remove low-end tones completely and reduce mid-tones on the black plate and (2) increase the mid-tones and deepen the low-end tones for both the yellow and magenta plates.

Price comparison

Ink selection

$$$$$	HiFi inks*
$$$$	Process colour inks*
$$$	Metallics and fluorescents
$$	Pantone colours
$	Black ink

* Colour separation costs included

the traditional process exactly. As a result, the flower was becoming distorted and interrupting the eye's perception – there were small white 'holes' visible in the image due to the inaccurate screen angles.

Stochastic screening avoided the issue of screen angling because the random placement of its pixels achieved the same effect of mixing the colours.

HiFi colour

High fidelity (HiFi) colour is a successful but expensive attempt to increase the spectrum available in printed colour (or the colour *gamut*) by printing an extended range of colours that usually includes the four process colours but adds special colours. The extra colours enhance the ability of print to represent more of the real colour spectrum.

Some HiFi technologies are based on CMYK + RGB, making a seven-colour process, referred to as *extra trinary separation*. However, Pantone's Hexachrome process uses only six colours, made up of CMYK + orange + green.

This technology is linked to the enabling technology of stochastic screening, because the random pixels can include the extra colours, whereas traditional rosette screening has some difficulties posed by the screen angles for the extra colours.

The original image is scanned traditionally to create the four process-colour separations, but other colours are fed into the software to scan the image to separate those additional colours as well. In this way, six or seven plates are created.

For most of the 20th century, fine art reproductions used the principle of employing extra colours to increase the colour fidelity to the original work. The predominant colours in the original image determine the extended colour palette chosen. In works by Gustav Klimt, for example, gold is often used as a fifth colour.

For posters, packaging, point-of-sale and promotional materials, annual reports and collectors' editions, HiFi colour is grand, but it costs.

Mixing specific colours

When specifying mixes of process colours for background colours, blocks of colour, logos or coloured type, provide a 'recipe' to the colour separator for the colour you want to

DOING IT FASTER
Solid colours only
Solid colours tend to make a faster and cheaper print job. As soon as you introduce a screen ruling, more care needs to be taken with the preparation and printing process.

achieve. You can look to colour charts, select the printed colour you desire and create that colour in your colour menu. When your file is separated, it will use the recipe embedded in the description of the colour.

Coloured type will always be better defined if one of the colours is specified as solid (100%).

Black backgrounds in process-colour work should always have another colour placed underneath the black, usually 50% cyan or solid cyan. The black will look less washed-out. Create it as '50C.100K' or '100C.100K'. The richest black in full-colour images is equivalent to '100C.100M.100Y.100K'.

If your job will be printed in the four process colours, select the colours by looking at a printed process-colour selector. If your job will be printed with Pantone inks, look at the appropriate Pantone colour selector. If your job will be published on-screen, such as on a website or CD-ROM, select the colour on your computer. If your job will be produced by digital printing, run a proof on the same machine to check the colours. In this way, you will know what to expect. Remember, in all cases, your computer screen and your computer's printer can give only an approximation of the printed product.

Do not specify Pantone colours on-screen when you are printing only in process colours. You should use a process-colour selector rather than a Pantone colour selector and build the colours you need. The Pantone colour equivalents that are defined in your computer will often reproduce more 'muddy' colours than you wish, because they will have small percentages of every colour in order to come close to the actual Pantone ink mix. The Pantone company has released a selector with the specifications for each Pantone colour in the nearest match available in CMYK.

Sometimes, to compensate for ink absorption on particular papers, printers will vary the mix of inks by mixing, for example, fluorescent yellow with process yellow or fluorescent magenta with process magenta to maintain or increase brightness.

Under-colour removal

One of the problems for high-speed printing is the overlapping of colours in the shadow or dark areas of colour separations. This means that printing presses must be slowed down to accommodate the drying time of the numerous layers of ink. To avoid this, there are processes

DOING IT SMARTER
Soy inks
Inks are traditionally made from petrochemicals, but environmental concerns have encouraged the development of vegetable-based inks. Soybeans have provided a useful base for ink production, particularly with the four CMYK inks.

DOING IT SMARTER
Coloured type
Particularly in the four-colour process work, type in colour reads best when it has a clean edge, which can be achieved only with a solid colour. If the colour is made up of two or three process colours, ensuring that one of the colours is solid or 100% strength will help the type's readability. With this technique, it is best not to rely on 100% yellow as it's usually too weak in tone against the paper stock, though it will work when reversing out of other colours.

that have been developed to lessen the amount of cyan, magenta and yellow ink that are deposited on the paper under the black areas of a photo. They are under-colour removal (UCR), greyscale conversion (GSC) and grey component replacement (GCR).

Note that although these processes are widely used for speedy production of catalogues, newspapers, magazines and other long print runs, there is a trade-off where the density of their blacks is lost. One of the great attractions of four-colour printing is the rich blacks that are created by those layers of cyan, magenta and yellow ink on which the black ink sits.

Quadratones

This is a method of producing a rich black-and-white image with the CMYK process. Scan a black-and-white photograph and reduce the resulting levels in the cyan, magenta and yellow channels, so they are contributing to the density of the print, but not colouring it. Without UCR and GSC, the blacks are richer and there is a greater range of tone through the mid-tones and more detail in the highlights.

Pantone colour system

Printed colour is mostly specified in either Pantone colour matching system numbers or mixes of the four process colours. Other colour systems are not as widely used.

Pantone is a brand name that defines a range of specific colours that are usually used in limited colour work. The colours are based on a series of standard ink colours that are combined (by a printer in amounts specified by the Pantone company) to create the Pantone range.

Pantone is a proprietary system of colour developed in the United States and launched on 30 September 1963. More familiar as 'PMS' (Pantone Matching System) colours, the system is used by printers throughout the world as a de facto international colour standard.

Ink companies around the world are approved by the Pantone company to mix the Pantone inks and the colour selectors are available through art material shops and bookshops, and by mail or online order through some book companies.

The colour selectors are available on both white gloss art paper and white offset paper so you can see the way the colour will vary on different types of paper stock. With gloss art paper (a 'coated' paper), the ink sits on the surface, and with the offset paper (an 'uncoated' paper) the ink is absorbed to a certain extent so the colour alters, sometimes becoming darker, sometimes becoming lighter.

Expect paper to absorb ink to some extent. Use the selector as your guide. If you know the sort of paper you are printing on, choose a colour that will look right when printed. The only safe way to do this is to look at a Pantone colour selector, not your computer screen or your printout.

The Pantone mixers (the standard set of inks from which all the others are created) are upfront in the selector and given sensible names like Pantone Yellow, Pantone Warm Red, Pantone Reflex Blue.

The Pantone original set of colours is identified by a three-digit number, under which there is a mixing guide for the printer to create that colour. The four-digit colours extended that set at the end of the 1980s to fill some gaps in the original set. There are 1114 colours made up from 14 base colours and a transparent white in this range.

In October 2007, Pantone introduced its Goe System of a further 2058 chromatically arranged new colours that were mixed from nine new base colours and one clear extender. It includes about 40% of the original colour set.

Specifying tints

Tints are always specified as percentages of the colour. Create tints by reducing the percentage from 100% (or 'solid' colour). This was previously done in even steps of 10% as shown in Pantone Tint Selectors, but can now be finely tuned with the tint selection controls of most software. Try to avoid the extreme tints, <5% or >95%, as these have a tendency not to print or to fill in when printed, respectively.

Metallic inks

There is a Pantone metallic colour selector that has more bronzes, silvers, coppers and party-hat colours than you could possibly ever need – over 200. They are reasonably opaque but usually print better with either a 'double hit' of the metallic ink or with a colour printed beneath them on which the metal sits. There is also an extended drying time with their use as well as their aversion to accept overprinting. Any colour you wish to put 'on top' of them

Metallic inks have fine suspensions in their mix that produce their metallic sheen. Other effects are achieved in a similar manner. Heat-reactive inks, for example, change colour when handled. Microscented capsules carrying a selected fragrance can be suspended in ink, which when brushed lightly with a finger, enables you to smell them. In this example, the coffee aroma is released when you rub the surface of the coffee.
Client: Franklin Web
Publication: *Printing Matters*
Studio: Adstract Art

DOING IT SMARTER
Pastels
If you want a pale colour in a background, do not print a solid of the specific Pantone pastel; print a light tint of a more intense Pantone colour. A tint deposits less ink on the sheet and saves de-inking chemicals, which would need to be stronger to get rid of the solid colour in the recycling process. However, remember that stippling can sometimes compromise fine detail.

will usually need to be reversed out of them and then printed.

Sadly, these beautiful metals came out just when designers were becoming environmentally aware, so this set is doomed because they contain metals suspended in the ink that are environmentally unfriendly and which cannot be recycled appropriately.

There is another glitch. A computer cannot show you what a metallic colour will look like when printed. To show your client what the job will look like, get a good range of metallic nail varnishes and paint your rough or find a metallic giftwrap that you can run through your printer!

However, some great special effects can be achieved with metallic inks and designers are trying many tricks such as replacing a colour in the four-colour process with a metallic equivalent or printing halftones in metallic ink or on metallic backgrounds.

Talk with your printer about achieving metallic effects.

Fluorescent inks

Although your computer screen has a different intensity from a printed piece because of the light that is being projected out of the screen dots, it cannot give an accurate effect of fluorescence.

The fluorescent colours are at the back of the standard Pantone selector and are shown twice. The second print is where they have been printed twice (a 'double hit'), which intensifies their fluorescence (this is indicated by a 2X following the colour code). Fortunately, there is a range of fluorescent highlighters available for mocking up the effect for a client to see.

To extend the range of available fluorescent colours, you can mix other Pantone mixers with the Pantone fluorescents but this can be a bit hit and miss and sometimes compromises the fluorescent effect too much.

Pastels

There is a Pantone pastel colour selector that extends the range of pale, gelato colours. The colours in this range were missing from the original Pantone set. Previously, when pastels were printed they were temperamental and quite uneven through a print run – sometimes heavy, sometimes light. The new mixers are more reliable through a print run.

The pastels are particularly good for fine detailed backgrounds in stationery and brochures.

RGB and hexadecimal colour

Computer screens, like television screens, are RGB monitors, where the colours you see are made up of varying intensities of a pattern of small red, green and blue lights. When all the lights are at full intensity, we see white. When all the lights are at lowest intensity, or off, we see black.

The standard for RGB colour description is the hexadecimal system. It describes a colour by specifying the combination of intensity of red, green and blue lights that create that colour on-screen, resulting in a six-character colour tag.

The sequence is given as two characters for each of the three colours: effectively RRGGBB. Consequently, red is #ff0000 (describing the red lights at 'full' intensity, the green and blue lights 'off'), green is #00ff00, blue is #0000ff.

So, when all lights are on full, the screen will appear white, described as #ffffff. Equally, when all lights are off, the screen will appear black, described as #000000.

Other colours combine the lights; for example, yellow is described as #ffff00.

Hexadecimal descriptions use the numbers from 0 to 9 and letters from a to f. So, for example, orange is #ff6600.

Anti-aliassing

Aliassing creates the 'jaggies' on a shape, most noticeable in curves and circles, angles and diagonals. This is because the image is made up of a series of square pixels.

All type and most graphics produced for a screen will be anti-aliassed, so they read as smooth shapes. It blurs the 'jaggies' by filling in pixels close by with colours that blur the edges of the shape.

You will need to limit the intermediate colours used in your anti-aliassing or you will find your file size increases.

Also make sure that the background colour on your text is the same as the background in your site so the anti-aliassing will smooth the text against the actual background.

Alternative colour specifications

For corporate identities particularly, it is important to consider all likely colour uses and specify the corporate colour palette for all output options:
☐ Pantone colour system
  – coated
  – uncoated
☐ CMYK for four-colour process production
  – coated
  – uncoated
  – newsprint (the colours will be brighter again to compensate for the high absorbency and off-white tint of the paper)
☐ RGB for on-screen production
  – hexadecimal specification
  – web-safe 216 alternative.
As the print colours specified here assume production on white paper, there will also be occasions when you need to re-specify to take account of a tinted paper stock, for example.

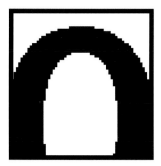

A raster image
is bitmapped in pixels

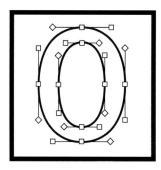

A vector image
is mathematically described and
resolution-dependent

Anti-aliassing
bitmaps with intermediate tones

Web-safe colours

While websites can use up to 16 million colours described
in hexadecimal alphanumeric codes, in older computer
hardware and browsers, they are sometimes limited to the
216 colours in the Netscape colour cube (sometimes called
the 'Web 216'). It features colours with the light intensities
described only in this limited set of hexadecimal codes:
00, 33, 66, 99, cc, ff. Set your monitor to 256 colours to
see approximately what web users will see. You would only
use these colours if you knew a number of users in your
intended audience had older hardware that limited their
monitors to only 256-colour display.

Dithering colours

To achieve a greater range of colours than the limited
web-safe 216, those colours are 'mixed' on-screen by
a process called 'dithering'. This is achieved by either

Dithering
by interlacing stripes of colours

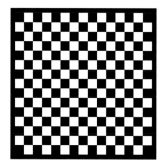

Dithering
by chequerboarding two colours

interlacing stripes of two colours or by chequerboarding two colours that will create the colour you want when seen from a distance.

The problem with colour systems

You are designing a two-colour print job. You create the design on-screen, selecting the colours from the palettes on-screen and it looks great on-screen. You 'soft-proof' it for your client by sending it as an attached file in an email so they can preview it on their computer screen. You print the design to your colour printer to proof it for them. You send the job to a printing house which prints it in the Pantone colours specified by the computer printout. The printed result is neither the colours you saw on-screen, nor the colours of the computer printout.

Why is it that with 16 million colours, you still can't get the colour you want?

Let's visit the scenario again, step by step.

You created the job for the colours that looked good on-screen. Your monitor uses the RGB (red, green, blue) colour system developed for television. When all the red, green and blue lights are on at full power, the screen is white. When they are all off, the screen is black. When they use varying intensities of red, blue and green light, they create all the colour you can see on-screen.

Next, you soft-proofed it by sending to your client's computer which was maybe a different brand with a slightly different colour screen – but most likely also calibrated differently according to your client's personal preferences.

Next, you proofed the design on a colour printer that uses the four-colour process similar in principle but not identical to the printing industry's four-colour process. When all the colours are printed together, they produce black. When there are none of them, the image is white (or whatever the colour of the paper you have printed the image on). When you use dots of varying size of the four colours, and overlap them, they create all the colours you can see in most magazines and catalogues.

Finally, when the piece was printed using the Pantone colours, your printer used colours that were mixed from chemicals different from those used in the four process colours and with an entirely different system of colour generation from the way colour is created on-screen. Being transparent, as most inks are, the colour surface and density of the paper on which they are printed alters them as well.

There is room for error.

So sometimes a simple thing like matching a single corporate colour across a range of corporate material is impossible. That corporate red that has a hint of burgundy in the washroom towels with corporate insignia; it's a lighter dyelot for the corporate umbrella (and fades); on that west-facing exterior awning, it has faded to almost yellow; in the annual report it looks like a ripe tomato; in the raffle tickets it look like a jaffa orange; in the *Yellow Pages* ad, it is a murky rust; and on the website, it is a luminous beacon of pulsating light.

Got the picture? You do not have colour control.

Prepress

Prepress describes the preparation process between design and printing. It is a point in the schedule where you collect all the materials that will enable accurate translation of the design into a printed document.

For example, when you are preparing your document, place low-resolution images into the document to be able to move around it faster without waiting for each large image file to download. At prepress, these are replaced with their equivalent high-resolution scans that will ensure their printed quality. So you must identify and supply both the low- and high-resolution images to your printer's prepress facility.

Because of typefaces being supplied by many companies and each company's font description being slightly different, you will need to list and possibly supply your prepress operator with all the fonts needed in your document.

Some programs will create a list of everything that your prepress operator needs to reproduce your document, but it helps if you understand the process.

For example, when you go through the proofs noting down the font usage, you need to list not only the face but also each weight of the face you use. Also, you may sometimes forget to list the expert font sets, dingbats, symbol and picture fonts you used. They are easy to overlook, but you will not recognise your document if they are not supplied.

In website and multimedia development, the equivalent process to prepress falls between completion of design and uploading and is called *flight checking* and can include *alpha* and *beta testing* phases.

Finished artwork preparation

Preparation of a file in readiness for prepress is called finished artwork. It includes the detailed collection and

What you need to supply to your printer

In addition to your disks, proofs or printouts, you must supply a printout or sheet listing the following:

☐ Contact details:
  . your name
  . your organisation
  . your direct phone number
  . your mobile phone number
  . your e-mail address
  . your billing address and details
  . your street address for deliveries
☐ Materials supplied:
  . disks and the files contained on each that pertain to the job or match the approved quotation
  . transparencies and their label or code
  . image scans at reproduction resolution (not compressed for screen display) and their format and file name
☐ Format used: Mac or PC
☐ Program/s used:
  . version number/s
☐ Fonts used:
  . exact name of typeface as listed in font menu and weights including bold, italic and expert sets
  . any dingbat, picture or symbol fonts
  . you might save all fonts as outlines
☐ Hard copy (must be prepared from the supplied digital files – not earlier versions)

☐ Final reproduction requirements, requesting as appropriate: digital files, separated film positives, film negatives, proofs
☐ If it is a specialist prepress house, the name of the printer or reproducer who will use the final files or film:
  . name of contact and direct phone number, for queries.

Ensure you have removed earlier versions from working folders so there is no confusion.

When they receive your files, they'll do a 'preflight' test that will identify any problems like missing fonts or images.

Ensure you have back-up copies of everything you supply. It is also a good idea to have additional back-up files off-site (if there is a fire, for example, you do not lose your work).

checking of everything: text, typefaces, scans, layers, backgrounds, page numbers, files.

When you are supplying scans, check that the resolution is appropriate for their final reproduction, otherwise you may see jaggies in your final print job. This often occurs where you made a last-minute substitution or decision to increase the size of an image to improve your layout, but forgot to rescan it at a correspondingly higher resolution for its new sizing.

Have your scans been saved as CMYK for printing, instead of RGB? Have you converted all Pantone colours into CMYK mixes for your CMYK file? Have you checked you don't have any rogue or unexpected Pantones in your Pantone file?

Have you limited the range in your black-and-white scans appropriately for reproduction? Often this required setting the highlights at 5% and the shadows to 90% or maybe 95%.

Have your scans compensated for dot gain as advised by your printer? On some uncoated stocks, this might require reducing the 50% mid-tone dot to 45% and a 90–95% shadow dot to 85%.

If printing on a cream stock, you might also uniformly reduce the amount of yellow in order to compensate for the yellow content of the stock to maintain a more realistic colour. On other coloured stocks, consult your printer or paper company for advice on colour correction.

Check alignments and make any adjustments to kerning and other optical corrections. Also check that each text block contains the text it is supposed to and links to the correct page.

Ensure that any product, catalogue or job codes and required image credits are included on the final artwork.

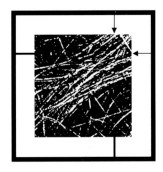

An image that bleeds
off a page needs to print over the page area by at least 3 mm and be trimmed back to its final size.

Bleed

Any image, rule, graphic, logo, background or colour – or even type – that continues off the edge of a page is said to 'bleed' and, in order for it to print correctly, it must extend beyond the page area by at least 3 mm on each side. This is then trimmed back to the page edge during the finishing processes of guillotining or die-cutting.

Check that all scans have been correctly positioned for the trim. Their picture boxes now include an extra 3 mm of image. For example, you should not recentre a portrait

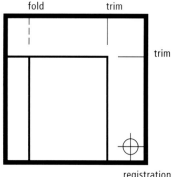

fold   trim

trim

registration

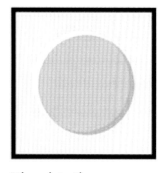

Misregistration
where one colour accidentally overlaps
another, leaving a fine white gap,
could be compensated for by spreading
the lighter colour and choking the
darker one.

READ MORE ABOUT IT
Agfa produced a range of excellent
    publications including these
    titles: *An introduction to digital
    color prepress*; *A guide to color
    separation*; *An introduction
    to computer-to-plate printing*;
    *Color bytes: Blending the art and
    science of color*; *The secrets of
    color management*.
Mark Gatter, *Getting it right in print:
    Digital prepress for graphic
    designers*, Laurence King, London,
    2005, ISBN 1 85669 421 6.

– it should be centred on the trimmed width, not the bleed
width that you see on-screen.

Because bleed is so dependent on accurate trimming for
its effect, it is wise not to have too fine detail on the edge of
your sheet – even just a coloured stripe parallel to the edge
can be dangerous if it is, say, 3 mm or thinner. Note that,
with bleed, a 3 mm strip would be drawn at 6 mm thick and
placed over the trim edge.

Trim marks, fold marks and registration marks

Most page layout programs will automatically apply trim
marks and registration marks to your file. They are required
to help the printer when the job is on the press.

Trim marks need to align through the page if the pages
are backed up. They will guide the guillotine operator who
will trim the final job. They usually start 3 mm from the
trimmed edge and are about 5–7 mm in length.

There will not automatically be *fold marks* on your job.
These are similar to trim marks. They start 3 mm from the
edge of the page and are fine dashed lines (rather than the
fine solid line of trim marks).

Registration marks are needed whenever there are two or
more colours in a print job. They are small cross-hatches
that are in exactly the same position on the artwork for
each colour. They need to overprint exactly on press. They
ensure the colours are printed in their exact placement or
'in register'. They should be placed off-centre, one to the
left, one to the right, partly to be out of the way of spine fold
marks, but also for alignment purposes in imposition. It
can quickly be seen if a page is the wrong way up.

Trapping

Trapping is a technique where you prepare each colour in
a separated set to take account of small discrepancies in
register that can occur with paper stretch or misregistration
in printing. Spreading – or flooding – and choking adjacent
colours achieve this.

With trapping, there will be a slight printed overlap –
often as small as 0.25 point. Briefly, the principle is that the
darkest colour can print tightly ('choked') and the lightest
colour can bleed into it by being 'flooded' or 'spread'.

File management

Ensure you name files in a way that clearly identifies yourself, the job, the file and type of file.

At the end of the code there will be a full stop and an abbreviated file description: *.doc* for Microsoft Word files, *.pict, .tiff, .gif, .jpeg* or *.jpg, .pdf, .eps* for image files as appropriate; and various extensions for proprietary page layout and web software documents.

Always keep a back-up of your files and never give your only copy to another supplier. It is recommended that it be stored off-site (in case of fire, flood or theft).

Labelling the disk for quick retrieval is important also. You might create folders for each job to keep all picture, text and document files together. You might create a disk for each client. You might simply back-up by date.

Imposition

Printers prepare the imposition for books. Because of folding, some pages will be upside down when printed on the flat sheet and pages that will be seen together in the booklet may be far away from each other in the flat plan.

In an A6 booklet, page 8 will be to the left of page 1, page 2 to the left of page 7, etc. Notice that even-numbered pages are on the left and odd numbered pages on the right. Also note that the numbers will equal one more than the total number of pages: in this case $8 + 1 = 9$; $2 + 7 = 9$.

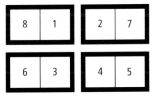

It is usual that books are made up from sections of four, eight, 16, 32 and 64 pages. If you had a book with 36 pages, you might print a section of 32 pages and a further section of four pages to produce the 36 pages. However, it is often better to massage the page count so it will sit within a standard section.

For magazines and books that have coloured sections and different colour distribution through the book, a flat plan helps to identify where the colour falls in the imposition. The designer can then design accordingly.

Long-8s

A variation on a standard imposition is the long-8, so called because it doubles over itself to the side, with no upside-down pages. This means that alignment of pictures on a double-page spread is easier to achieve even if they

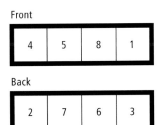

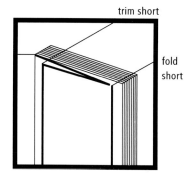

trim short

fold
short

Foldouts

A page that folds out to accommodate a map, table, photograph or illustration needs production planning to be successful and cost-effective. The page should fold shorter than the full width, so that when the book is guillotined, the fold is not cut off; and the flap will also be anything from 1–5 mm shorter again, so it sits snugly into the spine. In the case of ring binders, it will usually be 15 mm shorter.

are some distance apart in the imposition, because the alignment is no longer as dependent on the folding process.

Sheet

Two colour one side	A	1	2	3	4	5	6	7	8
	B	9	10	11	12	13	14	15	16
Full colour section	C	17	18	19	20	21	22	23	24
	D	25	26	27	28	29	30	31	32

Flat plans

enable you to clearly see the distribution of different colour specifications according to where they will fall on the printed sheets and sections.

Dummies

Assemble and supply the printer with a photocopied or laser-printed dummy (sample) of the finished job. If they have any queries about the imposition or order of pages, they can quickly refer to the dummy.

Quick print preparation

Much quick print is now exclusively digital or photocopied, rather than printed traditionally. In the case of digital printing, you simply supply a digital file. To save money it should be prepared with no bleed and 3–5 mm clearance on all edges.

For photocopying, provide a master that:

- uses black ink only with no screens unless you provide screened artwork to be shot dot-for-dot (or better, some other halftone technique such as a line screen – detail needs to be rugged for quick print)
- has no bleed
- has a 10 mm grip edge on at least one edge – the same edge on both sides of the sheet
- is a standard size (A4), or is bled artwork to fit on a standard size (e.g. so it will print bleeds and trim marks on an A4 sheet) and guillotine it to a smaller size

- has no registration marks – trim the artwork to actual size and do not mount it (slip it into a folder, plastic sleeve or envelope).

Output resolution

There are two measurement systems used to generate output. They are both expressed similarly and are often confused. One describes the quality of digital output from printers: dpi (dots per inch). The other describes the resolution of the halftone dots for print reproduction: lpi (lines per inch).

Dpi (dots per inch)

The resolution of your printer is defined in *dpi* or *dots per inch*. An inch is approximately 25 mm. Office laser printers have standard dpi settings at 300 or 600 dots per inch or higher. Of course, with digital production, these aren't really 'dots' at all, they are *pixels*, or tiny square picture elements. So 600 dpi means 600 pixels per inch or roughly 24 pixels per millimetre.

When you look at output from high-end imagesetters that are used for print negatives, you are looking at a resolution of 2400 or 1200 dpi. This means that the pixels that make up the image are finer – at 2400 dpi there are about 96 pixels per millimetre. You get a much smoother appearance to curves, circles and, of course, the dots that make up halftone images.

Lpi (lines per inch)

Lines per inch or *lpi* refers to the resolution at which you choose to reproduce an image. It depends on the printing method and the paper chosen. For example, in newspapers, it was standard for photograph reproduction to be set at 60 lpi, which is why the halftone dot screen in old newspapers is so plainly visible.

In exclusive packaging, you might find 300 lpi or higher, but the dot in this is barely visible with the naked eye. The difference between a 300 dpi pixel and the 300 lpi halftone dot mentioned here is that the pixel is a specific-size square but the halftone dot is a variable-size circular dot. As a result of the need for this variable-size dot, you use a machine with 2400 dpi to create a 300 lpi output.

Effective resolution

If you reduce an image, its effective resolution increases. If you enlarge an image, it will have a lower effective resolution.

To calculate the effective resolution of an image, divide the actual resolution of the original image by the percentage of scaling required to get the image to its final size.

60 lpi
300 dpi

60 lpi
2400 dpi

60 lpi
stochastic screening

Comparing different output resolutions

While stochastic screening is described in microns, lpi equivalents have been used here for ease of comparison.

100 lpi
300 dpi

100 lpi
2400 dpi

Conventional halftoning
an enlargement

200 lpi
2400 dpi

200 lpi
stochastic screening

Stochastic screening
an enlargement

300 lpi
2400 dpi

300 lpi
stochastic screening

Proofing

Do as much checking on-screen as possible throughout the production process. This is called 'soft-proofing' and can be used for all but the final clearance of a printed job. This avoids unnecessary printing and paper waste.

Proofing is undertaken in stages that progressively inform the production process.

The first of these is at editorial stage, where the final text content is read and corrected by an editor.

The next stage is page proofs. Pages are assembled with the revised text document flowed in and pictures, typefaces and all design elements added. At this point, the editor may be brought in to recheck the document and the client checks the text and image positioning and alignment. When the client approves this stage, the indexer can start the index.

The final proofing stage should be imposed proofs from the printer, which are often made into a physical dummy of the final product.

Designers check that images have reproduced appropriately – that their resolution is even, their colours correct and they are correctly positioned in the picture boxes. They also check that colour for backgrounds and text are correct and that trapping is correct. They will check that all the typefaces have translated correctly without default fonts appearing (where the output device could not recognise a font, often because it was either not loaded, identified inappropriately, or not supplied). They check there are production flaws in the film or output that may have been caused by scanned dust or lint, imperfections or scratches in the film.

Anyone involved with the job has their final check. It is signed off by the client as being 'ready for print' or 'requiring revision'. If there are many corrections, a revised proof will be needed.

Proofing systems

Never do your final check of colours on-screen for printed output. There are many proofing systems available and most will do an acceptable approximation of the printed result, but none are perfect. You will need to try a few to see the variations and to compare them with the actual output to decide which best suits your requirements.

Press checks

Designers often wish to see the colours on press, because it is so difficult to mock up exactly how colours will look when printed. When the job is being printed, you might do a 'press check' so that, if there is an unforeseen problem, it can be rectified 'in-run' rather than reprinting. You will be expected to sign-off a copy when it is right. It will then become the referral copy for the printer throughout the print run. Print shops have lighting booths specifically to ensure that you are checking colour in standardised lighting conditions.

A Chromalin or chemical proof is made up by exposing each piece of separated film onto a layer of plastic and coating the resulting image with a chemical dust that approximates the desired print colour. In process colours, the four plastic layers are sandwiched together to create a composite image. The process cannot match Pantone colours but is comparatively accurate for process-colour checking. There are often small particles of dust caught in the processing, which look like errors in the image, but are just a part of the proofing system. Always ask the printer to check the film to confirm that they are not visible on the plates.

Printing

It is most important to develop a good relationship with your printer and discuss the most appropriate printing processes to achieve what you want.

There is a reason the apprenticeship and training time for prepress, printing and finishing was more extensive than the time it takes for most graphic designers to graduate – there is much technicality to cover with many nuances of application. You should not expect to know it all by simply reading about it.

In the prepress area, do not expect to be able to do it to the same level of expertise just because you have a software program that can prepare materials similar to some of those processes.

The best advice for learning about printing is to visit printers and prepress personnel and ask questions. Heed the advice you receive and your product will benefit. Sound production knowledge enables you to create innovative design solutions that are founded in a production reality – your client will be able to afford to produce your design and you will be able to produce the finished artwork for its manufacture.

Here then, are just brief descriptions of the main processes you will encounter in printing and finishing. There are a few tips and hints included but the most important one is talk with your suppliers.

Preprints

If you wish to maintain your corporate colours across a range of material without having to print them each time, think about preprinting some standardised sheets on an appropriately coloured and weighted sheet of paper with one or more of your corporate inks. You can then overprint in black as required. Black is used for ease; you can print directly from your laser printer or photocopy, saving time and money. You can repeat the logo or some motif from the graphic identity.

DOING IT CHEAPER
Ganging-up

Maybe you could get together a group of people or organisations that could use their combined buying power to increase their print options, such as using process colour. All people would need to agree to use the same colours on the same paper, and have the same number of copies (remember, if everyone wants 5000 copies and you want 10 000, it just means you print 'two-up' of yours). If you print two, four, eight, 16 or 32 originals at once, you start seeing printing economies and you can share the savings.

DOING IT SMARTER
Environmentally friendly trimmings

If you avoid bleeding images and bands of colour off the edges of a cover or poster, the printer's waste (the trimmings off the sheet) will be cleaner and require less de-inking, thereby avoiding use of further chemicals in the processing prior to recycling.

Overs

A printer will always print some extra sheets of your job in case of spoiled work throughout the process – colours might get scuffed, the folding machine may use up a few, or some may get trimmed crookedly. The 'overs' enable the printer to guarantee you get the full print run you ordered without having to rerun the job on the press.

Other printing terminology
- *Duplex:* to print both sides of a sheet in one press pass; that is, concurrently
- *Triplex:* to print black and one colour on the front and black only on the back
- *Back-up:* to print one side of a sheet then prepare the press again to print the back; that is, not in one pass
- *Transactional printing:* bill or account printing usually overprinting by a digital printer on an offset preprinted shell
- *Inline finishing:* finishing processes are connected to the printing press and converted in a single pass or workflow process

DOING IT CHEAPER
Production planning
Rush work is expensive – give printers, finishers and prepress operators (and even photographers, illustrators, designers and photo libraries) as much time as possible. It is not unusual to pay double rates for high-priority late work that jumps the queue.

If your job jumps the queue, other clients of your supplier will be inconvenienced as a result. You pay for the flak that will result from your lack of planning.

Even if material will be received very late for a tight production deadline, you can plan a production schedule with most suppliers that will gear up the minute they receive final materials. You can still expect to pay a premium for this sort of work, but there should not be as much disruption to other clients' schedules if you have planned appropriately.

By preprinting, you can save printing two or three colours for every issue of your newsletter or pamphlet series – you need only overprint the information that changes each time. It is worth considering the possibility of preprinting newsletter shells or pamphlet shells – blanks that have only the standard information on them. Usually you include the corporate logo, the masthead of the newsletter (not the edition number and date), the contact addresses, phone number, website URL and email addresses (if they are not likely to change in the near future) and a contents box (without the contents list). Then each time you come to print again, you need overprint only one colour.

If you produce 1000 newsletters every month in two colours, preprint the second colour and leave the text colour (usually black) off. Print the annual supply (12 000 sheets) at the beginning of the year as a one-off, one-colour job. The paper is purchased upfront and stored, and you will save significantly over the year. For the 12 issues, you can overprint 1000 of the preprinted sheets as a one-colour job (in this case, probably black). Your newsletter will look like you printed two colours but, because the paper was pre-purchased, you pay only for one-colour printing monthly.

Entertainment organisations and promoters regularly use this technique for theatre, concert and event posters – leaving a blank area on the poster for overprinting the details of local performances. In this way, they can afford to have full colour in all venues without the cost of individual print runs. The same savings can be made in programs, flyers and pamphlets; just leave an area or a panel for overprinting the changing details.

READ MORE ABOUT IT
Alan Pipes, *Production for graphic designer*, 4th edn, Laurence King Publishing, London, 2005, ISBN 978-1-85669-458-2.
Constance J Sidles, *Great production by design: The technical know-how you need to let your design imagination soar*, North Light Books, Cincinnati, 1998, ISBN 0 89134 838 7.
Constance Sidles, *Printing: Building great graphic design through printing technique*, Rockport, Massachusetts, 1999, ISBN 1 56496 601 1.
Michael Barnard, John Peacock & Charlotte Berrill, *The Blueprint handbook of print and production*, Blueprint (Chapman & Hall), London, 1994, ISBN 1 857130 04 9.
Australian Print Finishers Association, *Finish first: A complete reference to the print finishing industry*, Australian Print Finishers Association, Melbourne, 2006.

Astrid Sweres (ed.), *d4p: Design for print*, CRC Smartprint and Australian
  Scholarly Publishing, Melbourne, 2005, ISBN 1740970969.
Trevor Wilson, *Printmate: A graphic arts reference book*, T. Wilson Publishing
  Company for APPM, Melbourne, 1989, ISBN 0 85828 0140.
David Bann, *The print production handbook*, Macdonald & Co., London, 1985,
  ISBN 0 356 10788 4.
Alastair Campbell, *The new designer's handbook*, Little, Brown & Co., London,
  1993, ISBN 0 316 90658 1.
Martin Greenwald & John Luttropp, *Graphic communications: Design through
  production*, Delmar Publishers, New York, 1997, ISBN 0 8273 6459 8.
Australian Paper, *The printer's enemies*, Australian Paper, Melbourne [brochure].

Offset lithography

Lithography is based on the principle of oil repelling water.
The inks are attracted to the image area that has been
exposed on a photosensitised plate. The exposure is often
produced through a photographic negative on film that
exposes only the desired print area of the plate. This can
also be achieved *direct to plate* through digital imaging. This
is also referred to as *CtP* or *computer-to-plate* production.
The water, or dampener, sits on the plate in the areas where
there is no image. Lithography is therefore a planographic
process, where there is no raised or sunken ink area.

The plate is often aluminium, sometimes plastic or
even paper, because each of those can be wrapped around
a revolving cylinder, which is the basis of a rotary printing
press.

Offset lithography is based on an image being offset or
transferred to a rubber cylinder (called the *blanket*) as an
intermediate step between the transfer from plate to paper.

DOING IT SMARTER
Work-and-tumble
A variation of printing two-up, work-
and-tumble or work-and-turn describe
cheaper and faster ways to print a
piece. Let's say you have a double-
sided poster. The printer may ask you
to prepare the artwork side by side for
the front and back sides of the poster.
The printer then prints them in one
print run on half the sheets you need,
tumbles the sheets once printed and
puts them at the front of the machine
again to print the other side. Then they
are trimmed up and your whole print
run is complete.

The process can save some costs
such as making two proofs (there is
only one proof to make, even though
it is twice the page area). It also uses
only one set of printing plates, so it
saves on materials, prepress and set-
up time on the press.

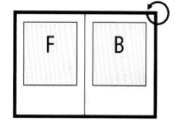

Tumbled for second pass to back up

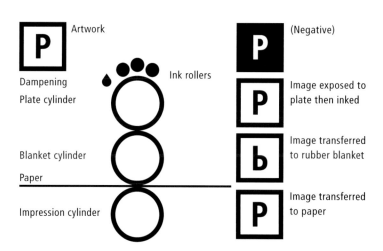

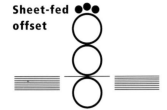

Sheet-fed offset

The paper is fed into the press either as single sheets, called *sheet-fed offset*, or from a reel, which is called a *web*, hence *web-fed offset*.

Waterless printing

Without the use of dampening, waterless printing or dry lithography achieves a better quality reproduction than conventional 'wet' offset printing. The image area is etched out of the silicone coating on an aluminium plate, which allows ink to sit on the aluminium substrate. This is effectively a hybrid printing style somewhere between offset lithography and engraving. The quality is evident in its ability to print finer screens that define more details in the image. Waterless printing requires different inks from conventional inks and also does not run on conventional offset printing presses without conversion.

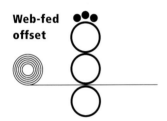

Web-fed offset

Web offset

For catalogues, newspapers and other large print runs, web-fed offset is used where a web of paper from a reel is drawn through the printing press and continuously printed. This is often connected up for in-run collation, folding, stapling, trimming and wrapping as well. Web presses can run at high speeds, though their speed is limited by ink drying times, which is why under-colour removal and greyscale conversion processes were developed.

Screenless printing/collotype

Collotype printing, like lithography, is also a planographic process but uses a light-sensitive gelatine film on a glass plate, which is exposed to create areas that will attract more or less ink. It is a slow process but can achieve almost photographic quality due to there being no halftoning process, hence the term *screenless printing*.

Laser printing, photocopying and xerography

Photocopying is based on the principles of positive and negative charges repelling each other and attracting like. Photocopying relies on charging the paper through recognising and translating data on an original image. The information about the image is reflected through lenses to an electrostatically charged drum, breaking down the

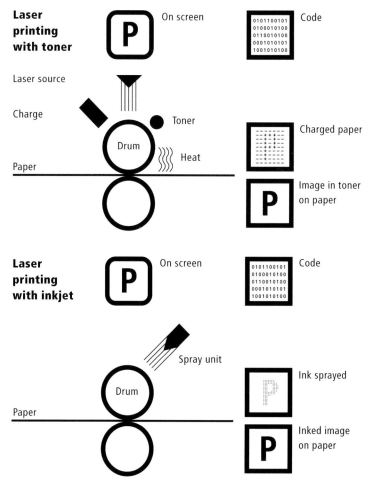

Laser printing with toner

On screen

Code
```
0101100101
0100010100
0110010100
0001010101
1001010100
```

Laser source

Charge

Toner

Drum

Heat

Paper

Charged paper

Image in toner on paper

Laser printing with inkjet

On screen

Code
```
0101100101
0100010100
0110010100
0001010101
1001010100
```

Spray unit

Drum

Paper

Ink sprayed

Inked image on paper

Printing two-up

It is often worth printing two or more items at once. Why not print a pamphlet series all together? You need not distribute them until they are required, but the print cost per unit should be cheaper if they are printed at the same time.

This is often a good way of being able to afford all elements of a corporate identity to be printed with the same number of colours. You might print the letterhead, the continuation sheet, the 'with compliments' slip, an invoice, and maybe even a flyer on the same large sheet of paper with the same colours and then guillotine it into the separate pieces. If each piece is produced separately, you can have significant costs in set-up each time.

The only drawback to this scheme is that you must want the same amount of each piece. But you can even resolve that. For example, by getting two of the letterhead printed which will give you double the number of letterhead to continuation sheets and, in the same way, three invoices, a single print run of 1000 sheets will cut down to give you 2000 letterheads, 1000 continuation sheets and 3000 invoices.

Printing business cards

With most organisations and businesses, there are many people who need cards. The best way to keep unit costs down is to print all the cards together in one print run. This is how printers can supply 250 full-colour business cards for a very small price – if 20 people answer their ad, they print 20 cards side by side and trim them up.

Talk to your printer and ask how they want the card artwork supplied.

charge on the image areas. Then a fine resin dust called *toner*, which also has been charged, is attracted. This is translated to the paper sheet which runs through the heating unit, effectively toasting the toner to the page.

You can enlarge or reduce artwork swiftly with a photocopier and can set it to increase or decrease the amount of toner. There is also a level of distortion you can expect, making alignment uncertain from copy to copy or page to page in a multipage document, though this is a minor inconvenience for the cheap and quick quality xerography achieves. Incidentally, *xerography* comes from 'Xerox', the corporation that developed photocopying.

There can be problems with laser toner printing. For example, with textured specialty stocks, the toner won't always adhere and will simply brush off. This is usually to do with the heating unit. Another problem can be heat-induced shrinkage which can cause uneven rippling of the paper. This is due to the heat required to seal the toner drying out some of the water content of the paper.

Inkjet printing tends to be more reliable.

With some electro-ink technologies, coloured particles are suspended in oil and attracted or repelled by different charges for even greater clarity.

There are also web-fed digital printing presses.

Digital printing

By contrast with photocopying, digital printing translates a digital file that describes a page directly to the printing equipment. The page is recreated each time, which is why variable data handling is so easy.

There are a number of competitive technologies, based on various ink properties, usually based on particles that are fused or sprayed on paper, having been placed with digital precision on the paper's surface. Some digital machines use 'offset' or *indirect* methods, with a blanket that transfers the image; some are direct to the sheet.

There are some issues with digital printing that you might watch out for. Sometimes there will be a resolution issue where, instead of a smooth graduation of colour, you will get a stepped graduation or a 'banded vignette' where a pattern of stripes appears. Also digital inks will often crack and flake when folded and sometimes when trimmed.

'On-demand' or 'just-in-time' printing

Printing on-demand or just-in-time means storing a document in a digital form and printing and binding it only when a customer requires a copy.

For university subject handbooks, corporate training and procedures manuals, Acts of Parliament and legislation – and even class textbooks – on-demand printing is an option that solves storage and warehousing issues, updating issues (because the digital file can be updated when required), distribution and inventory control. It is even environmentally sound.

In most cases, it is achieved with digital printing equipment, sometimes with variable data.

Variable data printing

Only the depth of an organisation's database of clients and prospects limits the possibilities for the personalisation of print. Direct marketing or CRM (Customer Relationship Marketing) relies on sufficient database controls and digital printing as its main printing choice.

This is more than just inserting a person's name at the top of a form letter, their total use and the payment due on their electricity bill, even more than mentioning the suburb from their address in the final paragraph. This is more like those options you have to generate a child's book for a special, personalised birthday or Christmas present – the child's name and the names of all family members, two best friends, pet, favourite colour and where they holidayed last year added to a story that has standard pictures, standard plot and gaps to fill.

'But I know you want more!' Not only this, but in full colour with personal photographs, monograms, perhaps an avatar as a character and specific content choices as well!

There is no reason societies and associations – and any organisation with subscribers or members – could not gainfully use this technology. Of course, it will take database management and time, and probably a bit of extra finance, but that will be a small investment compared with the potential revenue that can be generated by providing a truly personalised service.

Consider a personalised magazine. What does it mean for content development? You will need to address articles to each of the different reader segments you identify within your readership. You can do this by asking their preferences in a questionnaire. Match a reader's profile with a particular set of content preferences and possibly throw in a randomly selected article from another area. It means you will develop more content that will be keyed to a particular reader profile.

But how do you provide advertising space? Set the articles in groups of pages that have advertising contained within particular articles. An advertiser could then niche-market more effectively to the reader who requested that type of content. This should enable more finely tuned advertising with greater chance of translation into sales or interest in the product. So advertising is secure – though perhaps a little more expensive per piece (again, greater expense is trading off greater success through better profiling of readers).

Readers could submit digital photos of their own to be scaled and cropped by the magazine into set formats like cover designs. The name of the magazine could also be personalised. The trend for magazines with initials only as titles gives a clue to how this can be achieved. If *GQ* can be *Gentlemen's Quarterly* and *GH* can be *Good Housekeeping*, why not *EW* for *Elizabeth Whitbread*'s magazine? And, if you can have *Dolly* and *George*, why not *Nicola* and *Tyler*?

When you are compiling the magazine for the reader, program the database to select articles from their preference list and work into the number of pages they have selected. The computer will generate teaser copy for the cover based on the reader's selections and a personalised contents list. It will flow the reader's name through the document with the new pagination. The ads will fall as appropriate for the reader's selected content. Supplied personal photographs will be inserted. The editor's letter will be personalised with something like, 'Dear Claire, Welcome to your third issue of *CR* magazine ...' You might even have a comic strip with generic characters and created avatars of your readers based on photos they have supplied, creating 'The Adventures of Lachlan and Danielle'. Subscriptions to this magazine could be very high indeed!

Commercially, imagine a company with a new appliance to market. It is an upgrade of an existing kitchen product that has been on the market for a number of years. The company believes that many purchasers are beginning to consider an upgrade because of the flow of calls to service centres and the average cost of fixing it.

The company can use its guarantee database to send a questionnaire to those who have purchased the appliance previously and tell them about the new product. In order to get a higher response, a kitchen refit can be offered and an extra prize of a free upgrade of the appliance to the test recipe or story about the product, asking each consumer their preferences about the product. Would it need to be operated by other members of the family? What are their names and ages? What colour from this range would best suit the kitchen décor? What textural finish would they like on the base: marble, leather or woodgrain? Customers could even send in a photo of their current appliance on their kitchen bench, stating why their kitchen needs a facelift.

Imagine their surprise when in the following week they receive a letter thanking them for their response and apologising for them missing out on the main prize, but with a special offer that shows the exact model they described in their questionnaire in a photograph on their own kitchen bench (in place of the old model), with extra attachments for Maggie and Kathleen to use, shown and described. A full-colour brochure that mentions the benefits of the new product to their family and retells Maggie's classic tale of using the appliance or reprints Auntie Brigid's favourite recipe could accompany this. A reply card would complete the pack – with only a single tick and payment details needing to be added.

Personalisation to this degree can be very persuasive.

READ MORE ABOUT IT
Joyce Rutter Kaye, 'Magazine 2000: Monogram', *U&lc*, vol. 19, no. 4, International Typeface Corporation, New York, Winter 1992.
Susan E Davis, 'Designs for a custom textbook revolution', *Step-by-step graphics*, vol. 8, no. 4, Dynamic Graphics, Peoria, Illinois, July/August 1992, ISSN 0886 7682.

Lenticular printing

You possibly first experienced lenticular printing in a children's book cover or a postcard. It's a moving image on a printed object – and used to be just two images (a before and after) – but can now feature up to full-motion video! Just by tilting the printed surface ...

The trick of these stereograms is based on the lens design that is printed on its reverse at very fine resolution. The lenses are made of clear optical plastic with a series of parallel lenses called *lenticules*.

The principle that allows the image to change is the same *interleaving* concept used in web colour blending. Fine stripes of two or more different graphic images are interleaved in register with the appropriate lenses.

What is truly amazing is that these images can bend and even be up to 2.4×1.2 metres in size – and even be tiled at that size. So, walking along a corridor in an exhibition, you might have a life-size image of a person on the wall that actually moves as you pass by!

There are four possible types of movement:
- *The 'flip' effect:* two pictures as a before and after
- *The 3-D effect:* which is like a hologram, with the third dimension, where the viewer can move from side to side and feel there is a solid object suspended in the print
- *The 'morph' effect:* comprised of between two and 12 images where one image changes fluidly into another
- *Full motion video:* again comprised of between two and 12 and even up to 20 images.

The lenticules may be up and down or left to right, depending on the type of transformation. However, they will need to be horizontal for animation or you may see more than one image. Discuss this with your lenticular printing expert.

There are a few general artwork hints to help maximise the success of lenticular images:
- Don't use small type, serif or italics.
- Avoid horizontal stripes.
- Use colour theory: cool colours recede and warm colours advance.
- Avoid white backgrounds which can create ghost images.
- Artwork files should not be flattened as layers will be used to generate the print.
- You need to extend the background for the 3-D effect – so increase the bleed.
- Elements that are supposed to advance should not bleed.

READ MORE ABOUT IT
OuterAspect.com.

Letterpress

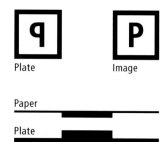

Plate   Image

Paper

Plate

Printing from a raised image, letterpress is the process that Johannes Gutenberg used and is based on the principles of wood-block printing or linocut printing. A raised, backwards image is inked and transferred to paper. It is also called relief printing.

Paper money and playing cards were printed by this method in China in 960 AD and a book *Tripitaka* was printed there as early as 868 AD.

Later, movable type, where individual letters were assembled into the lines of text and placed into a forme that incorporated any illustrations on wood block, was invented by Pi Sheng between 1041 and 1048 in China and used

in Korea as early as 1241 before Gutenberg brought the
technology to Europe in the 1400s.

A plate of metal or plastic is now coated with a light-
sensitive material, which is exposed through a photographic
negative of the desired image area. The area that was
exposed is sealed and the area that was not exposed is
etched away by acid, leaving a raised reversed image ready
for inking. The plates are then locked together in a forme
and bedded in the press.

There are three types of printing presses. The *platen
press* is where two flat surfaces are brought together like
the action of your elbow when your hand touches your
shoulder. A *rotary press* is where the forme is curved
around a cylinder and paper brought to it by an impression
cylinder. A *flatbed press* has a flat forme that moves under
ink rollers and paper is drawn across the forme by the
impression cylinder.

Gravure

Printing from a surface with variable depths of sunken
image area, gravure is based on the etching process or
intaglio printing. After a doctor blade has swept the excess
ink off the shiny metal non-image area, the deeper cells
in the plate hold more ink than the shallower cells and
transfer it to the paper, making a tonal variation within each
dot size variation. This gives gravure images a greater depth
of tone. There is also a slight blurring around the deeper
colours, which in process colour can even start to mix,
creating a softer dot, and almost an illusion of continuous
tone.

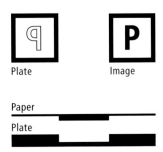

Plate   Image

Paper

Plate

The plate cylinder sits on an ink roller in a trough of ink.
As it turns the doctor blade cleans the non-image surface
of the plate and paper is drawn through the press by the
impression cylinder above.

The gravure process is used in the packaging industry
because it can deposit a larger amount of ink in one *pass*
(run through the machine) than, say, offset printing which
may take two or three passes to deposit an equivalent
amount.

Engraving

Also an intaglio or sunken-image process, engraving can attain a mesmerising level of fine detail. It is very similar to gravure in principle, but the flat engraving plate is applied to the paper with considerable pressure, not only transferring the ink, but also creating a raised image on the front of the sheet and indents on the back. Engraving ink colours are also more opaque than most others, enabling light colours to be printed directly onto dark papers. In the case of metallic inks, they can be burnished (restamped) to look polished.

Stencil   Image

Squeegee squeezes ink through stencil to paper

Screen   Ink

Stencil

Paper

Screen printing

By forcing ink through a stencil image that is adhered to a screen made of fine silk or polyester, screen printing can achieve remarkable detail and also deposit a remarkable amount of ink.

This stencil printing process is used in some finishing processes, such as laminating, and is also used commercially for packaging and printing on various substrates like metal, fabric and plastic.

An image is photographically transferred to a screen by exposing a photosensitive stencil with ultraviolet light. The stencil is then washed to remove the image area. This is applied to the screen and leaves a fine mesh for the ink to penetrate. The screen is placed on top of the paper and ink is drawn across the screen by a squeegee. The screen is then lifted to reveal the printed piece. Multiple colours can be applied using separate screens. The inks are thicker and more opaque than most, although you can also print transparent inks and varnishes.

This process is capable of remarkably fine work: up to 60 or even 75 lpi screen work on the right substrate. For example, on translucent polypropylene it can print both sides to create an almost three-dimensional effect. But, if printed on the underside in reverse order, the polypropylene surface means the print cannot be scuffed or scratched. A final hit of white over the image area seals the colours and makes them appear solid. (Polypropylene by-products are carbon dioxide and water, so it is 100% recyclable.)

Silkscreen printing is also used by cost-conscious community-based printing ventures for posters and other materials because stencils cut by hand can be applied to the screen.

Flexography

Used commercially in packaging (such as chip packets) and to print on uneven surfaces such as containers, plastics, foil and corrugated substrates, flexography is based on the letterpress process. The term comes from the raised plate made of flexible rubber or polymer. It's like a huge rubber stamp. Due to the huge number of copies typically printed by this process in the foodstuff packaging area, and the flexible nature of the plate, there can be distortion throughout a print run so fine detail and small type should be avoided. Sometimes artwork will need to be distorted to accommodate the packaging requirements. You will need to work closely with the print manager to prepare material for this process.

Selecting a printer

A prospective client can expect to see samples of work produced by the printers they visit or contact. Many will have websites that describe the services they offer, list clients they have worked with, and show recent work, and some will have online quoting.

In addition to the *Yellow Pages*, there are directories and listings by other organisations, including chambers of commerce and printing associations.

Identifying the cause of print problems

There are occasional print imperfections. They include:
- *pinholes* or *scratches:* these may be a fault on the plate or the negative film
- *hickies:* where dirt or dust is caught in the ink and causes a little glitch in the colour (sometimes like a halo)
- *picking:* a small feathery mark that is left where fibres of coating have been lifted off the surface of the paper after the ink was printed, often due to the quality of the paper or a problem with the blanket on the press
- *skew:* where a paper sheet has fed crookedly or the plate has been prepared with a crooked image

CHECKLIST
What you need to supply your printer
In addition to all the material you would supply your prepress operator (see p. 298), you must supply your printer with the following:
- ☐ Number of copies required
- ☐ Number of pages
  - – double-sided?
  - – bleed?
  - – plus cover?
  - – print inside cover?
- ☐ Paper specifications
  - – cover/text/specialty
  - – colour, weight, brand of each
- ☐ Number of colours
  - – Pantone
  - – process/HiFi
- ☐ Finishing processes required
  - – laminates (gloss/matt)
  - – varnishes (gloss/matt)
  - – trimming details including final size
  - – folding details
- ☐ Embellishments
  - – foils (metallic/patterned/clear/coloured)
  - – embossing/debossing
  - – thermography
  - – die-cutting/scoring/perforation
  - – laser cutting
  - – pop-ups and hand assembly
- ☐ Binding processes
  - – saddle stapling
  - – paperback/soft back/perfect binding/burst binding
  - – hardback/case binding
  - – ring binding
  - – spiral binding/wiro binding/half-Canadian binding
  - – side stapling
  - – plastic comb binding
  - – thermal binding
  - – post-and-eye binding
- ☐ Date required
- ☐ Delivery instructions
  - – packing
  - – address/es
- ☐ Any security or embargo issues.

- *striping:* caused by uneven inking or uneven pressure on the printing plate
- *ghosting:* where some ink has been left on the print roller from the previous print and prints slightly out of line with the next print
- *curling:* where the heat of a process might dry and stretch a paper, causing it to curl
- *set-off:* caused by stacking the sheets while they were still wet, causing transfer of a reverse image to the sheet they are stacked against.

Printers will rarely let these escape the print room and will fix them inline during the print run as much as possible.

Paper

Paper can represent more than 25% of the invoice for most printing. Appropriate paper selection and awareness of paper terminology and the different qualities available can enable you to choose the right paper or *stock* for a printing task. Seek advice from your printer and paper company representative about the suitability of the chosen stock for the project.

As a design element, paper not only brings colour and visual texture to a printed piece, but also has a tactile quality that communicates subtle messages through the sense of touch. Take advantage of tactile contrasts when you are selecting paper, not necessarily contrasting papers within the same product but contrasting with the papers your audience is likely to be handling most of the time. In this way, distinctive paper selection can help to achieve separation from other paper products.

Most paper merchants are suppliers and distributors who carry a variety of papers from Australian and international paper mills. The papers fall into generic categories, which will be briefly explained. These generic categories define different qualities for different uses.

If you want to see specific papers, call the paper house reps and ask for *swatch books* (a stapled set of sample sheets labelling all the colours and weights in a particular range) and printed samples of the papers they carry. Ask for the generic category and they will let you know the full range of papers they carry in that category.

You will find that some papers are identical but called different names and charged at different prices, according to the paper company that supplies them. This is because the paper suppliers buy stocks from paper mills around the world. Sometimes a particular paper will become very fashionable, so each company will want to carry its own version. The amount of paper each purchased from the mill will be one of the reasons the price may vary from supplier to supplier.

'I love paper. I love paper because it's sensual and tactile and the internet really isn't. Paper has surface, weight and texture. Sometimes it makes noise – it rustles or snaps. Usually it smells good. It bends, wrinkles, folds and drapes. It's opaque and translucent. It's sleek, shiny, matte or textured. It has soul. But best of all, it is a time-honoured repository for artwork.'

Paula Scher, The Mohawk Show 2008 announcement

Paper selection

The qualities you are looking for when selecting paper are its:

☐ colour
☐ weight (particularly if mailing)
☐ bulk (thickness; you may need a bulky paper to make a smaller number of pages seem more substantial)
☐ show-through (opacity)
☐ suitability for its task
☐ brightness and whiteness (level of light reflection)
☐ gloss (surface finish)
☐ tactile quality (texture)
☐ printability (how it will take ink; absorbency and drying time)
☐ strength and flexibility (to withstand its expected handling on press and by the ultimate user; to not easily crease or tear)
☐ suitability for binding and embellishment processes
☐ archival quality (durability)
☐ wastage from the sheet size
☐ cost
☐ availability
☐ environmental impact.

Doing it environmentally smarter

To be kinder to the environment, reduce the size of your printed piece and print both sides of the paper. A poster can work even at A4. The back of the poster can have further details, ordering or booking information on it.

You might also choose a lighter paper rather than a heavy one. With recycled paper being a little more bulky, you can go a grade lighter in weight without sacrificing the feel or opacity of your sheet.

Papers are made from *pulp*, mostly composed of plantation wood and other natural fibres such as cotton or hemp. The paper industry's environmental awareness means that there will be fibres from mill waste and printing offcuts, used papers and even fabric scraps, in most paper pulp.

As the fibre is processed, it is cooked and cleaned with water, bleaches and a chemical cocktail that eventually colours the pulp ready for paper production. Bleaching is often achieved using part oxygen substitutes – sometimes chlorine-free – rather than the chlorine gas bleaching used previously.

Gradually, paper is formed along a fine wire mesh by removing the water and moving it through presses and driers, eventually coating it with various substances to improve its print performance, and rolling or embossing it to create its specific surface quality. It is then cut into sheets or rolled onto reels for web printing.

As the fibres trundle through this process, they become aligned in the direction of the flow and this creates what is called the *grain* of the paper. Paper will roll or bow along the grain and will fold and tear easily along the grain. Books should be folded along the grain (it should run parallel to the spine). When folded against the grain, some papers might crumple or crack.

There are also some synthetic papers available.

When selecting paper, look for weight, colour, texture, strength and opacity, and its ability to perform. *Strength* is needed for papers to survive the printing, folding and binding processes and eventual use by the consumer. *Opacity* defines the paper's level of transparency. This depends on both the thickness of the paper and the composition and density of its pulp. Some low levels of opacity will allow you to see the print on the reverse of the page, or even the page behind that. You might design around this feature, but there are times when you will not want it.

When ordering paper, *ream* is the term for 500 sheets. That is 500 *leaves*. It is also 1000 *pages* (as a page is one side of a sheet). In a book, the right-hand pages are the *recto* pages and the left-hand pages on their reverse side are the *verso* pages.

READ MORE ABOUT IT

Nancy Williams, *Paperwork: The potential of paper in graphic design*, Phaidon, London, 1993, ISBN 0 7148 2802 5.

Catherine Fishel, *Paper graphics: The power of paper in graphic design*, Rockport, Massachusetts, 1999, ISBN 1 56496 563 5.

Paper specification

Paper is mostly defined by its weight using *gsm* ('grams per square metre') or g/m². This is called its *grammage*. To give a rough idea of comparative weights, photocopier papers are usually 80 gsm; letterheads and pamphlets, around 110 gsm; posters, around 170 gsm; lightweight covers, about 220 gsm; and boards are over 300 gsm.

In the United States, weight is expressed in *lbs/ream* (that is, pounds per 500 sheets). Standard papers are about 80 lbs/ream. Light papers are about 60 lbs/ream and heavier stocks, 100 lbs/ream.

Some heavy boards will be referred to as 3-ply or 6-sheet boards. These are boards that have been created by laminating three or six sheets together, respectively.

Paper is also defined by its thickness, which can also be termed its *caliper* or *bulk*. It is measured in *microns* (micrometres, or one-millionth of a metre) or μms by callipers. This measurement is useful for calculating the width of a spine, for example. But often a dummy is made of blank sheets of the exact paper specified, bound in the same manner as the design specifications, so you can see, feel and measure the exact width. A dummy is also useful for your client to visualise the final product. Paper houses usually provide this service.

The sequence of specification is usually colour, paper name and weight, and it is usually best to identify the paper company in brackets at the end.

If you specify generic grades such as 'A2 matt art', or even a specific stock from a particular paper merchant, on some jobs you should include the additional specification of 'or equivalent'. You can also request that printing does not start until the stock selection is approved.

Competing paper companies will have an almost identical range of generic papers and may even carry the same specialty stock produced by the same paper mill under a different name.

Dot gain

When dots are printed with ink on paper, there is often a small increase in their size due to the paper's absorption and possibly some slight distortion during the printing process. This is termed *dot gain* and it is often compensated for in prepress. During film preparation, the dots will be made slightly smaller, making the proof seem slightly lighter overall, but accommodating the expected dot gain comfortably on press.

DOING IT SMARTER

Duplexes

Instead of printing a full-bleed colour on one side of a paper to contrast with the other side, you could select a duplex sheet from a paper manufacturer. Duplex describes any sheet that has a different surface or colour on each side. A different surface can be produced by polishing only one side of the sheet. A sheet with a different colour on each side is made from two sheets of paper that have been laminated together to create a hybrid stock. They are usually thicker and therefore used more as cover stocks where one colour is the outer cover and one is effectively the endpaper or inside cover stock. If you use a concertina fold in a pamphlet with a duplex stock, both sides of your pamphlet will show off the two stocks.

DOING IT CHEAPER

Ask your printer what stocks are 'out the back' that they want to get rid of. There might be enough of one of them for the print job you're preparing. That stock will often be cheaper, because the client it was originally ordered for may have already paid for it, due to minimum order and mill standard requirements.

Art or coated grades

Art papers are excellent smooth white surfaces for reproduction of fine details and full-colour screened images. The smooth surface is achieved by coating the paper with fine mineral clay compounds, which are then dried and *calendered*. Calendering is where the paper passes through heated rollers to polish the paper's surface. The amount and type of both coating and calendering determines its relative smoothness and shine.

In Australia, art papers are graded from A1 – the highest quality surface and most expensive – down to A2 and A3. The grade is determined by the amount of coating on each side. An A1 sheet includes upwards of 20 gsm of coating on each side; an A2 grade, over 10 gsm of coating on each side; and an A3, less than 10 gsm of coating each side.

In the United States, there are five levels from A#1 to A#5, with the grade determined by the amount of light reflected by the stock. An A#1 sheet reflects slightly more light than an A#2 sheet.

Note that these gradings have nothing to do with the international sheet sizes called A1, A2 or A3.

For most applications, a grade A2 art paper is an acceptable standard and cheaper than the A1 stocks. But for high-quality posters and publications, the A1 sheet is recommended as a superior surface.

Gloss art or calendered paper

Gloss surfaces are created by calendering or super-calendering. Ink will take longer to dry on gloss papers, because it sits on the smooth surface. This usually gives the best reproduction of colour photographs, because the vibrancy of the colours is maintained. The categories of gloss include ultragloss and *cast coated* (the glossiest).

Matt and dull art

Matt or *dull* art papers are coated papers that do not have a gloss finish. They have been *blade coated*, where a thin metal blade smooths the surface after the coating has been applied. Matt art papers might also be called *satin*, *suede* or *velvet*.

Uncoated and specialty grades

Uncoated grades include:
- *newsprint*, which includes a large amount of mechanical pulp where the wood fibres have not had lignin removed and therefore will yellow with age and exposure to light
- *bond papers*, weighted from 70 to 90 gsm
- *offset papers*, treated to perform well in offset presses, starting at about 90 gsm
- *laser grades*, designed to perform well in photocopiers and laser printers and to reduce curl when they pass through heating units
- *specialty grades*.

Specialty grades include transparent papers and rough or antique papers, onion skin (semitranslucent) and egg-shell papers, archival and permanent papers, and paper with texture embossed into them. The texture might mimic woodgrain, linen and other fabrics, stucco or leather, or they might be rippled, hammered, mottled or ridged. They might also feature inclusions such as confetti, grass clippings, petals, leaves or contrasting fibres such as silk, or denim. They will often come in a suite of colours and weights that can be mixed and matched.

Some specialty papers are still handmade.

There are other specialty papers like NCR (no carbon required) pressure-sensitive papers for forms printing and account books; continuous papers for computer systems; and security papers with various metallic or chemical inclusions.

In some cases, you might choose to make a feature of a paper's *deckle edge* – the feathery edge of a sheet that is not trimmed off in some specialty grades.

Handmade

Many exotic papers are available with inserts of leaves, bark, seeds, petals, grasses, fabrics, threads, printed pieces and even sequins and glitter. These are mostly handmade but some companies are producing them in relatively commercial quantities. They will often be hand-dyed with natural dyes, herbs and spices – and some may be marbled or preprinted.

Recycled grades

Environmental concerns should have been partly solved by the 'paperless office' that the personal computer was to have heralded. But the increase in paper usage brought forth considerable pressure to at least 'reduce, reuse or recycle'.

The paper industry quite rightly noted it had always recycled post-industrial waste, but the issue was more how to recycle post-consumer waste.

The process of creating paper is tough on fibres and recycled paper keeps going through this process, each time making the fibres finer and weaker. So paper will rarely have a totally recycled content. In order for paper to have the strength it needs to survive the industrial processes and consumer use required of it, new fibres will be required. So most paper companies will now be able to tell you percentages for how much post-consumer, post-industrial and virgin fibre (wood pulp) is contained within each stock they carry.

Recycled stocks will often have an increased absorbency and greater bulk due to their softer fibres. So fine detail and spindly serifs often don't print well on them. The printer will probably run more ink to compensate for the absorption, but this may cause more dot gain than usual. Solids may look mottled, due to the different absorbency levels within the recycled and virgin fibres.

When designing a product, certain decisions can limit the paper product's recyclability. The main offenders are usually finishes, such as UV and other laminates, any plastic coatings or self-adhesive glues. Try to achieve the same effect with different processes.

Post-industrial waste
Most papers have a percentage of post-industrial or pre-consumer waste in them. This includes mill broke and other mill waste – the waste paper created in the paper-making process itself, which contains trimmings and damaged paper. But post-industrial waste also includes paper trimmings that have never been printed, which are returned from printers to the paper mill for repulping. These papers will mostly have undergone some manufacturing process, but will have been discarded, largely unchanged.

Post-consumer waste

This is the content most people think of when they say 'recycled'. It is paper that has been printed, finished, bound, purchased and used by a consumer and returned to the paper mill for recycling. After cleaning and de-inking, the fibres are still a greyish colour, so they will often be bleached before being repulped to make new sheets of paper.

Stationery grades

Most paper companies produce stationery ranges of a series of papers with different surface and colour qualities but with matching weights in each range that include:

- a *writing* or *letterhead* grade with a weight of 90–100 gsm
- a *text* weight, which is designed for two-sided printing and therefore has less show-through (or greater opacity), weighing in at 100–150 gsm
- a *cover* weight suitable for business cards, starting at about 200 gsm
- matching *envelopes*.

Your printer or paper rep can show you samples.

Laid/wove

Created by patterns in the wire mesh while the paper is pulp, laid papers are often used for stationery and have a fine pattern of horizontal or vertical lines within them. You can see it more clearly when the paper is held up to the light. Wove papers are created with a woven mesh.

Watermarks

Watermarks are created during the making of the sheet of paper. The pulp passes underneath a dandy roll, a roller of fine wire mesh that has wire artwork built onto it. Where the wire logo or type is raised, the paper will be thinner and therefore when the sheet is dried it will allow more light through so a soft image called a watermark can be seen.

This is an expensive process and economically viable only if an enormous amount of paper is being milled for an organisation. Basically, an organisation can commission a paper company to prepare a wire frame of the logo and produce the paper.

Finishing processes and embellishment

Price comparison

Gloss/matt finishes

$$$ Celloglaze
$$ Liquid laminate
$ Varnish and aqueous
    coatings

Finishing processes and embellishment come at the end of a print run and put the final touches to a print job. Many can be expensive and time-consuming, so you need to plan your production schedule accordingly. They have varying degrees of impact on the environment, which are only briefly noted.

Varnishes

A solvent-based coating, varnish is run like an additional ink, after all the colours have been printed. The finish can be gloss, semigloss, satin or matt. If you want to contrast matt and gloss finishes, it is best to print two varnish runs. This is often done to gloss photographs and matt the background on which they appear.

In order to create a printing plate, a separate piece of artwork is needed to define the area where each varnish is to appear.

Most varnishes contribute to air pollution.

Tinted varnish

You may want a logo, type or pattern overprinted in varnish, but sometimes a clear varnish is too subtle. So a small amount of ink is added to the varnish to alter its colour and an artwork plate is used to enable the logo, type or pattern to be seen.

Glitter varnish

Glitter can be suspended in varnish and printed like any other varnish. Often used in greeting card design, the fine speckles are available in numerous coloured metallic reflective finishes. They should not print across folds or creases.

Glow-in-the-dark varnish

Used in greeting cards and novelty items, a varnish that contains light-sensitive particles is overprinted on light-coloured areas of a design. After exposure to light sources for up to 20 minutes, it emits a 'glow' in the dark or low-light areas.

Laminates

A plastic surface laminated onto a printed sheet gives the highest gloss finish. Both gloss and matt laminating plastics are available. A laminate gives a protective surface to a printed piece, but can also be applied in different areas using its liquid form. It is sometimes referred to as *cello-glazing* (pronounced 'sell-o-glazing') or *cellosheening*.

Laminating is not kind to the environment, as the plastic cannot be effectively removed from the paper fibres. It cannot be recycled after use, and ends up in landfill.

Liquid/UV laminate

Laminating is now mostly achieved by printing a liquid laminate over a printed sheet. This is then cured by exposure to UV light, which is also an air-polluting process.

You can print from an artwork plate or just apply a solid laminate across the entire surface.

Sheet laminate

By heat-sealing the laminate from a reel of plastic sheeting to a printed sheet, the surface is sealed.

Coatings

Other finishing processes similar to printing include gumming and latex coating.

Gumming

When you receive a form that needs to be sealed with gummed tabs, the 'gum' or glue has been printed along the edge in a manner similar to spot laminating.

An alternative is double-sided tape (or 'peel-and-seal' tape) that adheres to the edges (where you remove a layer of thin, high-gloss paper that adheres to the tacky surface of a glued strip).

Latex coating

The familiar silver-grey ink that you scratch away with a coin to reveal winning numbers on instant lottery tickets, 'scratchies' and other promotional items is printed with a latex-based ink.

Folding

The sum total of folding technology is that paper can be folded either forwards or backwards. In diagrams, these two folds are shown with a dotted line and a dashed line (a solid line is a cut).

In various combinations, particularly with gluing and die-cutting, 3-D objects and pop-ups can be created. To help the folding process, use a score (indent) or a double score. Sometimes a form of perforation to fold sections without getting crumpled edges is used.

Guillotining/trimming/drilling

Trimming is a separate process at the end of a print run that happens on an industrial guillotine. The operator places the material under a straight blade and cuts off the unwanted extra paper.

Although the guillotine usually trims only at 90°, trimming can be done at angles by creating the appropriate chocks. For curved edges, however, you need to look at die-cutting techniques.

The holes in documents produced for ring binders are drilled at high speed.

Collating and gathering

Collators stack multiple sheets in order, ready for binding and trimming. For larger publications, collation is sometimes called *gathering*. Large publications that are produced in 16-, 32- or 64-page sections need their sections to be collated in order.

For saddle-stitched (stapled) publications, gathering is done inline on a conveyor, where the saddle catches each section in order from the centre of the book to the cover on top, and the lot is then stapled at the end of the line. The thickness of the paper at the spine, through which the staples are stabbed, causes the phenomenon known as

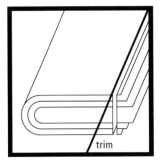

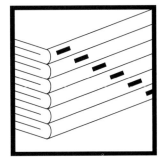

Paper creep
is determined in prepress and
appropriate compensation made.

Signature marks
on the spine of each section align to
show the collation sequence.

paper creep – where the text block on pages in the centre of the book will appear closer to the outer trim edges. This is usually counteracted at page imposition stage.

For a section-sewn book or perfect-bound book, the sections need to be piled in order. Each section will have a section identifier (signature mark) down the spine so the printer will know the sections have been collated in the correct order.

Numbering

Applying numbers to invoice books and raffle tickets can be done in-run by attaching a small letterpress automatic numbering machine to the press. The numbering device can be told how many times the same number must be struck, in the case of forms being produced in triplicate, for example.

Binding

Publications that need to be bound are usually printed not as single sheets but in signatures of eight, 16, 32 or 64 pages. These are then collated into the correct reading order and bound with their cover. There are numerous binding processes available that are briefly described and illustrated in this section. Your printer can show you examples.

Saddle stapling/saddle stitching

Pre-folded sections or sheets are collated and placed on a saddle, which is like an inverted V. The cover is added and the staples or stitching applied.

Price comparison

Binding

$$$	Hardback/case binding/ section-sewn
$$	Soft cover/paperback/ perfect-bound/burst-bound
$	Saddle/side stitching

Hard case binding steps

1   Trimming
2   Folding
3   Endpapering
4   Collating
5   Sewing
6   Smashing the spine
7   Gluing spine
8   Drying
9   Nipping the text block
10 Three knife trimming of the text block
11 Rounding the spine and backing
12 Glue spine
13 Apply mull (the cheese cloth that seals the spine)
14 Glue spine
15 Apply head and tail bands and paper lining
16 Create the 'case':
    • Cut the boards or printed paper case
    • Cut the cloth
    • Make the case
17 Foil blocking on the case
18 Case in
19 Press in and groove the cover
20 Stacking and checking
21 Dust jacketing
22 Packing

From *Finish First* by the Australian Print Finishers Association

Paperback/soft cover/perfect binding

The most imperfect binding technique, perfect binding is the one that doesn't fold flat, and when you force it to open flat, the glue breaks and the pages all fall out. This is, of course, the worst-case scenario, but it readily identifies the technique. Part of the problem is caused by the fact that the pages start off in sections, but the fold is trimmed off and the inside edges are roughened so the glue can adhere to each page. There are many glues that can be used and some are close to perfect.

Perfect binding also allows papers of differing weights and qualities to be collated and bound into a publication, so it has an attraction for magazine producers who want to bind in preprinted advertising sections, samples and subscription cards.

The other attraction of perfect binding is that it gives a square-backed spine, but it is best to do this with about 96 pages. It can be done with 64 pages, but is less successful.

Burst binding

A variation on perfect binding, burst binding seeks to rectify perfect binding's main problem of guillotining the fold by retaining the fold and forcing glue through notches or punctures along it. Sadly, it is still imperfect and sometimes too much glue is forced through, further limiting the ability of the book to be opened.

Hardback/case binding/section-sewn

As implied by one of its names, the book's sections are collated and sewn in order. This is then bound into a cover. Section-sewn books can have a paper cover drawn on, so not all section-sewn books are case-bound.

But all case-bound books are section-sewn. The 'case' referred to in case binding is the hard covers that are created to wrap around the spine of the sewn sections to protect the book's pages. The case consists of boards covered and connected by cloth, paper or leather. This is attached to the sewn sections with cloth and endpapers. It is often then decorated with head and tail bands and sometimes a ribbon for bookmarking.

Often the case will be further protected by a dustjacket, which is a wraparound paper cover with flaps that tuck inside the covers.

Ring binding

A ring binder allows material to lie flat inside a binder. The pages are drilled two, three or four times to align with standard 'rings'. The binder and its cover might be printed before assembly or they might have printed sheets bound into plastic pockets on the spine, back and front covers. There might be a set of dividers supplied or collated into the text.

This is an excellent solution for material that is likely to be regularly updated. You simply remove the page that is out of date and replace it with the revised page.

Often the text is shrink-wrapped for distribution, so the pages aren't harmed in the process.

Spiral binding

A series of fine holes is punched down the side of the guillotined and separate pages of the publication. Then a spiral of wire coated in plastic is threaded through the holes. Spiral binding (sometimes called 'plastic coil binding') allows pages to lie flat; different weights and qualities of paper – even different sizes – can be bound together.

Wiro binding

Wiro binding is similar to spiral binding but the wire is doubled up and fed through the holes in a different pattern.

Half-Canadian binding

Half-Canadian binding is wiro binding with a cover that has been bound and which folds out over the wire from the back to the front, creating a square-backed spine.

Binding

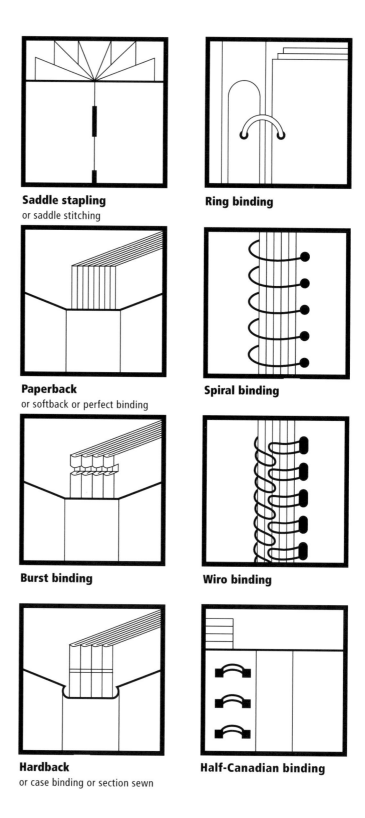

Saddle stapling
or saddle stitching

Ring binding

Paperback
or softback or perfect binding

Spiral binding

Burst binding

Wiro binding

Hardback
or case binding or section sewn

Half-Canadian binding

Office binding styles

Side stapling

Separate sheets that are collated with separate back and front cover sheets are stapled two, three or four times through the left-hand side of the front cover and out the right-hand side of the back cover. The staples are sometimes covered with a strip of binding cloth, which gives a relatively square back and protects the reader's hands from the staples.

Remember that side-stapled documents cannot be opened flat and material that is too close to the spine may be lost.

Reinforcing

Sometimes a strip of glued cloth is added to reinforce side-stapled binding. This can also be added to folded bindings to strengthen folders or covers that are likely to be used extensively.

Ensure that you take account of the area of the cover that will be obscured by the cloth when you create the cover artwork.

Plastic comb binding

Another side-binding process, using a comb binder, cuts a pattern of rectangular holes through the collated document. A plastic comb is then uncoiled, the pages inserted, and the comb recoiled to bind the document. These documents lie almost flat.

Plastic strip binding

This is another side-binding process that uses a series of punctured holes down the left side of the collated document. A plastic strip with protruding plastic spikes is fed through the holes and another plastic strip placed at the back. The excess length of the plastic spikes is trimmed and the back strip melted to the remaining spike. Although this is narrower than side stapling, the document still cannot be opened out flat.

Thermal binding

This is an office version of perfect binding, using heat to melt a glue strip to a document within a pre-folded cover.

Post-and-eye binding

A variation on ring binding, post-and-eye binding uses a small post with an internal thread that takes a screw on the other side of the document. The post goes through the holes drilled down the side of the document.

Craft bindings

Japanese binding

A sewn side-binding technique that has long been used commercially in Japan creates patterns with contrasting thread and secures the pages effectively. The book will not open flat.

Zigzag binding

Zigzag binding is a binding style from China that connects concertina-folded pages to pockets in separate front and back covers. The covers then protect and strengthen the book, often enabling it to stand.

Twigs

This is a side-binding technique that simply passes looped twine through two holes drilled through the book and its covers. A twig is then passed through the looped twine and the twine is tightened and tied at the back of the book. Many different objects can be used in lieu of twigs or twine, including chopsticks and pencils, ribbons and rubber bands.

READ MORE ABOUT IT

Shereen LaPlantz, *Cover to cover: Creative techniques for making beautiful books, journals and albums*, Lark Books, Asheville, North Carolina, 1995, ISBN 0 937274 81 X.

Kathy Blake, *Handmade books: A step-by-step guide to crafting your own books*, Bulfinch Press, Little, Brown & Company, New York, 1997, ISBN 0 8212 2220 1.

Angela James, *The handmade book*, New Holland, London, 2000, ISBN 1 85974 437 0.

Jean G Kropper, *Handmade cards and books*, Lothian, Melbourne, 1995, ISBN 0 85091 708 5.

Office and craft bindings

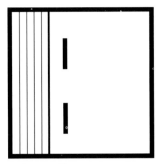

Side stapling

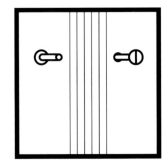

Post-and-eye binding

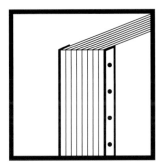

Plastic comb binding

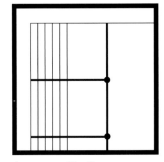

Japanese binding

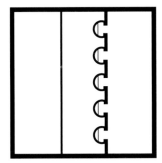

Plastic strip binding

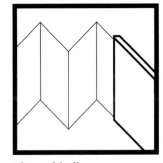

Zigzag binding

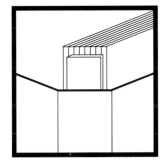

Thermal binding

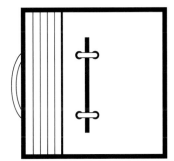

Twig binding

Foils

Foil stamping or foil embossing is based on the letterpress principle, but uses metallic and non-metallic 'foils' on a plastic mylar substrate or 'carrier'. When stamped onto paper by the raised image die (the metal plate), the foil is transferred from its plastic carrier to the page. This is achieved through heating the metal plate in order for the adhesive on the foil to melt to the paper. The pressure from the press usually leaves a fine indent along the edge of the image area in the softer surface of the paper.

Foiling can combine with embossing or debossing to create some impressive effects.

Metals, vinyls, clear, holograms, printed foils

Foils used to be thin metallic sheets, but the term now refers generically to any material transferred in this way. Therefore, coloured vinyl 'foils' and even clear plastic 'foils' can be stamped onto papers. White vinyl, for example, can be stamped onto a navy textured sheet of paper to provide a smooth surface on which to overprint in process colour.

Metallic foils come in a broad range of metallic colours and finishes, from shiny and reflective to matt and low sheen, from traditional gold, silver and bronze to brushed aluminium and anodised colours. Some have holograms embedded within them or have been overprinted with patterns created by laser.

Hologram preparation is very expensive and can take a long lead-time.

There can be limitations on the area that is able to be printed in one stamp: the foil comes in reels of particular sizes and you may want to discuss wastage with your embellisher before getting too carried away.

Embossing and debossing

Embossing creates a raised image by stretching the paper itself. Conversely, *debossing* presses an image into the paper. This is achieved by a variation on the letterpress process, where male and female dies clamp and stretch the paper's fibres by a combination of heat and pressure.

Blind embossing is where the paper is raised with no printing on the image area.

Price comparison

Raised levels

$$$$$	Hologram/sculptural emboss
$$$$	Foil stamp
$$$	Emboss/deboss
$$	Laminated stickers (hand-applied)
$	Thermography

Sculptural embossing is where there are many sculptured levels in the male and female dies, rather than one lift. A sculptural die is much more expensive because it is actually sculpted by an artisan – it cannot be created photographically because it is not simply one level raised or lowered like embossing and debossing.

With all embosses, there is a minimal interruption to the paper sheet, making the process one of the most environmentally friendly because all it does is stretch the fibres involved. If a cover is just blind-embossed, it can go straight into repulping, because there isn't even a need for the de-inking process.

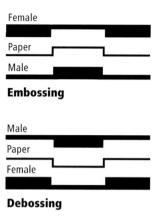

Embossing

Debossing

Thermography

At the conclusion of an offset print run, a fine resin dust can be applied to a printed piece. It sticks to the wet print area and excess dust is removed from non-image areas by vacuum. The sheet is passed through a heater where the dust pools and swells on the inked area. When cooled, the resin sets as a solid plastic raised image. This is known as thermography and is used regularly on business cards.

The technique should always be used on solid ink but does not always work on large flat areas.

Thermography should be avoided on items that might pass through the heating units in laser printers or photocopiers, as the resin will melt.

Die-cutting, scoring and perforation

A *forme* is created which includes a plan for scores and cuts, using dulled metal for the scores and knives or sharp blades for the cuts. This forme is called the die and it is then stamped out of a sheet, using a variation of the letterpress process.

If you want a perforation in a shape other than a straight line, it is prepared in the same way but with knife blades that have notches in them. Where the notch is, the paper is not pierced.

Straight-line perforations can also be added to a print job with a perforating wheel that is added to the press at the end of the run.

With die-cutting (sometimes called 'forme-cutting'), notches are used at regular intervals so that cut pieces will

A die-cut used on a brochure cover.
Client: Rosanna Golf Links
Studio: Adstract Art

DOING IT CHEAPER
Die-cut folders and brochures
Use existing dies for folders and
brochures – most printers save the
formes of previous jobs 'out the back'.
Ask to see your printer's collection
of dies and see if any of them can be
used. This will save you the cost of
preparing the die.

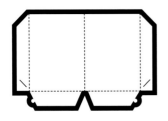

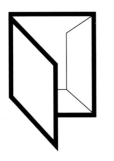

not fall into the machinery of the printing press, which
explains why die-cuts need to be pushed out of the paper
that surrounds them.

Window-facing

In packaging design and some specialty book covers, a
transparent 'window' is added to a die-cut hole. Usually
this is a square-cut piece of acetate or PVC that is glued
to the back of the die-cut printed card. Always discuss the
production specifications with your supplier.

Laser cutting

Die-cutting is limited by the flexibility of the blades used
to cut the shapes and the cost of creating the die forme. If
you require greater detail, you might consider laser cutting.
It is capable of intricate detail and burns the paper away
according to the digital file created for the cut. It can also
cut sharp corners. You can also cut intricate outlines on
sticker bases, where the laser only cuts the top layer, leaving
the base intact.

Sometimes if the paper stock is too light it can be
scorched by the laser on the edges of the cut. Always
discuss the artwork with your supplier to ensure you
prepare the artwork as required. For example, it will need
small 'bridges' to avoid a complete cut-out of the images,
similar to die-cut shapes. The bridge should be at least
1 mm.

Pop-ups

The novelty of pop-ups is a method of engaging the reader
with a print product. It can be so unexpected and effective.
There are some simple pop-ups that you might consider
using in a printed piece. Their application is limited only by
your imagination. As far as stretching your budget to pop-
ups, simple ones might be able to be created with just a bit
of handwork, rather than expensive dies and scores.

READ MORE ABOUT IT
David A Carter & James Diaz, *The elements of pop-up: A pop-up book for
aspiring paper engineers*, Little Simon, New York, 1999, ISBN 0 689 82224 3.
Any book by Robert Sabuda.

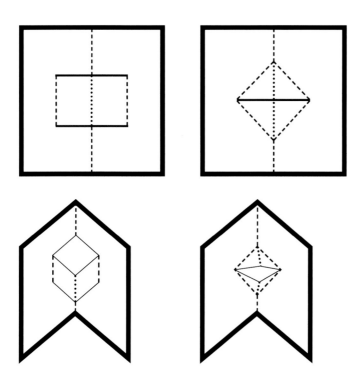

Pop-ups

These plans show cuts with a solid line; forward folds or scores with a dashed line; and backward folds or scores with a dotted line. When cut and folded, they make the two pop-up forms below.

Professionalism

Using a designer

Selecting a contractor

A prospective client can ask to see a portfolio of current work from a designer, an illustrator, a photographer, a multimedia producer, and an advertising agency (which will also have a 'show reel', a video of television and radio commercials). Many will also have websites that describe their work processes, show recent work, and list other clients they have worked with, some of whom may provide testimonials.

In addition to the *Yellow Pages*, there are industry directories – often online.

In directories, you might look up the following categories:
☐ Advertising agencies
☐ Artists – commercial
☐ Designers – graphic
☐ Illustrators
☐ Internet services
☐ Multimedia services
☐ Photographers – advertising and fashion
☐ Photographers – commercial and industrial

Assessing a portfolio

In a portfolio, look for an appropriate production quality, a conceptual approach that shows rigorous creative thinking, and the sorts of clients the designer has previously worked for.

Discuss the audience the material was designed for to try to gauge its effectiveness. There should be some performance statistics, which may be anecdotal, as it is rare to have hard statistics on design effectiveness.

References should be supplied which will help a client ascertain the work practices and professionalism of the service provider.

Commissioning a contractor

Throughout *The Design Manual*, there are lists of information required when commissioning designers and printers. The basic requirements are much the same for most contractors – they all require client contact details, approval and delivery details, briefing, and so on.

When contracting image-creation contractors like illustrators, cartoonists, photographers, film-makers and

other artists, there are requirements that you must ensure
are clear:

- the output required (often an original work at a certain
  size)
- the resolution required for any digital files (often digital
  files are preferred to original images)
- representation issues like the portrayal of diverse
  nationalities and casting variety
- colour palettes
- style preferences (as indicated from the contractor's
  portfolio).

You should also ask for roughs for approval – but be sure to
define the acceptable standard for a rough. The whole point
is to not make a contractor produce a final piece in order
to secure your commission. Usually a composition sketch
with annotations and a sample of style is sufficient.

Provide research materials if possible. For example, you
may provide picture research for illustrators and cartoonists
of famous people or politicians who need to be depicted.

Contracts

Usually a designer will prepare a contract in letter form as
part of an initial proposal which at this point may or may
not include any design work. The contract will cover a job
description, fees, scheduling, copyright, conditions and any
other agreements.

There will often be two copies, one for the client to keep,
and one the client will be asked to sign and return. It is
standard practice to initial each page.

It is also standard practice for a designer not to
commence work until the return of that agreement.

There will often be a statement that the estimate is valid
for a limited period of time, usually 90 days to a year.

Payment is usually made on invoice within seven, 14,
21 or 30 days, as agreed at the briefing or in the contract.
There may be staged payments worked into the production
schedule. Depending on how payment is to be made, there
may be payments on completion of each stage or hourly
rates plus expenses to date.

Some designers will request payment of a
commissioning fee of between 10% and 50% of the total
job cost before commencing the job. This is often the case
when there will be many subcontractors to be paid by the
designer.

Rates

A client may request that all production, including printing, finishing, replication and distribution, be included in design fees, or may just buy the design and negotiate the production separately.

A client should expect to pay for:

- briefing and liaison meetings (except the initial contact meeting)
- design and research
- preparation of an initial proposal including competitive submissions
- preparation of roughs
- materials used
- corrections at client request
- print brokering and handling of subcontractors (often there will be a 5–15% handling fee for this)
- job recording and administration
- any changes to the job
- any work completed even if the job is halted
- any further security requested
- any additional proofs prepared at client request
- all costs of commissioned authors, editors, photographers, calligraphers, illustrators, film-makers, sound recordists and programmers, including art direction and briefing time
- any photography, illustration, film footage and sound file usage fees
- rush work or overtime requested
- any price increases for materials or suppliers that occur during the production period
- additional expenses arising from the assignment including any out-of-pocket expenses and travel expenses.

Production experimentation will often be cost-shared, but this needs to be agreed at the outset.

Basically, all of these costs should be either agreed at the outset – or at the point where it becomes obvious there will be an additional expense. It should not be assumed that the client will 'know' there is an additional expense if they ask for a service not in the original scope of the contract. It is wise to provide a revised estimate of costs and get sign-off from the client before commencing the new request.

A client will not usually pay for:

- initial contact meeting
- coffee and hospitality

Pricing strategies

Joy V Joseph, in 'Basics of strategic and tactical pricing' on MarketingProfs.com on 14 March 2007, summarised a number of strategies for pricing that included:

- *High volume, discount pricing:* low margins, many clients, regular product needs and volume-based profit
- *Every day low price:* consistent low prices but not the lowest, needing many clients and repeat visits to maintain volume-based profit
- *Penetration pricing:* low pricing to build a market for your services, usually when starting out
- *Loss leaders:* a particularly cheap price for a specific product that gets customers to come to you, hoping they will buy more products once they are there
- *Premium pricing:* high pricing due to being well-established and highly regarded, usually the market leader
- *Premium pricing in a niche market:* high-pricing in a market segment and value-adding, often with specialist market knowledge and high credibility
- *Skim pricing:* charging a high price in a niche or specialty market due to low competition.

- corrections where the designer is at fault
- the first proof at each stage
- overtime or rush work due to the designer not performing as promised
- work not performed at the halting of a project
- training sessions (unless requested or negotiated upfront)
- waiting time (unless caused directly by the client)
- filling in time sheets (except job records)
- cleaning up the workplace
- computer back-ups.

Copyright and intellectual property

Discuss ownership of concepts and artwork, since copyright rests with the creator unless specifically assigned. Usually copyright is considered to have been paid for the particular use negotiated with the job, and any use beyond that – including reprinting – needs to be renegotiated.

Illustrators and photographers own the originals of their images and need only supply them in transparency or digital form for use in the job, unless the original is specifically purchased and reproduction rights negotiated.

In some cases, like magazines, book series, websites, multimedia products and corporate identities, a client is purchasing the conceptual design for a product, including all the artwork files in multiple formats and full templates for its various incarnations. It may even commission a style manual for the product, in order to guide future designers or in-house designers in the production of materials that meet the design standard. This should be negotiated upfront and the rights discussed. Clients will want unlimited, exclusive rights to reproduce the materials in future – so you need to negotiate appropriate payment.

However, you might negotiate a non-exclusive licence to use the style sheets, coding or templates developed in the process.

In effect, a client is buying the right to reproduce an image, not the image itself. There are moral rights conventions that recognise a creator's right to attribution and that their work will not be defaced or compromised. It is best to seek legal advice on the interpretation of any suspected infringement here.

It is usual, however, for designers, illustrators and photographers and other contractors to reserve the right

Rates

Rates vary and can be charged as follows:

- Hourly rate + materials
- A flat fee
- Varying hourly rates for different types of work:
  - creative – normally charged at a higher rate
  - production
  - meeting time
- Varying hourly rates for different staff:
  - seniors – normally charged at a higher rate
  - juniors
  - technical – covers upkeep, upgrade and maintenance of technology

or a combination of any or all of the above.

to reproduce material produced for a client as samples or advertising material or to enter into competitions. They will normally credit the client as the source of the commission and, in the case of award entries, if selected, the client will often be recognised with a certificate of achievement as well.

In the case of high-security or confidential documents, this may not always be possible and this should also be noted in the contract's discussion of rights.

Any ideas, designs or illustrative material rejected by a client are considered to be the designer's property (unless rights are negotiated and purchased) and may be used by the designer freely.

While there are assumptions in copyright law, it is better to be specific and define that a product is covered by copyright by using the © symbol, noting the copyright holder and the date of the copyright taking effect. Look at the verso title page of this book to see a standard copyright notice for print. Most websites will have a link at the foot of each page that defines who owns the copyright.

While there are differences in legislation, the principles of copyright are much the same internationally. In New Zealand, a technology-neutral framework was introduced in 2008 that introduces the term 'communication' work and allows users, for example, limited rights to duplicate across different devices for personal use.

Conditions

The designer has a duty of care to protect and return to the client in original condition any property or materials required in the production of the job. The designer, though, is not usually responsible for the loss, damage, destruction or unauthorised use of such materials by others.

Designers are not usually liable for the failure of other suppliers such as printers, manufacturers, reproduction houses, photographers, illustrators, authors, editors or indexers, but this will depend on the arrangements made initially and contractual agreements.

Usually, if the designer has outsourced directly to designer-chosen suppliers and is charging a brokerage/handling fee, the designer will be liable for the failure of those suppliers.

Where the client has selected the suppliers and is negotiating directly with and being billed directly by those

'Clearly, clients are looking for lean manufacturing solutions ... creative firms are being asked to develop overall design frameworks, and are then faced with clients inclined to "take it from here," farming-out design execution and production to lower-cost production resources, found in-house, freelance and in small agencies.'

David Miller, 'The architect and the brick layer: Confronting choices for creative firms' in *Communication Arts* Design Annual, November 2004 suppliers, the client is more likely to be liable for the failure of those suppliers.

Scheduling

Normally, the timing of the various phases of the job, the production schedule and the payment schedule are agreed at acceptance of a proposal or estimate.

At any stage, if the schedule is broken, for whatever reason, the original timings will often need to be renegotiated and rescheduled.

When circumstances change and the client wants the work finished sooner, any additional costs (for overtime or queue-jumping in production) are passed on directly to the client, renegotiated at the point it becomes necessary.

READ MORE ABOUT IT

Ed Gold, *The business of graphic design: A sensible approach to marketing and managing a graphic design firm*, rev. edn, Watson-Guptill, New York, 1995, ISBN 0 8230 0546 1.

Barbara Ganim, *The designer's commonsense business book*, North Light Books, Cincinnati, 1995, ISBN 0 89134 618 X.

Jill Yelland, *The art of minding your own business*, Press for Success, Perth, 1994, ISBN 0 646 19850 5.

Cameron S Foote, *The business side of creativity: The complete guide for running a graphic design or communications business*, WW Norton, New York, 1996, ISBN 0 393 73031 X.

Ellen Shapiro, *Clients and designers: Dialogues with CEOs and managers who have been responsible for some of the decade's most successful design and marketing communications*, Watson-Guptill, New York, 1989, ISBN 0 8230 0639 5.

A career in design

After high school, graphic design studies at tertiary level qualify you for employment as a graphic designer. You will then apply to a number of design studios, advertising agencies, publishing houses, public relations and events firms, film-makers, website developers, multimedia and e-learning agencies, government departments and corporations.

Jobs are advertised online and in newspapers. There are also employment agencies that studios approach for emergency staffing or short-term contracts. But people often approach potential employers in the hope of an interview or portfolio review.

Employers are looking for reliable employees who have

DOING IT SMARTER
Job record

Designers and clients should each create a job record in a file (physical or online) or job bag with details of the following:

- Briefing
- Proposal, contract and schedule
- Roles and responsibilities: design staff, contractors, client's staff
- Cost: estimates and actuals, expense records
- Various approval stages: content, text, image, proofs
- Any correspondence: email printouts, faxes, letters
- Any contact: briefly noting telephone calls and the dates and attendance at any meetings, recording decisions, approvals and any changes to the task
- Research material and drafts
- Flat plans, wire frames
- Style book: style sheets, templates, roughs, samples, colours
- Suppliers' names and contact information
- Any quotes/estimates from suppliers/contractors
- Time sheets.

This will enable easy documentation if required, but will also make it easier for someone else to be briefed quickly if the job is passed to another person at any stage.

'In Australia, employability skills are defined as the skills required to gain employment or establish an enterprise, and also to progress within an enterprise or expand employment capability, so as to achieve one's potential and contribute successfully to an enterprise's strategic directions.' The eight employability skills are:

1 Initiative and enterprise
2 Learning
3 Self-management
4 Communication
5 Teamwork
6 Problem solving
7 Planning and organising
8 Technology.

> Dr John Mitchell, *Campus Review*, 19 February 2008

Malcolm Garrett says a graphic designer should be 'jack of all trades and master of one' so you can 'work well in a team with other people who do things well.'

> *Eye* Forum No. 3 'Design and Education', London, 22 January 2008 (online)

'Because of their role as intermediaries between research and production, designers often act as the main interpreters in interdisciplinary teams, called upon not only to conceive objects, but also to devise scenarios and strategies. To cope with this responsibility, designers must set the foundations for a strong theory for design – something that is today still missing – and become astute generalists. At that point, they will be in a unique position to become the repositories of contemporary culture's need for analysis and synthesis ...'

> Paola Antonelli in 'Design and the elastic mind', *Seed*, 15, March/ April 2008

CHECKLIST
Your work preferences

Self-knowledge will help you to seek the right position for you – and allow you to negotiate the most effective work contract and conditions. You might want to consider your areas of expertise. You might consider:

☐ graphic design specialising in:
  – corporate identity
  – print
  – web and multimedia
  – packaging
  – exhibition design and signage
  – typesetting and coding
☐ image making specialising in:
  – photography
  – illustration
  – film or animation
☐ marketing and advertising
☐ production management
☐ teaching or training.

Regarding work preferences, if you prefer working alone, you might consider freelance or self-employment or working as a sole designer 'in-house' in an organisation or corporation. If you like bouncing ideas off others and enjoy collaboration, you might prefer a design studio in a commercial firm, a government agency or a not-for-profit organisation.

Other preferences might be your approach to starting a project. Some designers start immediately while others need to research similar projects; some need silence while others need music or distraction. Some designers prefer a relaxed or still space; others need a high-energy or pressured environment.

You might also consider more prosaic preferences like the physical location (inner city, regional, suburban), climate, conditions and facilities, types of clients and projects, the interpersonal relationships ...

Incorporating some ideas from Philippa Hays

Skills designers lack the most

1 Business management
2 Understanding client's business
3 Verbal communication of ideas
4 Team working
5 Drawing skills
6 Creativity
7 Problem solving
8 Software skills

> [UK] Design Skills Advisory Panel in *High Level Skills for Higher Value* (online), Design Council and Creative and Cultural Skills, London, 2007

sound technical skills and efficient production skills. They are also looking for a spark of creativity that may develop into useful – read 'saleable' – design skills.

Initially, you can expect to be a production designer. But, once you have proven your ability to produce precision artwork for either print or online production – and liaise successfully with suppliers to achieve a quality job – you will find you are given the opportunity to demonstrate your creative solutions to client briefs.

You will be expected to quickly understand and use the studio systems and software accurately to ensure your hours, jobs and leave are recorded appropriately.

However, arguably, your most valuable asset will be your 'people skills' – how you relate to clients, suppliers and co-workers, how they respond to you and how easy it is to work with you.

READ MORE ABOUT IT
Shari Davies, *Career FAQs: Design professionals*, Career FAQs, Sydney, 2006, ISBN 978 1 92110 619 4.
Tricia Austin & Richard Doust, *New media design*, Laurence King Publishing, London, 2007, ISBN 978-1-85669-431-5.
Steven Heller (ed.), *Teaching graphic design: Course offerings and class projects from the leading undergraduate and graduate programs*, School of Visual Arts and Allworth Press, New York, 2003, ISBN 1-58115-305-8.

Creativity

When clients commission graphic designers and other creative professionals, they are often commissioning a stranger to provide a service they do not understand entirely and are a little uneasy with. They want something enigmatic called 'creativity' that is almost a magic ingredient – and the designer is their alchemist.

In our mystical art, what our clients are looking for is a return on their investment (ROI) and value-adding, beyond the ordinary. Something special. A 'wow'.

So how do you manage to meet or exceed this expectation?

Illustrators and photographers will often have a unique 'style', 'attitude' or 'atmosphere' that is commissioned.

However, what does a graphic designer have? It is most likely to be an approach to an issue or a particular way of interpreting a message. It might be reliability and trust that they understand the needs of the client's business.

You need to think as broadly as you can. You need to question each small request or wish the client expressed and examine them in relation to what you've learnt about their business, their particular project and their audiences.

Yet, while you are expected to come up with a unique perspective, interesting juxtaposition of images and engrossing visuals that underline the main messages, artwork that translates seamlessly to print or screen, on deadline, you might also offer a few 'freebies' along the way.

You could, for example, make decisions that reduce the production budget, double the audience, decrease the carbon footprint, add a web solution for regular updates, animate the illustrations for web or CD-ROM, prepare cool corporate gifts, add extra giveaways or souvenirs using offcuts of the printed sheet at no additional expense. This is considered 'value-adding'. And, while they won't be appropriate or able to be offered for every project, there is usually something you can do to provide an additional 'oomph' to your presentation.

'There's another unspoken truth about creativity: It isn't so much about original creation as it is about using old ideas in new ways, places, and combinations.'

Polly La Barre in *Fast Company*, issue 54, January 2002

'In design we're always trying to get designers away from the computer and back to tearing and ripping and achieving tone through touch and feel.'

Ian Wingrove in *AdNews*, April 2007

'Creativity demands whole brain thinking. The process circulates all four quadrants of the brain, each of which initiates distinct processes. These are: Desire and Conception (right brain processes that are infinite; no holds barred), and Incubation and Delivery (left brain; rational and non-emotional). If we genuinely desire something, we conceptualise it, we incubate the idea, and finally deliver it.'

Lloyd Bond, creative director of the opening and closing ceremonies at the Sydney Olympic Games in 2000, quoted by Anna Kassulke in AIM's *Management Today*, August 2006

READ MORE ABOUT IT

Julia Cameron, *The artist's way: A course in discovering and recovering your creative self*, Pan Books, London, 1993, ISBN 0 330 34358 0.

Michael Michalko, *Thinkertoys: A handbook of creative-thinking techniques*, 2nd edn, Ten Speed Press, Berkeley, California, 2006, ISBN 978-1-58008-773-5.

Michael Michalko, *Cracking creativity: The secrets of creative genius*, Ten Speed Press, Berkeley, California, 2001, ISBN 978-1-58008-311-9.

Rosemary Herceg & Tim Flattery, *Ideas generation: Tools for being constantly fresh, creative and original*, Lansdowne Publishing, Sydney, 2000, ISBN 1 86302 701 7.

Jordan Ayan, *Aha!: 10 ways to free your creative spirit and find your great ideas*, Three Rivers Press, New York, 1997, ISBN 0-517-884003.

Robin Landa, Denise M Anderson & Rose Gonnella, *Creative jolt*, North Light Books, Cincinnati, 2000, ISBN 1-58180-011-8.

Rose Gonnella, Denise M Anderson & Robin Landa, *Creative jolt inspirations*, North Light Books, Cincinnati, 2000, ISBN 1-58180-012-6.

Tom Kelley with Jonathan Littman, *The ten faces of innovation: IDEO's strategies for beating the devil's advocate and driving creativity throughout your organization*, Doubleday, New York, 2005, ISBN 0-385-51207-4.

Chris Baréz-Brown, *How to have kick-ass ideas: Get curious, get adventurous, get creative*, Harper Element, London, 2006, ISBN 978-0-00-722094-6.

Michael Schrage, *Serious play: How the world's best companies simulate to innovate*, Harvard Business School Press, Boston, Mass., 2000, ISBN 0-87584-814-1.

Ernie Schenck, *The Houdini solution: Put creativity and innovation to work by thinking inside the box*, McGraw Hill, New York, 2007, ISBN 978-0-07-146204-4.

Daniel H Pink, *A whole new mind: Moving from the information age to the conceptual age*, Allen & Unwin, Crows Nest, NSW, 2005, ISBN 978 1 74114 738 4.

The Disney Imagineers & Peggy Van Pelt (ed.), *The imagineering workout: Exercises to shape your creative muscles*, Disney Editions, New York, 2005, ISBN 0-7868-5554-1.

Twyla Tharp, *The creative habit: Learn it and use it for life*, Simon & Schuster, New York, 2003, ISBN 978-0-7432-3527-3.

John Kao, *Jamming: The art and discipline of business creativity*, Harper Collins Business, London, 1996, ISBN 0 00 638682 2.

Mihaly Csikszentmihalyi, *Flow: The psychology of optimal experience*, Harper Perennial, New York, 1990, ISBN 978-0-06-092043-2.

Studio management

Often a designer starts a business as a *sole trader* or joins with another designer to form a *partnership*. The business gets under way and gradually increases until it becomes necessary to add some support staff. These could include other designers but will likely also include administrative staff like a receptionist, bookkeeper or account (or sales) manager.

Often one of the partners or staff will take the lead for sales negotiations, tender preparation and proposals; while another will become responsible for maintaining production schedules and production management, quoting and contracting suppliers; another may become more involved in the management of staff and day-to-day operations of the studio.

Most design studios remain small – the average is between three and five employees.

However some can become quite large – particularly in-house studios for major corporations or government bodies. And, as a studio becomes larger, it takes on all the usual administrative practices and procedures for similar-sized operations.

Most businesses will also have a series of allied professional service firms who advise them on the development and management of the business – accountants, financial advisers, lawyers, bankers, cleaners, suppliers, Internet service providers, technical support services, and so on.

Terms and conditions of employment

You will need to decide what hours your staff will be able to work and how flexible you are going to be about when they work them – will you allow people to start late in the

CHECKLIST
Staffing options

- ☐ Full-time (usually 7–8 hours per day for five days per week in standard business hours)
- ☐ Part-time (a set number of hours per week, usually on agreed days)
- ☐ Casual (occasional hours on call)
- ☐ Shift worker (can be full-time or part-time and for the hours outside standard business hours, possibly including nights and weekends)
- ☐ Trainee/apprentice (a supervised junior staff member who usually undertakes a training component at a college, which may or may not be paid for by the employer)
- ☐ Subcontractor (worker running a separate business)
- ☐ Outworker (work from home and paid per hour or for each project)
- ☐ Seasonal worker (often itinerant worker or holiday staff)
- ☐ Worker on retainer (paid a guaranteed amount per week/ fortnight/month to produce whatever is required in that time – like a reserve on stand-by).

CHECKLIST
Leave

Local legislation will usually define the amount of leave required in contracts:

- ☐ Annual leave or recreation leave (usually between two and four weeks per year)
- ☐ Special leave or personal leave (usually includes compassionate leave and sick leave and may include leave for religious observation)
- ☐ Public holidays (include decreed national and local holidays)
- ☐ Maternity/paternity leave and parenting leave.

Flexible work and work/life balance

- Telecommute: staff can work from home one day a week or more regularly (and it's environmentally friendly too)
- Satellite staff: people who work in another location permanently
- Network with other designers to offer services to companies in multiple cities without the cost of flights – and getting referrals by giving referrals
- Hot-desking: allows multiple shifts for workers without additional outlay for workstations or maximises use of resources with multiple part-time workers
- Video-conferencing: instead of face-to-face meetings, wasting time in traffic or on flights
- Share your workspace with complementary professionals to enhance each others' business
- Working holidays: enable staff to be refreshed by new experiences (you could swap staff with studios in other cities, states or nations)
- Employ for diversity: different ages, races, languages and cultures can enhance the diversity of design solutions and even the types of work you can attract and handle.

morning and continue late into the night? Or do you want staff in standard business hours?

What about overtime? Will it be paid or based on time off in lieu of pay? After a full day at work, will overtime attract a penalty rate like an additional 50% ('time-and-a-half')?

What holidays will you offer and when will staff become eligible for them? Will they start accruing immediately or will your employee need to work a month, quarter or year before they are eligible for leave? Will you have an annual shutdown period? What are the local regulations regarding employment? hours worked? public holidays? sick leave? training? allowances? parking? lunch and other work breaks?

Then how will you manage security of the premises? Who will be responsible for locking up? What about the personal security for staff if they are working late?

What and when will staff be paid? Will it be weekly, fortnightly or monthly? Will you pay bonuses? If so, for what?

Then there will be questions around the use of equipment for personal projects, the policy on charitable work, the potential for study leave ...

READ MORE ABOUT IT

Marcus Buckingham & Curt Coffman, *First, break all the rules: What the world's greatest managers do differently*, Pocket Books, London, 1999, ISBN 978-1-4165-0266-1.
Tom Peters, *Re-imagine!*, Dorling Kindersley, London, 2003, ISBN 1-4053-0049-3.
Jennifer White, *Drive your people wild without driving them crazy: Leadership lessons for a chaotic world*, Capstone Publishing, Oxford, 2001, ISBN 1-84112-143-6.
Stephen C Lundin, Harry Paul & John Christensen, *Fish! Omnibus: A remarkable way to boost morale and improve results*, Hodder Mobius, London, 2006, ISBN 0 340 92458 6.
Rosamund Stone Zander & Benjamin Zander, *The art of possibility: Transforming professional and personal life*, Penguin, Camberwell, Victoria, 2002, ISBN 0 14 300122 1.
Disney Institute, *Be our guest: Perfecting the art of customer service*, Disney Editions, New York, 2001, ISBN 0-7868-5394-8.

Ethical considerations

It is reasonable that designers, their clients and suppliers expect ideas, interests and privacy to be respected. They expect that confidentiality will be maintained.

As an employee, your boss also expects that you will not steal clients, their contact details or projects when leaving;

nor will you divulge their business secrets or practices, either while you are working on the project, in employment at the studio or when you leave.

Copyright on the work you produce is usually owned by the business you work for (though the 'moral right' is yours, which allows you to be acknowledged as the creator).

Don't infringe another designer's or image-maker's rights. Respect intellectual property by giving due credit and do not misrepresent the work of another by omission of such credit.

Declare relationships with suppliers, including any financial interest or arrangement, when recommending them to clients.

Another issue that can arise is a perceived or actual conflict of interest when, say, two clients in the same industry or locale who are competitors approach your business for design work. This can become complicated when you are developing a specialty in a niche market. You should discuss the potential new client with your existing client, noting your intention to provide a specialised service to others – and how that broader experience will likely add a further dimension to the work you will do for them. With the new client, have it noted at the outset that you have a competitor of theirs as a client so they can make an informed choice of whether to do business with you. If you continue working with them both, you will need to assure both clients that you will maintain confidentiality of their interests.

There are also political choices that individuals and organisations can make. It can be appropriate to remove your services if you are asked to do something that is making you uncomfortable either legally or morally. You may refuse a contract if you are politically opposed to the messages it is sending, either as an employee or as the owner of the business.

READ MORE ABOUT IT
Relevant local legislation on copyright, moral rights and trade practices.
American Institute of Graphic Arts, *Business and ethical expectations for professional designers*, New York, 2001, (sponsored by Aquent), available: www.aiga.org.

Index

The letters *sc*, which follow some page references, indicate subjects discussed in side columns only; subjects discussed in both main and side columns on the same page are not highlighted. Roman numerals in **bold** type refer to the colour section.

abbreviations and other shortened
        forms 244, 246–48
    Bible references 253
abbreviations lists, in order of
        publication 57
abstracts in journals 62
A/B testing 44
accessibility 34–35, 110*sc*, 155, 228
    see also cultural traditions
acknowledgments 57
    image credit lines 186–88
acronyms *see* abbreviations
addresses and contact numbers 246
    area on envelopes for 97
    in catalogues 69
    newsletter, journal and magazine
        publishers 61
    on pamphlets 66
    in small-space press ads 149
    URLs 247, 249, 263, 264
advertising and marketing 8, 143–55,
        164
    corporate identity manual standards
        and specifications 89
    cover design and 58–59, 151–52
    custom magazines 63–65
    deletion of folios on full pages 269
    freestyle layout 173–74
    HiFi colour 288
    latex coating 330
    personalised 25, 152–53, 313–15
    placement/positioning lines 15–16
    promotional characters/mascots 85
    promotional events 106–8
    right-hand page premium 161
    small-space 97, 149–50, 220, 258
    sound (audio) 26

    using vehicles 106
    see also catalogues; magazine
        advertising; posters
A4 paper 92–93
    pamphlets and brochures 65, 67
A4+ paper size 98
aged people 35, 228
aircraft names 240
aliassing 293, 294
alignment 171*sc*
    proximity 158, 169
all-capitals settings 242, 271
    with capitals and small capitals
        244
    em rules 252
    en rules 251
    hyphens 250
    leading (linespacing) 233
    not italics 239
    tracking (letterspacing) 236
alphabet *see* letters (alphabetic)
ambient sounds 111
America 180, 249, 323, 324
American Psychological Association
        (APA) system 265–66
AM screening *see* screens (printing
        devices)
angled ovals 223
animated GIFs 116, 129
animatics 114
animation 115–23, 136
    colour sequencing 281*sc*
    diagrams, graphs and charts 195*sc*
    lenticular printing 315–16
    websites 126
    see also 3-D animation
annual reports 52–59
    colour in 86, 288
    display setting 233
    layouts 203
    typefaces 213
anti-aliasing 293, 294
antonyms 42
A paper sizes 179
apostrophes 240, 246, 247*sc*

    smart quotes and 249*sc*
appendixes 57
appreciation/acknowledgments 57
approvals 47
    see also copyright
arcing 117
area, in graphing 191
art *see* imagery
articles 61–62, 63
    contents lists 60
    custom magazines 65
    personalised magazines 313
    referencing 264
art (gloss) papers 213, 324
artwork, finished 297–300
ascenders 224, 227, 231–32, 233
Asian traditions 32, 161, 162, 172–73,
        336
asymmetry 172–73, 174*sc*, 256
    display lines with negative leading
        (linespacing) 233
attention-getting devices 9–12, 27, 28
    covers 58–59
    horizontal bar charts 193
    pamphlets 67
    pop-ups 330, 340–41
    see also separation
attitude 59, 87, 168–69
audiences (readers, markets) 4–35
    discussion in briefings 39–40
    discussion in presentation meetings
        46
    editorial asides/notes to 240, 252
    forms 99, 102
    magazine covers 58
    magazines 144, 152
    research into 41
    testing 44–45, 86*sc*, 102
    type sizes for comfortable reading
        227–28
    see also attention-getting devices
audio 111–12, 136
    in advertisements 26
    file size 125
    icons 134

loops 129
audits 79–80
Australian flag 287
author biographies 56, 62
author–date style 265–66
author names 56, 59
    articles 60, 61, 62
    in bibliographic references 265–67
    programs 72
    in reading lists 252
    series 55
author portraits 56
auto-leading 231, 232
avatars 120

back covers 56, 58
    CD jewel cases 180
    magazine advertisements on
            151–52
    newsletters, journals and
            magazines 61
    pamphlets 66
back dustjacket flaps 56
backgrounds 163, 281
    boxed text 268
    lenticular printing 316
    photographs 184
    in process colour 289
    websites 126, 129, 293
back margins 181
backs of business cards 97
backs of posters 147
back-up 308sc
backward eye movement 161, 162–63
balance 171–73
    see also asymmetry
ballet titles 239
banners (mastheads) 60, 65
bar charts 171, 192–93, 195sc
bar codes 56, 60
baselines 231–32
bastard title pages 56
Bible references 253
bibliographies see references
binding 331–37
    catalogues 67
    proposals 76sc
biographies of authors 56
bitmap fonts 223
black-and-white photos 173, 184, 285
    tone 197, 290
black-and-white pictures 164
black-and-white scans 299
black (extrabold) fonts 226, 237–38
blackletter typefaces 218, 219, 220
blade coating 324
blankets 309

bleed 166, 299–300, 307sc
    lenticular printing 316
    part-title pages 57
blind embossing 338, 339
blinking graphics 126
blocked paragraphs 54, 258–59
blurbs 56, 58
boards 323, 332
body copy see text
body size of type 224, 227
bold type 226, 237–38, 271–72
    rules in 199
    in small-space press ads 150
    tracking (letterspacing) 236
    using HTML 137, 139
bond papers 325
book catalogues 58
book fonts 224
book racks 58
booths at exhibitions, trade shows and
            conferences 106–8
borders 168, 169, 199, 220, 258
    classified ads 151
    small-space press ads 150
    see also bleed
bottom (foot) margin 181, 182–83, 207
boxes 200
    all-capitals headings in 242
    angled ovals 223
    on forms 101, 102
    pictures in 176sc, 180, 188sc
    text in 267–68
B paper sizes 179
braces 253
bracketed serif 216sc
brackets 251, 252–53, 265, 266
braille 155
brand advertising 144
branding 78, 79sc
    extension 87sc
    touchpoints 145
briefs and briefings 39–41, 46
British paper sizes 180
brochures see pamphlets and brochures
budgets 49, 50sc, 345–47, 348–49
    discussion in briefings about 41
    finishing costs 328sc, 331sc, 338sc,
            340sc
    image purchases 186–89
    ink prices 287sc
    paper costs 308, 321
    post office charges 63
    printing costs 308, 309sc, 311sc,
            323sc
    see also price details
bulk (paper) 323, 326
bullets see dot points

burst binding 331sc, 332, 334
business cards 96–97, 180, 339
    advertising on 97, 220
    folder pocket for 98
    paper stock 327
    printing 311sc
bus shelter posters 180
by-lines 62

© 56, 348
calendered papers 324
calipers 323
cap height 224, 227
    optical correction and 214
capitals 241–45
    abbreviations and other shortened
            forms 244, 246–48
    comic and graphic novel scripting
            convention 74sc
    starting footnotes 264
    in heading hierarchy 271
    in Internet documents 139
    kerning (letterspacing) 235
    starting list entries 261sc
    see also all-capitals settings; lower-
            case letters
captions 269
    newsletters, journals and
            magazines 60, 62
    rules above or below in unjustified
            text 176sc
    sequence diagrams 195
    see also photograph captions
carbon dioxide emissions 30–31
car signage 106
cartoons 189
    comics and graphic novels 73–75,
            281sc
cascading style sheets 86, 139–41,
            215sc
case binding (section sewn) 331, 332,
            334
cast coated papers 324
catalogues 23, 67–70, 185
    for books 58
    for personalised type 230sc
cataloguing-in-publication data 56
CD-ROMs 180
    website prototyping using 45
    see also multimedia
ceiling signage 104–5
celloglazing (cellosheening) 328sc, 329
centred settings 255
Chairperson's statements 57
chapters 57, 269
charts 171, 189–96
check boxes 101

chemical proofs 306
children 4
    books for 228
China 10–11, 316, 336
Christmas catalogues 68
Chromalins 306
church services, orders of 73
circles *see* shapes
clarity 12–13
classified ads 150–51
clearance (approvals) 47
    see also copyright
clear foils 338
client publishing 63–65
clip art 188–89
closing quotes 246
clothing (uniforms) 86, 92
CMY 287*sc*
CMYK (process colour) 287–91, **II–IV,
    VI, VIII**
coated (gloss) papers 213, 324
coatings 328–30
codes 224*sc*
    colour systems 287, 291, 292, 293
    inventory 68–70
    see also colour coding
collating and gathering 330–31
collectors' editions (souvenirs) 72–73,
        288
collotype 310
colons 246, 252
    in bibliographic references 265,
        266, 267
colophons 56, 57, 61
colour 164, 168–69, 280–96
    art grade papers 324
    boxed text 268
    business cards 97
    catalogues 67, 68
    corporate palette 86, 89
    discussion in briefings 40
    discussion in rationales 46
    foils 338
    forms 99–100, 101, 102
    heading levels in 237
    icons 83
    lenticular printing 316
    in logos 21, 92
    multimedia products 113
    packaging 154, 288
    posters 147, 168–69, 288
    prepress 299–303, 305–6
    printing 307–8, 311*sc*, 312, 315–19
    'secret' messages 27
    symbolic 21–22, 32–33
    in 3-D animation 123
    see also website colour

colour blindness 35
colour coding 171, 281–82
    elements in charts 191, 192, 193
    forms 99
    parts of organisations 86
    series 55–58
    websites 125
coloured paper 284, 321, 323*sc*
    cream stock 299
    stationery 26–27
colour photography 168–69, 184, 280*sc*
colour separation 287–90, 300, **II–IV,
        VIII**
columns 181–82, 207
    boxed text alignment with 268
    grids 175, 176–77
    paragraph styling 259
    printed publications distributed
        online 141
    in tables 262–63
    see also narrow measures
comb binding 335, 337
comics 73–75, 281*sc*
commas 246, 248, 251
    in references 264, 265, 266
commissioning *see* contracts and
        contractors
compatible typefaces 229
competitions 152, 154, 314–15
compliments slips 97
compressed (condensed) fonts 223–24,
        226, 231
computer animation *see* animation
computer files *see* files
computer games 117, 120
computers 30–31
    colour selection 289, 292, 293–95
    keyboard shortcuts 210*sc*
    time expressions 249, 252
    vertical justification operation 183
    see also screens; websites
computer-to-plate production 309
conceptualisation 42–44
concertina folds 65, 66, 323*sc*
concert posters *see* posters
concert programs 72–73
conclusions and recommendations
        (publication part) 57
condensed fonts 223–24, 226, 231
conferences 106–8
conflict of interest 355
conservation *see* environment
consistency 159, 168, 198
    grids 174–77
    website design 125–26
constant page depth 182–83
contents lists *see* lists of contents

continuation lines 62
continuation sheets 93–94
contoured text 175*sc*, 183, 198, 258
contractions 247–48
contracts and contractors 344–49
    authors 59
    cartoonists 189
    photo clearances 188*sc*
contrast 196–99, 206
    between typefaces 229
    see also bold type
copyright and intellectual property
        186–88, 347–48
    discussion in briefings 41
    line and notice 56, 61, 132, 348
    orders of service and 73
    typefaces and 214
corporate documents 81
    identity manuals 87–92
    proposals 75–76
    style manuals 40, 89
    typefaces for 85–86, 88–89
corporate identity 77–108
    custom magazines and 65
    graphic detailing 171
    grids 177*sc*
    image advertising 146
    launches 48
    preprints 307
    publishers' information 56, 60
    in small-space press ads 149
    two-up printing 311*sc*
    websites 86, 125–26
    see also branding; logos
corporate publications 81, 86
    custom magazines 63–65
corporate wardrobes (uniforms) 86, 92
costs *see* budgets
coupons 67, 69, 152
    scissors along broken line 220
covers 56, 58–59, 60, 160–61
    contrasting with text paper stocks
        27
    DVDs 180
    freestyle layout 173–74
    menus 70
    pamphlets 66
    paper specification 323
    personalised magazines 314
    proposals 76*sc*
    publication series 55
    see also back covers; binding
C paper sizes 179
craft bindings 336, 337
creativity 351–52
credit lines 186–88
cropping 168, 170–71, 185–86, 187

clip art 188
cross-references 54, 230, 239, 278
cross-rules *see* rules
cross-sections (exploded diagrams) 192, 195
C6 envelopes 93
CSS 139–41
CtP production 309
cultural traditions 10–11, 32–33, 172–73
    craft bindings 336
    eye flow 161, 162
    see also international audiences
curl 325
curricula vitae (proposals) 75–76
Customer Relationship Marketing
        (direct-mail advertising) 25,
        152–53, 313
custom magazines 63–65
cutaways (exploded diagrams) 192, 195
cutting 339–40
    see also trimming

dandy rolls 327
dark tone 197–98, 206
dashes (em rules) 250–52
dates 56, 249, 250
    in bibliographic references 264,
        265–67
    newsletters, journals and
        magazines 60, 61
    in small-space press ads 149–50
deadlines *see* production management
debossing 338–39
deckle edge 325
decorative indenting 258
decorative typefaces 220, 221–22
dedications 56
'default' (system) fonts 95, 215*sc*
deliverables, discussion in briefings
        about 41
delivery 48
demi fonts 224
departmental names 241*sc*
descenders 224, 227, 231–32, 233
design audits 79–80
design effectiveness 49–50
design files 159*sc*
design justifications 46–47
desktop publishing 209–10
diagrams 189–96, 239
Didot point system 227
die-cutting 339–40
'digital natives/immigrants' 5
digital printing 312, 313
dingbats 170*sc*, 220–23, 262*sc*
direction 199
direct-mail advertising 25, 152–53, 313

disability access 34–35, 155
display ads 151–52, 161
display type 220, 221–22, 272–75
    asymmetrical text 256
    leading (linespacing) 233
    letterspacing 235, 236
    punctuation 246, 247*sc*, 250, 251,
        252–53
    see also all-capitals settings;
        headings
distribution methods 39, 48
    custom magazines 63
    flyers and handbills 148–49
    letterbox drops 66, 67, 149*sc*
    online 141
dithering colours 294–95
diversity, cultural 32–33, 110*sc*, 161, 162
DL envelopes 65, 67, 93
documentary note system 266
domestic scenes, sound in 111
dominance 164
dot gain 299, 323*sc*, 326
dot leaders 71
dot points 260–61
    boxing 267
    varying 171, 220, 262*sc*
dots 163
double columns *see* columns
double-em rule 250*sc*, 252
double-page spreads 68, 152
    eye flow 161–62
    grids 175
    margins 181
double quotes 248–49
double-sided tape 329
dpi (dots per inch) 303, 304
drawings *see* imagery
drilling 330, 333
drop capitals 244–45
dry lithography 310
dull art papers 324
dummies 167*sc*, 302*sc*, 305, 323
duotones 285–86, 287, **V**
duplexes 323*sc*
dustjackets 56, 332
DVDs 180
    see also multimedia
Dwiggins, William Addison 2

e-books 239, 278
editorials 60–61
    custom magazines 64
editors 56, 305
    asides/notes to readers 240, 252
educational multimedia 110–11
effectiveness of design 49–50
electro-ink technologies 312

ellipsis, points of 247
email 126, 134
    viral advertising 145
email newsletters 141
'embargoed' copies 48
embellishment and finishing processes
        30, 308*sc*, 328–41
embossing 338–39
employment 349–54
    see also contracts and contractors
em rules 250–52
em spaces 54, 246*sc*
endmatter 57
endnotes 263
endpapers 27, 56
energy use 30–31
engraving 318
enlarging *see* scaling
en rules 250–51, 261
en spaces 246*sc*
entry points 19
    websites 132
envelopes 26–27, 93, 97–98, 179
    for direct-mail advertising 153*sc*
    for pamphlets 65, 67
environment and environmental impacts
        28–31, 40, 292
    finishing processes 30, 326, 328,
        339
    paper 29–30, 322*sc*, 326–27
ethical considerations 354–55
    see also copyright
Europe 32, 155
evaluation 49
event logistics 48–49
event posters *see* posters
exclamation marks 246
executive summaries 57
exhibitions 106–8
exit sequences for websites 133
Ex libris block 56
expanded fonts 224
expanded font sets 225
expenses *see* budgets
exploded diagrams 192, 195
exponential axes, in graphs 190–91
external links from websites 126
external signage 105–6, 236
extrabold (black) fonts 226, 237–38
extralight fonts 224
extreme leading 84, 233
eye flow 161–63
e-zines 141

faces 164*sc*
fake duotones 285*sc*
fake watermarks 327*sc*

fallow areas 162*sc*, 163
family trees (tree diagrams) 194–95
fax sheets 94*sc*, 95
fees *see* budgets
fiction 17, 18, 59, 213, 240
    comics and graphic novels 73–75,
        281*sc*
figure/ground interaction *see*
        backgrounds
files 136, 301
    finished artwork 297–300
    for odds and sods 159*sc*
    size 34, 112–13, 125
film and film-making 8, 19–20
    expression of time in referencing
        252
    mood boards 6–7
    movie posters 180
    quoting titles 239, 241*sc*
    storyboarding 114–15, 118–19,
        281*sc*
    transfers to DVD 109
    see also animation; video
finance *see* budgets
financial highlights/statements 57
financial years 250
fine fonts 224
finished artwork 297–300
finishing processes 30, 308*sc*, 328–41
first letter of text block 244–45
first lines of paragraphs 54, 182*sc*,
        258–59
first (lead) paragraphs 62, 259
fixed spaces 246*sc*
flag, Australian 287
flaps 46*sc*, 47*sc*
    dustjackets 56
flashing graphics 126
flatbed presses 317
flat mounting 46*sc*, 47*sc*
flat plans 301, 302
flat-tint duotones 285*sc*
fleurons (dingbats) 170*sc*, 220–23,
        262*sc*
flexography 319
flight checking 297
floor signage 104–5
flow charts 193
flow lines 175
fluid design 140–41
fluorescent inks 287*sc*, 292, **VIII**
flush left unjustified 253–55
flush right unjustified 255
flyers 148–49
FM (stochastic) screening 283, 287–88,
        304, **I, IV**
focus groups 44

foils 338
folder dies 98*sc*
folders 98, 340*sc*
folding 330
    imposition 301–2
    letterhead 93
    newsletters and newspapers 63
    pamphlets 65, 66, 323*sc*
fold marks 300
foldouts 302
folio (paper size) 180
folios *see* page numbers
fonts *see* typefaces and fonts
food packaging 155
foolscap 180
footers 61, 270
foot (margin) 181, 182–83, 207
footnotes 263, 264
fore edge 181
foregrounds *see* backgrounds
foreign audiences *see* international
        audiences
foreign words 240
forewords 56
formats 178–83, 253–68
    discussion in briefings 40–41
    printed publications distributed
        online 141
    triangular 67
    see also imagery; justified and
        unjustified text; margins;
        paper; paragraphs
formes and forme-cutting 339–40
forms 81, 98–103
    gumming 329
    identity manual standards and
        samples 89
    for ordering 66*sc*, 69–70, 153*sc*
    paper stock 102, 325
founts *see* typefaces and fonts
four colour (process colour) 287–91,
        II–IV, VI, VIII
frames per second 115
free-form layout 173–74, 256
front covers *see* covers
frontispiece 56
full-capital settings *see* all-capitals
        settings
full (process) colour 287–91, **II–IV, VI,**
        VIII
full stops (full points, periods) 54,
        246–48
    in bibliographic references 265,
        266, 267
    footnotes 264

gate folds 65, 66

gathering and collating 330–31
genre titles 59
ghosting 208, 320
GIFs 116, 129
glitter varnish 328
glossaries 57
gloss finishes 328–29
gloss papers 213, 324
glow-in-the-dark varnish 329
glues and gluing 329, 330, 332
Goe System 291
Golden Section 178
grades of paper 323–27
grain (paper) 322
grammage 323, 324, 325, 327
graphical use interface (GUI) 131–35
graphic detailing 169–71
graphic novels 74–75, 281*sc*
graphics *see* imagery
graphs 189–96, 267
gravure 317
greeting cards 328–29
grey component replacement (GCR)
        290
greyscale 35
greyscale conversion (GSC) 290
grids 174–77
Griffo, Francesco 238
gripper edge 159*sc*
gsm 323, 324, 325, 327
guillotining *see* trimming
gumming 329
Gutenberg, Johannes 218, 316, 317
Gutenberg diagram 162*sc*
gutters 181–82

half-Canadian binding 333, 334
half-title pages 56
halftones 282–83, 285, **VII**
    see also screens (printing devices)
handbills 148–49, 173
hand-held devices 218, 223
handmade papers 325
handwriting *see* writing
hanging indents 55, 259–60
'Hansard' 240
hardback (section sewn) 331, 332, 334
head (margin) 181
headers 61, 270
headings (headlines, display lines)
        270–75
    in advertising format 164
    boxed lists, tables and graphs 267
    first paragraphs after 259
    forms 99
    Internet documents 139
    letterspacing (tracking and kerning)

234–36, 247
linespacing (leading) within 233–34
in lists 199
menus 70–71
with multiple lines 15–16, 233–34,
          236, 242*sc*, 274*sc*, 275*sc*
newsletters, journals and
          magazines 61–62
overprinting or reversing out in
          photographs 197
pamphlets 67, 234
punctuation in 247, 251
report style with numbered
          paragraphs 54
rules above or below in unjustified
          text 176*sc*
spaces around 200
see also display type
height of letters *see* type size
hexadecimal colour 293–95
HiFi colour 288
high-speed printing 289–90
highway signage 236
holograms 338
home pages 125–26, 132
    intranets 135
    links to and from 124, 128, 132, 134
horizontal bar charts 193
horizontal rules *see* rules
'How to use this book', in order of
          publication 57
hue 280–81
hybrid images 10
hymns 73
hypertext 19–20
    see also navigation of websites
Hypertext Markup Language (HTML)
          137–39
hyphens and hyphenation 249–50, 255,
          257–58

icons 82–83, 125, 126–27, 131–35
    on forms 100
    reusing 181*sc*
    see also logos
idea generation 42–44
identity manuals 87–92
illustrated strip books 74–75
illustration *see* imagery
image advertising 146
image GIFs 116, 129
image libraries 186–89
imagery (pictures, graphics) 136, 158–
          59, 164–74, 183–96
    acknowledgment of sources
          (publication part) 57
    author portraits 56

comics and graphic novels 73–75
conceptualisation and idea
          generation 42–44
on covers 58, 59
deletion of folios on full pages 269
discussion in briefings 40
discussion in rationales 46
email newsletters 141
on envelopes 97
inclusivity 110*sc*
list of illustrations 56
magazines 58, 60
multimedia products 113
prepress 297–306
separation from competing 9–11
small-space press ads 150
storyboarding 114–15, 118–19, 166,
          281*sc*
titles of arts works and paintings
          239, 241*sc*
type over 167
in unjustified text settings 176*sc*
websites 124–27, 129
see also animation; bleed; captions;
          colour; corporate
          identity; photographs;
          symbols
imperial measures 180, 249*sc*
imposition 301–3
imprint pages 56
in-betweening 115
inclusivity 110*sc*
indents and indenting 164–65, 258,
          259–63
    boxed text 268
    foils 338
    footnotes 264
    hanging 55, 259–60
    measurement unit 180
    scores 330, 339
    tab set for numbered paragraphs
          54
indexes 54, 199
    in order of publication 57
    when indexers can start 55, 305
Indigenous traditions 32–33
information architecture 127–28
information organisation systems
          12–13, 14*sc*
    see also headings
information packs 75–76
information sheets 76*sc*, 148–49
initialisms *see* abbreviations
initials 84–85, 246
    in bibliographic references 265,
          266
inkjet laser printing 311, 312

inkpads, coloured 284
inks 287–93, **I–VIII**
    colour used to fill in forms 99
    digital 312
    latex-based 330
    novelty 10
    in printing process 309, 310, 312,
          317–18, 319, 323*sc*
    soy 30
    thermography 339
    tinted varnish 328
    see also tone
inline finishing 308*sc*
inserts 27, 284
inside margins 181
instructional multimedia 110–11
instructions on forms 100, 101
intellectual property *see* copyright and
          intellectual property
interactive tests and quizzes 111
interactivity testing 129
interest, conflict of 355
interim reports 75–76
internal links in websites *see* navigation
          of websites
internal signage 104–5
international audiences (markets)
          32–33, 34, 100
    American dates 249
    American papers 323, 324
    copyright provisions 348
    European pharmaceutical packaging
          155
    paper and products sizes 179–80
    see also cultural traditions
international paper sizes *see* paper
          sizes
internet sites *see* websites
interview transcripts 240
intranets 86, 135–37
    multimedia web-parts 110
introductions to publications 57
    custom magazines 64
inventory codes 68–70
inverted commas *see* quote marks
invitations 66*sc*
    to weddings 26, 73, 218–20
invoice books, numbering of 331
invoices 93*sc*
ISBN/ISSN 56, 61
italics (obliques) 226, 238–40, 271–72
    in display type 273
    editor response to letters to 61
    journal abstracts 62
    in narrow measures 231
    using HTML 137

jaggies 293, 299
Japanese binding 336, 337
Japanese books 162
Japanese Industrial Standard 180
Japanese *tatami* mats 173
job records 47, 349*sc*
journals 59–63
justifications (rationales) 46–47
justified and unjustified text 207,
        253–58
    captions 269
    decorative indenting 258
    fixed (thin, punctuation) space
        246*sc*
    footnotes 264
    gutters 181
    picture boxes and rule setting
        176*sc*
    vertical justification 183
'just-in-time' printing 312

kerning 234–35, 247
keyboard shortcuts 210*sc*
key frames 115

labels *see* packaging
laid papers 327
laminates 328*sc*, 329
language 34
    used in rationales 47
    see also text
large-format 180
laser cutting 340
laser printing 311–12, 339
    papers for 325
last lines of paragraphs 182*sc*
latex coatings 330
launches 48–49
    media kits 98
layering 20
    audio 111–12
layout 10–11, 158–205, 253–72
    discussion in rationales 46
    hypertext and film technique 19–20
    see also boxes; formats; space and
        spacing
leader dots 71
leading 84, 198, 231–34
lead (first) paragraphs 62, 259
leads, in advertising 152
lead times, in advertising 143
Learning Management Systems 111
left- and right-hand pages (recto and
        verso) 56, 57, 175
    eye flow 161–62
    running heads 61, 270
left margins *see* margins

legal documents, lists in 260
legal requirements 132
    packaging 154–55
    see also copyright
legibility 20, 242–43
    forms 101
    small-space press ads 150
    typefaces 216, 230, 236, 241
    website background and 126
    see also readability
length of lines 55, 230–31
lenticular printing 315–16
letterforms 84, 170, 273–74
    see also logos
letterheads 26–27, 92–94, 327
    blocked paragraphs 258–59
letterpress 316–17, 331
letters (alphabetic) 22–23, 241
    hyphens separating 249–50
    inventory coding in catalogues
        68–69
    ordering lists by 260
    paragraph numbers incorporating
        54
    see also capitals; lower-case letters;
        type
letters (correspondence) *see* mail
letterspacing (kerning and tracking) 84,
        198, 234–36, 238, 247
ligatures 84, 273–74
light and lighting 197–98, 206
    external signage and 105
    in 3-D animation 117, 123
    of 3-D graphics at trade shows
        etc. 108
light fonts 224, 226
limited colour 284–86
    dithering 294–95
    forms 101, 102
    printing and printing costs 308,
        309*sc*
    see also tone
line graphs and charts 190–91, 192*sc*,
        195*sc*
lines 160–64, 165
    in diagrams, graphs and charts
        190–95
    flow lines 175
    see also rules
lines of text 55, 230–31
    breaking words at end 250, 255
    em rules/dashes at end/beginning
        251
    headlines with multiple 15–16,
        233–34, 236, 242*sc*,
        274*sc*, 275*sc*
    non-breaking spaces 246*sc*

spacing (leading) 84, 198, 231–34
    see also paragraphs
liquid design 140–41
liquid laminate 328*sc*, 329
lists 258, 259–62
    punctuation 252, 261*sc*
    rules in 199
    see also catalogues; dot points;
        references
lists of contents etc. 56, 57
    indents 261–62
    magazines 60
    rules in 199
lithography 309–10
LMS 111
lofting/loafing 117
logos (logotypes) 82–83, 84–85, 90
    animating 120–23
    colour in 21, 92
    on custom magazines 65
    full stops (periods) not used in 247
    ghosting 207–8
    identity manual sections discussing
        88, 89, 92
    kerning 234–35
    layout 165
    in mastheads (banners) 60
    on posters 147
    publishers' 56, 60
    'Registered trade mark' under 218
    reproduction at different sizes
        (tracking) 236
    on signage 104, 106
    on stationery 93, 95, 97, 98
    as watermarks 327
    on websites 125–26, 129
long-8s 301–2
loops 116, 126, 129
loose tracking 235, 236
lottery tickets, instant 330
lower-case letters 241–42, 243
    ascenders and descenders 224, 227,
        231–32, 233
    comic and graphic novel scripting
        convention 74*sc*
    headings 271
    leading (linespacing) 231–32,
        233–34
    signage 106
    small-space press ads 150
    starting list entries 261*sc*
    see also x-heights
lpi (lines per inch) 303–4, 318
lyrics 73

Macquarie Dictionary 240
magazine advertising 144, 151–52, 169

lead times 143
personalised 313–14
right-hand page premium 161
small-space ads 149–50, 258
magazines 59–65, 180, 220
binding 332
boxed text 267
covers 58, 151–52
e-zines 141
flat plans 301, 302
inks and finishes 10
quoting titles 239
mail 63
artwork specifications 98
direct-mail advertising 25, 152–53
letterbox drops 66, 67, 149*sc*
letters to the editor 61
postcards 98, 147–48
see also addresses and contact
numbers; envelopes;
letterheads
manuals 53–55, 312
corporate identity 87–92
Manutius, Aldus 238, 239
margins 180, 181, 207
letterhead area for overprinted
letters 93
menus 71
numbered paragraphs 55
see also columns; indents and
indenting
marketing *see* advertising and
marketing
markets *see* audiences
mascots 85
mash-ups 142
mass-market paperbacks 59
mastheads 60, 65
American meaning of term 61
mathematical settings 220, 252, 253
matt papers 102, 324
maximal capitalisation 243
maximal punctuation 246–47
measurement 180
on-screen 140
output resolution 303
paper specification 323–27
see also size
mechanical spacing *see* tracking
media kits 98
media releases 96
medium (roman) fonts 224, 226
memoranda sheets 95–96
menus 70–72
metallic foils 338
metallic inks 287*sc*, 291–92, **VII**
metaphors 23–24

graphical user interface (GUI)
131–35
metaverse 120
metrics, audience 5–6
microns 323
military histories 240
minimal capitalisation 243
minimal punctuation 243, 246
minute papers 95–96
mission statements in publications 57
mixed column grids 175, 176
mocap suits 117
models, photographic 58
modern layouts 203–5, 255
modern serif 216*sc*
modular grids 175, 177
moiré 283*sc*, 285
Mondrian, Piet 173
monograms 85
mood boards 6–7
motor vehicle signage 106
mounting techniques 46*sc*, 47*sc*
movie posters 180
multicolumn setting *see* columns
multimedia 19–20, 110–24
animating diagrams, graphs and
charts 195*sc*
flight checking 297
prototyping 45
typefaces recommended for 218
see also screens; websites
multivariate testing 44–45
musical works, titles of 239, 241*sc*

names 56, 61
capital letters 241*sc*, 244, 246–47
on forms 100
italics 240–41
menu dishes 70–71
paper stocks 321
punctuation 246–47
see also author names; titles
narrow (condensed) fonts 223–24, 226,
231
narrow measures 228, 231
text 182, 255
navigation of websites (internal links)
132–33, 137–39, 141*sc*
developing architecture 127–28
to and from home pages 124, 128,
132, 134
icons 82–83, 125, 126–27, 131–35
interactivity testing 129
negative leading 233
nesting 141*sc*
netiquette 142
Netscape colour cube 294

newsagencies 58, 60
newsletters 59–63, 220
advertising lead times 143
e-zines 141
inserts 284
layout 165, 175
preprinting 308
registered self-mailed 98
newspapers 63, 175, 303
advertising in 143, 149–52, 161
colophons (mastheads) 61
mastheads (banners) 60
quoting titles 239
newsprint 325
New Zealand 348
non-breaking spaces 246*sc*
novels *see* fiction
numbers and numbering 248
documentary note system 266
footnotes 264
invoice books and raffle tickets
331
lists 260–61
newsletter etc. issues 60, 61
paragraphs 53–55, 260–61
'scratchies' and instant lottery
tickets 330
sliding scales on forms 101
see also codes; dates; page
numbers

object/space interaction *see*
backgrounds
oblique fonts *see* italics
octavo 180
office binding styles 335–36, 337
offset lithography 309–10
offset papers 291, 325
older audiences 35, 228
'on-demand' printing 312
one-colour design *see* limited colour
ongoing projects 40
'on-product' and 'on-shelf' advertising
154
opacity 322
opening quotes 246, 249*sc*
open (loose) tracking 235, 236
opera titles 239
optical area 191
optical centre 172
optical spacing (kerning) 234–35
order forms 66*sc*, 69–70, 153*sc*
order of publication 56–57, 60–62,
132–33
orders of service 73
'or equivalent' paper stock 323
organic layout 173–74

organisation charts 57, 194
orphans 182*sc*
output resolution 58, 299, 303–4
outside margins 181
'out the back' stock 323*sc*, 340*sc*
ovals 268
    angled 223
overprinting 307–8
    finishing processes 328–30
    templates 94
overs 307*sc*
overseas audiences *see* international
    audiences

pace 201–3
packaging 153–55
    freestyle layout 173–74
    HiFi colour 288
    identity manual specifications 92
    output resolution 303
    printing 317, 318, 319
    prototyping 45
page design *see* layout
page imposition 301–2
page numbers (folios) 269–70
    in bibliographic references 265,
        266, 267
    indexes/cross-references by 54, 55
    magazine contents lists 60, 61
    roman and arabic 56, 57
page proofs 305
paintings *see* imagery
pamphlets and brochures 65–67, 323
    cross-rules 175
    decorative indents 258
    die-cutting 66, 339*sc*, 340*sc*
    in direct-mail advertising 153*sc*
    duplex sheets 323*sc*
    freestyle layout 173–74
    multiple-line headings in lower
        case 234
    preprinting 308
    two-up printing 311*sc*
Pantone colour system 287*sc*, 289,
    290–93
paper 25–28, 321–27
    business card stock 97
    dot gain 299, 323*sc*, 326
    form stock 102, 325
    ink absorption 289, 291
    for laser toner printing 310–11
    in offset printing 310
    post office charges 63
    prepurchased 308
    for proposal production 76*sc*
    see also coloured paper; folding;
        stationery

paperbacks *see* soft covers and
    paperbacks
paper creep 330–31
paper sizes 179–80
    business cards 96–97, 180
    with compliments slips 97*sc*
    envelopes 65, 67, 93, 179
    folders and 98
    for pamphlets and brochures 65, 67
    posters 147
    stationery 92–93
paragraphs 258–60
    long, in narrow column measure
        182
    numbered 53–55
    widows and orphans 182*sc*
parentheses and parenthetical
    statements 251, 252, 265,
    266
part-title pages 57
pastels 282, 292–93, 327*sc*
pattern formation 198–99
    see also shapes
payment *see* budgets
'peel-and-seal' tape 329
perfect binding 331, 332, 334
    thermal 335, 337
perforation 330, 339
periods *see* full stops
personalisation of print 25, 152–53,
    313–15
personalised web output 142
personas 5–6
PERT diagrams 195
'petite' capitals 244
pharmaceutical packaging 155
phone numbers 246*sc*
phone symbols 220
photocopying 302–3, 310–11
    papers for 323, 325
photograph captions 19*sc*, 62, 269
    image credit lines 186–88
    pictures in contents lists 60
    positioning for photographic series
        68–69, 167
    reversing out or overprinting
        68–69, 197
photographs 166–71, 183–88, 285
    alignment 158, 169
    asymmetical layouts 173, 174*sc*
    borders 168, 169, 199, 200, 258
    in catalogues 68–69, 185
    copyright and intellectual property
        186–88, 347–48
    on covers 58, 168–69, 314
    ghosting 208
    organisation charts containing 194

    in pamphlets 66
    quadratones 290
    tone 197
picas 180
pictograms 22, 90, 134
picture boxes 176*sc*, 180, 188*sc*
picture fonts 223
pictures *see* imagery
pie charts 192, 195*sc*
pi fonts (dingbats) 170*sc*, 220–23, 262*sc*
piggyback marketing 149*sc*
Pi Sheng 316
placement lines *see* headings
plain language 15*sc*
planes *see* shapes
plastic coil (spiral) binding 333, 334
plastic comb binding 335, 337
plastic strip binding 335, 337
platen presses 317
play titles 239
plurals 240, 246
PMS 287*sc*, 289, 290–93
poem titles 239
points 180
    see also full stops; type size
'point size' 227
points of ellipsis 247
polypropylene 318
pop-ups 330, 340–41
portfolios 344
portraits of authors 56
positioning lines *see* headings
possessive punctuation (apostrophes)
    240, 246, 247*sc*
post *see* mail
post-and-eye binding 336, 337
postcards 147–48
    reply paid 98
posters 146–47, 160–61, 180
    with colour photographs 168–69
    freestyle layout 173–74
    HiFi colour 288
    printing and printing costs 308,
        309*sc*, 318–19
prefaces 57
preliminary pages 56–57, 60–61
prepress 297–306
preprints 307–8
presentation boards 6–7
presentations 46–47, 75–76, 351–52
press ads 149–52, 258
press checks 305*sc*
press kits 98
press releases 96
price details 56, 60, 61
    on menus 71–72
primary audience *see* audiences

printers (machines) 308–19, 339
    output resolution 299, 303–4
    quick print preparation 302–3
printers (people) 56, 307, 319
    materials supplied to 297–306,
        319sc
printer's flowers (dingbats) 170sc,
    220–23, 262sc
printing 25–30, 307–20, 322sc
    colour reproduction 282–96, 324
    forms 99
    pamphlets 65
    proposals 76sc
    trim edges and 171sc
process colour 287–91, **II–IV, VI, VIII**
process diagrams 194
processes 38–50
    exhibition design 108sc
production 158–340
    details included in publications 56,
        57, 61
    forms 102
    proposals 76sc
    see also contracts and contractors
production management and scheduling
    47–48, 308, 349
    advertising lead times 143
    indexing 55, 305
product measures see measurement
professionalism 344–55
program evaluation review technique
    diagrams 195
programmed animation 116
programs 72–73, 271–72
projects 52–155
promotion see advertising and
    marketing
proofing 305–6
proofreading 253sc
proofreading marks 254
proper nouns see names
proposals 75–76
prototyping 45
proximity (alignment) 158, 169
publication, order of 56–57, 60–62,
    132–33
publishers 56, 61
    acknowledgments/appreciation 57
    logos 56, 60
pull-quotes 19, 171, 220
punctuation 145–253
    hyphens and hyphenation 249–50,
        255, 257–58
    italic usage and 240
    for lists 252, 261sc
    paragraph numbering 54
    references 263–67

punctuation space 246sc
puns, visual 43
purpose of design 2–35

quadratones 290, **VI**
quarto 180
question marks 240, 246
quick print 302–3, 310–12
    pamphlets 65sc
quoted material 239–40, 248–49, 252
    Bible references 253
    pull-quotes 19, 171, 220
quote marks 239–40, 246, 248–49
    in display setting 247sc

radio buttons 101
raffle book numbering 331
ragged left 255
ragged right 253–55
rag zones 255
raised capitals 244–45
range left 253–55
range right 255
raster images 294sc
rationales 46–47
readability 20, 230–31, 243
    captions 269
    forms 100
    italics 239
    justified and unjustified text
        255–57
    menus 70, 71
    numbered paragraphs 54, 55
    signage 106, 236
    typefaces and fonts 213, 218–20,
        223, 230
    website backgrounds 126
    website italics 137
readers see audiences
reading 14–20, 22–23
    eye flow 161–63
reams 322
recommendations and conclusions
    (publication part) 57
recommended retail price 56, 60
recording sound 111–12
recordkeeping 47, 349sc
rectangles see shapes
recto pages see left- and right-hand
    pages
recycled paper 322sc, 326–27
reduction see scaling
references, reference lists and
    bibliographies 57, 263–67
    double-em rule 252
    style used in this book 243, 260
registration 171sc

registration marks 300
reinforcing 171
relief printing 316
religious services, orders of 73
repetition 198–99, 207–8
reply paid cards 98
reports 52–59
    interim 75–76
    'under embargo' 48
    see also annual reports
reprint information 56
reproduction permissions see copyright
research 41–42, 46
    at project end 49–50
    see also testing
resolution 58, 299, 303–4
response areas of forms 100, 101–2, 103
reversed type 138, 242, 268
reverses 283, 292
review quotes 56
RGB 293–95
right-hand pages see left- and right-
    hand pages
right margins see margins
ring binding 330, 333, 334
    fold outs 302
    post-and-eye 336, 337
    publications with numbered
        paragraphs 54
rivers of space 256sc
roadblock ads 145
roman fonts 224, 226
roman numerals 260
    page numbers 56, 57
rotary presses 317
roughs 43–44, 47, 345
rule of thirds 178
rules 175, 199–200
    in forms 99
    in Internet documents 139
    in menus 71
    separating footnotes from text 264
    in tables 262–63
    technique for judging thickness
        273sc
    unjustified text setting 176sc
runarounds 175sc, 258
running heads 61, 270
run-on addresses 246
rush work 308sc, 349

saddle stapling/saddle stitching 330–31,
    334
samples, for briefings 40
sans serif typefaces see serif/sans serif
    typefaces
satin papers 324

scale, contrasting of 11, 196*sc,* 197, 207
scaling 186, 188*sc*
   output resolution and 58, 303*sc*
   small capitals 244
scans 299
scheduling *see* production management
scientific and technical reports 231
   lists in 260–61
   numbered paragraphs 53–55
   Vancouver system of referencing
      243, 266–67
scientific names 240
scissors along broken line 220
scores 330, 339
'scratchies' 330
screen-based media 109–42
screenless printing 310
screen printing 318–19
screens (printing devices) and screening
      283, I–VII
   limited colour 285–86, V
   output resolution 58, 299, 303–4
   process colour 287–88, II–IV
   waterless printing 310
screens (viewing devices) 110, 124
   all capital display lines 233
   colour 289, 293–95
   forms on 99, 100, 101–2, 103
   italics 239
   measurement units 140
   publications viewed on 141, 239,
      278
   reading on 137, 163*sc*
   reverse type 238
   storyboard frame sizes for 118
   typefaces and fonts 137, 218
   type size 227
   wide formats on television 109,
      112*sc,* 113*sc*
script typefaces 218–20, 253
sculptural embossing 339
seals 98
seasonal catalogues 68
secondary audiences 4–5
'secret' messages 27
sections 301
section-sewn books 331, 332, 334
security 48
semicolons 246, 252, 267
senior audiences 35, 228
sentence case 243
sentences *see* punctuation; text
separation 9–11
   classified ads 151
   colour 287–90, 300, II–IV, VIII
   packaging 153–54
   photo subject and background 184

posters 147
small-space press ads 149
text in Internet documents 139
see also attention-getting devices;
      boxes; rules; space and
      spacing
sepia 287*sc*
sequence diagrams 195
series 55–58
serif/sans serif typefaces 213–18, 226
   fax sheets 95
   on forms 99, 100
   italics 238–39
   leading 232
   lenticular printing 316
   parentheses in display setting 252
   point sizes for setting 228
   with script typefaces 220
   small-space press ads 150
service, orders of 73
set solid 231, 233–34*sc*
shapes (planes) 164, 165
   anti-aliassing 293, 294
   cropping 168, 170–71
   cutting 339–40
   in diagrams, graphs and charts
      192–95
   dingbats 170*sc,* 220–23, 262*sc*
   direction implied by 199
   imagery 183
   pamphlets 67
   see also boxes; folding; formats;
      symbols
sheet-fed offset 310
sheet laminate 329
ships' names 240
shortened forms *see* abbreviations
shows 106–8
   quoting titles 239, 241*sc*
side columns 182
   vertical mastheads (banners) in 60
side stapling 335, 337
signage 81, 104–6, 236
   at exhibitions 107
   identity manual specifications 92
   posters 146–47
signature marks 331
silkscreen printing 318–19
simplicity 164–67
single quotes 248–49
site maps 127–28
6-sheet boards 323
size 167, 179–80
   files 34, 112–13, 125
   folders 98
   leading (linespacing) 84, 198,
      231–34

line length 55, 230–31
   see also paper sizes; scale; screens;
      type size
skinning 117, 142
'skite box' 61
slab serif typefaces 213, 216, 252
   not in small-space ads 151
slash/slant 249, 254*sc*
small capitals 236, 243–44
small-space ads 97, 149–50, 220, 258
smart quotes 249*sc*
Smith, Webb 114
soft covers and paperbacks 180, 331*sc,*
      332, 334
   fake endpapers 27
   mass-market 59
'soft-proofing' 305
solid colours 238, 278, 283, 288*sc,*
      289, 291
   see also tone
solid setting 231, 233–34*sc*
solidus 249, 254*sc*
song lyrics 73
song titles 239
sound *see* audio
souvenirs (collectors' editions) 72–73,
      288
soy inks 30
space and spacing 163–64, 200–203,
      206–7, 246*sc*
   blocked paragraphs 258–59
   boxed text 268
   between columns (gutters) 181–82
   above and below headings 270
   between initials 246
   between letters (tracking and
      kerning) 84, 198, 234–
      36, 238, 247
   between lines (leading) 84, 198,
      231–34
   logos 84
   measurement unit 180
   menus 71
   numbered paragraphs 54, 55
   page depth 181
   punctuation marks and 246
   between words 253, 256
   see also margins
spaced em rules 251
spaced en rules 250–51
specialty papers 27, 323, 325
   laser printing 311–12
specialty typefaces 220, 221–22
spell-checks 253*sc*
spines 56, 59, 180
   collating and gathering and 330–31
   newsletters, journals and

magazines 60
publication series 55
square-backed 332, 333
width 323
spiral binding 333, 334
spot colour 280*sc*
square brackets 252
squares *see* shapes
squint test 273*sc*
stage shows 239, 241*sc*
standard sizes 179–80
stands at exhibitions, trade shows and
conferences 106–8
stapled publications and documents
330–31, 334, 335, 337
state names, shortened forms for 244,
246–47
stationery 26–27, 91, 92–98
freestyle layout 173–74
paper grades 327
sizes 179–80
specifications in corporate identity
manual 89
stereograms 315–16
stereotypes 5, 7*sc*
stickers 98
stipples 283
stochastic screening 283, 287–88, 304,
I, IV
storyboarding 114–15, 118–19, 166
colour sequencing 281*sc*
street names 246
street signage 236
strength of paper 322, 326
strip binding 335, 337
studio management 353–54
style books 182*sc*
style manuals 40, 89
style sheets 181*sc*, 275–79
cascading 86, 139–41, 215*sc*
styling 7–8, 11
see also rules
submissions 75–76
subtitles 55, 56
in bibliographic references 265
suede papers 324
sumi-e 10–11
summaries 252
executive summaries 57
supplementary information (publication
part) 57
suppliers 47–48
surprise, elements of 10–11, 27, 28
swash characters 274
swatch books 321
symbol fonts (dingbats) 170*sc*, 220–23,
262*sc*

symbols 21–23, 43
© 56, 348
cultural differences in meaning 32
in footnotes 264
for imperial measures 249*sc*
indicating end-of-articles 62
for people with colour blindness
35
proofreading marks 254
see also icons
symbols as corporate identifiers 82–83,
84, 90
identity manual standards and
specifications 88, 89
on posters 147
on stationery 93, 95, 97
see also logos
symmetry 172
see also asymmetry
synonyms 42
system fonts 94, 215*sc*

tables 56, 262–63, 267
taboo subjects 33
tabs *see* indents and indenting
tactility 26, 27–28
tape, double-sided 329
target audience *see* audiences
tatami mats 173
tax invoices 93*sc*
teaser copy 56, 58
on envelopes 97, 153*sc*
newsletters, journals and
magazines 60
teaser mailing 147
technical and training manuals 53–55
technical reports *see* scientific and
technical reports
technologies 5
bar codes 56, 60
environmental aspects 29–31
ink 291–92, 312
mash-ups 142
see also computers
telephone numbers 246*sc*
telephone symbols 220
television 109, 112*sc*, 113*sc*
advertising 145
animating diagrams, graphs and
charts 195*sc*
quoting program titles and episodes
239
storyboarding frame size for 118
templates 89, 92–95, 181*sc*
grids 174–77
tender documents 75–76
tension 2*sc*, 33, 160, 173

territory names, shortened forms for
244, 246–47
tertiary audiences *see* audiences
testimonials (publication part) 56
testing 44–45, 86*sc*
forms 102
websites 129
tests and quizzes in instructional
multimedia 111
text 52–55, 158–61, 253–68
accessibility 34–35, 155
capitals in continuous 242
contoured imagery 183, 198
direct-mail advertising 152–53
discussion in briefings 40
discussion in rationales 46
letterhead area for overprinted
letters 93
magazine and display ads 151, 152
measurements of area 180
moving typography 116
newsletters, journals and
magazines 61–62, 165
organisation charts 194
postcards 148
posters 147
reading 14–20
in rough layouts 167*sc*
separating footnotes from 264
small-space press ads 149–50
type sizes for comfortable reading
227–28
websites 126, 137–39, 227
see also justified and unjustified
text; paragraphs
texture 198
texture mapping 83, 123
theatre posters *see* posters
theatre programs 71–72, 271–72
thermal binding 335, 337
thermography 339
thickness (bulk) of paper 323, 326
thin fonts 224
thin space 246*sc*
3-D animation 116–20, 122–23, 136, 330
lenticular printing 316
lighting at trade shows etc. 108
use in signage 104
3-D graphs and charts 192, 193
3-ply boards 323
tick boxes 101
tight tracking 235, 236
time 249, 252
in sequence diagrams 195
tinted varnish 328
tints 281, 291
stipples 283

title case 243
title pages 56, 57
    series 55
titles 56, 61, 314
    articles 60, 61–62, 239, 264
    in bibliographic references 264,
        265–67
    capitals 241sc, 243
    on covers 58, 59, 60
    display type 251, 274–75
    films, when transferred to DVD 109
    italics or quote marks 239–40
    kerning (letterspacing) 234–35
    using letterforms in to create layout
        patterns 170, 273–74
    mastheads (banners) 60, 65
    programs 72
    series 55, 56
tone 197–98, 206, 280–83
    coding charts 191, 192, 193
    sepia 287sc
    typecolour 198, 253, 256
    see also screens (printing devices)
toner 311–12
top margins 181
touch 26, 27–28
touchpoints 145
tracking 198, 235–36, 238
tracking research 50
trade catalogues see catalogues
trade shows 106–8
traditional layouts 203–5
training manuals 54, 312
training multimedia 110–11
transactional printing 308sc
trapping 300
tree diagrams 194–95
triangles see shapes
trim marks 300
trimming 299–300, 307sc, 330
    deckle edge 325
    see also bleed
triplex 308sc
tritones 286, 287sc
twig binding 336, 337
2-D animation 115, 120–23, 195sc
2-Ls cropping method 185sc, 186
two-colour design see limited colour
two-up printing 311sc
type and typography 209–79
    discussion in briefings 40
    discussion in rationales 46
    measurement unit 180
    moving 116
    over images 167
    scale relationships 207
    tonal value 198

typecolour 198, 253, 256
typefaces and fonts 168, 212–31
    cascading style sheets 86, 139–40,
        215sc
    corporate 85–86, 88–89
    dingbats 170sc, 220–23, 262sc
    footnotes 264
    lenticular printing 316
    letters to the editor 61
    logotypes and 84
    mastheads (banners) 60
    menus 71
    for overprinting 94
    paragraph numbers 54
    programs 72–73
    readers' associations and
        perceptions 209–10
    system ('default') 95, 215sc
    see also bold type; italics; serif/sans
        serif typefaces
type size 224–28
    authors' names 59
    business cards 97
    captions 269
    footnotes 264
    headings 200
    indent size and 258
    leading (linespacing) and 231–33
    lenticular printing 316
    magazine advertising 152
    optical correction and 214
    on packaging 154
    paragraph numbers 55
    script typefaces 218
    titles 58
    tracking (letterspacing) and 235,
        236
    typefaces and 213, 216–18
    see also x-heights
type variation 237–44
    paragraph numbers 54
    see also bold type; capitals; italics
typewriters 209, 210sc

uncoated papers 291, 299, 325–27
under colour removal (UCR) 290, III
'under embargo' 48
underlining, signalling hypertext link
    137–39
Unicode 224sc
uniforms 86, 92
United Kingdom 180
United States 180, 249, 323, 324
unity 168–71
    see also consistency
unjustified text see justified and
        unjustified text

upper-case letters see capitals
URLs 247, 249, 263, 264
UV (liquid) laminate 328sc, 329

Vancouver system 243, 267
variable data printing 313–15
variable page depth 182
varnishes 328–29
vector images 294
vehicle names 240
vehicle signage 106
velvet papers 324
verso pages see left- and right-hand
        pages
vertical centring 172
vertical justification 183
video 111sc, 112–13, 145
    cover size 180
    expression of time in referencing
        252
    website files 136
video literacy 17
vinyl foils 338
viral advertising 145
virtual reality environments 120
vision statements in publications 57
visual art see imagery
visual literacy 21–24
visual processing see legibility;
        readability
visual puns 43
visual research 42
volumes 60
    series 55–58

wall signage 104–5
wardrobes (uniforms) 86, 92
waterless printing 310
watermarks 327
Web 2.0 128–30
'Web 216' 294
web-fed offset 310
website colour 86, 293–95
    coding 125
    logos and 129
    people with colour blindness 35
    signalling hypertext link 137
    text and 126
website maps 127–28
websites 19–20, 124–41, 200–201
    accessibility 34–35
    animating diagrams, graphs and
        charts 195sc
    boxed text 267
    cascading style sheets 86, 139–41,
        215sc
    colour 86, 125, 126, 129, 137

columns in web pages 207
dashes in text setting 250–51
flight checking 297
icons 82–83, 125, 126–27, 131–35
metaphors for 23–24, 131–35
numbers 246*sc*
online publications 141, 239, 278
on-screen forms 99, 100, 101–2,
    103
product catalogues and 68
prototyping 45
referencing 264, 265, 266
resolution of book cover design
    published on 58
typefaces 86, 218
video downloads 112–13
see also home pages; navigation of
    websites
web URLs 247, 249, 263, 264
weddings 26, 73, 218–20
weight (layout elements) 168, 171–73,
    271
see also bold type
weight (paper) 323, 324, 325, 327
    binding papers of differing 332,

    333
    recycled 322*sc*
Western traditions 32, 33, 161
white space *see* space
wide measures 228
widescreen formats on television
    screens 109, 112*sc*, 113*sc*
wide (loose) tracking 235, 236
widows 182*sc*
width of capital letters 241, 243
width of spines 323
window mounting 46*sc*, 47*sc*
windows added to die-cut holes 340
wine packaging 154
wireframes 116–17, 127–28
wiro binding 333, 334
with compliments slips 97
words 14–16
    en rules separating 250
    foreign 240
    hyphens in 249–50
    plurals 240, 246
    spacing between 253, 256
    synonyms and antonyms 42
    see also lines of text

work 349–51
    see also contracts and contractors
work-and-tumble (work-and-turn)
    309*sc*
working titles 39
wove papers 327
writing 22–23, 32*sc*, 151
    on forms 69
    on menus 71
    script typefaces 218–20
    see also italics

xerography *see* photocopying
x-heights 224, 228, 232
    in display setting 250, 251, 252
    'petite' capitals 244
    small capitals 243

years, financial 250
Yellow Pages advertisement 148–49,
    220

'zebra striping' 262–63
zigzag binding 336, 337